Poor and Pregnant in Paris

RACHEL G. FUCHS

POOR and PREGNANT in PARIS

*Strategies for Survival
in the Nineteenth Century*

RUTGERS UNIVERSITY PRESS
New Brunswick, New Jersey

Library of Congress Cataloging-in-Publication Data

Fuchs, Rachel Ginnis, 1939–
Poor and pregnant in Paris : strategies for survival in the
nineteenth century / Rachel G. Fuchs.
    p.   cm.
Includes bibliographical references and index.
ISBN 0-8135-1779-6 (cloth)—ISBN 0-8135-1780-X (paper)
1. Poor women—France—Paris—History—19th century.   2. Unmarried
mothers—France—Paris—History—19th century.   3. Maternal and
infant welfare—France—Paris—History—19th century.   4. Welfare
recipients—France—Paris—History—19th century.   5. Birth control—
France—Paris—History—19th century.   I. Title.
HV1448.F82P375   1992
362.83′92′094436109034—dc20   91-29887
                                                                          CIP

British Cataloging-in-Publication information available

For Norman

Contents

Illustrations

Acknowledgments

From the time that I first conceived of this project in the summer of 1983, numerous people have sustained and encouraged me in many ways. I wish to express deep appreciation to the colleagues I have met over the years in Paris whose friendship I continue to enjoy, both in Paris and at the annual meetings of the Society for French Historical Studies. These friends have provided an important sense of community in an otherwise isolated professional world. The insights, information, critiques, and lasting friendship they have unstintingly offered have been crucial to me over the years.

My research time in Paris has been made more pleasurable and less arduous not only by the support of friends but also by the help of particular archivists, among whom Brigitte Lainé and Philippe Grand have been most important. They offered assistance in securing documents at the Archives de la Ville de Paris et Département de la Seine, made working conditions much more agreeable, and provided delightful collegiality and companionship. In many ways Brigitte Lainé has been *une marraine* to American historians working in the Archives de Paris. I also greatly appreciate the help of Mme Martine Bui and the staff of the Archives de l'Assistance Publique for making it such a congenial place to work. In addition I wish to acknowledge the staffs of the Bibliothèque Marguerite Durand, the Bibliothèque Nationale, the Bibliothèque Historique de la Ville de Paris, the Archives de la Préfecture de Police, and the Archives Nationale for their cooperation and assistance in the research for this book. Closer to home, Sheridan Harvey has combined friendship with facilitating my work at the Library of Congress; and the staffs of the

National Library of Medicine and of Interlibrary Loan at Purdue University have helped make some research possible in the United States. I owe special appreciation to John Contreni and the History Department of Purdue University for welcoming me during the year I spent writing this book in Indiana.

Research trips to Paris and the time to write this book would not have been possible without the support of several fellowships and grants. The National Endowment for the Humanities has supported me with both a summer research grant and a fellowship year during which I completed the first draft of this book. During other summers my research has been generously supported by Arizona State University: the College of Liberal Arts and Sciences Faculty Summer Research Program (1985, 1987), the University program of grants-in-aid for junior faculty (1984, 1986), and the Women's Studies Summer Research Grant (1988).

I have previously published several portions of this book and wish to thank the editors and publishers for permission to reproduce excerpts from those articles: "Preserving the Future of France: Aid to the Poor and Pregnant in Nineteenth-Century Paris" from *The Uses of Charity: The Poor on Relief in the Nineteenth-Century Metropolis,* edited by Peter Mandler, copyright 1990 by the University of Pennsylvania Press; "From the Private to the Public *Devoir:* Henri Monod and Public Assistance, 1870–1914," Western Society for French History, *Proceedings* 17 (1990), 373–382; "Women in the Paris Maternity Hospital: Public Policy during the Nineteenth Century" (with Paul E. Knepper), *Social Science History* 13, no. 2 (Summer 1989): 187–209, copyright 1989 by *Social Science History* and reprinted by permission of Duke University Press, Durham, North Carolina; "Legislation, Poverty, and Child Abandonment in Nineteenth-Century Paris," reprinted from *The Journal of Interdisciplinary History* 18 (Summer 1987): 55–80, with permission of the editors of *The Journal of Interdisciplinary History* and the MIT Press, Cambridge, Massachusetts, copyright 1987 by the Massachusetts Institute of Technology and the editors of *The Journal of Interdisciplinary History;* "Morality and Poverty: Public Welfare for Mothers in Paris, 1870–1900," *French History* 2 (September 1988): 288–311, copyright 1988, Oxford University Press; and with Leslie Page Moch, "Pregnant, Single and Far from Home: Migrant Women in the Metropolis," *American Historical Review* 95 (1990): 1007–1031, American Historical Association, 1990.

Several very special people combined friendship with collegiality by reading the manuscript, offering helpful criticism, and encouraging me in every way. I am very grateful to them all. Mary Lynn Stewart and Lois Magner offered many useful suggestions on the too lengthy first draft. Jim Farr also critiqued all 700 pages of that draft and then later had the good grace to say that the manuscript did not seem that long. Leslie Page Moch not only read the first and later drafts but also, during the entire research and writing process, offered a sympathetic ear to my triumphs and woes along with important friendship. Karen Offen and Charles Dellheim willingly read several chapters and offered good suggestions. Elinor Accampo read the entire penultimate draft during most trying circumstances and provided acutely insightful conceptual criticism. During the final stages of the manuscript preparation three exceptional graduate students, Andrew Davies, Gavin Lockwood, and Tina Weil performed countless tasks with intelligence, humor, and kindness. My stubbornness alone, and not these wonderful friends and colleagues, is responsible for any faults in this book.

My understanding family has been immeasurably supportive during the long gestation of this book. Daniel read the entire manuscript with the keen eye of a political scientist and editor. He pointed out places to cut, helped clarify passages, and took an interest in the book far beyond what filial duty commanded. Mindy had to use her training as a doctor to put up with my ceaseless phone calls and answer my seemingly endless questions about childbirth, disease, abortion, and general medicine. My husband Norman not only read this manuscript when I was in despair about how to cut it yet further but also provided computer expertise and tolerance when the book sometimes took over our lives. It is therefore dedicated to him.

Poor and Pregnant in Paris

Introduction

To be poor and pregnant in Paris during the nineteenth century placed a woman in an extraordinarily difficult position. Her options for managing this crisis were few. She had to depend on her own emotional strengths and on her severely limited financial resources. Until late in the century, charity and public welfare took little notice of her and shunned her if she was not married. One common picture of the poor and pregnant is the young woman thrown out of her house and job, standing solitary on the banks of the Seine and contemplating suicide. In another setting she is alone carrying a tightly swaddled bundle in her arms as she walks away from a public hospital on a cold, gray, snowy day. Thousands of people familiar with Victor Hugo's *Les Misérables* see her as Fantine struggling to survive. The women in these portraits are isolated; but other images suggest mutually supportive generations of single mothers. What influenced the situation of the poor and pregnant of Paris? What were their strategies for survival?

The very word "strategy" implies that these women had information providing them with the power to make rational decisions about their lives. It would be erroneous to assume that the poor and pregnant of Paris, whether married or single, sat around a kitchen table with lists of available options, deciding on what strategy to adopt. Their lives were too precarious to allow such orderly decision making, and their list of alternatives would be short. It would be equally erroneous, however, to assume that the women were powerless and lacked ability to govern their own lives. Women made choices, albeit without adequate information, without many options, and without much planning. This book

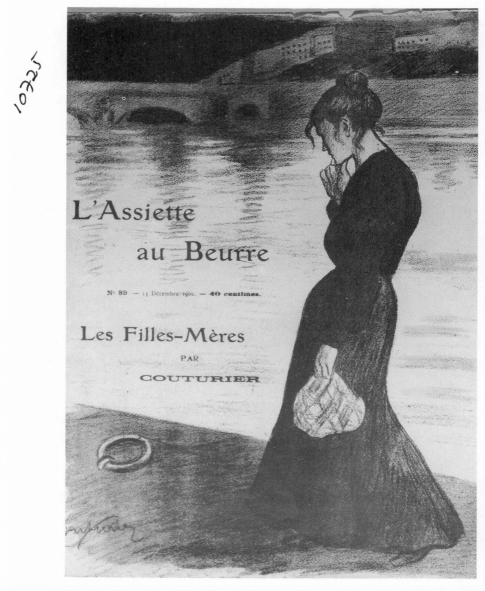

Fig. 1. Couturier, "The Unwed Mothers," cover illustration, *L'Assiette au Beurre,* 13 December 1902.

10724

Fig. 2.   A. Demarest, *Leaving the Maternity Hospital.* La Maternité–Baude-
loque at the end of the nineteenth century. Reproduction courtesy of Centre de
l'Image de l'Assistance publique.

attempts to show how women negotiated their environment and, in
some respects, helped shape it.

The issues surrounding women and poverty that were critical in
nineteenth-century France bear remarkable resemblance to many of
those in twentieth-century United States. Then as now legislators, moralists, and clergy were concerned by the problems of cohabitation, children

born out of wedlock, homelessness, endemic poverty, and single mothers. One hundred years ago in Paris people lived together in consensual unions which ranged from nonmarital monogamy to liaisons of shorter duration and lighter intentions. In moral and economic terms, politicians, social reformers, and religious leaders criticized unions which resulted in children born out of wedlock. Present day complaints about immorality are, therefore, not new. Sexual relations in late twentieth-century America would have the same consequences as in nineteenth-century France were it not for contraception. Indeed, the problems of housing, family relationships, numerous poor children born within and out of wedlock, and the problems of poverty and welfare in American cities are amazingly similar to those in Paris more than a century ago. Poor women, then as well as now, sought ways of coping with their problems of poverty.

A study of pregnancy and motherhood among the poor has implications far beyond the lives of these women. How women dealt with pregnancy and motherhood reveals more than individual or group motivations. The frequency, methods, and location of childbirth, and women's methods for dealing with the resultant infant, reflect the level of social development, economic growth, medical advancements, and the place of women in a culture. A study of how women have experienced their fertility also speaks to class relations since many of the choices of poor women were circumscribed by rich men—what male legislators and social reformers believed about the women, how the men viewed poor women in the society, and what steps upper-class men (and to some extent, women) took to influence the lives of poor women. A study of poor mothers in society illuminates both class and gender relations in Paris and illustrates the connection between social policy and the way ordinary people lived their lives.

When I first began research on this topic, my goal was to investigate how urban, working-class women resolved the conflict inherent in managing their productive and reproductive lives. I was interested in family structure among the poor and the impact of industrialization and urbanization upon the family; the problems of motherhood and of the poor and pregnant were central to those issues. The illegitimacy rate was one barometer by which to assess changes in the family. Throughout the nineteenth century at least one-quarter of all births in the department of the Seine were to single mothers, and Paris had one of the highest illegitimacy rates in the western world. To nineteenth-century social commentators, the very presence of single mothers and their babies indicated the decline of the family and the disintegration of the moral foundation of society.

Other historical literature has concentrated on the relationships between industrialization and family life and on attitudes toward working-class women.[1] My earlier book on abandoned children and child welfare did not attempt to explore the options women had, what it was like to be pregnant and deliver a child in the nineteenth century, or the alternatives mothers had to child abandonment. Why did half the single mothers in Paris abandon their babies at the beginning of the nineteenth century? Why did that proportion decline to less than 20 percent by 1900? Why did an increasing proportion of mothers keep their babies, and what was life like for the women who kept them? The answers to all of these questions seemed to lie with the expansion of welfare programs toward the end of the century; mothers' lives appeared changed by the development of the welfare state.

It soon became apparent that I could not understand the women without first trying to fathom the world in which they lived. The attitudes that politicians, writers, and social commentators held about them in many ways circumscribed the women's lives because these were the people who shaped welfare and charity policy. Public figures perceived poor mothers and their infants within the context of a larger political and cultural context. Changing national demographics, religious beliefs, cultural constructs, medical technology, and political climates all affected women's lives in unanticipated ways. Politicians and reform-minded individuals possessed the power to hammer out concrete policy that affected women's lives; but the men were not operating on their own whims. They were responding to a visible and staggering problem of destitute women and children.

One of the major challenges in writing about the Parisian poor is that sources are sparse and seldom written by the poor themselves. Poor women become visible only when they meet the policymakers through their interactions in the public arena. Much of the central drama of the poor and pregnant is played on a stage in which the women confront legislative and administrative rulings, public welfare, charitable institutions, public hospitals, and the criminal courts. The women are illuminated only when on stage with people who ran these institutions and kept the records. The men have the power of interpretation because in this drama they are the actors, playwrights, producers, and directors. The poor women, however, have major parts which they can develop to their fullest extent. Once they step off that stage the poor women exit through the side door, down the narrow streets and back alleys on which they live, and on which little historical light shines. The men, however, exit the theater through the front door, into the glare of the spotlights; they grant the interviews, meet the press, write the reviews, and shill their production. This book is an effort to balance the paucity of direct evidence of the enormously difficult material struggles of the poor and pregnant against the disproportionate information available about elite male discourse.

The story of these women's lives begged to be told, and I tried always to keep the women on center stage of this changing drama and not relegate them to supporting roles or to the wings of a greater production. The poor and pregnant of Paris had neither a room of their own nor the income and leisure which might permit them to tell their own life stories. In the views of their contemporary male social commentators, poor women of Paris were workers (women of "doubtful" morality) or mothers (the moral ideal).[2] Neither view takes into account the complexities of these women's lives and how they managed to be both workers and mothers under what were often the most adverse circumstances. That these women survived and managed to eke out a life testifies to their amazing strength and resourcefulness.

The poor and pregnant of Paris included both married and single mothers. They lived in a complex, changing, and often hostile world in which regulations and laws, often detrimental to them, ordered their lives. This book concentrates on the single mother, who faced the more severe and complicated set of problems. Her coping mechanisms, however, cannot fully be understood without comparison with the married poor. Crucial to this study is an understanding of who adopted particular survival strategies, why they made certain choices (or had the choices made for them), and what effect the specific survival strategies had on their lives. The women were at once victims and survivors. Many even managed to make the best of the terrible role society assigned them.

This book has four specific objectives: to analyze nineteenth-century French attitudes toward urban, poor, and single mothers; to examine how these attitudes influenced the nature of charity, welfare, and women's lives in one metropolis (Paris); to explore cultural and structural problems of poverty as reflected in mothers' responses to their pregnancy and to charity or welfare; and to bring to light one aspect of the female experience. Behind these lies an implicit consideration of how moral and ethical values affected public policy, and, in turn, how public policy imposed values. Exploring the issue of who should deal with the problem of single mothers—the individual, the family, the church, private charity, or the state—will contribute to an understanding of the roles and status of women, the strength and function of the family, the connection between private philanthropy and public welfare, and the development of the national social welfare system. In these ways, I hope this book will further our knowledge of the strategies of survival among the poor, thus shedding light on how that group interacted with the state and dominant social groups.

A study of the poor and pregnant in nineteenth-century Paris clarifies our understanding of the realities of life for thousands of poor women in one of France's most important cities, the city that set the pace for developments throughout the nation and the one which contained a large presence of workers, rootless population, and single mothers. This study first introduces the women, then describes the changing ideology and juxtaposes women's experiences to it.

The book opens with an analysis of the socioeconomic and demographic characteristics of a major group of the poor and pregnant, both the married and the single. Information comes from a random sample of almost 1,500 women who gave birth between 1830 and 1900 at la Maternité, Paris's free, public maternity hospital. Throughout the century it was the largest and most important such institution. Chapter 1 includes a discussion of how and why the women entering this hospital shifted or remained constant over the century, and the changing nature of their childbirth experiences and utilization of public institutions. The cast of characters is augmented by a sample of women who gave birth at another public hospital, l'Hôtel-Dieu, and by yet another sample of women who went to a midwife paid for by Public Assistance, the government agency responsible for public welfare. The stories of women on trial for the crimes of infanticide and abortion at the Paris Assize Courts bring a few individuals to center stage to shed light on their strategies and their support network of kin and neighbors.

The next five chapters examine some of the multiple connections among state power, class hierarchies, and gender relations within the sphere of charity and welfare for women. They seek to explore how social and political elites viewed the problems of single motherhood and examine the solutions they proposed. These chapters analyze some middle-class assumptions about working-class women and focus on why, and how, attitudes, programs, and policies toward mothers, particularly the unwed, changed during the nineteenth century.

Chapters 2 and 3 concentrate on the changes and consistencies from 1830 to 1914 in prevailing attitudes toward single and married mothers mired in poverty. The views of prominent leaders of various social and political groups played a significant role in both shaping and mirroring dominant attitudes. They also helped define the world in which the poor and pregnant lived, limiting these women's options. From 1870 to 1914 the issue of depopulation shaped the debate over the poor and pregnant, and attitudes changed from the earlier period. Chapter 3 concentrates on the views of leading politicians across the political spectrum, public assistance officials, physicians, and other advocates of reform. Issues of nationalism, anticlericalism, and demographic change became the concern of rich men and influenced attitudes toward poor women.

Middle-class and elite women historically have been in the forefront of philanthropy. Chapter 4 explores the attitudes that bourgeois and philanthropic women held toward single mothers, the impulse toward charity that drove these women during the century, and the relationship between these women and the working-class women they were seeking to aid.[3]

Chapters 5 and 6 discuss the evolution of private charity and public welfare, from the charities facilitating marriage among the poor, to the few shelters for the pregnant poor, to charities providing in a minimal way for the married poor. Private charity was largely destined for married mothers and may have been the catalyst in the formulation and implementation of public policy for single mothers. Welfare for single mothers fell upon Public Assistance, the government's welfare agency, especially after 1870. The French welfare state started with programs for women and children, and it involved a set of assumptions about class and gender. These chapters detail the development of aid to unwed mothers to prevent abandonment, the growth of maternity and convalescent homes, the nature of public hospitals, and protective legislation for mothers. Poor women appear in these chapters when they share the stage with charity and welfare personnel.

The major questions concern how the mothers dealt with their situation, what it meant to have a baby under conditions of poverty, and how women responded to the social programs aimed at them. The remaining three chapters attempt to answer those questions through an examination of the women's behavior and their choice of options—sending their baby to a wet nurse, keeping their baby with the assistance of public welfare or family support, abortion, infanticide, or child abandonment. These chapters explore the relationships among changing perceptions of unwed mothers, legislation affecting them, and the survival strategies of the mothers themselves. They will also demonstrate how the availability of new options, provided by a change in public and private policy, gave an increasing proportion of unwed mothers the choice of keeping their children. Welfare-inspectors' reports, combined with the women's testimonies at the Assize Courts provide a body of evidence that allows the historian to go into those narrow streets and dark alleys inhabited by thousands of poor women in order to catch a glimpse of their lives— what their courtship, work, and living arrangements were, and what kind of family and neighborhood networks were available to them.

Based on Public Assistance records and on the manuscript reports of inspectors working with Public Assistance's programs of aid to unwed mothers, chapter 7 explains how public welfare changed from 1870 to 1914, how the governmental inspectors viewed the programs and the welfare recipients, and how the women themselves perceived them. Chapter 8 begins with a brief discussion of the methods of contraception known to the poor of Paris. Since these women lived in an era without available effective contraception, abortion served as a method of birth control for many. This chapter details what was known about abortion and what the consequences may have been. The records of Paris's Assize Courts provide rich dossiers of information on the women who were tried for abortion, their methods, their information networks, and their interactions with midwives and doctors. Chapter 9, based on an analysis of almost 100 cases of infanticide brought before the Paris Assize Courts from 1867 to 1891, examines infanticide as a strategy for the poor and pregnant—although perhaps not a rational one.

Any discussion of the poor and pregnant and of single motherhood is fraught with value-laden terms. Throughout the nineteenth century, the term for a single mother was *fille mère,* a pejorative phrase meaning an unwed mother. Feminists at the turn of the century wanted that term abolished, and starting around 1920 that term was dropped for the more acceptable phrase of *mère célibataire;* today the terms *mère abandonnée* or mère célibataire are the terms of choice applying to any single mother regardless of whether she has ever been married. In English, the phrase "single mother" is more acceptable than "unwed mother" and I have used it whenever possible. When I use the phrase "unwed mother" it is because the woman's marital status was important to the policy makers or to the implementation of charity and welfare. Throughout the nineteenth and twentieth centuries, the French term for a consensual union was "living in *concubinage.*" Unless directly quoting, I have used the phrase "consensual union" as a translation for *concubinage.*

Prostitutes in Paris are absent from this analysis because single mothers were not synonymous with prostitutes.[4] Many single mothers worked in legitimate jobs (such as domestic service and garment making) but during periods of seasonal unemployment or economic crises turned to prostitution as a means of subsistence, selling their bodies in exchange for food. It is often difficult to separate temporary, clandestine prostitutes from other working-class women. If a woman had sexual relations with several different men, her critics would accuse her of prostitution. The very phrase *femme isolée* in the nineteenth century described a woman working as a seamstress or dressmaker in her room as well as a woman engaged in clandestine prostitution.[5] Should such a single woman have a baby, she became one of the single mothers who so preoccupied many nineteenth-century social critics. The blurring of the line between prostitutes and single mothers occurred when women working in respectable jobs became pregnant as a result of encounters with men in exchange for money or goods, which often happened during the "dead season." At such times, prostitution might have been the only means by which she could keep the wolf from the door.

Finally, the terms "morality" and "illegitimacy" are problematic concepts and are treated as such. All children of single mothers, regardless of the long-term stability of the relationship, received the label of "illegitimate." To American ears at the end of the twentieth century, the language of the last century is derogatory or has pejorative connotations. I have tried to be sensitive to the value of language, but when necessary to convey nineteenth-century sentiments I have used the value-laden words; no negative implication is implied.

No matter what language is used, the lives of the poor and pregnant in many cases were grief-ridden. At the same time, those lives illustrate the indomitability of the human spirit in women's attempts to survive despite terrible odds. Many women could not survive independently, and relied upon hospitals, shelters, or home welfare services. Yet others had sufficient resources to avoid dependence on public institutions. Not all families were devastated. Even single mothers could sometimes rely on their own mothers, many of whom were married. Indeed, there is little evidence for a "bastardy-prone sub-society" indicating generations of single mothers.[6] Nevertheless, many women could not rely on the father of their child for any support. In late nineteenth-century France, in the absence of a male head of family in the person of the child's father, the state assumed the patriarchal role through its welfare programs. State paternalism assumed some of the support tasks of the absent fathers, making female-headed households permeable to state intervention. Implicit in the last chapters of this book are the theories regarding discipline and control of the working classes derived from Michel Foucault and Jacques Donzelot.[7] Still, social control theories are limited when looking at social welfare and the survival strategies of the poor and pregnant of Paris. The women's very survival and their ability to use public welfare for their own ends speaks to their inordinate strength and limited power.

CHAPTER

1

The Poor and Pregnant

Ernestine Pallet's unwed mother died soon after giving birth to her in 1862 at the public hospital, l'Hôtel-Dieu. Ernestine was released to her aunt who soon abandoned her at the public foundling home, the Hospice des Enfants Assistés. Foundling home authorities sent Ernestine to a wetnurse and foster family who worked as farmers in Burgundy. When Ernestine was twelve, her aunt reclaimed her and placed her as an apprentice metal polisher. In 1878, at the age of sixteen, while still living with her aunt and working as a metal polisher, Ernestine met Eugène Légault, a twenty-two-year-old whom many accused of being lazy and brutal. When drunk, he chased Ernestine with a knife. Ernestine quarreled with her aunt who vehemently opposed the liaison, so she moved into a cheap furnished room in the eleventh arrondissement in the Belleville section of Paris. She soon became pregnant, and in November 1879, when she sought admission to nearby l'Hôpital Saint-Louis, the admissions officers brought her to a nearby public-welfare midwife where she gave birth to a baby boy. Pallet was just seventeen at the time.[1]

Not wanting to abandon her baby, as she herself had been abandoned, she breastfed her infant for two months, then weaned him so she could go back to work. Ernestine wanted to marry, but whenever she suggested it to Eugène, he laughed at her. He provided no child support and also squandered all of Ernestine's earnings on drink and gambling. On January 31, 1880, Eugène took all their money, Fr 65, and left her and their infant son without food or resources. Ernestine had no money and neither she nor her baby had anything to eat. Not wanting to beg in the street, she asked a neighbor for help, but that neighbor refused her. She dared not ask her aunt for help because of the argument over her relationship with Eugène. His mother, with whom he lived much of the time, had helped out with child care and food, but had refused further help without remuneration because Ernestine and Eugène earned good wages. She could earn 4 francs, and he earned Fr 7, on days that they worked.

On the second day without food, as she later testified, she had gone to the offices of Public Assistance. She went to one office where she hoped to abandon her baby; but officials deterred her. At another office she sought immediate assistance, and when she finally saw an official, he told her to return in a week because he had to conduct an investigation to find out if it were true that she "was dying of hunger." She left in tears, denied help from Public Assistance and without any food for her hungry and crying baby. In desperation, overcome by madness, she claimed, she strangled her baby and then told everyone that she had abandoned him to Enfants Assistés.

Ernestine loved this man who battered her, and she became pregnant again. In May of 1881, almost nine months pregnant, she finally left Eugène because of his abuse. She sought admission to la Maternité, but was refused because she was not in labor. Not wanting to return to her violent lover, she turned herself in to the police for the crime of infanticide that she had committed in February 1880. The jury convicted her of murder, but with extenuating circumstances. She had to serve five years in prison, in part because of testimony from public officials that there was no record of her asking for assistance, and that bureaucrats at Public Assistance never tell a woman that she has to wait eight days. Furthermore, officials averred, Ernestine could have employed other strategies to save her son and herself.

The story of Ernestine Pallet illustrates the limited choices open to a desperate woman who was poor and pregnant in Paris. It shows the failure of neighborhood and family networks to help her and the failure of private charity or public assistance to come to her relief in 1880. It also highlights the importance of public hospitals and midwives to Ernestine in 1879 and in 1881, and to her mother in 1862, while it raises questions about how poor women managed in France's largest city.

Support Systems and Living Arrangements

Poor women's information and support networks remain obscure. Women left no records detailing how they knew about charity or welfare, how they survived without assistance, or what their survival strategies were. Yet it is possible to catch a few glimpses of evidence, often

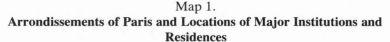

Map 1.
Arrondissements of Paris and Locations of Major Institutions and Residences

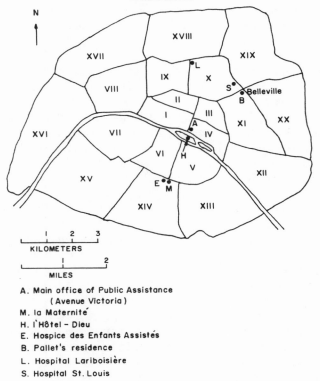

A. Main office of Public Assistance
   (Avenue Victoria)
M. la Maternité
H. l'Hôtel – Dieu
E. Hospice des Enfants Assistés
B. Pallet's residence
L. Hospital Lariboisière
S. Hospital St. Louis

indirect and played out in the wings, off the main stage of the drama known to historians. Women, especially those without family in Paris, depended on the kindness of neighbors. To obtain certificates of morality from their mayor's office in order to receive charity or welfare, they needed two witnesses who could attest to their habits. Neighborhood shopkeepers and others who rented rooms in the same building often testified for such women.[2] Domestic servants and women toiling in workshops or sewing in their rooms had access to information from their neighbors and from other workers. Local welfare bureaus and public hospitals never strove to remain hidden from view and publicized their activities with posters detailing their regulations. Women's knowledge of shelters and welfare programs seems widespread, even among women who would not, or could not, use them. Ernestine Pallet knew enough either to make the trip to the offices of Public Assistance, or at least to allege that she had, and tell Légault that she had given the baby to Public Assistance. She had many ways of finding out about available assistance: from the midwife who delivered her, from her neighbors in the building where she lived, and from people at work. Having been a child of Public Assistance herself until a teenager, that agency was probably never far from her mind.

Midwives played a pivotal role in the lives of poor women. They directed poor women to charity and welfare services or to the public foundling home, informed needy postpartum women about available aid, and even told them how to apply. Mothers who did not deliver their babies in one of the public hospitals usually found out about Public Assistance from the midwives. Midwives often knew the pregnant woman through connections with a neighborhood herbalist if the pregnant woman had sought to abort.[3] Midwives were the link not only between the destitute mother and Public Assistance, but also between bourgeois women and their objects of charity. It was they who usually told charitable women about needy pregnant and postpartum women. Midwives were instrumental in directing the poor women's strategies of reproduction and motherhood. Except for the women who were tried for infanticide, most women delivered their babies with some assistance from a midwife, and strangers to Paris virtually depended on these women.

Of all the people in the neighborhood, concierges and laundresses were second only to midwives in their importance in the networks of the poor and pregnant. Concierges responded to queries from welfare officials and the police. Laundresses gave depositions in cases of suspected infanticide and abortion as to the amount of blood they found on the sheets (indicating an abortion or childbirth) or when a woman had not brought sheets tainted with blood for several months, thereby indicating a pregnancy.[4] They could keep secrets and help, or gossip and hurt, the poor women. A laundress was partly responsible for the infanticide trial of Marie Merlin. Merlin lived with her father and siblings. Through her father, the family received assistance from their local welfare bureau; the Société de Saint-Vincent-de-Paul furnished their apartment and paid the laundress. This laundress washed Marie Merlin's sheets bloodied by a recent childbirth, and turned her in to the police.[5] Female networks did not always offer support, especially when possible complicity in a crime was an issue or the family was indigent and entirely dependent on a variety of charities, thus perhaps pariahs in the community.

An out-of-wedlock pregnancy did not necessarily divide a woman from her family. A young woman from the provinces sometimes could engage her parent or relative to raise her first out-of-wedlock child while

Fig. 3.　*The Mothers*. Reproduction courtesy of Centre de l'Image de l'Assistance publique.

she sought employment in Paris. Marie Beurette, a nineteen-year-old domestic servant, already had an out-of-wedlock daughter whom her family was raising at home in the Côtes du Nord. She stated that in her home town, to have one child is "the best thing of all." She came to Paris to get work to help her parents support that child but soon got pregnant again. This time she drowned her baby because she was already sending thirty francs home every month and could not afford to support another child.[6] Some women came to Paris only when pregnant for the second time: one baby was acceptable, and affordable, but more would go unforgiven and unsupported.

Maria Forney's family not only helped her raise her first child but also provided information on the termination of an unwanted second pregnancy. Forney and Eugène Bouton, from families of "poor but honest cultivators," had intended to marry as soon as he fulfilled his compulsory military obligation. Their entire village seemed to know of their arrangements. In the meantime, they had one son. Her parents helped raise him for three years while she continued to live at home and earn her living as a seamstress. When Marie became pregnant for a second time, just before Eugène was scheduled to depart for his military service, his sister advised her how to secure an abortion in Paris.[7]

Young women raised in Paris differed little from their rural counterparts in the support they received from their mothers for their first out-of-wedlock pregnancy and their avowed fear that a second pregnancy would incur the wrath of their families. Marie Moran, living with her parents in Paris, first became pregnant at age sixteen. Her parents kept and raised the infant despite seven children of their own. Moran continued to live at home, sharing a bed with a sister. When she became pregnant again three years later she successfully hid this pregnancy, to spare her parents. She maintained that she had intended to go to a public hospital and then work far from her family, so that she would not cause them further pain and financial burden.[8]

The stories of individuals reveal the wide range of family relations. Mothers could be more supportive of their sexually active daughters than fathers could be and spoke in a different voice from the men. Louise Martin represents one unwed woman who had a sympathetic mother and hostile father. When pregnant at age twenty she left her village for Paris to avoid the reproaches of her father. Her mother knew she was pregnant and tried to facilitate Louise's stay in Paris by helping her find a place to stay and by sending her letters and packages. Louise wanted to return home, and the only thing that kept her in Paris was the fear of her father beating her.[9] Not all fathers were to be feared. Even after her arrest for infanticide one father stood by his daughter and wrote that God and he would not abandon their poor girl and that she should take courage, and another's helped raise her first child.[10]

Widows could rely on help from their families for their legitimate children but had to conceal a subsequent out-of-wedlock child. Magdalene Guyot, a thirty-six-year-old widow from the Yonne, had two children but left her home town, to save her honor and that of her family, when she got pregnant after the death of her husband. She left her children with her parents and went to Paris where she contacted her married sister.[11]

Parents readily acknowledged consensual unions and helped support the children of those unions. Living in a consensual union was not always a stigma. What the bourgeois family would not allow, the working-class family could not avoid.[12] Even if a couple did not marry, an unwed mother could receive child care help from those who would have been her in-laws—even if the father of the child failed to provide support. For example, Ernestine Pallet had the help of her lover's widowed mother who raised her baby for almost three months—for a fee. The unwed father's parents seemed more likely to support his child if he had been called to military service, because he could not marry until he fulfilled his military obligations. Twenty-four-year-old Anastasie Siredey planned to marry a young man, Jobert, and they had a son together, whom he legally recognized and his mother helped support. When he went off to fulfill his military duty, Anastasie left her son with Jobert's mother, whom she paid a small sum, and went to Paris where she found work as a laundress. While in Paris she had a brief affair, and claimed that she had intended to abandon this baby at Enfants Assistés so she could marry Jobert.[13]

Even without the support of their parents, women in Paris sometimes had the support of other relatives. Cousins found jobs for one another and even testified that they would have cared for the out-of-wedlock infant of a relative.[14] Mélanie Briolet, orphaned at fourteen, supported her younger brothers with the help of her cousin, a laundress, who gave her work for over ten years.[15] Parents, or other relatives, who helped a new mother with child care received some payment, sometimes as much as Fr 30 a month—what a good wetnurse charged.

In all but two of more than fifty extant court cases of infanticide and abortion from 1867 to 1891, the women who had out-of-wedlock pregnancies were themselves products of married parents.[16] This suggests that the cases of women tried for infanticide and abortion represent an exceptional subset of the poor and pregnant of Paris. Those women who felt a need to hide their pregnancies were not part of a "sub-society" in which nonmarried mothers were themselves offspring of a nonmarital relationship. Some did, however, fulfill other criteria of the "bastardy prone sub-society" in that they bore more than one illegitimate child; but in several cases of abortion and infanticide, the second and subsequent pregnancies were what had caused the consternation.[17]

Having an out-of-wedlock child did not preclude eventual marriage or support from the child's father. Louise Belvel, for example, had two children before her marriage, and Elisa Boutonne's mother married her father two years after she was born. Several women tried for abortion had children before and after their marriage. Some men were willing to marry women even though they were not the father of the woman's child. A worker who found Marie Durovin on the street agreed to marry her even though she was having a child fathered by another, although he never promised to legitimize or support the infant.[18]

Women who gave birth in the hospitals of Paris lived in a variety of domestic arrangements. In midcentury, fewer than 3 percent were homeless. As many as 25 percent of the patients lived with friends or relatives. Another 20 percent, mostly domestic servants, lived with their masters or patrons. The remainder lived in consensual unions or lived in a *garni*—that is, in the cheap furnished rooms and crowded lodgings clustered around the railroad stations, in the central portions of the city, and in the newer, very poor working-class areas on the edges of the city which developed toward the end of the century. The lodging houses rented miserable furnished rooms, and sometimes just beds, to the poor. About 33 percent of the patients in Paris's maternity hospitals in 1862 lived in a garni; another 18 percent lived in their own small rooms or apartments.[19] Ernestine Pallet lived first with her aunt, then moved into a cheap furnished room, and then lived in a consensual union in a garni.

Domestic servants resided away from hometown kin and compatriots. The servant's sexual vulnerability was based on her housing situation and the structure of her employment. Domestic servants for each apartment in a building typically lived together on the top floor in small, often windowless, rooms along one hallway; sometimes women shared a room under the eaves of the building's mansard roof. Without insulation these rooms were cold in winter, hot in summer, and offered little privacy. On errands for the household, servants met the shopkeepers and workers of the neighborhood, and at public dances and other large gatherings, they came in contact with strangers. Neither her mistress's family, nor other servants, nor neighborhood tradespeople could protect the chastity of the female servant. Rather, she was vulnerable to seduction and rape, not only because she was poor but also because she generally lived apart from her family and friends; many slept in unlocked rooms to which others had access.[20] Thus domestic service, the largest single female occupation in nineteenth-century Paris, offered little protection for the woman, which is why domestic servants appeared among the poor and pregnant in proportions exceeding those in the general population.

A domestic servant's support system was grounded in her living arrangements. The most consequential person was her employer, who could take advantage of the maid or protect and support her. Tales of employers or their sons seducing their servants are legion, but rarely were these seductions mentioned in court testimony. Far more commonplace were employers who fired a servant when she became pregnant as a result of relations with a person of her own social standing.[21] Less well publicized are the times when an employer retained her domestic throughout the pregnancy and even took her to the hospital or brought in a doctor when labor began, and then promised to take her back after the baby's birth, provided the domestic gave her baby to a wetnurse.[22] Domestic servants also had contact with one another; if they were the only servant in the household they met others in the course of their duties. They performed tasks outside the house which brought them in contact with peddlers, laundresses, neighborhood merchants, and other domestics, some of whom probably liked to gossip and dispense advice. Cooks especially knew merchants on the street.[23]

The living arrangements and social situation of seamstresses and garment workers differed from those of domestic servants, even though the housing of young women who worked in the needle trades (either sewing at home alone or in sweatshops) was no more luxurious than the servants' rooms. In fact, the cramped, cold and dim single rooms they rented were often similar to the attic rooms that housed domestic servants; but seamstresses and women in various needle trades frequently lived in a garni. The key difference was that seamstresses' housing, whether in a garni or in less wretched rooms, allowed young women greater independence from their employers and coworkers than servants had; what separated the two was the servitude experienced by domestics. However, garment workers' extremely low salaries (exacerbated by seasonal unemployment which could last three months), in combination with the freedom to change residence without losing employment, led more needleworkers than servants into consensual unions. Contemporary observers as well as modern scholars see a "blurred boundary" between consensual unions and prostitution, both engendered by needleworkers' dismally low salaries.[24]

Consensual unions were common in nineteenth-century Paris, but it is impossible to know exactly how prevalent they were. The direct evidence about what the French call *concubinage* derives from the records of the charitable Société Saint-François-Régis, in part based on a midcentury municipal inquiry that found one consensual union for every four married couples in Paris. Drawing on this report, historian Michel Frey argued that working-class cohabitation was founded on sexual attraction and was in that sense a product of sexuality freed from familial and rural constraints. Frey argued, however, that consensual unions were part of a culture in which sexual freedom was only one aspect of the accepted behavior. Court records and the municipal inquiry demonstrated that these unions were grounded in women's economic, legal, and physical vulnerability; the women perceived them as failed courtships. Frey concluded that "illegitimacy and concubinage are not in contradiction to marriage for the working class. The two are linked, and it is the *non-realization of marriage* that determines the position of the concubine."[25]

In 1880 and 1891, close to one-third of Paris's illegitimate births were to couples in stable consensual unions. Emile Levasseur estimated that about one-half the children born out of wedlock in 1884 were the fruit of consensual unions, one-quarter were born to countrywomen who entered Paris to give birth anonymously, and one-quarter were "the real product of Parisian immorality."[26] Given the high frequency of consensual unions, it is likely that many of the poor and pregnant lived in such arrangements—some of which proved to be short and unstable, others of which were stable and long term equivalents to a legal marriage. Seamstresses and laundresses were more likely than domestic servants to have lived in consensual unions because of the nature of their work.[27]

The mother's partner and father of the child rarely entered the scene. The mother probably went alone to the hospital and had no visitors while there. Sometimes the father did not even care for the older children in the mother's absence and simply disappeared. An unwed mother could not name the father of the child on the birth certificate unless he legally recognized his offspring, an action which gave the unwed father the rights and responsibilities over his offspring that a married man had. If the father did not legally recognize the child, as was usually the case, the child's birth certificate provided the mother's name, but instead of the father's name was the simple phrase "father unknown."

Women who came to Paris pregnant presented another picture. Toward the turn of the century, Public Assistance officials interrogated hundreds of postpartum women who were not eligible for assistance because they had lived in Paris less than a year, and these women revealed what they had done upon arrival in Paris.[28] Just over 25 percent of them lived with their employer and worked as domestic servants for a wage that the authorities recognized as extremely low. A slightly smaller group (22 percent) stayed with friends and relatives until delivery, and the same percentage lived in cheap furnished rooms (garni), such as the one Pallet rented when she left her aunt. A few more found small apartments or unfurnished rooms to let. Only one in thirteen was accompanied by the father of the child. Some who arrived near term—about one in seven—were able to stay in one of the shelters for the pregnant homeless; some stayed in more than one shelter, before and after they delivered their baby in la Maternité, the major, free, public maternity hospital in Paris and the surrounding area. Between 1852, when homeless pregnant women were denied admission to la Maternité, and the 1890s, when shelters for them opened, many women met an unfortunate fate. Procurers of prostitutes recruited new arrivals at the city's railroad terminals.[29] Not every story was grim, however, thanks to the few religious and philanthropic organizations that exhibited a concern for domestic servants and recent arrivals in Paris.[30]

La Maternité's records are mute on how long the women had lived in Paris, or whether the women came to Paris pregnant. There is thus no way of knowing exactly where the women conceived. On the one hand, single women were vulnerable to pregnancy in the city; on the other hand, pregnancies in the provinces did not always result in marriage. Instead, failed relationships and pregnancies forced many women to migrate.[31]

The records of the welfare midwives who delivered the babies of women sent to them by Public Assistance officials and by administrators of la Maternité from 1869–1880 provide evidence about where women had the sexual relations resulting in pregnancy. The vast majority of women they delivered had become pregnant in Paris. Only one-fifth had lived in Paris fewer than nine months before delivery. This finding matches Levasseur's conclusions that one-quarter of all the city's illegitimate babies were conceived outside the city.[32]

Neither the city nor the surrounding department of the Seine wanted to bear the cost of aiding indigent mothers from the rest of France, nor did they want to support the abandoned children. Yet, difficult as Paris was for the pregnant woman or single mother, migrant women rarely chose to return home. New mothers even refused the travel funding for "repatriation" to their home department that Public Assistance started offering in 1888. Fewer than 20 percent of those offered repatriation accepted the offer, despite the threat of ineligibility for Parisian Public Assistance.[33] They stayed in Paris, and many of them delivered their babies at la Maternité.

The Women of la Maternité

Public hospital records afford an unparalleled look at the poor and pregnant of Paris over the course of the nineteenth century. No hospital provided a more complete portrait of impoverished pregnant women during the entire century than did la Maternité. For more than a century la Maternité served generations of desperate pregnant women who could not qualify for any other type of public or private relief, and who could not afford to pay a midwife on their own. Many of these women did not even have a room of their own in which to have a baby; they were among the poorest of mothers. Parisian women associated this hospital with death and destitution, and for most of the century anyone who could avoid going there would shun it, preferring to pay a midwife.[34]

The age of women admitted to the maternity hospital remained stable during the entire century: most women were between twenty and twenty-seven years of age when admitted, with an average of twenty-five. The range included women throughout their childbearing years (from sixteen to forty-four). Fewer than 12 percent were under twenty years old and less than 2 percent were over forty. The average age for single women was twenty-four and that for married women was twenty-seven; married women probably were having their second or subsequent child.[35] Since the hospital was for indigent women, married women would likely face a crisis of poverty not so much with their first child, but with their subsequent ones. Single women, in contrast, would face a crisis with the birth of their first child as well as with subsequent births.

During the last third of the century almost half the women in la Maternité were having their first baby; another third were there for the second baby; and the rest were having their third or subsequent children. Similarly during the early 1880s, in all the hospitals of Paris, including la Maternité, more than half the 23,000 women giving birth were delivering their second or later baby.[36]

Over the century most of the patients at la Maternité were single, in their mid-twenties, worked as domestic servants or in the sewing trades, came from the provinces, and lived in the working-class neighborhoods of Paris. More detailed examination, however, reveals significant, but subtle changes over time.

One of the greatest changes in the characteristics of maternity hospital patients over the century was in their marital status. From 1830 to 1860 roughly 85 percent of the poor and pregnant admitted were single. Only two years during that era proved exceptional. In 1847 and 1848, years of economic depression and urban unrest, the percentage of married women admitted increased to 25 percent from the norm of 16 percent in that generation (1830–1855). Furthermore, the percentage of married women entering prior to their eighth month nearly tripled to 20 percent from only 7 percent in the 1830s. A third of both married and single women entered in their eighth month. This reflects the dire economic straits that married mothers experienced during this time of revolutionary upheaval and high unemployment. Economic dislocation and poverty may have forced many married women to seek hospital shelter earlier, or increased deprivation may have resulted in premature labor.

In 1852 when a midyear hospital decree designed to prevent abandonment of legitimate children greatly restricted the admission of married women to the maternity hospital, the percentage of married women temporarily decreased to 10 percent. Beginning in 1869, however, there was a gradual increase in the percentage of married women, reaching 28 percent in the last decade of the century.[37] The increase in married women coincides with the years of economic depression in France—1847 and from the mid-1880s to the mid-1890s.

The increase in the percentage of married women in la Maternité was not a result of an increase in marriages in the city and department, which remained stable. Nor was it a result of the decrease in the illegitimacy rate, since the concurrent decline in the percentage of single mothers in the hospital lags well behind the decline in the illegitimacy rate in Paris and the surrounding area.[38] Rather, more married women entered the hospital as a response to legislation and medical advances in obstetrics that made the hospital a place no longer to be shunned at any bearable cost. The legislation of 1893 defining childbirth as an illness made a free hospital stay more acceptable. That 1893 legislation particularly affected the percentage of married women admitted to la Maternité; 32 percent of women admitted during the years 1895 and 1900 were married compared with 25 percent in 1885 and 1890. Married mothers could apply to their local welfare bureau for the services of a free midwife, and many did; but the stigma of going to la Maternité lessened sufficiently for them to have chosen the hospital over the services of a midwife, particularly if they experienced a difficult pregnancy.

Married women tended to use the hospital differently than did single women. At the beginning of the century they sought admission closer to the time of delivery than did those single. Those few who entered the hospital before their eighth month usually arrived as a result of problems such as miscarriages. After 1875, the differences in the behavior of married and single poor and pregnant women became more apparent. Married women more frequently sought admission for general reproductive and gynecological problems, and left without having a baby more frequently than did single women.[39] Across the decades, of those who came to the hospital with a miscarriage half came in the 1890s, and half of the miscarriages occurred in the third month of pregnancy. Women leaving the maternity hospital without having a baby tended to live in the surrounding area, and used this institution as their neighborhood hospital (see map 1). Only one-tenth made the long journey into Paris from the poor, working-class suburbs.

At the beginning of the century, la Maternité served as a shelter for unwed mothers as well as a maternity hospital. It admitted indigent women as early as their seventh month of pregnancy. In the 1830s almost half the single women admitted used this hospital as a shelter during their last months of pregnancy and stayed in the hospital from 3 to 121 days until they delivered their baby. These women were "without any resources," "without shelter," or in "danger of premature delivery."[40] Pregnant women using the hospital as a temporary shelter were expected to do some light work such as sewing infants' layettes. The rest delivered within three days of admission to the hospital; they either arrived in labor or had labor induced. During the 1830s and 1840s single women, in general, entered the hospital earlier in their pregnancy and stayed longer before delivery than did married women.[41] Of the married women, only 7 percent were admitted before their eighth month (compared with 32 percent of the single mothers); only one-third stayed more than one week before delivery. Most married women did not need the hospital as a shelter and had other children at home who required their care. Those married women who stayed in the hospital longer were frequently widows or were ill. For both married and single women, about two-thirds of those admitted in their eighth month of pregnancy were in labor.[42]

Public policy had a profound effect on the poor and pregnant of Paris. Starting in 1852, hospital administrators strictly enforced an 1845 regulation requiring that women have resided in the department of the Seine for at least a year or be in "imminent peril of delivery" at the time of admission. As a result, the number of women entering la Maternité before their eighth month shrank from slightly more than one-fourth of all women admitted in the 1830s and 1840s to less than one-tenth from 1852 through the end of the century. Since almost all who were admitted in their eighth or ninth month gave birth either the same day as admission or within two days, they were probably in labor when admitted or the doctors induced their labor. The few who had been admitted before their eighth month had been suffering from a miscarriage or gynecological problems.[43] Hospital authorities no longer permitted the poor and pregnant to use that institution as a refuge for unwed mothers. Women had little choice but to change their strategies.

A woman not "in imminent danger of delivery" seeking admission to la Maternité was required to present certificates of indigence from her local welfare bureau or mayor and a certificate from her local police commissioner stating that she had resided in Paris at least one year. To acquire the residency certificate she had first to secure a statement from all landlords as to how long she had rented a room from them. Or, if she were a domestic servant, she had to obtain a statement from each employer she lived with over the course of a year. If a woman changed jobs or residences during the year, as poor women in Paris (especially pregnant ones) frequently did, she had to track down all her landlords and employers for that year. If she did not have the certificates and was not in hard labor when she presented herself at la Maternité, the hospital authorities would turn her away. If delivery looked imminent, however, she would be admitted even without those certificates. In times of severe overcrowding or of the brief closings for puerperal fever epidemics, all women, except those presenting the most dire emergency, were denied admission and sent to another institution or a public-welfare midwife.

The case history of Jeannette Pazy, a patient at la Maternité in 1857, illustrates the predicament of a midcentury woman and her coping strategies. Pazy, a day laborer from the Nièvre, southeast of Paris, left home pregnant at twenty-three. She worked on the outskirts of Paris as a domestic servant for two months before delivery, first in one location, then another. After she went into labor, Pazy hastened to la Maternité where she bore a son on October 17, 1857. While at the hospital she asked for assistance for herself and the baby, or, in the absence of aid, she asked how to abandon her infant. The director of the hospital informed her that because she had not lived in the area for a year, the only form of assistance to which she was entitled was free transportation home; she could not even abandon her baby at the Paris foundling home. Only Pazy's father remained at home because her mother had died. Lacking family support, without money for a wetnurse, with no chance for a job as a domestic servant because she had a baby, and despairing of welfare or the possibility of legal abandonment, Pazy took what she thought was her only recourse. She did not leave the city but, within hours of her discharge from la Maternité, left her infant near the entrance to the foundling hospital across the street.[44]

Domestic servants like Pazy constituted one of the largest occupational groups of single women entering the hospital. The percentage of domestic servants increased from one-fifth in the 1830s to roughly two-fifths by 1900, an increase greater than the increase in domestic servants in the Paris population. Their low wages (despite receiving room and board) and frequent job changes made them susceptible to economic coercion and vulnerable to seduction.[45] Because domestic servants were without a room of their own, or the resources required for a midwife-assisted home birth, they had nowhere else to go to have their babies. Servants' births in all Parisian hospitals remained more than one-third of total births and almost half of out-of-wedlock births throughout the last decades of the century.[46]

Domestic service, which entailed that the servant live with a family, in principle offered protection to the young women, often as young as twelve or fourteen when they left home, and could also provide an avenue for upward social mobility.[47] Almost all domestic servants were from the countryside, a smaller town, a village, or a foreign land. Domestic service provided a semidependent life with a family which included food and lodging, an element of protection, and a meager wage in return for service. In effect, it did not always afford protection to a young woman. Servants were vulnerable to sexual advances both from members of the employer's family and from other servants in the household or apartment building. Jules Simon, in his treatise on female workers, described servants whose seducer was "in the same house. . . . A lackey, a coachman have only too many occasions to do ill to the servants who spend the most part of their free time with them, far from all supervision; and sometimes it is the master himself who corrupts the morals of a poor girl, doubly seduced by his authority and by his fortune."[48]

Marie Renard was just such a vulnerable woman. When she first arrived in Paris from the distant alpine province of Savoy, she stayed with her aunt and uncle for about ten days until they found her a position as a domestic servant with a family around the corner from them. Renard asked her employers for a key to her room to protect herself from the advances of their seventeen-year-old son; she was denied a key. The young man entered her room and asked to share her bed. She said that she tried to prevent him from doing so, but he forced himself upon her. After this initial rape, unable to lock her door to keep him out, she acquiesced to continued sexual relations. Renard became pregnant within four months of her arrival in Paris.[49]

In the first half of the century, women working in the various needle and garment trades represented as large a percentage of patients in la Maternité as domestic servants. In the 1830s, seamstresses (*couturières*) represented 19 percent of the women in la Maternité, and women working in a variety of other needle trades constituted another 10 percent of the total. Thus, 29 percent of the women in la Maternité were in garment or needle trades. Day laborers and general workers not specifically in a needle trade comprised 17 percent of the women. As the century progressed, the proportion of hospital patients who were domestic servants increased steadily to more than one-third of the total by the 1890s, while the proportion who worked as seamstresses or in the needle trades declined to one-fifth. Cleaning women (*femmes de ménage*), saleswomen, merchants, artificial flower makers, and those without a job all appeared as parturient women in the hospital in much smaller numbers.[50]

While before 1875 no woman stated her occupation as *ménagère,* or homemaker, 10 percent did by the 1890s. Almost all of these women were married. These ménagères were not the unmarried, destitute, domestic servants and needle workers who dominated hospital admissions before the 1870s (and who still entered that hospital in great numbers). Ménagères were likely artisan or working-class women whose family income enabled them to stay at home. They were above the poverty level, yet faced a financial squeeze because of their young children, and they were therefore poor enough to qualify for free medical care; they chose the hospital over a midwife. Often, as may have been necessary, they did part-time work (such as sewing, laundry, or ironing) in their own homes to supplement the family income. They tried to balance their productive and reproductive lives.[51]

Explanations for changes in the occupations prevalent among women entering la Maternité remain speculative. It is possible that since the hospital continued to serve the poorest women, as the century progressed domestic servants remained the most poverty-stricken while general workers experienced a rise in their standard of living and thus were able to afford a midwife. More important, domestic servants had no private living quarters and therefore could not use a midwife. The arrival of ménagères at the hospital indicates acceptance of that institution, and after the 1893 law neither the women nor the institution were marked with the stigma of inadequacy or poverty.

Mothers in la Maternité overwhelmingly originated in regions of France outside the department of the Seine and the percentage of women born outside the department of the Seine fluctuated in accordance with general migration to Paris, economic conditions, changes in hospital rules, and the marital status of the women. Before 1870, as many as 89 percent of all mothers in la Maternité had been born in one of France's other departments and moved to Paris. From 1870 to 1900 that percentage decreased to 80 percent. Married mothers in the hospital were more apt to have been born in the department of the Seine: the percentage of married women born locally remained constant at roughly 25 percent during the century; that of single women increased from 13 to 18 percent. Throughout the century, domestic servants tended to be born outside the Paris area while women in a particular trade, such as laundry workers and specialized garment workers were more often born in the department of the Seine.[52]

From 1830 through 1848, women who delivered in la Maternité generally reflected trends of migration to Paris.[53] The areas sending the most women to Paris's maternity hospital were the nearby areas of the Ile-de-France and Picardy. Lorraine, Burgundy, and the populous Nord also contributed to the wards of la Maternité, but in fewer numbers (see map 2). During the middle decades of the century, 1852–1869, more distant provinces sent women to la Maternité. Picardy and Lorraine still dominated, but Burgundy and the Centre (southwest of Paris) sent the next highest percentage, followed closely by the Ile-de-France (see map 3). In the last decades of the century (1880–1900) the pattern changed dramatically. Brittany, which before this time contributed under 3 percent of the women in la Maternité, now sent the highest percentage of single women; the Centre was second, followed by Burgundy, Picardy, and Alsace. The Nord, Ile-de-France, and Normandy sent proportionately fewer women than before. The pattern of migration shifted from east to west, and reflected the increasing presence in Paris of people

Map 2.
Birthplace of Single Migrant Mothers in la Maternité, 1830–1848

from farther afield by the end of the century (see map 4). With little variation throughout the century, women from the nearby areas were as likely to have worked in the needle trades as in domestic service. In contrast, most women from the more distant regions worked as domestic servants.[54]

Breton women's occupations in Paris reflect the increasing importance of domestic service in the city. Although over half the single mothers in la Maternité worked as domestic servants, almost all the Breton mothers served as domestics. It is likely that the Breton women came to Paris as a result of the poverty of their area. They sought to earn their living, and perhaps contribute to their family economy, by one of the few occupations open to them: domestic service. Their sparse education and rural background did not prepare them for the urban environment, making these unfortunate young women particularly vulnerable. Brittany furnished Paris with only 5 percent of its migrant women; but 15 percent of the single mothers in la Maternité came from that region. This is particularly striking, because illegitimacy rates in Brittany itself were low

Map 3.
Birthplace of Single Migrant Mothers in la Maternité, 1852–1869

□ < 1 %

▦ 1 – 2.9 %

▨ 3 – 4.9 %

▧ 5 % or more

throughout the nineteenth century. Given the conservative and religious nature of Brittany, the women probably remained celibate while living at home and then became pregnant in Paris, although some doubtless left their homes because they became pregnant. Their refuge in time of childbirth was la Maternité or one of the other public hospitals.

Poor and Pregnant Elsewhere in Paris

Women at la Maternité were similar to those of the poor and pregnant who gave birth in other public institutions in the city. Throughout the century, l'Hôtel-Dieu admitted all indigent people in need of medical services, regardless of sex, illness, or duration of residency in the department of the Seine. It admitted pregnant women only if they were in labor. Most of its maternity patients came between 1852 and 1862, after la Maternité imposed stricter admission requirements, and before l'Hôtel-Dieu temporarily closed its maternity wing because of deaths from

Map 4.
Birthplace of Single Migrant Mothers in la Maternité, 1890–1900

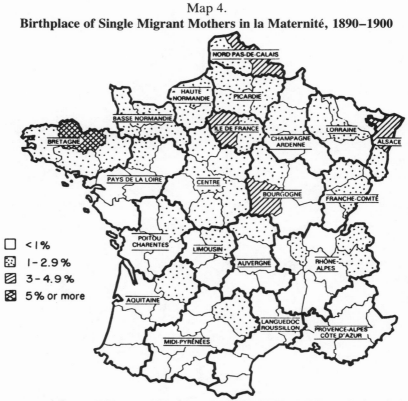

puerperal fever.[55] From 1850 through 1865, l'Hôtel-Dieu admitted the second highest number of parturient women of all the public hospitals in Paris, and in 1861 and 1862 almost half of the more than 7,000 births in public hospitals in Paris (44 percent) occurred in la Maternité and l'Hôtel-Dieu, with 30 percent of the total births in la Maternité alone.[56] The average ages of both married and single women at l'Hôtel-Dieu were precisely the same as that for women of similar marital status at la Maternité, but la Maternité admitted a slightly greater percentage of single mothers.[57]

The occupations of mothers at l'Hôtel-Dieu in the 1850s and 1860s differed only slightly from those in la Maternité or any of the other public hospitals of Paris.[58] Because there were fewer single women in l'Hôtel-Dieu, fewer domestic servants appeared as patients than at la Maternité (only 18 percent worked as domestics compared with 35 percent at la Maternité during the same years), but there were more seamstresses, laundresses, garment workers and day laborers, sometimes working in the metal and woodworking trades located in the nearby areas, at l'Hôtel-Dieu. Occupations of women who delivered in Paris's many other hospitals during the 1860s and 1880s were similar to those of women at la Maternité, however there were fewer domestic servants. Of all the hospitalized pregnant in Paris, only 27 percent were domestic servants compared with 37 percent at la Maternité.

The different areas of residence tends to explain some of the variations in the occupations. Almost an equal percentage of women delivering at la Maternité hailed from the more distant, poor, working-class arrondissements such as the second, ninth, tenth, eleventh, eighteenth, nineteenth, and twentieth arrondissements and working-class suburbs as from neighborhoods surrounding the hospital (see map 1). Each of the other hospitals in Paris primarily served working-class women of their neighborhood. For example, l'Hôpital Saint-Louis drew from the tenth arrondissement in which it was located and the contiguous eleventh.[59] Ernestine Pallet's cheap furnished room in the eleventh arrondissement was only about five blocks from Saint-Louis, the closest hospital.

The slight differences between the pregnant women who entered la Maternité and those of l'Hôtel-Dieu indicate that women used l'Hôtel-Dieu, Paris's major general hospital, more as a neighborhood hospital. L'Hôtel-Dieu also had fewer regulations restricting admissions to women who had resided in Paris at least a year. Women had only to be seriously ill, or in labor, to be admitted. As with women at la Maternité, the vast majority of those at l'Hôtel-Dieu came from areas such as nearby Picardy, the Centre, Ile-de-France, Lorraine, and Burgundy and only 16 percent had been born in the department of the Seine.[60]

Some women may have preferred l'Hôtel-Dieu to la Maternité because at the latter they were subjects for student midwives. Other women arrived at l'Hôtel-Dieu after encountering bureaucratic difficulties and being denied admission elsewhere. Such was the situation for a young woman who came to l'Hôtel-Dieu in April 1853 to have her baby. Since she presented no medical emergency and was not about to deliver, the intern who examined her sent her to the nearest hospital with an obstetrical service—la Clinique, just across the river. Because the maternity service of la Clinique was temporarily closed, the intern there sent her to la Maternité. After a wait, the midwife in charge at la Maternité examined her and gave her a "ticket" to be admitted. At the admissions desk, they demanded her certificates stating that she had lived in the city for at least one year, that she was nine months pregnant, and that she was too poor to pay a midwife or have the delivery at her home. Since she did not have the documents and was not in labor, they would not admit her and sent her to the police of her area, the faubourg Saint-Antoine, over a one-hour walk from la Maternité, where in turn the police demanded proof that she had lived in Paris at least one year. Exhausted and tormented, she then sought her absentee landlord who was unavailable. The next day, she had labor pains, and fearing to deliver her baby in her room, she first set off for her landlord in Belleville, then went directly to l'Hôtel-Dieu where she delivered her baby, without certificates of residence and indigence, three days after she first sought admission. L'Hôtel-Dieu admitted her on grounds of imminent delivery.[61] It was necessary to have all of the required certificates in hand before labor and delivery. This became especially difficult if, as was common, a young woman did not live in one place for more than a few months and needed to obtain statements of residency from several different landlords or employers.

Since the mid 1850s, doctors and hospital administrators realized that the incidence of maternal death was lower among women giving birth with a midwife outside the hospital than among women at la Maternité.[62] Recognizing the advantages of midwife deliveries, more than a decade later, starting in 1869, the administrators of la Maternité and other public hospitals, in cooperation with Public Assistance, paid local licensed midwives to deliver many parturient women who sought hospital admission. Hospital admissions officers sent many women presenting uncomplicated labor and delivery to publicly supported welfare midwives. Between 1869 and 1900, Public Assistance employed as many as 96 midwives at any one time, who helped a total of 25,958 poor women deliver their babies. These midwives were subject to regulations, inspection, and daily visits from a Public Assistance doctor to ensure cleanliness and antiseptic measures. They were named by the administration of Public Assistance and served on a three-year, renewable appointment. They had to live in the arrondissement in which they practiced and could be dismissed for malpractice. No midwife could have more than five to seven women in her establishment at any one time, and new mothers and babies had to stay eight to ten days after delivery.[63] Occasionally there were complaints that the patients left the midwife too soon, when they were still weak. Some midwives had a reputation of verbally abusing their patients; a rudimentary information network may have existed among the poor and pregnant of the city, because some women tried to avoid certain midwives. Public Assistance furnished each woman who delivered at a welfare midwife's establishment with a layette for her infant, just as it did for women who delivered in the hospital.[64]

The poor and pregnant whom the hospital authorities sent to Public Assistance midwives resembled those who delivered at la Maternité in every way throughout the last three decades of the century; la Maternité patients were not atypical.

Not one women at a maternity hospital, or who had the assistance of a public-welfare midwife, gave her occupation as that of prostitute, but the question remains as to whether these women engaged in sex for money, either on a regular basis or as a temporary means of survival during periods of unemployment. Women in the maternity hospitals held the same occupations as most prostitutes claimed: domestic servants, seamstresses, laundresses, and linen launderers and menders. Given the poverty of women in these occupations, and their long periods of unemployment, many women must have exchanged sex for money in order to survive. As the historian Alain Corbin stated, "In Paris, kept women were generally linen menders, seamstresses, laundresses, dressmakers, or some flowermakers who worked in the ateliers of the city; victims of insufficient salaries, they sometimes had to use their charms to complement their resources."[65] Garment workers, for example, comprised at least 20 percent of all female laborers in Paris, and 30 percent of the known prostitutes. Domestic servants were at least 20 percent of the labor force and 39 percent of prostitutes. Some of the women in la Maternité claiming a legitimate occupation, especially in the garment trades, may have been clandestine or occasional prostitutes, pushed toward it by desperate poverty, often prompted by her abandonment by family or lover.[66] Both groups, women in the maternity hospital and prostitutes, claimed occupations common among the working-class female population as a whole.

Poor women who did not seek admission to a hospital but who gave birth at home with the assistance of a midwife furnished by their local bureau de bienfaisance differed in their occupations from those who sought admission to la Maternité, another public hospital or a public-welfare midwife.[67] In the 1890s almost 36 percent of the women giving birth in la Maternité were domestic servants. This contrasts with only 2 percent of the women who delivered their babies at home with a bureau de bienfaisance midwife. Daily maids who did not live with their employer and were more likely to be married constituted 10 percent of the clientele of the welfare bureau's midwives but only 1 percent of those in the hospital.

In the last decade of the century, between 20 and 25 percent of the women who gave birth at home with the help of a midwife from their local bureau de bienfaisance did not work for wages outside the home and were listed as "sans profession;" this included ménagères. During the same decade, only 13 percent of those at la Maternité were either ménagères or without a job. Day laborers (*journalières*) represented about 17 percent of home births with a midwife from their bureau de bienfaisance and only half that in la Maternité.[68] The high percentage of women who claimed no profession, and the low percentage of domestic servants who delivered their babies at home, confirmed that those women who used a bureau de bienfaisance midwife were married, as regulations stipulated those using the bureaus should be.

The poor and pregnant of Paris included more than the hundreds of thousands of visible women who appeared in the scenarios set by the criminal justice system, the local welfare bureaus, the public hospitals, and the associated public welfare midwives. The enormous cast presented here is not unique, but rather representative of many of those in Paris. These women are discernible because at one crucial point in their lives they came into contact with public institutions who recorded the women's passage. Countless others were not included in the productions managed by public authorities because either they could not obtain admission or they chose not to apply. They remained in the dark alleys of Paris, obscured from view because they had no way of letting the world see who they were. They somehow managed on their own.

Because the average income of poor working women in Paris during most of the century ranged from Fr 250 to Fr 600 a year, the economics of work and single motherhood presented a staggering problem for the women. The estimated annual minimum cost of living for a worker during the last decades of the century ranged from Fr 850 to Fr 1200 a year.[69] Lodging alone cost from Fr 100 to Fr 150, food cost from Fr 550 to Fr 750, laundry from Fr 100 to Fr 150, and clothing, heating, and lighting all cost from Fr 100 to Fr 150 a year. A female worker who earned Fr 375 per year, the average wage for an unskilled worker, ate poorly. Her milk for breakfast and her bread for the entire day cost 25 centimes. She ate fried potatoes and some sausages for a cost of about 20 more centimes. Cheese cost another 10, totaling 55 centimes per day. During the long period of seasonal unemployment all meat disappeared as did her breakfast. Thus, she ate for less than Fr 200 a year, but her diet was completely lacking in fresh fruits or vegetables. It also left her just Fr 150 to pay for her lodging, heat, clothes, and light.[70] If she had a baby, she could not survive without assistance. It is not hard to understand why a woman allowed a man to pay for her lunches in return for sex, why she lived in a consensual union, or why she might despair if she became pregnant.

The lives of the poor and pregnant were determined by poverty, despite their constant work. Furthermore, their choices were constrained by whatever institutional structures were available. The texture of their environment changed profoundly over the century and reflected the dominant attitudes that politicians, bureaucrats and social reformers held about the poor and pregnant, especially the single mother. The women's daily struggles, their constant battle for survival, their strengths, their strategies, and their restricted options can not be fully appreciated without an understanding of the cultural, political, and institutional milieu of the city and country in which they lived. Institutions that helped these women had changed over time, and that change directly reflected changes in moral perceptions and prescriptions.

CHAPTER

2

Immorality and Motherhood: 1830–1870

The poor and pregnant of Paris lived in a society dominated by men who held strong views about what constituted moral behavior. These views helped shape both the script that included poor women and the direction the women were to follow. Male ideas about moral behavior set the parameters for women's lives, but those ideas changed during the course of the nineteenth century and so, too, the parameters changed.

As Victor Hugo began his well-known romantic story of Fantine in *Les Misérables,* "she had been born at Montreuil-sur-mer, but nothing was known of her parents. She was called Fantine because she had never been called anything else. . . . At the age of ten she had left the town and gone into service with a farming family in the neighbourhood. At fifteen she had gone to Paris 'to seek her fortune.' She was beautiful and had stayed pure as long as she could. . . . She worked in order to live, and presently fell in love, also in order to live, for the heart, too, has its hunger. She fell in love with Tholomyès. For him it was a passing affair, for her the love of her life." Hugo underscored her innocence and virtue, because her relationship with Tholomyès was a result of love, not licentiousness. She and Tholomyès had been lovers for two years when he abandoned her and returned to his parents in Toulouse. Fantine "wept bitterly. It was her first love. . . . She had given herself to Tholomyès as to a husband, and the poor girl had a child."[1] Hugo's sympathetic image found few echoes during his time but resonated later in the century.

Throughout the first three-quarters of the nineteenth century the poor and pregnant of urban France, especially single mothers, were central to any discussion of the social question: What should be done about the problem of the poor, the so-called dangerous classes, characterized by depravation, immorality, and crime? The problem of the urban poor was equated with the fecundity of impoverished women who lacked morality and had children even though they could not support them. Social analysts described an epidemic of illicit relationships rampant in the city, generating urban malaise, immorality, and deviancy. They feared working-class promiscuity and regarded illegitimacy as a barometer of immorality. Indeed, it was the perceived problem of illegitimacy, not the plight of the poor mothers themselves, whether married or single, that occupied the minds of early nineteenth-century social commentators.

In nineteenth-century Paris, the poor were highly visible, and their conspicuous presence compelled social reform campaigns. Parisians lived in a world in which illegitimacy was an overwhelming social problem. During the first half of the century the illegitimacy rate in metropolitan Paris exceeded 30 percent; throughout the century, it never fell below 24 percent.[2] Furthermore, the city grew rapidly from 548,000 in 1801 to over 2.5 million in 1900, less from a natural increase than by an influx of migrants, many of whom were unemployed and without a permanent home. The population growth was not distributed evenly over the city, but concentrated in the working-class areas. Migration and illegitimacy symbolized the geographical and familial instability that separated the dangerous classes from the honest laboring classes.[3] Especially unsettling to property holders was the population increase immediately following the 1830 and 1848 revolutions. The vivid memory of urban unrest, aggravated by a visible increase in the population of the working classes of the city, agitated the middle classes to seek social reform.

Attitudes toward the poor and pregnant were part of individual and community belief systems that sought to reinforce and defend bourgeois cultural values. The dominant moral values of politicians and social reformers helped organize the social order; their perceptions fueled ideologies, which in turn empowered politics. According to the reformers of nineteenth-century France, the well-ordered state depended upon a well-ordered family; to have a well-ordered family there was a need to control women's sexuality and reproduction.[4]

Prominent social critics and reformers wrote treatises and reports that, though they cannot be taken as evidence for the actual conditions, are rich with indications of elite perceptions of the working-class situation. Their writings influenced policy and consequently set some of the parameters within which poor women had to lead their lives. Middle-class observers provided the initiative and set the tone for specific family policies that applied to women.

The poor and pregnant abound in the reports of social reformers, charitable organizations, and public officials, each with its own characteristic point of view, but when taken together they span a spectrum of opinions. Whether it was the women themselves, unscrupulous men, or economic conditions that were to blame for single motherhood was a subject of dispute. Depending on the position of the writer, the single mother was morally corrupt—degenerate, drunk, and a threat to the sanctity of the family and to social order—or a sinner but redeemable, or an innocent victim of circumstances. Toward the end of the century the image of the single mother as a depraved woman receded to the more dominant image of her as a victim of society who must be protected for her children's sake—if not for her own.

Writers defined the single mother by her relationship with her child without more than a hint of the father or the mother's own circumstances. Although fathers could legally recognize their out-of-wedlock children, almost none did until late in the century. The single mother alone bore legal responsibility for her child. Article 340 of the Napoleonic Civil Code on *recherche de la paternité,* enacted in 1804, distinctly prohibited the mother from seeking child support for any of her children born out of wedlock. This law removed all legal, fiscal, moral, and social responsibility from the father if he was not married to the mother of his child, or did not legally recognize his child. It specifically prohibited a mother or child from seeking paternity support. The child, however, was always entitled to maternal support. This law circumscribed the world in which the single mother could act. The Code's interdiction against paternity searches reversed centuries-old Church and civil laws which often required that a father financially support his child whether he married the mother or not.[5]

The Napoleonic Code, by expressly forbidding *recherche de la paternité,* represented the triumph not only of Napoleon's male chauvinism but also of Rousseau's antifeminist philosophy. Rousseau maintained that the "law of nature" leaves men uncertain of the paternity of the children they are expected to maintain; women, therefore, should be subject to men's judgment and laws.[6] Forbidding *recherche de la paternité* accommodated the bourgeoisie's desire to protect marriage, the family, and inherited property. They feared that "legitimate" sons would have to share the patrimony with children the men bore out-of-wedlock and thus lead to the breakdown of the family. Furthermore, the law's supporters argued that if a working-class woman could not pursue the father of her child for financial support, she would restrain herself from sexual behavior before marriage.

As a result, reformers and politicians of the nineteenth century concerned themselves mainly with working-class women who became single mothers. They paid less attention to poor married mothers, to widows, or to middle-class single mothers for they did not perceive these women as a danger to traditional values or a threat to the social order.

The Fallen Woman, 1830–1848

Poverty, immorality, and single motherhood became a focus of concern in Paris in the 1830s when reformers tried to analyze and contain perceived social deviance. Following the 1830 Revolution, Parisian authorities feared working-class militancy and the spread of radical ideas. In seeking to remove the causes of social deviance, reformers became concerned with the problem of poverty and its apparent associated "depravation of morality" especially among women. Social critic H.A. Frégier intoned in 1838, "The poor and vicious classes always have been and always will be the most fertile crucible for all categories of wrong-doers." He articulated the widespread assumption that the poor women of Paris carried in their wombs the potential for reproducing the "dangerous classes" and maintaining a cycle of immorality and poverty. As mothers, they bore essential responsibility for establishing family ties and for raising future generations. They formed an integral part of urban life; but, he complained, many were not living in an accepted family. Only one-third of the women in the needle trades were married to the men with whom they were living. The other two-thirds, living in "concubinage," represented the "disordered morals" and potential danger of the big city.[7]

Frégier was not alone in blaming single mothers for an increase in poverty and alleged immorality in the cities. In seeking to remove what they thought of as the causes of social deviance, reformers became concerned with the causes of *misère,* or extreme poverty, and misery among the working classes, and they based their remedies on the perceived causes. To ameliorate the social problems of poverty and illegitimacy, they generally preferred "moral tutelage and social control" to economic reforms or acquiescence to workers' demands.[8] During the first half of the century, political or social economists, moral economists, and social Catholics, dominated the discourse. Within each group subtle differences marked individual philosophies; occasionally there was a great deal of overlap, especially between the moral economists and the social Catholics. Rather than regarding these schools of thought as monolithic, they are best seen as useful constructs for understanding the varying, sometimes divergent, and frequently overlapping attitudes toward poor mothers.

Social Economists

Political economists originated, and initially dominated, the debate over industrialization and its effects on society. They believed in the industrial system, advocated free trade, and favored laissez-faire policies. In the 1830s some French political economists wanted political economy to embrace the whole social system and they added human relations to traditional political economy, differentiating their system of beliefs from more doctrinaire political economists. They referred to their philosophy as social economy.[9] Social economists rejected government intervention either in economics or in family life. As modified Malthusians, many believed that much of the misery derived from the improvidence of the people: women workers did not restrain their sexuality, bore children whom they could not support, often did not marry, or married before they could afford their children.[10]

The social economists led the discussions about the ills of society, including single motherhood. Attention to unwed mothers grew out of their analysis of the "dangerous class." They believed that almost all forms of social deviancy, including unwed motherhood, arose from segments of the poor and uneducated working population and the unemployed "floating population." In analyzing the danger posed by the laboring population, social economists studied the origins of economic suffering and the influence of industrialization and urbanization on morality. Since they could not explain indigence by referring to the economic system alone, social economists asserted the moral origins of poverty and particularly faulted the women. Extreme poverty was the result of moral weakness, lack of religion, decline of family ties, and relaxation of personal hygiene—all the woman's responsibility. The system was not at fault, they said, rather it was the moral defects of the working classes—their laziness, debauchery, drunkenness, and lack of foresight—that led to poverty. Add passion unchecked by reason or education, and the poor moved from poverty to deviance. To the social economists, single mothers were deprived because they were depraved; moral corruption caused poverty. The victims of poverty were themselves responsible.[11]

Louis René Villermé's inquiries and reports from the 1830s and 1840s supported and sanctioned by the Academy of Moral and Political Sciences, influenced political and social thought for generations. After on-site investigations of workers' lives, he concluded that "inadequate income more often than not was the root cause of a host of misfortunes . . . that befell the working classes."[12] However, inadequate income was a result of moral disorder. True to the philosophy of social economists he insisted that "the corruption of morality . . . had the indirect but equally deadly effect of reducing family income. The young male worker gave little thought to the future and came to marriage penniless; the single woman, whose income was at best barely sufficient for her needs, foolishly wasted even that small sum on fashion." To Villermé, debauchery was the major threat to a family's balanced budget.[13]

Social economists frequently blamed the growth of cities, industry, and the increase in urban working population for leading to an increase in poverty and illegitimacy. Foremost among the urban problems was the indifference to religion and relaxation of public morals occasioned by large numbers of men and women together in the work place. According to social economists, the relaxed morals were primarily the fault of women workers. Young women established irregular relationships with their co-workers and easily succumbed to seduction by their employers and foremen. Villermé believed that immorality was contagious and spread from one person in the workplace to another, by example and by peer pressure. According to Villermé, conditions in industry led to bad language, corruption of morality, promiscuity, and cohabitation or "concubinage." Women's immorality created too many more newborns and continued the downward social spiral; industry and urbanization only created the environment in which this was more likely to occur.[14] Villermé's moral indignation leaps out of his report. He especially attacked the unwed mother as a symbol of moral decay. He did recognize, however, that in some areas of France, men living in "concubinage" often legally recognized their children, and lived as if they were married. When Villermé made a statement that could be a positive one, he used the word "men;" when writing about a lack of morality he usually mentioned women or young girls specifically.[15]

The social economists' answer to the problems of poverty did not lie in alms-giving, religious charity or regular public assistance from the state (called *charité légale*). They believed that charity and welfare was to be avoided because it interceded in the responsibilities that parents and children have toward one another, and encouraged imprudent behavior, excess population, and a "flood of misère." Social economists did admit, however, that in certain circumstances there could be some charity or welfare. The government should take care of the misfortunes that "man" could not prevent. For example, hospitals for the deaf, blind, physically incapacitated, or insane would not actually increase the number of disabled people. All charity, however, should consist of face-to-face interaction between the charitable donor and the recipient to encourage a sense of foresight, saving, planning, and morality among the poor. Above all, aid must encourage neither laziness nor childbirth.[16]

As a leading social economist, Villermé condemned most charity and welfare in 1840 because he believed that then the able-bodied would refuse to work, thus denying industry a potentially productive segment of society. He declared that individuals were morally responsible for their own well being, and the best charity was the least. The only exceptions he made were for abandoned and orphaned children, the insane, those too old or too sick to work, and those morally deserving poor who face a sudden disaster. For example, he argued that if both a husband and wife worked, had no vices, and bore no more than two children then they could survive without aid, but usually without sufficient income to save. Unemployment, sickness, or the birth of another child would plunge them into horrible poverty; then it was necessary for charity to aid them temporarily. He noted that women received half the wages of men, but even for them charity would be useful only if it were offered to the most worthy, given only temporarily, and only in extraordinary circumstances, such as to married mothers at the time of childbirth and the first few months after.[17] To social economists, aiding single pregnant women and indigent mothers disrupted family ties, encouraged mothers to abandon their babies, led to an increase in disordered morality, and produced more children.

Social economists were of two minds about fecundity. On the one hand, a nation's strength and status were often measured by its population size. On the other hand, an increase in population among the denizens of Paris inspired fear. For several social economists, an excess of population, or an "unfortunate birth" among the working classes was one of the prime causes of their misery, along with disorder, laziness, debauchery, or a physical calamity.[18] Prudent behavior on the part of the lower classes could prevent poverty. Workers had a choice: prudence in marriages and childbirth, or a miserable existence. If poor women had too many children, it was their own fault, a result of early marriages or loose sexuality.

How could morality be improved? Villermé proposed a paternalistic, controlling solution in which individual manufacturers and factory owners should create situations that did not contribute to immorality. Most important, manufacturers should keep young men and women separate. Although social economists showed no sign of understanding a poor mother's plight, abhorred public welfare, and sought no measures to alleviate her misery, by the same token they did not urge state interference or seek control of her private life—except, of course, by the powerful means of moral censure.

Moral Economists

The moral economists, the second group of social reformers, highly influential and widely represented in the Academy of Moral and Political

Sciences, incorporated "moral science into its discourse on the production of wealth."[19] The moral economists in many instances resembled the social economists. They examined the relationship between morality, especially that of women, and the nation's wealth. Primarily concerned with working-class family life, moral economists placed high value on stability and financial security. They viewed cleanliness, hard work, sex only within marriage, and limited childbearing as the keys to survival and happiness. Like the social economists, they extolled the virtues of the hardworking, prudent family.[20]

Yet, inherent in the analyses of the moral economists was a reversal of the relationship between poverty and immorality hypothesized by the social economists. Rather than moral weakness leading to poverty, moral economists believed that poverty, especially among women, led to vice. The sin of a "fallen woman" resulting in single motherhood, was not due to a woman's innate depravity, but rather to the conditions of poverty that engendered such behavior. Moreover, they advocated limited state intervention into private spheres in the interests of improving industrial society by creating a stable and moral working class. Intervention into working-class family life was to be limited in order to avoid suggesting that workers had a right to public resources to see them over hard times. Moral economists wanted workers to learn that the family, and not the society at large, was the seat of financial and moral solidarity. Both moral and social economists expressed awareness that the preservation of the social order required some judicious assistance to the needy, but only to the *deserving* poor—the orphans, the aged, the insane, and the genuinely infirm. Those able to work should not receive assistance.

Moral economists particularly underscored the marriage problem which lay either in consensual unions or imprudent procreation within marriage. In neither case could the workers afford their children. Moral economists argued that marriage and childbearing should be postponed until workers had saved enough, but they preferred early marriages to illicit unions. They perceived illegitimacy as both a cause and symptom of social disorder, fundamentally problematic as a rejection of legal marriage and of the family, the essential foundations of social organization. Equally important to the moral economists, consensual unions were the source of illegitimate children who might well rebound to the public ill—either as criminal instruments of social disorder, or as budgetary liabilities such as abandoned children or juvenile delinquents. Rather than focus on prohibiting short term sexual relationships, however, moral economists sought to encourage legitimate marriage among long-term cohabitants who could be redeemed. Unlike the social economists, the moral economists had no qualms about state intervention in a woman's private life if it facilitated a legal marriage.[21]

Joseph Marie de Gérando represents the most prominent moral economist of the 1830s and 1840s. He demonstrated that the number of births was the greatest in the poorest quarters of Paris, and he argued that indigence, morality, and a high birth rate were thus inextricably intertwined. He recognized the problem of the cities where men and women lived and worked in close proximity. He condemned improvident indigent women who had an "excess of sensuality," and entered into precipitous marriages. Yet, he counseled against early marriages because they led to children and misery. His solution to reduce the numbers of needy was to teach good morality, have the workers avoid an imprudent marriage and postpone marriage until they could support children. Gérando focused on the behavior of poor women within their physical environment of poverty and placed them in an untenable situation. He believed that women were destined to live for someone else. He saw them as a daughter, sister, wife, mother, or nun. There was no place in his ideal system for a woman worker living outside a family environment, except as a domestic servant.[22]

Like other social analysts, Gérando expressed neither sympathy nor charity for women who gave themselves to "licentious living," but he felt sorry for the naive women who succumbed to men who gave them false promises of marriage and then departed. He worried about how the honest poor women, seduced and abandoned, would live; but Gérando never suggested that the man had any responsibility or obligation to the child, society, or to the woman he seduced. He recognized, however, that once a woman became pregnant, she often lost her job. Without resources she could not even find shelter and fell into a downward spiral of debauchery. Gérando's solutions rested on the moralization of women and provision of shelter for them, with no effort to do anything to or for men. He proposed refuges for unwed mothers where they would be received, rehabilitated, and put to work under the veil of secrecy. The staff would support the good sentiments of the poor women, seek to reconcile the new mothers with their families, and try to find them work. In several respects these refuges for unwed mothers resembled reform schools with the goals of making the women repent and saving them from "libertinage" after "the first fall." These refuges would save the honor and pride of their families and also of their infants. The "moral rehabilitation" of the single mothers would prevent the corruption of their babies who would otherwise repeat the patterns of their mothers and became a menace to society. Thus, charity and public welfare would save more than one victim from an abyss.[23]

Gérando was not quite so charitable toward women in consensual unions. He sought ways to preserve the urban family from "the plague of concubinage which is a flagrant insult to religion and morality, at the same time that it brings misfortune to the children it produces and puts disorder in society." Cohabitation, he averred, often began by seduction, with the woman giving in to degradation by living with the man. Away from the moral authority of her family "she became the most dangerous instrument of depravity." Her licentiousness produced a *"femme vicieuse"* who had no dignity or self-respect, knew no bounds and whose vices were very contagious. He was, however, a harsh critic of both members of the consensual couple. "Those who abandon themselves to these sinful liaisons substitute sexual pleasures to obligations, caprice to fidelity. Men think they are free, but it is a baneful liberty which permits the sacrifice of those around him to his own passions. For [the woman's] entire life she has compromised her honor and is stripped of virtue."[24]

Unwed mothers who had already fallen "into the abyss of corruption" received even less pity and charity from Gérando. He conveyed little understanding of women's vulnerability by blaming the women, not their seducers, for a breakdown in the family—they led men astray and spread disease. Although admitting that sometimes indigence led to a woman's fall, Gérando also believed that it had become a mere excuse.[25] Yet, even "fallen women" were not beyond redemption. Gérando offered them incarceration in an institution administered by private religious charity and supported with public funds. There they would work, in silence and solitude, apart from their old environment. Although Gérando's ideal institution sounds like a detention center, he indicated that he wanted it to be a safe shelter and not a dark, dank prison. As a social reformer who practiced what he preached, Gérando founded the Asile Gérando, which received young unwed mothers ("victims of a first 'fault' ") who were abandoned and exposed to possible corruption and misery.[26]

Such institutions were supplementary to what Gérando considered the best form of charity—home relief from religious and philanthropic people. Capricious alms-giving, he argued, without restrictions involving a change in behavior for the recipient, would only degrade the recipient and encourage immorality. He justified home assistance to unwed mothers as leading them back to a path of virtue.[27] Gérando and other moral economists thought poverty was not so much a cause of immorality as were poor women, and they saw moral reform of poor women as a solution. Such moral reform justified intervention, and it is this intervention that distinguishes the moral economists from the social economists. Although Gérando represented the ideas of the moral economists, his views also resembled those of the social Catholics.

Social Catholics

Social Catholics equaled the social and moral economists as important social reformers and policy advisers. They emphasized the moral, spiritual and social centrality of the nuclear family as the base of the moral community. Intrinsic to their argument was the belief that "the solution to the great problem of misère was impossible without a purification of morality." Fundamentally critical of industrial capitalism, and reacting in part to political economy which extolled the virtues of industry, social Catholics blamed the new industrial and urban society for loosening family bonds and thereby facilitating the demise of the nuclear family. In their eyes the breakdown of the nuclear family was symptomatic of the spiritual and moral decline of society.[28] Social Catholics of the early- and mid-nineteenth century sought to employ Christian principles in their solutions to the social question. They based their argument on moral reform, and in this they were not so different from the moral economists.[29]

Stating that "immorality is the sister of misère," social Catholics argued that with moral reform would come an alleviation of misery.[30] Social Catholics therefore usually advocated private, voluntary charity under the inspiration of Catholicism and strongly urged individualized personal contact between charitable donors and recipients, in order to allow the devout bourgeoisie to educate and reform the working-class, especially the women. They eschewed state intervention to alleviate poverty. Like the moral economists, they strongly believed that the poor did not have a right to charity or assistance.

Visiting the poor in their homes had long been an important duty of a pious Catholic, and this continued to be the primary social Catholic strategy throughout the nineteenth century. Home visits were to prevent abuses and ensure that the aid was used properly, but an equally important function was to support and educate the deserving poor as well as to spiritually uplift both the recipient and the donor. Social Catholics opposed indiscriminate alms-giving, because the donor did not know the exact use to which the recipient put the aid or if she was deserving. Furthermore, alms-giving provided no chance for moral education. Religious charity was more effective than alms and better than the coldness of philanthropy or public assistance.

One of the most influential Catholic critiques of the industrial social order was the 1834 study of poverty by Count Alban de Villeneuve-Bargemont. He advocated a return to rural areas and agricultural life "based on values of human solidarity."[31] Villeneuve-Bargemont argued that urban industrial manufacturing led directly to the two specific causes of misery: a lack of work and immorality. He differed markedly from the social economists who said that the poor bore sole responsibility for their indigence in arguing that the rich were responsible for the misery of the poor because of egoism and lack of charity. His solution was the creation of agricultural colonies for workers. Without the reversal of economic development, he believed, Christian charity would reduce immorality and ignorance so that the poor would rise from dire poverty. Charity to the honest poor was inseparable from religion. Villeneuve-Bargemont implicitly raised the question of the extent to which women at the time of childbirth were deserving poor, physically unable to work. He combined his commitment to the concept of parturient women as deserving of Christian charity with the more general belief that aid to these women would contribute to population growth and further working-class misery.[32]

Villeneuve-Bargemont advocated population control by means of abstinence. He insisted that "governments do not need to encourage an increase in population. Their interest is to possess a robust, intelligent, moral, and economically comfortable population rather than a large but miserably poor and unhappy one." From this desire to produce a more comfortable population, combined with genuine Christian ethics, he advocated charity to both married and single women in childbirth and for some unspecified time afterward. He believed that they should be given aid because they were unable to work yet obliged to feed and care for their infants. This charity began with home visits from devout Christians to bring relief along with religious moralization to poor mothers.[33]

Villeneuve-Bargemont urged marriage among the poor. "Conjugal charity," he believed, should not only strive toward the marriage of people in consensual unions, but such charity should also persuade single workers that an early marriage and children would compromise their happiness and have dire effects on their future.[34] He did not believe that the law should forbid marriage among poor workers, as it did, for example, in Bavaria. He maintained that "such an exclusion would be completely contrary to liberty and to natural justice. But, without infringing on these rights, the law can impose conditions of marriage on the workers who solicit and receive public assistance. The government should call on the Christian ministry to advise the poor to . . . fortify their resolve to delay marriage [and remain chaste]."[35] He believed that work is a virtue that leads to happiness and that poor women should be productive rather than reproductive.

Other Catholics writing during the first half of the century were not as charitable toward the poor and pregnant as Villeneuve-Bargemont. The influential representative of conservative Catholics on the issues concerning single mothers, the Abbé Adolphe-Henri Gaillard, minced no words when he castigated single mothers for their "corrupted morals." He blamed neither the economic system nor the male seducers for illegitimacy, and he adamantly opposed all paternal responsibility for an illegitimate child. Single mothers, according to Gaillard, should not be placed on the same exalted plane as married mothers, nor should their illegitimate children be given the same rights as legitimate children. The question of marriage, however, was delicate. He abhorred people living together without a legal marriage, especially when they had children. On the other hand he opposed people entering into a "brutal" marriage just because the woman was pregnant, and, like the moral economists, he counseled against unwise marriages when people did not have adequate wages or saving. Still, in an imperfect world, an early and imprudent marriage was preferable to people living together "in sin."[36]

Despite the alleged immorality of single mothers, Gaillard could not let them or their infants die. He argued that the consequences of the doctrines of the social economists would lead to many deaths; therefore he contended that Catholics must come to the aid of the deserving poor by fostering the improvement of their economic and moral condition. Like the social Catholics, he advocated discerning charity, but opposed charity for single mothers. To him, charity would enable single mothers to show the world that they have received aid for their bad behavior and the aid would make women indifferent to their "fault."[37]

Another devout Catholic whose beliefs directly affected mothers living in consensual unions, Jules Gossin thought that cohabitation was worse than a *liaison dangereuse;* he referred to it as a *"liaison criminelle."*[38] Gossin had three goals: rescue unfortunate women from the degradation of illicit cohabitation; give their children the benefit of legitimacy; and lead the family to the practice and love of the Catholic religion. Helping the poor to have a Catholic marriage would combat "disordered morals" and make useful citizens of those degraded and prone to crime.[39]

The belief in the sanctity of marriage and the family as a "magnificent institution" was essential to the ideology of almost all social and moral economists and social Catholics. In 1846 the 192 members of the Academies of the Institut de France joined in the condemnation of cohabitation by signing a statement that in the interest of public tranquility, the government, as well as all friends of law and order, should strive to overcome the obstacles that hinder marriage among the poor. The statement noted that in the criminal courts, of four people accused of crimes, three were living in "disorder." They stated that when men and women lived in disorder often they had no home; they did not economize and neglected their children. Mothers sold their daughters and fathers disappeared. Only a married couple created a home environment to nourish and protect their children.[40] Not only the social Catholics, but the moral and political economists as well, failed to understand consensual unions as a form of marriage for those unable to secure a legal marriage; rather they viewed such unions as dangerous and in opposition to the true family, upon which society was based.[41]

Some organizations urged marriage among the poor. The Société de Morale Chrétienne, founded in 1821 by the duc de Larochefoucauld-Liancourt, included prominent Protestants, social Catholic royalists, nondenominational philanthropists, and government officials. Although opposing dogmatic Catholicism, in some respects it served as an activist arm of social Catholicism and as a common meeting ground for elite social reformers who eschewed fanaticism.[42] Not a society limited to men, one of its most active members in 1848 was Mme de Lamartine. The wife of this Republican leader maintained the royalist practice of wives of heads of state serving as sponsors of charitable organizations.[43] By the 1840s the paternalism of ruling elites, especially social Catholics, toward the urban poor resembled the *noblesse oblige* of the traditional aristocracy from whose ranks many of the members of the Société de Morale Chrétienne descended.[44] The Société operated on the principles of mutual assistance, of human fraternity, and institutional charity to assure "the provident society."[45] Members combined the ideas of charity inherent in the philosophy of social Catholicism with the concept of limited state obligations that formed part of the philosophy of the moral economists.

Sounding sometimes like a social Catholic and at other times like a moral economist, Eugène Sue used the vehicle of the novel to agitate for social reform. His voice, along with that of Victor Hugo, dominated other novelists who used their craft to discuss the social question. Sue's enormously successful *Mysteries of Paris* serves as a prime example of a social novel that treated the plight of the poor in light of new ideas for reform. This novel, serialized in the *Journal des débats* from 1842 to 1843, reached a wide audience. Sue continually extolled honest work, honor, and a loving heart as the virtues enabling the poor to survive the circumstances of their poverty. In the novel, orphaned seamstress Rigolette was the model of virtue. She fended off seducers and hunger, sewed by candlelight in her room late into the night, remained cheerful, saved some money, did not marry until she could afford to, and took pride in remaining chaste so that she could marry an honest workman. She represented the bourgeois ideal of the honest poor, the virtuous heroine.[46] Yet, not all of the women in Sue's novel walked this particular rocky path of virtue.

Two women in the novel became single mothers, but because they loved their babies Sue did not accuse them of depraved morals. Once seduced and abandoned, it was loving maternity that morally lifted the otherwise fallen woman. The character La Lorraine, an indigent laundress, sought admission to la Maternité. Told there was no room, she had her baby in a cellar and friends nursed her back to health. She resumed work and tried to care for her baby, but because of her poverty both La Lorraine and her baby died. Sue presented this case in a straightforward way as one of the unfortunate circumstances of urban poverty. The character Louise Morel, a domestic servant drugged and raped by her employer, became pregnant. During the short time from the birth of her child until Louise realized it was dead, she loved her newborn. Remarked Sue, "she has been unfortunate, but not guilty."[47] Because of the "honest sentiments in her heart" she was redeemed and became an honest worker. Sue argued:

> Women, the most criminal, preserve at the bottom of their heart, two holy ties which the violent action of passions, the most detestable, the most impetuous, never break entirely—LOVE AND MATERNITY! To speak of love and maternity is to say that, with these poor creatures, a soft and pure emotion can still light up here and there the profound gloom of wretched corruption.[48]

Sue also implied that not all single mothers were innocent victims, and that alms demoralized them and therefore should not be given blindly.[49] *The Mysteries of Paris* combined elements of a social Catholic reform tract with aspects of a romantic morality novel. Voluntarism, good will, and good intentions were the essesnce of both. Sue sought philanthropy to redeem the poor urban women, much in the tradition of other reformers, and also in the paternalistic mode that resembled the noblesse oblige of the traditional aristocracy. Sue also subscribed to some ideas of the moral economists in advocating "preventive measures of provident legislation" for the urban poor.[50]

Socialists and Mothers in Misery

Although bemoaning the inequities of the industrial system and the misery that accompanied it, especially for women, none of the social Catholics or moral economists sought to change fundamentally the nature of the economy. Only socialists viewed impoverished mothers in light of a restructured economic system.

Some subtle similarities exist between utopian socialism and social Catholicism. A type of religiosity figured in both movements, and there was some limited overlapping membership, until 1851. Utopian socialists of the 1840s also wrote of the degradation of women workers, but rather than condemning women working outside the home, and single mothers in particular, the socialists predictably blamed the capitalist industrial system. Etienne Cabet, for example, bemoaned the plight of the "daughter of the proletariat. She must work for her family to survive but under conditions in which she is brutalized, loses her beauty and health, and is threatened constantly by the 'plague of libertinage.' She is often unable to marry, for economic reasons, and is forced into concubinage or prostitution."[51]

Socialists did not uniformly condemn consensual unions. The Saint-Simonian branch of utopian socialism even called for free-love unions until they realized that "women's lives were unbalanced at the least, shattered at the worst, by their inability to provide support for themselves and their children." Charles Fourier believed that couples "should no longer be bound in the marriage of 'civilization,' marriage based on dupery for men and servitude for women." He advocated unions based on love for only as long as the attraction lasts; but in order to to realize his goals, the economy and society would have to change because women suffered disadvantages.[52]

Eugène Buret, whose essay critiquing political economy received a prize from the Academy of Moral and Political Sciences, represents alternative socialist views, especially with regard to a lack of blame he placed on women. Buret acknowledged that families with the most children were generally those in greatest need, but he argued that if the population increased faster than the means of subsistence the economic institutions were at fault, not the women. "Vices," he said, "are both a part and a consequence of misère;" they were not a cause.[53] Buret postulated causes of poverty that were independent of the will of poor women. The industrial setting created female poverty by underpaying women workers, and by allowing prolonged periods of unemployment. As a result, almost twice as many women as men (1.7 to 1) appeared among the indigent. Furthermore, the concentration of workers in the same place led to temptations, seductions, and bad health. The situation was so bad for women, that if "a man does not add his salary to the insufficient salary of his companion, her sex alone constitutes a cause of misère. It is not that she lacks strength or arms, she lacks remunerative employment."[54]

There is no moral, normative tone in Buret's discussion of consensual unions because he saw them as by-products of the means of production and as resources against destitution. It was not that women workers chose to live in an irregular relationship; rather they lacked the means to marry. For Buret, consensual unions were not the result of immorality of

men and women but of the inequities of the industrial economy.[55] Buret
believed that private charity alone was inadequate and often counterproductive; it benefited the donor more than the poor. In language
foreshadowing that of the Third Republic he wrote of a "harmonious
solidarity" of intelligent private and public charity. Public welfare, he
argued, was necessary for all industrial countries; but even that was not
enough. It would take education, work, a justly remunerative economic
system, and a change in the economic system and class structure to
alleviate misery.[56]

The socialists presented the only significantly different view of the
poor and pregnant during the first half of the century, and they had no
importance in setting policy. Only subtle differences existed among the
social and moral economists or the social Catholics when it came to
attitudes toward poor women. Following in the tradition of Jean-Jacques
Rousseau, the dominant ideology of these decades defined women in
terms of their uncontrolled reproductive sexuality. Reformers differed
little in their desire not to reward women's alleged promiscuous behavior. The political influence of these reformers resulted in few positive
programs to alleviate the misery of the poor and pregnant during the
first half of the century.

The Fallen Woman, 1848–1870

During the Second Republic (1848–1851) social and moral economists
became less prominent than socialists who sought to create jobs, Republicans who strongly favored public assistance, and the social Catholics.
Among the social Catholics of the Second Republic were antisocialist
militants for private charity who opposed those who allied with the Left
in calling for state intervention and public assistance. The early 1850s
was a watershed time for social Catholics. Some broke away and became
socialists; mainstream social Catholicism became conservative.[57]

Debates on morality and poverty in the 1850s legislature echoed those
of the earlier decades. Moral economists continued to argue that one
should alleviate poverty in order to improve morality. Political and social economists believed that giving aid to unwed mothers would only
encourage the debauchery of women and lead to more illegitimate children, prompting new cycles of immorality and poverty.[58] Although both
generations connected women to social disorder, the first generation of
commentators on the social question, roughly from 1830 to 1850, viewed
women's unregulated sexuality as leading to working-class disorder; the
second generation (1850–1870) shifted the focus to "mothers as the key
to orderly family and social life."[59] This later generation worried less

about overpopulation of the working classes than did the previous one. In the 1860s, advocates of temporary aid to unwed mothers became more outspoken, concentrating their arguments less on the women than on the deprivation of their children.[60] The social economists became a minority, in part because they placed limitations on what could be done. Their attitudes derived from the concept that the less government involvement the better, and they offered no plan, other than some private charity for the moral poor.

During the Second Empire, Jules Simon extolled the virtues of motherhood and insisted that women's primary duties lay as wives and mothers, not as workers in factories. Even single women were potential wives and mothers. With his emphasis on motherhood lending stability to the family and therefore to society, he echoed both the moral economists and social Catholics of earlier decades. He offered no solutions to the situation of mothers who, by economic necessity, must also work except that they could work at home. He wanted women to restrain their sexuality and not become mothers until they could afford to stay home, under the "authority" and "protection" of their husbands.[61]

The views of the social Catholics dominated the discourse from 1850 to 1870 and had a place in all but the most radical doctrines of social reform. The ideologies of moral economy and social Catholicism became virtually indistinguishable. Both spread their ideas through the same philanthropic organizations as well as by books endorsed by the Academy. Neither group looked to the government as an agent of charity or social reform and both promoted social and personal regeneration through paternalism and patronage. This social Catholic outlook reveals the strength of the conservative mainstream of that ideology which stressed the importance of religion, custom and paternal authority as guiding influences in society.[62]

Many social Catholics loosely organized into the Société d'Economie Charitable in the early 1850s under Armand de Melun. More interested in prevention rather than relief of social misery, it nevertheless advocated assistance and protection to children, the sick, and the infirm, and it suggested instruction in economic and family planning (the latter through restraint). Melun supported the idea of private charity, but eschewing alms, he preferred personal contact between donor and recipient.[63] The Imperial government's support for a combination of private charity and limited public welfare was the result of some of Melun's activities. Above all, the goal was the preservation of family life. Hostility to consensual unions remained.

P. A. Dufau, a leading social Catholic member of the Société d'Economie Charitable, exemplifies the dominant political and social ideology of the Second Empire. His work represents a compendium of the ideas from the 1830s through 1860s. Searching for the causes of misère and looking for remedies, Dufau compared the social body to the human body. While the medical arts heal the human body, charity was the social art of healing a society sickened by misère. Integrating the causal theories of the social and moral economists, he described a vicious circle of poverty leading to immorality, which in turn led to greater poverty. Adding the principles of social Catholicism, religion became the medicine with which private charity would doctor the sick society.[64]

Unlike social Catholics of earlier decades, Dufau did not blame industry as a cause of social ills, but he criticized married women working for wages outside the home. He questioned the ability of a woman to raise robust and healthy children when she was completely exhausted from work. He realized, however, that the salary of the woman was necessary for the family, so she had to work—at insufficient and degrading wages. The birth of a child put the family in dire need. Demonstrating the socialist component of his social Catholic background, he argued for equal pay for equal work and for society to help furnish necessities to needy children of working-class families without resources.[65]

Moral condemnation fell upon the single mothers from reformers of the Second Empire just as it did from analysts decades earlier. Dufau, like Gérando, believed that a woman should only live under the protection of a family to avoid becoming a victim of corruption. Like previous reformers, Dufau complained about the loss of innocence that came from mixing the sexes in the factories, where the young girl had no one to protect her. Unlike Villeneuve-Bargemont, Dufau did not propose a return to agriculture. Rather, the young female factory worker should be under the watchful eye of charitable protection societies that would imbue them with wisdom and inspire religious practices. Domestic servants, according to Dufau, lived in an environment not much better than factory workers. Even though a domestic servant became part of a new family, she could be seduced, and that could lead to crime and prostitution. Dufau criticized women in consensual unions for their irreligion and licentiousness. His solution to the problem of cohabitation was to encourage marriage; even though it may have been improvident, it was better than the immorality of "concubinage."[66]

Dufau and other social Catholics of the time pled for charity to rescue the single woman after seduction and a false promise of marriage. Echoing Gérando, they suggested refuge-workhouses run by religious and charitable women for pregnant and postpartum domestic servants and other female workers. The charity would assure proper employment for the new mothers after they left the refuge. Under the care of charitable religious women, the seduced and abandoned would be led back to the path of virtue.[67]

To Dufau, facilitating marriage of the poor was not charity; it saved the family. Likewise, the refuge-workhouses for pregnant single women were institutions of reform and moralization rather than charities. Although Dufau favored assistance to needy married women, he did not wish to extend the relief on a regular basis to unwed mothers. He stated that "private charity could assist a poor, unfortunate girl, victim of a fault in which there was one more culpable than she . . . but the organization of *fixed and regular relief* or *public welfare* in behalf of women who live outside the laws of society . . . would be immoral [and] dangerous for the entire society!"[68]

Intrinsic to Dufau's ideology was the reconciliation of individual liberty with social security, except for unwed mothers. Morally, the poor did not have a right to assistance, but the rich had a moral obligation to aid the poor. He stated that when the poor suffered, it was a threat to the entire community. Dufau argued that the "state is the expression of society" and should be beneficient, especially when individual charity is powerless to remedy the social plague, but it should leave plenty to private charity. Private charity, he insisted, was the best way to guarantee individual liberty.[69]

Liberty, however, was guaranteed for the men more than for the women. In general, men who caused single women to be mothers escaped the wrath of Dufau and his contemporaries. Furthermore, these writers generally condemned the women, but not the men, for "living in concubinage." At best, reformers of all political persuasions expressed ambivalence about the role of the fathers of out-of-wedlock children. A few reformers occasionally admitted that men seduced and abandoned women, gave false promises of marriage, or were as guilty as she. Given the law forbidding a mother or child to search for the father, thus absolving the illegitimate father from all obligation, it was futile for reformers to try to force the fathers to acquiesce to child support. The law, however, reflected dominant attitudes toward women. It was the woman who had loose morals and did not practice chastity; it was the woman whose sexuality enticed the men; and it was the woman who bore full responsibility for the pregnancy and the children. It was the woman whose morality needed reform.[70]

Throughout the first two-thirds of the century poverty was inextricably linked with concepts of morality. Attitudes toward single mothers ranged from that of castigation for "depraved morality" and "debauchery" to pity for a young, seduced girl who demonstrated virtuous maternal love and was therefore worthy of redemption. In the 1830s and 1840s moralists and reformers worried about the population increase, especially among the working classes, whom they perceived as debauched if not actually dangerous. This concern with population colored their perceptions of the poor and pregnant in Paris. They did not want the impoverished and improvident poor producing even more poor. Reformers differed as to whether poverty led to immoral behavior, or the other way around. They also disagreed about what kind of assistance to give, and who was deserving of that charity. Reformers addressed the ideas of freedom and independence of the working classes, but that freedom was illusory, especially for women.

CHAPTER

3

Depopulation and Motherhood: 1870–1914

With the establishment of the Third Republic, a leading group of government officials and nationalistic reformers became more concerned with infant mortality than with the issues of working-class morality and fecundity that had obsessed reformers earlier in the century. A perceived population crisis altered attitudes and redefined the social question. Instead of "what are the causes of misery and how can it be prevented?" people now asked "what are the causes of infant mortality and how can we prevent it?" A child's right to life became a major focus of the decades from 1870 to 1914. Reformers and politicians softened and modified their criticism of poor women for having so many babies, mostly illegitimate, and they began to interest themselves with keeping those babies alive.[1] All of these changes enabled legislative and programmatic action.

In several popular novels, Emile Zola encapsulated the changed attitudes toward the poor and pregnant that marked the last decades of the nineteenth century. In his 1877 novel, *L'Assommoir,* Zola presented Gervaise, a single mother morally acceptable as long as she cared for her children and kept her rooms clean. Zola reserved his opprobrium for her degenerate drunkenness after her marriage. It is as if she "fell" despite herself, a victim of her urban, impoverished environment. In *Nana* (1880), to the contrary, the central character showed no devotion to her son, whom she sent away to be raised by someone else. Nana served as an example of a single mother who did not nurse or raise her child, and therefore was unrehabilitated. Zola, the ardent nationalist, made Nana the symbol of national degeneration. The degraded courtesan, devoid of maternal love and morality, died a horrid death just as France entered the Franco-Prussian war. The way to national success thus lay through fecundity and maternal love, neither of which Nana demonstrated. In his didactic novel, *Fécondité* (1899), Zola did not care if the mothers were married or not, working class or bourgeois, as long as they had children whom they nurtured themselves. He condemned single women who had abortions, abandoned their babies, or gave them to wetnurses—regardless of circumstances or social class.[2] Zola put his literary naturalism in the service of social comment and reform. In advocating fecundity, Zola supported the dominant populationist mentality that shaped the Third Republic.

French concern with depopulation cast pregnant women and their offspring in a more favorable light than earlier in the century. This shift to a populationist mentality after 1870 led to a reconceptualization of unwed mothers and married poor women with many children. Through the filter of a populationist ideology, such women were no longer a symbol of urban corruption; rather, they appeared as physically and morally distressed victims of the industrial economy or of the men who seduced and abandoned them. Even the language changed, and at the end of the century reformers began to refer to single mothers as "mothers abandoned without resources, secret mothers, mothers weakened by misery" or "the poor seduced girls."[3] As a corollary, reformers viewed aid to single pregnant women as a way to save infant lives and prevent depopulation. They less frequently differentiated between the married and single mother than did their predecessors, because it was really the infant, regardless of origin, who required protection. This is not to imply that all social analysts expressed pity or sympathy for the poor single mother. Many, especially the devout, still believed that unmarried women who became pregnant committed a "fault" and they needed moral reform or religious training; but even conservative reformers began to advocate programs aimed at saving the babies by sheltering and protecting the unwed mothers.[4]

Although social critics no longer believed that immorality caused poverty, they still feared that without proper guidance the conditions of poverty might engender immorality. In recasting the discourse, portraying indigent mothers as society's victims, reformers viewed the women as potentially fit to raise a child alone and furnish the proper familial environment—provided, of course, that they did not beg, steal, drink, or walk the streets, and that they accepted proper middle-class guidance. Social commentators believed that "an unwed mother is too often the unjust victim of an immoral society, which, up to a certain point must be considered as responsible for the mistake committed and which has the duty to protect the unwed mother in her weakness."[5] Officials now wanted to make sure that babies, whether born of single or married women, lived to be hard-working, moral citizens in support of the Republic. Motherhood became a sacred national duty.[6] With proper guidance and welfare, reformers and government officials hoped that even poor single mothers could breastfeed and raise a child, thus contributing to the child's chances for survival—and ultimately to those of the French nation.

New attitudes toward the single mother also required a different perception of the acceptable family. If the state urged a single mother to keep her infant, then the single-parent family consisting of a mother and her children would seem to be tolerated by the state. Politicians and social critics were in a bind. They sought to reconcile their desire for saving infant lives with their equally strong desire to defend the two-parent family. Their solution was advocacy of supervision over single-mother families. The key to the acceptance of the single mother, therefore, was public oversight of her childrearing practices. Thus, while defending the "natural" two-parent family and paternal authority, reformers could seek support for women raising families alone.[7]

As the bourgeois family became more private, the family of the indigent and of single mothers became more public. The patriarchal state consisting of doctors, scientists, legislators, and public assistance officials substituted for the absent patriarch of a nuclear family. Moreover, the fundamental duty of the state shifted from protecting liberty to protecting life.[8]

These shifts in attitudes toward and policies about indigent mothers and their children occurred in England, Germany, and the United States at roughly the same time or slightly later than in France.[9] In Russia, the middle class similarly developed a new concern with infant mortality, morbidity, and child abuse.[10] In the United States, the social welfare movements of the Progressive Era were based on the idea that criminals and social deviants, including unwed mothers, could be rehabilitated. In these countries the specter of national depopulation played a more minor role than it did in France because they did not face a stagnant population as did France, although national leaders in other countries still engaged in populationist rhetoric.[11] Conversely, fear of depopulation was the major impetus behind a change in attitudes in France, but it was not the sole driving force.

Socialism and worker unrest in the industrial and mining centers shook many nations at the end of the nineteenth century. French republicans such as René Waldeck-Rousseau and Léon Bourgeois encouraged social welfare programs in order to undermine socialists' appropriation of these issues.[12] Socialists had proposed a spate of public welfare projects and after socialist electoral victories, republican politicians adopted many of the ideas and programs of the socialists as a means of gaining popular support. Moreover, the Catholics and Monarchists feared the socialist surge as much as did the staunch republicans. Christian charity, not socialism, they argued, was the way to achieve "social pacification."[13] A temporary coalition of social Catholics and republican politicians sought to address some of the needs of poor families, whether headed by a single mother or married couple, in an effort to win supporters away from the socialists. Yet, new attitudes and programs for poor mothers adopted by mainstream politicians were far more than a reaction to socialism.

The long depression of the 1880s and the first years of the next decade profoundly influenced attitudes toward poor mothers. The depression exacerbated social and economic problems in France's major metropolis and increased the fear of working-class unrest—especially among the new, and poorest, arrivals to Paris. Driven by rural poverty to already crowded urban centers, the poor became more visible as a homeless and mendicant population. They were perceived as a threat to law and order; but unlike earlier reformers who sought to limit the population of these "dangerous classes," reformers of the Third Republic feared national depopulation more than the increased urban poor population. The state emerged as the agency to defend the family and the social order, and the housewife/mother had a key role in generating and maintaining the spirit of family life in a strong nation.[14]

Furthermore, anticlericalism and positivism pervaded the ideologies of a large and important segment of republican politicians who sought to stabilize the regime in the last decades of the century. The church and monarchy were closely linked not only with antirepublican policies but also with the policies associated with hardships for all the poor. Thus, republican politicians sought to undermine the influence of monarchical and clerical power and wanted the minds of the poor free from antirepublican sentiment. Combining anticlericalism with the positivist belief that social ills could be remedied led to new attitudes toward poor mothers.

Secular republicans, with their ardent anticlericalism, resurrected the rhetoric of the First Republic for the centennial celebrations of the French Revolution. These politicians invoked the century-old words of Larochefoucauld-Liancourt, woven into Article 21 of the Constitution of 1793, which declared: "Every French citizen has a right to existence. . . . Public assistance is a sacred debt. . . . Society owes subsistence to its unfortunate citizens, either in providing work for them, or in assuring the means of existence for those who are unable to work." This forms part of the social contract between the state and its citizens.[15] The leaders at the International Congress of Public Assistance and Private Charity which met in Paris in 1889, considering themselves the "son[s] of the Revolution," repeated the maxims of 1793, and stated that "the French Revolution promulgated the new right (*droit*) of assistance by declaring public welfare a sacred duty, and assistance to the poor a national debt."[16]

Anticlericalism, the threat of socialism, a long and disruptive depression, and the ideals of the French Revolution all contributed to changes in attitudes toward motherhood; but it was an intense fear of depopulation that, in a fragile republic, led to important attitudinal changes affecting the lives of poor mothers.

The Shift in Attitudes

In 1891, Jules Simon, a prominent French politician, declared that France loses a battalion per year because it "lets the infants of the poor die. . . . We let 180,000 infants perish each year. Does France have 180,000 too many that we can allow such assassinations?"[17] With this statement Simon added his voice to that of numerous French politicians—of all political persuasions—who decried the high infant mortality rate. He exhorted politicians and mothers to combat the depopulation of France and avoid being economically and militarily vanquished by Germany. On a national scale, the politics of motherhood had become intertwined with the rhetoric of depopulation, of nationalism, and of national defense. The belief that a large population contributed to industrial and military power, elevated infant mortality and a declining birth rate to matters of keen national interest.[18]

Consternation over depopulation emerged more than two decades before Simon's 1891 speech. Between 1866 and 1870 members of the Academy of Medicine argued that the problem of depopulation caused by high infant mortality was endangering the nation. Depopulation rhetoric then accelerated from 1872 through the first decades of the twentieth century, when prominent French bureaucrats, reformers, and politicians wrote increasingly of an infant's right to life and made saving the children a national concern. In particular, a key group of public officials believed that it was the state's obligation to provide children with health care and welfare assistance in order to assure their health and survival. The idea of saving babies' lives thus became the uncontroversial linchpin of the social welfare programs developing in late nineteenth-century France.

Two major events informed France's preoccupation with its population: the agonizing loss of the Franco-Prussian war in 1870, and the census results of 1891. The shocking and crushing defeat of France by the Prussian army in 1870 forced many French nationalists to examine the reasons for that defeat. In part, they blamed it on the degeneracy of the French. Many avowed that this weakness was the result of urban French women failing to nurse their babies themselves, giving their infants to others to wetnurse, either directly or by abandoning them to the state. This practice, they argued, resulted in a high infant mortality rate and in weak children who were undernourished, being deprived of their mothers' breast milk.[19] Those babies who survived mercenary wetnursing by women who fed other women's babies for money, developed poorly, and as adults many were too small and weak to qualify physically for military service. In the bitter disappointment of the military loss, powerful politicians sought to increase the nation's strength through an increased population as they constructed new solutions to the old problems of the poor and pregnant.[20]

The 1891 census results intensified concerns about depopulation. This census revealed that for the previous five years, France had an excess of deaths over births. The gap between natality and mortality which had been narrowing since 1872 virtually vanished between 1886 and 1891, with very little population growth during those years. By comparison, the German population had increased more than four times that of France's from 1880 to 1891.[21] This portended an increasing German military and industrial strength that panicked many French politicians. Moralists, extreme nationalists, and religious conservatives wanted women to produce more babies. They extolled the virtues of motherhood. Others, primarily doctors and practical politicians, focused on reducing infant mortality. They argued that since they could not force people to have more babies, it was necessary to save the ones they had.[22]

Politicians and reformers alike fought the war against depopulation with military metaphors. The medical profession, and especially pediatrics, increased in expertise and power, and thereby provided new weapons in the arsenal of political intervention in motherhood. Prominent doctors bested Jules Simon's estimate, claiming that France lost one army corps a year to preventable infant death. To stop this drain on France's "armed strength" they advised the state to fund hygiene and health programs to reduce infant mortality and urged aid to poor single mothers to increase the survival chances of their infants.[23]

Doctors were among those who took the lead in the battle against infant mortality and depopulation. Late nineteenth-century advances in science and medicine increased the political power of doctors and facilitated the development of programs of hygiene to prevent infant mortality. In particular, newly discovered medical information about the pasteurization of milk and control of communicable diseases encouraged doctors to become politically active, associating themselves with political pressure groups and serving as effective lobbyists. They held seats in the national and municipal governments, served on extra-parliamentary national committees, and even held ministerial positions.[24] Furthermore, they sought to respond to the social question of the day by reaching children through the mothers. Mothers, whether married or not, became crucial agents for the realization of medical programs because it was mothers who dealt with infants' health and hygiene on a daily basis. In late nineteenth-century France the "moral model of behavior as motivated by ethical and cultural imperatives was increasingly replaced by the medical model."[25]

Starting in the late 1860s, and continuing into the twentieth century, the national Academy of Medicine advocated maternal nursing, especially among the poverty-stricken, as a means to reduce infant mortality and the incidence of debilitated children among the survivors. In so doing it promoted the right of an infant to his mother's milk and her duty to provide it. Doctors denied mothers the right to wean their children prematurely because the child's life was at stake. They argued that it was in the general interest of society that the state impose a certain number of duties and sacrifices on all individuals. They noted that everyone, in effect, pays taxes and men must fulfill their military obligations; therefore women should fulfill their social debt of having children and breastfeeding them. Doctors even invoked natural law when the Academy of Medicine voted the following resolutions in 1904: "Maternal breastfeeding is the only natural means of infant feeding. A mother has the duty to nurse her child. The milk of the mother is the property of the child."[26] Members of the Academy of Medicine, at a general meeting in 1907, declared: "It is indispensable to have men to make soldiers, and therefore it is equally indispensable to have the mother to make the men." They asserted that "obligatory military service makes our army strong: the obligatory maternal duty [that of breastfeeding their children] makes our race numerous, healthy, and powerful; these two things are equally necessary to the grandeur of the country."[27]

Prominent doctors with political connections, such as Jacques Bertillon and André-Théodore Brochard, participated in the fight against depopulation throughout the four decades before World War I. Supporting maternal breastfeeding as the major way to save infant lives, Brochard stated in 1876 that "God wanted a mother to nurse her child and also to love her newborn. That is why he gave her breasts with milk and placed them on her chest so she could press her baby to her heart."[28] Bertillon and other physicians, politicians, public health administrators, and philanthropists established the League against Infant Mortality in 1902. The league sought to prevent infant mortality by maternal rest before and after childbirth and, more urgently, by encouraging breastfeeding.[29]

Doctors, along with public assistance officials, became the newest patriarchs of French society, and they were instrumental in the shift of the patriarchy from the private to the public arena. In late nineteenth-century France, the reformist literature connected the health of the body politic with the physical body. This gave French physicians a peculiar ability to cure the ills of state, particularly depopulation, and made association with the medical corporation, and election to the Academy of Medicine, desirable for public assistance officials.

Depopulation and Politics

Preoccupation with depopulation, far from being limited to doctors, came from all bands on the political spectrum—from ardent conservative Catholics and nationalists, to a broad coalition of middle-of-the-road republicans, to socialists. The concern intensified from the 1890s to the war.

The question, "If France does not produce and save its children, where then will it get its soldiers?" had many answers, each grounded in a different understanding of the problem.[30] Camille Rabaud, an ardent anti-German nationalistic Protestant, writer, and politician, argued in 1891 that the population problem was worse in France than in other countries, not so much because of infant mortality (which he correctly estimated as the same as in Germany), but because of a "feeble natality," especially among the well-to-do. Seeking to reduce infant mortality as well as combat a low birthrate, he proposed changing the law to enable unwed mothers to seek out the unwed fathers to force them to pay child support. He also supported marriage-law reform to eliminate many formalities that inhibited marriage. To save infant lives, he favored anonymous child abandonment as a means of eliminating abortion and infanticide—all in the interest of saving the future generation.[31]

Within the political Right, traditional Catholics urged marriage and fecundity. For example, Deputy Abbé Lemire authored legislation to expand an 1850 law that facilitated marriage among the poor. This 1907 law eliminated a few of the many formalities that had been required for marriage, notably parental consent for marriage partners who were not legal minors. Lemire's goal was to reduce the number of illicit unions and their resulting illegitimate offspring, and thus to promote the repopulation of France through marriage and legitimate children. Morality and religion had motivated the passage of the 1850 marriage law; the motivation half a century later was to increase the birthrate and reduce the high infant mortality rate by reducing the number of those more likely to die—children born out-of-wedlock.

Many conservative Catholics, such as Othenin d'Haussonville, a right-of-center Orleanist and permanent Senator, echoed social Catholics of earlier decades and sought to regenerate France through the moralization of poor mothers in which Christian societies would be the main agencies.[32] Along with other social Catholics, Haussonville sought to increase religious education that encouraged marital fecundity. Catholics agreed with other politicians on the ultimate goals: more babies and reduced infant mortality. They differed only as to the means. The end result was so compelling, however, that Senators like Haussonville worked with their republican counterparts advocating measures to protect the mothers and prevent infant mortality.

On the political Left, the majority of socialists voiced their concern with depopulation. Only a vocal minority on the extreme Left, especially the neo-Malthusians and those surrounding Paul Robin, argued in favor of family limitation. Robin and the neo-Malthusians viewed limitation of births among the proletariat as one of the most efficacious and humane ways to bring relief to their misery. In addition, Robin stated, birth control would liberate women from the tyranny of men.[33] Eugène Brieux, the critically acclaimed, didactic playwright and member of the Académie française, in his 1911 version of the play, *Maternité,* supported neo-Malthusian views and countered the nationalistic, pronatalist stance of government officials. His protagonist Lucie Brignac complains, "You'll never make women understand why children must be created to be killed in battle." In the closing scene another woman cries, "We must start the great strike! *the* strike—the strike of the mothers."[34]

Offering a perspective more typical of the Left, socialist Robert Hertz urged the French nation to act to prevent the "relative diminution of the population of France compared with the more rapid growth of other European peoples."[35] Most socialists believed that depopulation not only diminished national strength, but also harmed the workers. Socialists vociferously advocated state action and state responsibility (as opposed to the private, religious charity initiatives espoused by the Catholics) to safeguard the children and prevent depopulation. They argued that maternity was a social function and must have a just compensation. Therefore, the state should honor and monetarily support motherhood just as it did the merchant marine or the raising of livestock. Socialists proposed a plethora of public programs to improve working-class families' lives, increase fecundity, and prevent infant mortality. Proposals ranged from a tax on those without children, to paid maternity leaves during pregnancy and after childbirth, to financial support to encourage breastfeeding, to day care and free well-baby clinics.[36]

Socialist physician Just Sicard de Plauzoles argued that a transformation of the economy would solve France's problems of "depopulation, degeneracy, and decadence. . . . But, in the absence of an economic revolution and the installation of a socialist order, only one means can stop this evil [depopulation] and save France: that is the organization of motherhood into a national service."[37] He complained that patriotic exhortations to have more babies and to marry would have no effect. Moreover, an increase in the birth rate among the poor would only lead to an increase in mortality. Among the prolific proletariat the birth of a child was a disaster, and their misery increased with each child. Poverty was the greatest enemy of infants.

The situation for abandoned unwed mothers was particularly miserable, asserted Sicard de Plauzoles. Single mothers, all of whom had to work, were paid a pittance and could not properly look after their own babies. They had to send newborns out to a wetnurse where many were likely to die. Furthermore, he argued, the unjust French law protected neither the single mother nor her child: he favored paternal financial responsibility for the out-of-wedlock child. He did not condemn women living in consensual unions.[38]

Sicard de Plauzoles advocated treating married and nonmarried mothers equally and paying them as public employees. The government must protect mothers to save the babies, he declared, by making motherhood a necessary national social service. A pregnant or lactating woman is performing a public function. Therefore she should be treated as a *fonctionnaire* and receive an indemnity. It is the duty of the nation to do it and the mother's right to receive it. This would make maternal nursing obligatory, and regulated by law, just as the Committee of Public Safety in 1793 said it should be.[39] In this way, socialist Sicard de Plauzoles invoked the ideological heritage of the First Republic just as centrist republicans did.

The concern with depopulation also inspired new attitudes toward motherhood among republicans in the important and powerful solidarity coalition. Solidarism was a belief in cooperation, mutual responsibility, and collective action in the interest of humanity and for the greater good of the nation.[40] Founded on a vision of a just society based on associative action, solidarism's beliefs in community responsibility coincided with the ideas about social action proposed by some socialists. Solidarists asserted that society as a whole was responsible for the conditions into which its members were born and that it was the social duty of each person to protect all others from injustices. These politicians' language did not center on the mothers, but rather emphasized the needs of the babies and the national urgency to save the children, if possible without destroying family ties.[41]

Emile Cheysson, a believer in solidarity and a "pioneer in social engineering" during his forty-year career, linked depopulation to all aspects of national security, economic conditions, political stability, and public morality. He argued that the largest contributing factor to depopulation was infant mortality, especially among poor illegitimate children who were wetnursed. Mercenary wetnursing resulted in Parisian infants crowding the cemeteries in the wetnurses' villages. Cheysson had more in common with social economists of the preceding generation than with either the socialists or left-of-center republicans. For Cheysson, the problem was women working outside the home rather than at home as mothers of the family, because infants of working mothers died from lack of proper care. The best solution, according to Cheysson, would allow the woman to remain at home, fulfill her role as a married mother, and strengthen her family.[42]

Saving the children was so much a part of mainstream politics that in 1902 Premier René Waldeck-Rousseau convened an extra-parliamentary commission to study depopulation. Many politicians whom Waldeck-Rousseau appointed to this commission had already supported assistance to pregnant, parturient, and postpartum women. The chairman of the subcommission on infant mortality, Paul Strauss, said as early as 1897 that the "protection of mothers and children is of such great importance that it must be in the first place in the preoccupations of governments and legislators."[43]

The report of the subcommission on infant mortality called for protection of poor pregnant women and new mothers, both married and single, so that their babies would not die. It specified a variety of measures such as reduced work during the last stages of pregnancy, prenatal medical care and rest, four-week paid maternity leaves, mutual maternity insurance programs, more convalescent homes for postpartum mothers, an increase in free maternity hospitals, and sufficient financial support so that women, regardless of marital status, could nurse their infants. The subcommission also recommended well-baby clinics, free sterilized milk to mothers who could not nurse, infant care centers, and a wide variety of maternal and family aid. The subcommission sought to protect a woman through her pregnancy and the first few years of her child's life, but one thing it did not protect: her right to chose whether or not she wanted to be pregnant. They agreed to outlaw the sale of contraceptives or any information pertaining to contraception and abortion.

Commissioners decided that legislative changes were necessary. They proposed that "anyone, knowing a woman was pregnant who, of their own free will, hit her, wounded her or did violence to her, or who deprived her of her means of subsistence" would be punished with from one to three years of prison and a fine. If the pregnant woman was incapacitated as a result of mistreatment, the penalty was more severe. Finally, without unanimity, but with a majority of voices, they called for changing the law so that single mothers could seek child support.[44]

The subcommission favored anonymous abandonment of the child as a measure to avoid infanticide for those women who could not and would not, under any circumstances, keep their baby. Child abandonment continued to be an alternative of last resort for most reformers because they still believed that "the unwed mother is moralized by the presence of her child who keeps her on the path of repentance, and who does not let her quickly forget her first fault. . . . [Furthermore] the infant . . . has a right to life . . . [and] also has a right to his mother. . . . The country, on its side, has a right to all these infants."[45] Saving infant lives, however, assumed such paramount importance that many reformers advocated making child abandonment easier, when all other options had been exhausted. A small but vocal number of doctors and politicians, on and off the commission, unsuccessfully advocated reestablishment of the *tours* (revolving cradles in an opening in the wall of a foundling home) to permit easy and anonymous child abandonment. Others preferred that each hospital or foundling home establish an office where a mother could abandon her infant, with no questions asked, as a means to combat infanticide and abortion.

Members of the commission on depopulation neither spoke with one voice, nor maintained consistency in their views. The popular playwright, Eugène Brieux served as a member of this commission and devoted two plays to the debate on depopulation and motherhood. In *Remplaçantes* (1901), he lent his voice to the struggle against mercenary wetnursing and the resulting infant mortality. (In advocating maternal breastfeeding and idealizing women's role as mother, this play recalls Jean-Jacques Rousseau's *Emile*.) In *Maternité*, first performed in 1903, Brieux reversed his pronatalist stand and ridiculed the hypocrisy of official bourgeois arguments extolling the necessity of motherhood. In sharp contrast to Zola's *Fécondité*, this play disparages the demands of the populationists for incessant childbearing; Brieux argues for the right of a woman to choose if and when she becomes a mother as a necessary component of measures to reduce infant mortality.[46] He was not a pronatalist and expressed his concern with depopulation by advocating measures to reduce infant mortality.

In the interest of saving babies' lives, politicians, on and off this commission, discouraged free unions and proposed legislation to encourage marriage by modifying existing requirements of residency and parental approval.[47] They argued that not only would fewer requirements for marriage produce more marriages but also such unions would yield legitimate children who were less likely to die than those born out-of-wedlock. It was especially hard, they explained, for illegitimate children to marry because their birth certificate recalled their shame and that of their mother by stating that their father was unknown. A leading solidarist politician and repopulationist, Edme Piot, proposed that the

Fig. 4.   Replica of the *tour* of the Hospice des Enfants Assistés. Reproduction courtesy of Centre de l'Image de l'Assistance publique.

birth certificate of an illegitimate child should have the name of the man
who recognized that child (if such was the case) rather than merely "père
inconnu." If it were easier for children of single mothers to marry, it
would become easier, in turn, for their children to marry.[48]

Contrary to the moral economists and social Catholics of the 1840s
who criticized workers for marrying too soon and having too many
children whom they could not support, populationists of the turn of the
century complained that workers married too late. Rather than fearing a
bundle of babies among the working classes, politicians at the end of the
century desired the greater number of children that early marriages
would bring. If the families could not properly ensure that all those
babies could live, the government and private philanthropy should come
to their assistance with maternal protection and indemnities to needy
women to encourage breastfeeding.[49]

Emblematic of new attitudes toward women, children, and the family
were increasing numbers of reformers at the turn of the century who
sought to modify Article 340 of the Napoleonic Civil Code that forbade
recherche de la paternité. Doctor Gaston Variot at a 1902 conference on

maternal feeding took the opportunity to argue for changing the Code to reduce infant mortality; he asked: "Why should a mother alone be the victim of easy morals and improvident behavior, and why must she alone support the burden of raising her child?"[50]

Socialist, solidarist, and even some social Catholic reformers argued that the laws did not sufficiently protect the defenseless unwed mother and her child, but allowed men to satisfy their passions without any risk.[51] Single mothers had no male providers, only the providers in the state patriarchy. Therefore, some politicians reasoned, legislators should reform the laws which protect the man and absolve him of his behavior as seducer. Paul Strauss, an advocate of searching for the seducer and making him responsible, said of the trial of a single mother accused of infanticide, "Where is the seducer, the cause of the pregnancy? Why isn't he with the accused? If the seduced girl has so odiously violated the laws of nature and of humanity . . . the fault is especially with the one who has abused her weakness and tenderness. . . . The seducer remains unknown. . . . Responsibility belongs to both."[52] Lack of child support, Strauss argued, led to infant deaths due to poverty and also to increased abortion, illegitimacy, infanticide, prostitution, and suicide—the evils of society and the sources of misery, corruption, depopulation, and the ruin of the social body. If the law allowed paternity searches to make the father responsible society would have the means to combat all these evils, but especially infant mortality.[53] This discourse seeking to change the law and make the men responsible increased and became stronger during the Third Republic.

In defending the single mother, however, politicians risked provoking general bourgeois indignation that to pardon and protect her would encourage illegitimacy. Only a tiny minority of the staunchest advocates of recherche de la paternité, wanted a return to the law of 1670 which permitted the mother to bring a complaint against any putative father for financial damages. Most late nineteenth-century politicians wanted to protect married men and feared scandals harmful to the "legitimate family" if married men were pursued for child support for the offspring of an adulterous relationship. Even reformers who argued that the lack of paternal responsibility for a child born outside of marriage led to male debauchery reasoned that forcing a child upon a recalcitrant father would not be good for the child. Therefore, the majority of legislators did not seek to enforce paternal responsibility beyond payment for the child's food and proposed only that the *single* male seducer pay child support for the infant he helped produce.[54] This became the essence of the 1912 law allowing limited recherche de la paternité. Reformers thus protected the "natural legitimate family" and at the same time appeared as champions of children.

Paul Strauss best epitomizes the patriotic and humanitarian perspective on preventing infant mortality through support of poor mothers. A leading member of departmental and municipal governments in Paris and the department of the Seine during the 1880s and 1890s, Strauss became an influential solidarist national senator representing a working-class quarter of Paris from 1897 to 1936. When he assumed national office, he maintained that the "depopulation of France has become one of the most important concerns of a legislator. . . . The evil of depopulation grows worse."[55] He authored legislation to protect women and children and was one of the most active social reformers and philanthropists of his time who fought infant mortality. He stated that "the future is in the children, the little martyrs."[56]

Throughout his career Strauss argued that it was not the woman whom society must aid and protect, but the child. Mothers were merely vehicles by which sustenance and protection could be offered to the infants. The state was responsible for the child's right to life, he wrote, and the principle of the mother's right to liberty would not stand in the way. By 1901 Strauss had outlined his comprehensive program to reduce infant mortality and prevent depopulation. Since he knew that infants of single mothers had the highest mortality rates, he sought to aid those infants by reducing the ignorance and poverty of their mothers and encouraging women to keep and nurse their babies. He believed that generosity toward the poor single mother at the right time would result in her "irreproachable" conduct and proper care of her baby. He argued that poor, single mothers should receive assistance in the name of "patriotism and humanity" and the "whole collectivity would profit."[57]

Depopulation, Strauss wrote, was a national peril, and teaching married and single working-class mothers to provide hygienic infant care was the battle for national defense. Patriots, pediatricians, and philanthropists had to cooperate in this battle by providing free clinics and guidance. He maintained that assistance to mothers of newborns to encourage them to breastfeed their infants was the foremost way to combat infant mortality. In addition, he advocated paid maternity leaves from work during the last weeks of pregnancy to avoid stillbirths. He also supported the establishment of shelters in which destitute and homeless pregnant women could live and work until their babies were born. Strauss ardently believed that maternity hospitals and midwives should offer free (and if necessary, secret) childbirth for the women. (He did, however, want to decrease the number of midwives: he accused them of being abortionists, or "angel makers.") He called for convalescent homes for destitute women, where they would receive education and guidance in childrearing while they were recovering from childbirth. In the interests of humanity, national solidarity, and the struggle against depopulation, he argued, the Republic had the responsibility to provide these facilities and protect the infants' "right to life."[58]

Strauss wrote to muster public opinion in favor of welfare programs to protect mothers and save infant lives, so he drew his images of mothers to engender sympathy. He, as others, believed that single mothers could be rehabilitated through maternal love. Strauss deplored the sad condition of the single mother as a poor girl seduced and abandoned by her lover. He accurately portrayed her as a domestic servant, freshly arrived in Paris from the countryside, who lived on the sixth floor, under the eaves. A male servant of the same house shared her room and even the same bed of straw. The servant protested that he loved her, won her heart, and promised to marry her. After much resistance, the poor, naive maid succumbed to his seduction. She realized some time later that she was pregnant, only to discover in a profoundly sad state of shock that her lover was married and had a family.

Often, wrote Strauss, the seduction took place in a more odious manner. The domestic servant "is taken by her master." The master's wife knew nothing of this seduction. One day she noticed that her domestic was pregnant and dismissed her with no regard for her maid's future. These seduced and abandoned domestic servants lived like vagabonds because they lost their jobs when their pregnancy became apparent. They could not go home again owing to the shame of their pregnancy. He argued that these unfortunate mothers must be sheltered for the health of their infant. Whereas some called a woman an "incorrigible unwed mother," Strauss referred to her as a "Magdalene, more or less repentant," and as a poor suffering woman deserving pity.[59]

Strauss called for cooperation between public administrators and private benefactors and assured his readers, particularly the traditional Catholics, that even though public welfare in France was becoming a "sacred debt," private charity would not disappear because the extent of poverty was so great. To the socialists, Strauss replied that "hygiene is not a struggle of classes but is on a neutral ground for humanity and love of country."[60] Strauss articulated the new political position, stressing state obligation for welfare rather than the sacredness of individual liberty. He emphasized the responsibility of all levels of society for compulsory public welfare to provide relief and to prevent poverty and premature death. He did not hesitate, on any issue remotely involving the lives of impoverished children, to advocate the intrusion of the state into the private realm of the family.[61] In families with no father, the state would become the patriarch. Strauss was not outwardly concerned with controlling the sexuality of poor women. Rather, he seemed indifferent toward women's sexual morality and was only interested in their morality as good nurturers of their children; he wanted to control and support their motherhood.

Typical of late nineteenth-century anticlerical solidarists, Strauss's political philosophy and activities capture the decline in the traditional, religious view of the family and the emergence of a new morality: practicing proper modern hygiene under medical guidance in order to save the children. Women were to provide France with children; their sexuality was important only because they bore children and lactated. The two-parent family was no longer the only respectable mode; the single-parent household was not only tolerable, but made possible through limited public welfare. This was a radical change from the first three-quarters of the century.

Protestantism and Social Catholicism

Protestants played a particularly prominent role in the politics of public assistance. They made up only 1.7 percent of the population of France in 1883, yet comprised approximately half the members of the Advisory Board to the Director of Hygiene and Public Assistance in the 1890s. Generally in the political Center-Left, Protestants endeavored to create a republic of social action.[62]

The notion of duty to God, one's family, the community, and the nation is central to an understanding of Protestant attitudes toward motherhood among the poor of this era. Some years earlier, Count Agénor-Etienne de Gasparin, a Protestant Minister of the Interior for Louis Philippe in the 1830s, had stressed the fundamental notion of individual and familial duty. For Gasparin, this meant that family members had the duty to pray, to love, and to support one another. These duties applied first to all family members, and then to those outside the family.[63] During the Third Republic, Protestant solidarists extended this position by arguing that France was a family wherein all members of the nation were required to fulfill duties to one another.[64]

Henri Monod, the Director of Hygiene and Public Assistance in France from 1887 to 1905, perhaps more than any other administrator of the Third Republic, took these personal duties and made them public and national. A devout Protestant, Monod combined the solidarist vision of a national collectivity with his Protestant notion of duties and outlined the collective duties of the state as the family of France. The state had the sacred debt, the right, and the humanitarian duty to intervene to assure that all its members were protected.[65]

The gospel according to Henri Monod can be summed up in a few words: "Public welfare, when all other assistance is lacking, is owed to the indigent who find themselves, temporarily or definitively, physically unable to provide for their necessities of life." Monod did not limit the role of private charity. As he wrote, "Kindness! Voilà for private charity. Justice! Voilà for public assistance. Solidarity! Voilà, one for the other." He also did not deny the work ethic of earlier social analysts. Public assistance was necessary only for those unable to work: babies, the aged, the infirm, the sick, and the incurable. Society is founded on an exchange of services whereby individuals who have fulfilled their obligations to society should partake of certain benefits, the most important of which is the right to life. Monod wrote that the state is the intermediary that assures the execution of these reciprocal obligations.[66] He included pregnant women and mothers among those whom the state had a duty to assist because they had to assure the lives of their babies. Elaborating, he avowed that aiding the children and their mothers was not only "a question of humanity in need of this assistance, it is also in the national interest. It is the indigent families with many children that infantile mortality ravages. . . . One should, at least, by a law of assistance diminish the chance of death for these infants who only ask to live."[67]

The secular public assistance of the Third Republic adopted two Protestant religious principles—reciprocity of services between the poor and rich and the duties of personal charity—into national goals and ideals, transforming them into secular components of the provident society. Visitors to the poor in the Third Republic were to bring a different kind of Bible: the book of hygiene and the gospel according to the doctors.

In the face of the onslaught of anticlerical sentiment, some conservative Catholics such as Eugène de Margerie renewed their support of traditional attitudes toward mothers in misery. Much as their predecessors had done, they sought to regenerate France through programs of moralization from the church. They enjoined good Catholics to love the poor but not unmarried mothers. Social Catholics, in contrast, became less dogmatic than before and maintained a more flexible attitude toward social programs for poor single mothers than did conservative Catholics. Social Catholics regrouped in an effort to preserve the social hierarchy and the central role of the church in private charity. This should be done, they said, by sheltering working-class women through programs of child support and by improving their moral conduct. Private, paternalistic, Christian charity, and not the state, however, should be the doctor for suffering societies.[68]

Some of Othenin d'Haussonville's attitudes typified social Catholic ideology. He believed in the need for the regeneration of France, not only by increasing its population but also by moral redemption of young working-class women. In language reminiscent of that used earlier in the century, Haussonville saw insufficient wages as the main cause of poverty, especially when combined with a "number of children disproportionate to the resources of the household." Unlike many of his contemporaries who feared depopulation, he opposed a too rapid population growth, believing it would increase misery. Like his social Catholic predecessors, Haussonville blamed social misery, in part, on the promiscuous behavior and the habits of debauchery that lead to too many children among the poorest classes. Even for married women, children produce suffering. Up to the birth of a child, with both husband and wife working, life is bearable. Then, "At the first child he beats her; at the second he leaves her. This is not the exception; it is the rule."[69]

Yet Haussonville, unlike his social Catholic predecessors, blamed the laws, male seducers, and women's meager wages more than he blamed the immorality of single women themselves. He excused the single mother's "fault" as resulting from the "immediate and pressing necessity to procure for herself a piece of bread" and from the need to satisfy the "appetites of nature" that included "a little fun, gaiety and happiness so legitimate at the age of twenty."[70] Women's salaries, he showed, were insufficient to support themselves, so women had only two choices: to live with severe economic deprivations, or to marry. To Haussonville, marriage was the natural solution because it was objectionable for a woman to live alone. Furthermore, women "ask nothing more than to marry." Unfortunately, however, in many instances their fellow workmen took advantage of their needs for bread and affection without ever having the intention of marrying them. Haussonville urged indulgence for those women who struggled on their own and only gave in to a lover after great resistance. Furthermore, he complained that even if a woman could find someone willing to marry her, the necessary legal procedures were tortuous and time consuming. Haussonville's solution was to abolish the need for written parental consent for a marriage of those who were no longer minors. Until the law was changed, however, private charities should financially rescue couples and help them marry.[71]

Private charity, according to Haussonville, should be judiciously dispensed; on moral grounds he opposed many public programs of aid to the poor and pregnant. He scorned use of a maternity hospital for married poor women because institutional care encouraged women to desert their homes, their children, and their husbands. He opposed shelters for unwed mothers because they would reward immorality. The state, according to Haussonville, should not be so preoccupied with creating "little soldiers" by sheltering unwed mothers. Rather, the state should encourage Catholic charities' special role in administering to poor women because allowing misery to progress would champion the cause of the socialists and endanger the "natural social hierarchy." He viewed state intervention in the lives of the poor as insufficient and ineffective.[72]

Paternalism prevailed in the polemics of Catholics such as Haussonville and among most male reformers. From solidarists Emile Cheysson and Paul Strauss to the army of reformers who fashioned programs to combat depopulation, reformers, to a man, envisioned women's proper place as in the home, taking care of children. The nineteenth-century's cult of true womanhood in England and the United States, and Bismarck's vision of German women as mothers in the kitchen and in church, had their distinctive forms in France. The republican language of extolling the virtues of a woman staying home was not to say that it was her "proper" or "natural" sphere, but rather that true motherhood, including breastfeeding, was the way to guarantee the future of the Republic and the nation. Despite differences of opinion about the source of the problems and the nature of solutions, on this they agreed.

In the writings of these late-nineteenth-century social commentators, affectionate, hygienic motherhood made the difference between a "fallen woman" and a rehabilitated one. It was an image of motherhood that represented at once a new focus on women's options and a restricting of them. Before the 1870s reformers viewed the single mother from the working classes as debauched or immoral, regardless of whether she was in a stable union or had several partners. She could be redeemed only through religion and marriage. After 1860, and especially after 1870, the road to rehabilitation ran through hygiene and breastfeeding. It did not necessarily include marriage or religion. By the late nineteenth century, social theorists no longer castigated the unwed mother for her immorality.[73] Reformers of the 1880s echoed the moral economists of the 1830s—alleviate poverty and morality would improve—but in the 1880s the definition of a single mother's morality shifted. She became a victim of social forces and poverty. Reformers and politicians viewed women primarily as reproducers and nurturers. As a consequence they emphasized eliminating the mothers' misery and ignorance, improving hygiene, and thus preserving their babies' lives. It was less important that poor mothers be punished for their immorality; it was more important that the children be nurtured. This focus led public officials to see themselves as the paternalistic protectors of the nation's children, and indirectly as protectors of their indigent mothers.

The legally married two-parent family remained the bastion of social law and order, but a single mother appeared to be a sign of urban corruption less often than she had been earlier in the century. A more complex image of the single mother emerged with the blurring of the lines between an *ouvrière* (worker), who traditionally was a woman of "doubtful morality," and a *mère* (mother), the social and moral ideal.[74] Even though single mothers still symbolized unregulated sexuality and disorder to some social commentators, to most they served more as vehicles for producing and nurturing children; they were necessary because of their fecund wombs and lactating breasts.

The Napoleonic Code remained intact—forbidding maternal search for paternal support and absolving the father of any responsibility for his out-of-wedlock child—until 1912, and then the law made only minor incursions on his freedoms. By the turn of the century the state assumed paternal responsibility, not in the interest of the mother, but to train and socialize the mother for the benefit of the child. According to François Ewald, the development of the "provident state" is rooted in this shift from the ideal of laissez-faire liberty to the emphasis on saving lives, and the transformation of organized relief from optional benevolence to obligatory responsibility of the state for welfare. Even old liberals acquiesced to state power in the interest of saving lives.[75]

Most politicians and social reformers agreed with Sicard de Plauzoles, but few as blatantly denied the principle of individual liberty for mothers. Quoting Article IV of the Declaration of the Rights of Man of 1789, which said, " 'Liberty consists of the right to do that which will not harm another,' " Sicard de Plauzoles asserted that "it is evident that the mother in depriving the infant of her milk commits an act which harms him. She therefore does not have the right to commit it."[76] The right to life of an infant was more important than the individual liberty of a mother. With an end to discrimination against poor married and single mothers, and with rhetoric proclaiming their equality and their entitlement to assistance, women suffered a loss of freedom in determining how to raise their children, and all the hardships a lack of liberty entailed.

CHAPTER

4

Morality and Motherhood: Women's Voices

By the end of the century, most middle-class women's attitudes toward mothers in poverty were much like those of male reformers. Most women subscribed to their male contemporaries' rhetoric of idealized motherhood and the proper behavior of women. When appropriate, they extolled the virtues of motherhood, argued for increasing the population, or proposed and facilitated charities for indigent mothers. During the first half of the century, however, elite women's writings about poor women reveal that their motives, tone, and emphasis differed in some significant respects from those of men.[1] With a softer voice, women emphasized a commitment to human relationships and reproduction more than rigid moral dogma, economics, or nationalism.[2] Female writers, reformers, and philanthropists expressed almost exclusive concern with issues relating to women, especially the poor with children.[3] Toward the end of the century, however, a few feminists emerged with strong critiques of a society that refused to recognize mothers' rights.

Elite women had long played an important role in the lives of the poor. Wives of heads of state—from Marie Antoinette to Empress Eugenie, to wives of Republican presidents such as Mesdames Raymond Poincaré and Emile Loubet—involved themselves in charity. Some merely visited the maternity hospitals or joined charitable institutions as honorary board members; others took a more active role in forming and supporting charities. Except perhaps for Empress Eugenie and Madame de Lamartine, elite women played little direct role in the establishment of policy, although they were often instrumental in its implementation.[4]

Middle- and upper-class women had personal contact with the poor in the administration of charity and welfare, and these elite women could convey their impressions to their politically prominent husbands, thereby influencing their husbands' ideologies and politics. Women engaged in charity and welfare also reported to, and influenced, powerful welfare officials. By 1910 women served in public assistance as inspectors and deputy inspectors, visiting social welfare workers, as members of national and local public commissions on women and children, as directors of small maternity hospitals, and as members of the National Advisory Council of Public Assistance.[5] It is not obvious that this activity always benefited poor women. A compelling sense of sisterhood, or matronage networks, among the elite women and the poor mothers could positively influence poor women's lives. Conversely, a sense of rivalry between the elite women and the poor with whom they came in direct contact, in the prevailing mistress-servant or donor-recipient relationship, might more negatively affect the lives of the poor. In either case, the impact was substantial.

Materialism and Charity, 1815–1870

Charity and concern with less fortunate women and children was a time-honored social activity for middle- and upper-class women whose primary roles were as wife and mother.[6] Priests, pastors, and husbands told their parishioners and wives that under divine law, "helping the poor was a mission for the upper classes," especially the women.[7] In fact, Christian charity was not an exceptional virtue, but a feminine vocation and a social duty. In the 1830s, Protestant Count Agenor-Etienne de Gasparin believed that women "received the mission of charity from God and have no equals in the accomplishment of this duty. . . . Here are the poor, the sick, the unhappy; here are the perverted souls and the families which vice has entered; here are the abandoned children and the others raised without dignity; what a realm for feminine charity!" Of all those to whom women should minister, children and their poor mothers ranked first.[8]

The Countess de Gasparin, his wife, appealed to her social equals to exercise their responsibility. Despite her heavily religious and moralistic tone she showed more sensitivity than her male contemporaries when she enjoined her readers to love the poor simply because the poor suffered from their poverty. Unlike many of her male compatriots who castigated working women for failing to save money for the future and for having children before they could afford them, the Countess painted a pitiful picture of their poverty: no food, a cold attic room, children who were pale and sickly, and the family facing uncertainty about the next day. Needle work, the predominant occupation of such women—when there was work to be had—often required sewing without a break and without food, in a cold room from dawn to eleven at night, and for a pittance of a franc a day. The Countess de Gasparin expressed great sympathy for married women who worked hard yet still could not earn enough to live on, let alone save. These women, she said, had neither time nor reserves for sickness, unemployment, or a child. According to the Countess, such long and hard labor did not lead to a happy family life but resulted instead in misery and the breakdown of family ties when the husband regretted having a wife and children and abandoned them. These poor did not even observe the Sabbath. Depravity did not cause the breakdown of family ties and the failure to observe the Sabbath; rather women's economic misery led to the failure to keep the faith on both counts.[9]

The Countess de Gasparin had less sympathy for single mothers. She criticized them for having "criminal relations" outside of marriage. Gasparin feared that such cohabitation contributed to the downfall of the Christian family, her major concern. Sexual relations outside of marriage, however, did not result from general immorality among working women (as men of her time believed); rather they resulted from poverty. The single poor mothers would be delighted to marry, Gasparin wrote, and charity should help them do so. Such charity began at home, with the mistress-servant relationship.

Gasparin believed that when a young girl "fell" her mistress was also culpable because she had provided bad models of vanity, egotism, and corruption.[10] Gasparin disparaged the unjust and un-Christian credo that domestics "formed a class apart," lacked morality, lied, stole, and were ungrateful. According to Gasparin, domestics should be treated as members of the family, not as "the enemy," or as "things"; a pious Christian woman should open her soul to her domestic servant, who is a creature of God who should be assigned an honorable place in the family. Christian women, by preaching to their domestic servants and setting a good example, would reduce the likelihood of their servants seeking a lover and becoming pregnant. Although she shared her male contemporaries' failure to place responsibility on male seducers, the Countess de Gasparin was unlike her male counterparts when, in asserting the religious responsibility of the nobility toward their servants, she held other women of her social class accountable.[11]

In assuming that all women wanted to marry if they only could, Catholic bourgeois women differed little from Protestants.[12] Mathilde Bourdon, a widely read conservative Catholic from the department of the Nord, argued in 1859 that poor women should not live sinfully in consensual unions and it was the duty of charity to help marry them. As an example, she recounted the life of the fictional Geneviève, whose cohabitant, Grandjean, was an honest worker in her book, *La charité en action*. In response to a question from an emissary of the Société Saint Vincent-de-Paul, Geneviève cried that indeed she would like to marry, "but it is difficult . . . one needs papers, money . . . one must make the requests. . . . Grandjean is from the Limousin [in south-central France] and I am from Normandy [in the north]." Bourdon did not condemn Geneviève for immorality in cohabiting or having children before she could afford them; she thought her guilty of nothing except poverty and the consequent inability to marry.[13]

Antoinette, the heroine of a novel by Mathilde Bourdon, was an honest seamstress who in a period of unemployment was forced to pawn some of her meager belongings to feed herself and her younger sister. At the pawn shop she met Augustine, a seamstress who had lived with the man she loved without marriage. One day he announced that their "mariage à la parisienne" was finished and he left her and their son to fend for themselves. Charitable Antoinette shared her meager money and food with Augustine, who was even poorer and more unhappy than herself. Eventually, Augustine came to regret her mistake, her sickly son died, and she regained a life of religious devotion and virtue.[14] Antoinette exemplified what Bonnie Smith refers to as the "cult of the virtuous heroine," a woman who defied all obstacles to remain chaste and virtuous. Augustine had succumbed to seduction, made a mistake and slipped, but she was redeemed through loving her son and with a little help from her friends. Like Eugène Sue and Victor Hugo, Bourdon saw the work of caring for a child as redeeming for single mothers. She exemplifies the attitude of Catholic and Protestant women writers in general, who argued that poor women who overcame the problems of poverty and temptation should be rewarded with subsistence.[15]

Leading Protestant and Catholic women enjoined other women to show charity to those less fortunate. It was not enough to give large sums of money and receive recognition for that; a woman must go among the poor, as one individual to another, with an evangelical charity.[16] The Countess de Gasparin told a didactic story about the ideal woman, Mme Dubois, who carried her Bible while visiting mothers in misery. Mme Dubois went to her local welfare bureau in Paris to volunteer her services and was sent to Justine, a young mother in need. According to Gasparin's story, Justine, a Protestant girl, had left her rural home for Paris, where she served as a domestic. She was dismissed and while unemployed she met a young man named Victor. They lived together, had several children, and sank into destitution. Victor drank and was unfaithful to Justine. Their children witnessed a drunken father and what Gasparin alleged was an insubordinate and immoral mother who sometimes worked outside the home rather than attending to her family duties. Mme Dubois visited Justine and told her either to leave Victor or to marry him because God would not help her if she continued to live in sin. Justine replied that she wanted to marry, but Victor did not want to relinquish his freedom. Mme Dubois eventually persuaded the two to marry and helped them obtain a religious and civil ceremony. After the marriage, Mme Dubois continued to attend to the moral life of Justine by frequent visits to bring assistance and read the Bible aloud. Victor continued his dissipated life until he received a blow on the head. Again, Mme Dubois, the faithful friend of the poor, brought assistance. Finally, with the help of a pastor and Mme Dubois, Victor and Justine returned to her hometown, away from the temptations of Paris.[17]

In this story, Gasparin stressed the role of religion and moralizing aid on the part of a bourgeois woman. Her story illustrated disapproval of couples cohabiting, the difficulties of securing a legal marriage, the corruption of life in Paris, and the benefits of hard work in a rural setting. Yet, unlike the rhetoric of male social reformers of the same time, in this story the man, not the woman, bore primary responsibility for the dissolute life. Justine became a dutiful wife, with help from the local welfare bureau, through personal contact by a visitor to the poor. This romantic morality story, written to encourage married elite women to engage in charity as one of their Christian duties, points out the benefits of this interaction to impoverished mothers.

Protestant and Catholic notions of a woman's charitable duty differed little. Both focused on commitment to family. Catholics, however, believed in a class-structured social hierarchy, one in which "sin, evil, and poverty existed as part of that hierarchical order";[18] for them, charity could only alleviate some of the worst problems so that people would not starve. Elite Catholic women believed that each recipient of charity should provide proof of good character, morality, virtue, and marriage. Mathilde Bourdon, in expressing the general belief that "charity is the perfect appendage of Catholicism," cautioned women to be charitable only to the honest poor—those who were destitute through no fault of their own. She warned charitable women against being taken in by the undeserving.[19]

Religiously inspired women, both Catholic and Protestant, served the cause of motherhood and a strong hierarchical and patriarchal family. They did not usually advocate assistance for single poor mothers unless those mothers sought redemption. They did advocate, and often facilitated, the marriage of an unwed mother to the father of their child as a means of aiding the mother's salvation.[20] Women served the poor out of a devotion to the Christian ideals of love and charity as well as from the tradition of noblesse oblige. Their devotion and sense of responsibility required face to face contact with the poor in order to moralize, scrutinize the household, and offer advice.[21] The approach of these women, then, was much like that of most men of their era. Religious devotion was not the inspiration of all female social critics however; a feminist movement of moderate strength was also active during much of the century.[22]

Feminism and Mothers in Poverty, 1830–1870

Early nineteenth-century feminist ideology defined women as mother just as did other ideologies of the time, but feminist ideals and goals differed from those of traditional social analysts in stressing equality within relationships and equal opportunity in education and work. According to historian Claire Goldberg Moses, the "image of woman as mother became the linchpin of the feminist rationale for sexual equality." To the feminists of the 1830s and 1840s, however, "women's unique role as mother would no longer explain her confinement to domestic life; it would justify her participation in the public sphere."[23] Saint-Simonian feminists, along with later feminists, believed that before they could be sexually emancipated, women must be economically self-sufficient. This feminist discussion of a woman's sexual self-expression was diametrically opposed to the contemporaneous social Catholic and moral economist contempt for single mothers' apparent lack of proper morality.

Fourierist and Saint-Simonian feminists complained of male seducers. Suzanne Voilquin, a Saint-Simonian working-class feminist of the 1830s, wrote not of woman's immorality or unbridled sexuality but of her fears of male seducers. Voilquin described her fear of sexual harassment and her vulnerability to rape during her late night walks home from sewing in the embroidery workshop where she was employed.[24] In 1841, the Fourierist feminist Zoé Gatti de Gamond also discussed women who had "corruption . . . forced upon them; they do not consent to it voluntarily; they do not stop detesting it, even as they surrender to it. They struggle against the fatality of circumstances and curse an unjust society that condemns them to degradation."[25] When these feminists discussed sexual issues they emphasized women's vulnerability to men's exploitation. Their voices differed from those of their male contemporaries.

Julie-Victoire Daubié was the most prominent feminist of the 1860s. She published an influential essay in the important *Journal des économistes* and authored *La femme pauvre au XIXe siècle,* which received first prize from the Academy of Lyon in 1859. Daubié did not resemble typical bourgeois women of charity. The daughter of the bookkeeper for a Vosges ironworks factory, she supported herself as a governess. She was a social analyst on a par with male contemporaries such as Jules Simon.

Daubié proposed reform of the capitalist economy to improve the position of women and make charity unnecessary. She argued that working women's salaries were inadequate for them to support themselves and that women lacked the education or training necessary for more remunerative jobs. She urged equal education for girls and boys, since if women had access to better education, their economic position in society would improve, thus obviating the need for charity. If women had the same remuneration for their labor as did men, their poverty would be reduced and their marriage opportunities improved. Daubié understood the plight of the poor, and pending a transformation of society, advocated shelters for homeless girls and unwed mothers. She enjoined philanthropic women to organize information bureaus so that a "poor stranger in Paris, without an introduction to a job, would not lie trembling without bread in an attic room."[26]

Marriage laws and customs required transformation just as did the economy, according to Daubié, in order to assure women equality on the marriage market and emancipation within marriage. She advocated the same age of majority for marriage for men and women as an effort to achieve gender equality and enable more women to marry without parental consent, thereby reducing the cost and facilitating marriage among the poor. Daubié railed against the dowry, since a woman with insufficient resources for a dowry "to buy a husband" was unable to marry and thus forced to provide for her own subsistence and that of her children.[27] The lack of a dowry, she argued, could force a woman to become a courtesan or an unwed mother.

Daubié gave a feminist twist to some familiar opinions. As many writers did, she disapproved of consensual unions and referred to them as "living in disorder." Unlike others, however, she wanted to reduce female dependency and consensual unions by improving the economic status of women and making men responsible for their offspring. She was among the first to advocate abrogation of Article 340 of the Civil Code forbidding *recherche de la paternité* in her effort to encourage legislation that made the father liable for an illegitimate child. Never using the word morality, but focusing instead on the economic deprivation single mothers suffered, Daubié wrote of their "horrible indigence" and their "miserable furnished rooms." She firmly argued "the martyrdom of these working girls is one of the supreme embarrassments of nineteenth-century France, and it remains a stigma that legislation tolerates it."[28] She sought legislative and administrative changes to eliminate prostitution and wanted both men and women penalized for debauchery. In addition, she wanted legislation that would guarantee the security of young women so that a debauched man would not be able to corrupt "a girl of the people" without bearing responsibility for his acts.[29]

As did many of her male contemporaries, Daubié blamed the economy for much female misery. In contrast with male social commentators, however, Daubié did not believe that a single mother was depraved either as a cause or consequence of extreme poverty: "as for depravity, it is often . . . the fruit of our laws and customs that render the salaried woman the direct object of all exploitation." Women's conduct was a response to larger social and economic forces. Daubié sympathetically described young girls in the cities, far from their families, greatly undernourished, working from 6 A.M. to 10 P.M. for under 250 francs per year. In winters they worked seven days a week; "in summer they are abandoned on the sidewalk by the patron who closes his shop and says to them: 'Feed yourselves as you can; I owe you nothing when you do not work.' . . . How can one blame these women if they succumb to the seductions which surround them or, if struck in admiration by the golden existence of the courtesan they prefer opulent leisure to unprofitable and repellent work."[30] In general, Daubié's writing lacks the moral condemnation of single mothers that is characteristic of the writings of many male moral economists and religious bourgeois women. Her feminist approach reveals a nonjudgmental sense of sisterhood with the poor mothers of Paris.

Maternalism, 1870–1914

The secular Third Republic did not end traditional religious attitudes toward the poor and pregnant, but both Catholic and Protestant bourgeois women couched their discourse increasingly in lay terms in tune with Third Republican anticlericalism. They maintained their conservative view of the Christian family as the bulwark of society and women's ideal role as mother, yet actively sought social reform and extolled the virtues of charity toward poor women. Many joined charitable organizations as patrons and benefactresses. They continued to favor poor married moral mothers over the unwed mother, unless the single mother sought rehabilitation through Christian marriage.

Some Catholic women during the last decades of the century, seeing their "mission as improving the morals of working-class women," did not criticize single mothers for moral transgression. For example, Julia Bécour, the wife of a doctor in Lille, "saw illegitimate pregnancies as a sign of human degradation," but "the presence of vice in society . . . was the result of male failure to adhere to morality, the result of male seduction of women, the result of male standards of force as they overpowered those women whom they should have cherished."[31] In her unequivocal castigation of male seducers, Bécour wrote in a different voice from her male contemporaries and identified across class lines with the vulnerability women felt vis à vis men.

Léonie Chaptal and Pauline d'Harcourt d'Haussonville, two devoutly Catholic women writing at the turn of the century, urged charity to the poor. Chaptal devoted her life's work to protecting the working-class family by supporting prenatal health clinics for pregnant women and well-baby clinics for newborns.[32] In 1912, Pauline d'Haussonville wrote of the overwhelming importance of charity for one's own, as well as for society's, salvation. She urged all women to think of those mothers who were poorer than themselves, beset by anxieties about tomorrow and unable to meet their children's needs.[33] She implored other women to console, love, pray for, and give to those who were the most unfortunate—and the most unfortunate were orphans. Poor women in childbirth should also be the object of compassion. In contrast to earlier Catholic writers, but consonant with her male social Catholic contemporaries, she never complained that the poor were having too many children.

Mademoiselle Marguerite Jules Simon, the granddaughter of the well-known politician, in a 1911 advice manual for Catholic girls, took a position somewhat different from that of her grandfather. She warned against free love but did not condemn the immorality or irreligiosity of sexual relations outside of marriage. Instead she stated that it was in women's self-interest to refrain from free love and cohabitation. Simon told her readers to "listen to the anguished cry of a poor girl who let herself be seduced by the profoundly antisocial and antifeminist thesis [of free love]: 'When I went to live with him,' she said, 'I climbed the steps of his stairway with all the sincerity of a Catholic bride who crossed the threshold of the church, with all the seriousness of a bourgeois girl who entered the room of the city hall. . . . I believed that we brought, this scoundrel and me, an equal desire to love each other, an equal conviction of the seriousness of our relationship, an equal respect for one another; five months later he abandoned me.' " Simon urged her readers to avoid such deception and "prepare for marriage. . . . Assure your livelihood by wise savings, look for . . . the means to diminish your expenses, [and] don't hesitate to use" the Catholic charitable organizations. She advised single women to be honest, work hard, go to mass each Sunday, and attend the Catholic patronage societies that provided moral and material protection to working women who had to support themselves.[34]

Protestant women differed little from their Catholic counterparts in their attitudes toward both marriage and single poor mothers and pregnant women. In 1900, the editorial board of *La femme,* the journal of

Protestant women, included Julie Siegfried (the wife of leading solidarist Jules Siegfried) and Sarah Monod (president of the Christian Feminine Conference at Versailles). *La femme*'s writers advised their readers to befriend and protect "these poor creatures who often live outside of all notions of morality" and the proper domestic sphere.[35] *La femme*'s editorial policy was less interested in helping poor unwed mothers generally than in educating, sheltering, and supporting poor young Protestant girls. Although the editors did not explicitly state that their goal was to prevent unwanted pregnancies, their moralizing rhetoric was directed toward preventing seduction and cohabitation and it was reminiscent of language used by earlier Protestant writers who did focus on unwanted pregnancies. In order to protect young Protestant girls from the dangers of life alone in turn-of-the-century Paris, Sarah Monod, Julie Siegfried, and other prominent Protestant women founded societies to befriend young girls newly arrived in the big city.

Religious Parisian women were not alone in voicing pity and sympathy for poor mothers. Women without a religious affiliation, especially after 1870, argued that women should act together to alleviate the misery of working-class mothers in order to protect the children and decrease the number of illegitimate births and infanticides. They wrote of the plight of seamstresses, "brave and honest girls who became pregnant," were abandoned by the father of their child, lost their customers, could not pay their rent, and thus were out on the street. They mentioned a "poor farm girl," a domestic servant who was shown to the door three days after giving birth. The words "humanitarian" and "hygiene" replaced "religion" and "morality," as a network of secular solidarist bourgeois women sought to provide support and shelter for homeless mothers and their babies. Though these women recognized the difficulties faced by poor women, their focus, like that of many of their male contemporaries, was on saving the child.[36]

By the turn of the century, bourgeois women's voices increasingly resembled their male counterparts' as many prominent men and women turned their attention to morally and materially assisting poor women in their last month of pregnancy, during childbirth, and in the first months after delivery. Like bourgeois men of their generation, they formed patriotic associations to counter depopulation. Wives of solidarist politicians dominated these associations. Having children, these women understood, intensified misery, thereby necessitating relief to help the mothers and protect the babies. Bourgeois mothers believed that they were the ones most qualified and able to come to the aid of the poor women, to instill in them the virtues of hygiene and thrift, and to teach them proper childrearing practices. Just as in earlier generations, bourgeois women saw great merit in visiting the poor, but they did so not in order to take the Gospel to the poor but to take them the word of doctors and social hygienists. Moreover, unlike their predecessors, they supported state-funded as well private efforts to address the problems of the poor.

Obstetrician/gynecologist Dr. Blanche Edwards-Pilliet is emblematic of solidarist bourgeois women who advocated state aid for needy mothers. At the 1900 congress on women's rights, she predicted that " 'the time will come when woman will be considered a veritable social functionary during her gestation and nursing period. At this time she is in the debt of society, which in exchange for the enormous effort of maternity owes her nourishment, lodging, and rest.' " Believing that poor women could not afford to wait until society fulfilled its duty, she fostered the establishment of shelters for homeless pregnant women, and a two-week paid leave before birth for pregnant workers, and a four-week paid maternity leave following birth for new mothers. As did the men of her generation, she argued that both soldiers and mothers were social servants owed support from the state.[37]

In 1902 one group of bourgeois women formed an association called le Dû aux Mères (the Duty to Mothers) with the motto: "To create is good, but to take care of someone is better." The members of this association believed that the state owed needy mothers support. As a solidarist women's group, this association functioned as a humanitarian and philanthropic organization, without preference for the religion, nationality, or political opinions of either its members or its aid recipients. Concluding that misery caused degeneration and depopulation, the association's broadly defined goal was to unite all those who were interested in working against depopulation by combating infant mortality. The association's approach was to give immediate assistance to needy new mothers in order to facilitate maternal breastfeeding. The women of this association asserted that charity was the most sacred of duties and they had a duty toward poor mothers. Moreover, they and the state both owed assistance to poor mothers, who had a right to it.[38]

In striking contrast to polemicists of fifty years earlier, but similar to male contemporaries, women in le Dû aux Mères expressed more sympathy for single mothers than for married ones. They considered their main mission to "combat the terrible prejudice against these most unfortunate mothers and release these women from the scorn that victimized her and her innocent child." Give the unwed mother the aid that is her due, they demanded, and remove the stigma of illegitimate births; this would reduce infanticides.[39] In an appeal for funding, they told the now familiar story of poor unwed mothers, misled by the promise of a marriage, abandoned by their families, and struggling to work and at the same time raise their languishing children by themselves in their miserable furnished rooms. In all of their discussions, the women of this Association expressed only pity for the unfortunate circumstances of the poor single mother. They wrote not a word about her morality.[40]

A single mother's morality was also of less concern than the evil of depopulation for the members of la Société de l'Aide Maternelle (the Society of Maternal Aid), an association founded in 1906 under the patronage of the wife of the president of France, Madame Emile Loubet. No moral condemnation of the single mothers, even a subtle one, appeared in the language of this organization. They were always "poor mothers" or "domestics seduced and abandoned." Any moral criticism was reserved for the men who abandoned them. The Society's directors believed that "a mother is sacred, no matter where she comes from . . . [and] a newborn is a future citizen, a future mother of a family."[41] Their goal was to help remedy the population crisis by providing hospital care for "poor abandoned women" as well as married mothers in misery. Hospital care was to last four weeks after childbirth so that mothers could have lodging, food, and most important, so that they could nurse their newborns and avoid sending their babies to a wetnurse. The philanthropic women of the Society of Maternal Aid regarded wetnursing as the primary cause of infant mortality.

In general, charitable bourgeois women regularly visited patients, including unwed mothers, in hospitals and then again after they had been discharged. The stories they heard were familiar: a poor mother left the hospital with her new baby to return to her former lodging only to discover that her husband had sent the older children to the foundling home or left them to wander the streets, sold the furniture, and disappeared to the cabaret or with his mistress. These charitable women, often religiously and politically neutral, informed mothers of their limited options and helped them secure housing, clothing, food, and jobs.[42] Other women, such as school teachers, introduced courses on proper child care into their classes to teach young girls the responsibilities of motherhood and to show them how to best fulfill their mission in life as mothers.[43]

Marie Béquet de Vienne achieved particular importance because she was a tireless philanthropist and publicist on behalf of poor mothers and had the respect of prominent politicians. Her political beliefs combined aspects of Christian charity typical of bourgeois men and women earlier in the century with the political nationalism and solidarism of the Third Republic. Sounding like her male solidarist counterpart and close associate, Paul Strauss, she wrote that France was the most civilized nation in the world, but France suffered from depopulation caused by high infant mortality. Echoing the solidarist belief that "our French society is a vast family" she argued that it must "intervene when the natural family no longer exists or cannot act."[44]

Since children were the strength of the country, she concluded, "assistance is due to the child. It has a right to protection. . . . Society must not recoil before any sacrifice to assure the life and health of the child, and to give the child a moral and vocational training." Children could best be protected through their mother, Béquet de Vienne argued: "any mother, widow or never married, has a right to relief from public assistance, relief that will permit her to breastfeed her infant or pay a wetnurse." Since at least half of the needy women in Paris received no public relief, in 1876 she established the secular Society for Maternal Breastfeeding (Société d'Allaitement Maternelle) to aid needy mothers, regardless of marital status or religious preference, so they would not have to work outside the home. In Béquet de Vienne's opinion, private charity had an important role to play in supplementing public assistance. For her, private charity was as "rational as public assistance, but it also brought heartfelt tenderness to the unfortunate and . . . allowed hope to shine on their black horizon."[45]

In marked difference from her predecessors earlier in the century, Béquet de Vienne did not speak of alms or religious charity; she asserted the rights that society owed the child, particularly the right to life. Society should pay that debt through assistance to mothers, regardless of their marital status. Above all, she urged that care be taken of the pregnant woman and baby so that the country would have the new people it needs.[46]

Marie Béquet de Vienne displayed some understanding of the productive and reproductive lives of poor women. She argued that proletarian women worked as hard as men in their struggle for existence, but they did not receive the equal pay they merited. A poor pregnant woman had to work relentlessly in order to survive. As a result, many of them went into premature labor; therefore they needed shelters where they could live while pregnant and thus work only as much as they were able. She expressed a great deal of sympathy for the women, despite her preoccupation with saving babies for the nation, and she did not condemn them. She did fault the men and society who had deceived the women and failed in their duties.[47] In referring to *la grève de la paternité* she stressed that fathers' abandonment of mothers was more likely the cause of depopulation than *la grève des ventres*. The birth of a child terrorizes the men, she stated; they flee. If they remain, they advise the women to abort or commit infanticide. In these crimes, the man is guilty, but the law blindly lets him abandon his responsibility. She bitterly complained in 1908 that "laws made by men protect the men."[48] In this criticism of the men she differed significantly from her male contemporaries.

Still, by the end of the century, bourgeois women's voices generally resonated with those of the men. Men and women of all political and religious ideologies focused on the appalling infant mortality rate, blaming poverty, ignorance of hygienic child care, mothers' economic need to work, and insufficient wages for the problem. Women's writings had a more sympathetic tone and a clearer understanding of the economic problems of work and motherhood than men's writings did. Furthermore, they faulted men and the state for acting irresponsibly. They sought to help mothers in need through philanthropy, public assistance, and changes in the laws.[49] Nevertheless, though bourgeois women built successful philanthropic institutions that helped individual poor women temporarily, they looked to the highly centralized, male-dominated French state to provide societal solutions to the problems of women's reproductive concerns.

This is not to say that women debated the issues on narrow grounds. The Second International Congress of Feminine Organizations and Institutions met in 1900 and was attended by people of all political persuasions. The agenda embodied the concerns of diverse women's groups, including feminists, ardent and religious social Catholics, and Protestant philanthropic women. Bourgeois familial feminists and philanthropic religious women dominated. They spoke of mothers in misery as "poor women" who, pushed by necessity, "risked succumbing to the anguish of their sad situation."[50] Most supported philanthropic societies, state subsidies, and public assistance programs for poor mothers, including the unmarried.

Members of the congress, divided on issues of child support and women's dignity, debated to what extent the father of an out-of-wedlock child should be held responsible for child support. Jeanne Chauvin, a doctor of law, led the debate advocating the right of mothers to seek child support. This was in marked opposition to the argument of some men present at the congress as exemplified by Jacques Bonzon. He argued that recherche de la paternité was against French customs, and that it should be authorized only in cases of rape resulting in conception.[51] In those cases the man, Bonzon agreed, should not only be declared the father of the child and liable for support but also punished for rape. Seducers should be punished, in Bonzon's view, not by recherche de la paternité but by a different law which would force anyone who had done damage to another to pay for the damages. Women who gave themselves freely could not then turn this free union back against the man. At all costs, he argued, the law must defend and protect the legitimate wife and family against an "odious union of bastards and legitimate children." In such cases, it is only the child, he argued, and not the single mother, who is worthy of sympathy. The mother and father were equally at "fault" and the mother should not bring charges to the detriment of the father.[52] Bonzon ignored the stress and burden that having and raising a child put on the single mother, and he demonstrated little idea of the nature of seduction, or of free consent, in relationships of inequality. As most other male reformers, Bonzon wanted to protect the married man who had a child outside the marriage.

Most of the proposals at this 1900 congress were moderate. The women who attended did not demand that fathers legally recognize out-of-wedlock children, or even that the law be changed; they just wanted men to share the financial responsibility of raising children. Jeanne Chauvin and Marya Chéliga would allow Article 340, forbidding recherche de la paternité to remain, but argued that an unwed mother who had recognized her child should be permitted to compel the father to provide child support in the name of the minor child. There was never a question, Chéliga argued, of the father being forced to introduce the child into his "legitimate family. The natural child belongs exclusively to the mother." The father should just help feed that child since he contributed to its creation. If a single mother's search for child support would create a scandal for a married man and his family, then allowing this search would be an excellent measure to prevent the seduction of single women.[53]

Chauvin wanted the father to pay an indemnity to the mother for her loss of time at work. The mother, she argued, should have the right to obtain damages from the child's father to pay the cost of childbirth and to provide a supplementary income. The latter would enable her and her baby to survive during the first six months after birth when she could not work as before because she was obliged to stay home and nurse her infant. Mme d'Abbadie d'Arrast, a conservative Protestant and a member of the League against Infant Mortality, thought that although this proposal was in advance of public opinion, she hoped it would have a practical result of maintaining order and morality.[54] D'Abbadie d'Arrast was primarily interested in maintaining social stability; she voiced not a word about single mothers' rights.

Only one member of this congress, Maria Pognon, speaking on behalf of the League of the Rights of Women, argued against the notion that single mothers ought to be able to collect child support from fathers. She insisted that for a mother to pursue the child's father in order to make him financially responsible was undignified. A woman with self-respect, she argued, would not consent to go before a judge and explain to him how she knew a certain man. Even after the woman received a judgment against the father, she noted, it was unlikely that the man could be forced to pay. The present law entitled married women with children to receive child support from husbands who deserted them, but they were unable to collect. Furthermore, paternity was difficult to prove. Pognon's goal was to help the single mother raise her child; the child was not the "bastard who dishonored the family," as Bonzon alleged, but a "respectable little person." She proposed that the state establish a maternity fund that provided child support for out-of-wedlock children up to age sixteen; conference members defeated this resolution.[55]

Members of the congress finally adopted an eight-point proposal. First, during the initial year after the birth of an out-of-wedlock child, a mother could take action in the name of the child to force the father to pay child support until the child's majority. Second, child support included food, the cost of childrearing, and job training for the child in conformity to the mother's status. Third, if the father were married, child support should come from his own property and not that of his family. Fourth, proof of paternity consisted of witnesses, written proof, or a mass of evidence. The conference adopted the first four measures easily, including limited responsibility for married men. Only after an extended debate did they adopt the last four points, including the fifth, which allowed a mother to take action in her own name to obtain an indemnity for damages to compensate her for loss of work in the first six months after the birth of a child. Sixth, an adult woman could not bring charges against an underaged male. Seventh, the penal code would punish women's actions introduced in bad faith, and eighth, these provisions would not be retroactive.[56] Social conservatives as well as feminists in the National Council of French Women accepted these proposals.

The national legislature hotly debated many of the ideas for recherche de la paternité that the Second International Congress of Feminine Organizations and Institutions brought forth. Between 1901 and 1910 some of the points the women raised formed part of the proposals to permit recherche de la paternité that Gustave Rivet brought before the Chamber of Deputies several times during those years. Rivet's compromise bill of 1910, which became law in 1912, was less comprehensive than the one proposed at the Second International Congress.

The 1912 law permitted a single mother, on behalf of her minor child, to pursue the putative father for child support until the child's majority only in some specific instances: rape and kidnapping if the time of these events coincided with that of conception; or if the mother had proof of a marriage promise from the putative father; or if she had openly lived with him in a consensual union at the time of conception; or if she had a letter indicating his paternity; or if he had openly acted in the capacity of the child's father by ever providing support. She could not seek child support if she had engaged in "notorious conduct" during the time of conception. Child support could not be retroactive, so the mother had to find the father while the child was still a minor, preferably within two years after the baby was born.

The law was sufficiently vague on a number of key issues to assure passage. Although it did not specifically exclude married men from responsibility for child support for their out-of-wedlock children, married men would not likely have been liable for a paternity search under any of the conditions set forth by the law, except for the possibility of rape and kidnapping. Furthermore, the law did not grant children of an adulterous or incestuous relationship the right of recherche de la paternité. The law left specifics about what constituted child support up to the judges to determine at the time that the mother took the putative father to court. Supporters of the bill argued that there should be one moral code and that marriage was the best protection for women and children. In the absence of marriage, however, to defend the "natural child" against the "unnatural father" is to do one's duty to the country and to moral law.[57] The drive to permit recherche de la paternité achieved success in 1912 in part because its supporters viewed it as a way to decrease the number of abortions, infanticides, and child abandonment cases resulting from the poverty of a single mother.

The vast majority of politically active women wanted to keep abortion illegal and endorsed several measures to gain more convictions for illegal abortions. Madame d'Abbadie d'Arrast led the antiabortion campaign as part of a continuing effort to prevent depopulation. Ironically, antiabortionists argued for reducing the heavy penalty for abortion— more than five years of forced labor for those convicted of performing abortions and several years of prison for those convicted of having had an abortion. Antiabortionists argued that if the sentence for those guilty of performing or having an abortion were less severe, judges would be more apt to convict and sentence. To enforce convictions and penalties, antiabortionists lobbied to move abortion cases out of the hands of lenient juries, who appeared to accept poor women's necessary recourse to abortion, and give them to reputedly sterner judges. They accomplished this in 1922. Only a few feminists argued for birth control or supported a woman's right to abortion.

Feminism and Motherhood, 1870–1914

Incontrovertibly feminist publications such as *La fronde* and *La femme affranchie* took up the call to protect working-class mothers and children. Deprived of the right to vote or sit in Parliament, women expressed their political agendas by promoting men's legislative proposals when they agreed with them. In *La fronde,* an article by Renée Rambaud supported Constant Dulau's proposal for a law designed to "protect the woman and the newborn."[58] Dulau stressed that the goal of this law was to combat depopulation by decreasing infant mortality; since the state cannot convince people to have more children, it must protect the ones it has by taking better care of poor children regardless of their mothers' marital status. He argued that "instead of being preoccupied . . . with whether a little citizen is natural, or legitimate, or the result of an adulterous relationship, society should receive it with great joy." Moreover, this "little citizen" began life within the womb; Dulau wanted to protect mothers in order to prevent them from taking "irrevocable acts" as a result of "absolute distress." Each needy and pregnant woman, from the beginning of her pregnancy, should be able to find a refuge where she could live in security, where she would not have to work above and beyond her physical ability. Dulau and Rambaud advocated maternity hospitals and refuge-workhouses to be established all over France for married and single mothers.

In 1900 Clotilde Dissard, in the column "Chronique féministe" in *La fronde,* supported Paul Strauss's proposal for a law to protect working pregnant women. Strauss had made a public appeal for bourgeois women of France to help their pregnant working-class sisters by taking the initiative and forming a national society for the protection of working mothers and their young children. Dissard felt that women could organize to help one another quicker and more effectively than could lawmakers: "the realization of his wish, so legitimate, would be so efficacious and will certainly be understood by French women; they would get together and also do some good while waiting for our esteemed legislators finally to do their duty."[59]

La femme affranchie advocated shelters for mothers abandoned by their husbands and for poor women and their children. Avoiding the rhetoric of redemption and rehabilitation, this journal espoused a sisterly, solidarist approach. In 1904 the editors argued that if legislators wanted to repopulate France, they should give mothers assistance in the form of money, food, and linens.[60] In the same year, the editor, Gabrielle Petit, asked all "abandoned mothers" to send their addresses to *La femme affranchie* so that it could organize and unite women in a union, the only means to force an increase in salary and a reduction of the hours of work for mothers and pregnant women.[61] In 1905 *La femme affranchie* published a poem by Raphaël Duffouic, titled "Unwed Mothers" (Filles mères), that was emblematic of an editorial policy urging that single mothers be given respect and sufficient assistance. The poem pointed out that despite fancy speeches and scientific advances, French society had made no progress toward aiding unwed mothers. Politicians engaged in rhetoric about humanity, but as soon as a woman "erred," society turned its back on her. The poem ended with a plea for bourgeoisie, grande dame, or dressmaker's errand girl to respect, aid, and give sustenance to all mothers in the name of humanity.[62]

The well-known feminist Hubertine Auclert, in *Le radical* in 1899, wrote about the lack of respect accorded unwed others and the burden they bore in raising a child alone. Auclert pointed out the contradictory position in which society placed the unwed, or "illegal," mother. On the one hand society treated her as a pariah. On the other hand, because the unwed mother alone bore responsibility for her child, she was effectively "elevated to the rank of a man." The only time, Auclert added, that a man did not have responsibility in the family and in society was in the paternity of his out-of-wedlock children. As a result, only the children of unwed mothers belonged to her alone, because the irresponsible father disclaimed the child. Auclert explicitly blamed the unwed father for disavowing the child and French law for legally permitting him to do so.

Auclert's sympathy for the single mother prompted her to argue that illegitimate children should be exempt from military service just as were the children of widows. "The Republic takes the natural son away from his mother, puts a gun in his hand and says that he must defend the country," she said. The unwed mother, "crucified by her motherhood," does not have general sympathy as the widow does. Why is the system so unjust, she asked, that the son of a rich widow is exempt from military service because he supports his mother, while the recognized son of a poor single mother is forced to serve though he, too, supports his mother? "When a child is a pariah in his own country, what right does the state have to make him pay a tax with his blood?" Auclert pointed out that only in the military draft was the distinction between natural and legitimate children abolished.[63]

In her book, *Amour et maternité* (Love and motherhood), feminist Claire Galichon argued that society should honor all mothers equally, regardless of marital status. Like Auclert, Galichon noted the strange legal phenomenon whereby the child of a married woman belonged to the father but a child born of a woman alone belonged to the mother. Under current law, she argued, if a woman lived with a man in a free union for several years, and if he walked out on her and their children, she would be condemned by bourgeois society and without legal recourse to obtain child support from him. Galichon bemoaned that "society" called the single mother "dishonored" even when she loved her child, as much as did a mother with a "certificate of honorability conferred by a legal husband." Because society never pardoned the "faults of these women against social morality," she is a shamed unwed mother to her grave and her child is a bastard for his entire life. The "fault," however, was not the woman's for having the baby, but that of the "social order" for calling it a "fault."[64]

Galichon believed in what she called "free motherhood." Anyone who wished should be a mother, regardless of marriage, without shame or dishonor on herself and her family. The moral code is unjust to address the morality only of women and treat them like criminals, Galichon argued. If maternity were respected, within and without marriage, then the worst "social ulcers would disappear: such as debauchery, prostitution, child abandonment, infanticide, and vengeance by vitriol or revolver."[65] Unwanted motherhood, whether the woman was single or married, constituted degrading servitude. Galichon argued that a woman should be free to refuse or accept maternity. She was one of just a few feminists who favored legalizing abortion. She argued that if the law forbids marriage of an underage girl, it should authorize the doctors to intervene on the same grounds—immaturity and insufficient physical development—if she is raped or seduced.[66]

The question of the "systematic depopulation of France" intrigued Galichon just as it did mainstream politicians, and she argued for many of the populationists' answers, but from a feminist point of view. It is not the women who must bear responsibility for depopulation, but the men—politicians and unwed fathers. She strongly complained that women had never been consulted in this question of "maternal function with its numerous duties and sacrifices."[67] Galichon's plans to increase the population in the national interest, and in the interest of women, necessitated a restructuring of cultural attitudes. Laws and customs must honor motherhood among single and married women and provide illegitimate children with the same legal title and rights as the legitimate. The national budget should also support motherhood, which must be voluntary. She urged making unwed fathers legally, morally, and financially responsible for their children. Until society changes, women need marriage as a protection and safeguard for them and their children. Claire Galichon also urged changes in language. The title of "fille mère" is degrading, she maintained, and must be abolished. All women with children should be called "Madame."[68] In her discussion of women's right to accept or refuse maternity, and in her advocacy of the right of a teenage rape victim to terminate the pregnancy, Galichon differed from mainstream populationists.

Feminists Madeleine Pelletier and Nelly Roussel opposed the populationist dogma of the time, but they argued, like Galichon, that maternity should not be imposed on a woman. It is the woman, and the woman only, who should decide if and when she wishes to become a mother. Madeleine Pelletier advocated legal abortion during the first trimester.[69] Pelletier asserted that a large number of children was a cause of poverty and misery and that voluntary family limitation marched hand in hand with civilization. Therefore, if France was less prolific than her neighbors, it was a mark of advanced civilization. Abortion was one means of voluntary family limitation.[70] Pelletier argued that women should limit the number of children they have, either by contraception, for which information should be available to the women, or by abortion as a backup method of birth control.

Concurring with Pelletier, Nelly Roussel, writing in a 1904 edition of *La femme affranchie,* declared that "it is not true, my sisters—as one would have you believe—that fecundity without limits is an asset and that it is in the best interest of the human collectivity to see its numbers increase indefinitely. . . . The evil from which we suffer, alas, is not depopulation, but to the contrary, it is overpopulation, the unique cause of our misery and of the lamentable parade of shames, vices and crimes." Roussel, like Pelletier, called for population limitation among the working classes as a means to decrease their misery. Moreover, it was "the duty and right of women to wisely and freely regulate their fecundity." (Repopulationists, in contrast, believed that it was women's duty to increase the race.) Nelly Roussel asserted that women should reclaim their rights and control their maternity. In an angry speech she exclaimed that if women do what others expect of them as a duty, making citizens and soldiers, giving birth to numerous children, "submitting to a martyr's destiny," even then, she will not be thanked and will receive no recognition.[71]

Like Galichon and Pelletier, Roussel criticized society's negative attitude toward single mothers, who bore the burden of what bourgeois society called their "fault."[72] She argued that society denigrated working mothers even while it asked them to take on the extra burden of having many children, and she criticized the state's focus on the duty of women to bear children at the sacrifice of their right to chose.

Among feminist novelists, Lucie Delarue-Mardrus added her voice to those of Pelletier and Roussel when she wrote about Marie, a victim of male brutality who became an unwed mother in a society intolerant of the single mother. Marie, wanting nothing more than to stay at home, have her baby, and marry the rich man who initially raped her, goes to Paris to have her son and avoid the wrath of her father. She desperately wants to keep her son whom she loves very much, but her family forces her to give him to her childless relatives. Marie serves as the aunt to her own son. Eventually Marie marries a man who promised to help her raise her boy, but both Marie and her son meet a terrible end as a result of this man's brutality. Delarue-Mardrus's moral to this sad tale is that unwed mothers were not at fault for their exclusion from respectable society. Rather, brutal men shared responsibility for unwed mothers with a society that provided no role, no respect, and no support to these women.[73]

During the entire nineteenth century, with the exception of a few feminists, even female social commentators rarely mentioned mothers' rights. Toward the end of the century nearly all major reformers wrote of the right of the child to life and the duty of the state to assure that right, even at the expense of the mother's rights. Nevertheless, feminists such as Galichon, Auclert, and Roussel advocated women's rights to voluntary motherhood and almost all feminists came to believe that unwed fathers should exercise some paternal responsibility.

Most women writers, throughout the century, expressed pity and compassion for pregnant women and mothers in poverty. They used terms that were maternalistic, but not harsh, and they concentrated on poor mothers' needs rather than on society's economic needs. Expressions of sisterhood were voiced by only a few feminists, mostly at the turn of the century. In general, women spoke of the single mother in terms that were softer, more tolerant, and more protective than those of their male contemporaries. Although women writers at the beginning of the century were more apt morally to admonish the single mother than were later writers, they were not as censorial as the men of their time. By the end of the century, as male social reformers came to see poor women in a less critical light, there was often little to distinguish the male and female voices.

CHAPTER

5

Charity and Welfare for the Pregnant Poor

What should be done to redeem or rehabilitate, punish, or provide for the poor and pregnant? During the nineteenth century politicians, social reformers, and philanthropists of all religious and political persuasions advanced diverse ideas about these women. At the beginning of the century they judged poor mothers harshly and the meager assistance they made available to just a few women came primarily from private charities. By the time of the First World War women were seen as the qualified recipients of a less judgmental, yet not necessarily more generous public welfare system. Emerging ideas about national needs and state responsibilities, as well as new medical information, an increasing concern for the plight of poor mothers, and a compelling desire to prevent infant mortality led to the beginning of public assistance for the poor. New programs and institutions helped poor women to marry, find shelter, deliver their babies safely, and provide for the babies during infancy. Of particular importance was the evolution of the primary child-birth facility in Paris, la Maternité.

The state welfare systems that developed to address the problems of poor mothers and their babies had their roots in initiatives begun more than a century earlier during the First Republic. From 1760 to 1789 the increasing number, visibility, and suffering of the poor had compelled attempts at state intervention. During the Revolution, the government leaders attempted to address the problems of poverty in order to reduce the number of indigents and try to control begging and poverty-related crime. Providing public welfare for the poor also fulfilled their sense of mission; they made it one of the top governmental priorities.

The Constitution of 1791 affirmed the right of the indigent to assistance and the duty of the state to provide it.[1]

In 1793, the Republic mandated state assistance to illegitimate children and their mothers; a subsequent decree of the same year stipulated that the public should bear the cost of childbirth for the poor unwed mother. Furthermore, she was entitled to a pension from the state to help her keep her baby and fulfill her duty of breastfeeding. With great fanfare and publicity, the government of the Convention authorized public support to unwed mothers in order to reform their morality and eliminate prejudices against them.

Officials of the First Republic believed that it was one's duty to have children in order to perpetuate the spirit of liberty and that the welfare of children should receive the highest priority. The First Republic, however, had few available resources and as a result of financial constraints welfare plans barely got off the ground. In 1811 a Napoleonic decree abolished assistance to mothers and babies; instead it encouraged and facilitated the abandonment of children to public institutions. In an effort to protect the nation's innocent children from neglect, exposure, and death, largely due to the dismal poverty of their mothers, the Napoleonic government created a system of foundling homes and wetnurses for abandoned babies. Ironically, it was a system that led to the death of over half of those children.[2]

The Revolutionary governments implemented three welfare institutions that addressed the needs of pregnant women or new mothers: public hospitals, local welfare bureaus (bureaux de bienfaisance), and foundling homes. The increase in public hospitals was facilitated after de-Christianization, when the government confiscated many former monasteries and convents; those they did not sell they converted to public hospitals. Such was the case with la Maternité, which had been the Jansenist abbey Port-Royal before the government took it over in 1795.

From the Bourbon Restoration in 1815 to the advent of the Third Republic, religiously inspired private charity worked to improve the morality of the poor and to remove the perceived threat that poor urban women posed to property, the family, and Christian morality. Many philanthropists acted according to the belief that "a Christian society is eminently charitable" and that enlightened generosity obligated society to provide for the moral rehabilitation of the poor and pregnant, thereby preventing immortality and deviance. Religious charitable and philanthropic groups begun in the early nineteenth century grew during the 1850s and 1860s, when social Catholicism, with its predilection for private charity, reached its apogee.[3]

During the first three-quarters of the century, except for public maternity hospitals, religious charities dominated the Parisian scene. These private charities directed their assistance at helping deserving married mothers and at enabling others to marry. Any responsibility to provide for the unwed devolved upon a rudimentary public welfare system. During the last quarter of the century, the public welfare system expanded and developed in response to politicians' and social analysts' transformed vision of the poor and pregnant—a vision inclined more toward practical intervention than judgment. It was a transformation in attitudes that increasingly affected private charities as well. Starting in midcentury, the demarcations between private charity and public welfare became less noticeable, and by the end of the century private and public assistance can not easily be separated. Private philanthropists bequeathed money and buildings to public welfare agencies; at the same time national, departmental, and local governments gave subventions to many hundreds of secular private charities and enacted legislation affecting the private charities. Furthermore, public authorities inspected and regulated those charities they subsidized. This symbiotic relationship between the private and public sectors of poor relief evolved over the century and touched all branches of women's lives.

Marrying the Poor

To religious philanthropists during most of the century, marriage was the first step in moral rehabilitation, and helping the poor and pregnant to marry was one of the earliest and most persistent forms of charity. To reformers of all religious and political persuasions, consensual unions remained the scourge of society. It was not that women rejected marriage in order to flaunt their freedom and defy conventional custom; rather, indigent couples lived together without marriage by necessity rather than choice. Just completing the forms for registering a marriage was both expensive and difficult.

A young couple wishing to marry first had to go to the marriage bureau at the mayor's office. This was closed on Sunday, necessitating that they lose a day's work to start the marriage process. Then they each needed their birth certificates and affidavits stating that each had lived in Paris for more than six months. Just the couple's birth certificates cost Fr 2.55 each, and the marriage certificate cost another Fr 3.30, more than several days' wages for women earning only Fr 500 a year.

Parental consent laws limited a couple's autonomy and made marriage more difficult and expensive. Every man under thirty years old and every woman under twenty-five had the legal and financial burden of securing either the written and notarized consent of their parents to marry or the death certificate for a deceased parent. If both parents had died, the couple needed the assent of grandparents or the family council. The law required parental consent even when an adult had not seen a parent for more than twenty years, or if a parent was a vagabond or in an asylum. Not until 1896 did the legislature lower the legal age to twenty-five for men and twenty-one for women and require the consent of only one parent of each of the betrothed. In 1907 the need for parental approval was abolished for any person no longer a minor. Each certificate required the appropriate official seals and related notarial fees. If one or both of the partners had to go back to the countryside to obtain the required parental approval, as was usually the case for couples in Paris, they suffered the additional financial burden of losing wages and paying transportation costs, often to distant areas quite different for each.

The laws had been designed to protect inheritance, but in effect they worked to prohibit many of the propertyless poor from marrying. The poor were often illiterate and unfamiliar with the regulations and negotiation tactics used with the civil authorities. If they managed to complete the paperwork and have the necessary documents notarized, the couple then had to post the publication of the intended marriage at the mayor's office where each lived and in the parents' commune if either were a minor. In some cases the couple had to replace lost birth certificates, or rectify unrecorded births and improperly spelled names. Moreover, a man could not marry until he had fulfilled his obligatory military service and furnished his discharge papers.

The overall cost of just completing the paperwork for a civil marriage represented more than one month's wages for a poor working couple in Paris. Each certificate and piece of paper required a stamp, which cost money, as did the notarization. The cost ranged from Fr 40 to Fr 200, not inclusive of securing the birth certificate of all children born before the marriage and the fees to recognize (Fr 9.38) or legitimize (Fr 3.75) each child.[4] Often a woman earned less than Fr 500 a year and sometimes as little as half of that. Even with her partner's wages, saving for marriage would have been difficult. The final obstacle to marriage for many couples was the lack of special clothing for a proper wedding and the money for the wedding feast. Many couples simply could not afford a legal marriage, and as a result, the "Parisian marriage" prevailed. For many women in Paris, a consensual union represented a failed attempt at a legal marriage. For some, it may have been tantamount to marriage; couples sometimes lived together more than twenty years, referred to each other as husband and wife, and occasionally the women assumed the name of the man without having a legal marriage.[5] Desertion was the divorce of the poor.

Jules Gossin contributed practical proposals to the question of the marriage of indigents. He combined the rhetoric of social and moral economists in ascribing immoral behavior to single mothers with the social Catholic ideal of charity. The rehabilitation of cohabiting women through marriage became his life's mission.[6] Toward that end, in 1826 he founded the Société Charitable de Saint-François-Régis de Paris to facilitate the civil and religious marriage of indigents and to legitimize their children. The Society emphasized the importance of marriage as a means of improving morality and rehabilitating single mothers. It reflected the concerns of the social Catholics and moral economists in that the Society aimed solely to "moralize" the women and legitimize the unions, thus helping to end the "plague of concubinage that threatened" the city. The Society's leaders saw their organization as a charitable intermediary, first between a couple who wanted to marry and their families in getting approval for the marriage, and then between that couple and the civil authorities in arranging for the marriage.[7]

Having heard about this charity from friends, neighbors, priests, or local officials, couples seeking aid to marry had to begin by securing a recommendation from a recognized authority such as their mayor, clergyman, a representative of a hospital or local welfare bureau, or a member of the Société de Saint Vincent-de-Paul or another Catholic or lay charitable society. Equipped with a letter of recommendation attesting to their residency, age, and good morality, the couple then, and only then, could appear at the headquarters of the Société de Saint-François-Régis, located in a poor working-class area near the Church of the Saint Sulpice, but only on a Sunday from noon to two or three o'clock.[8]

Lay volunteer counselors, *dames de charité,* usually religiously inspired bourgeois women, organized in each parish of Paris, then interviewed the couple at home with the instruction to "penetrate the couples'" hearts and inspire religious sentiments."[9] This meant making sure that the couple abstained from drinking, went to church and confession, and baptized their children. Counselors also found out the couple's occupation; date and place of birth; number, ages, and sex of their children; and the whereabouts of their parents. They refused to marry any man under eighteen or woman under fifteen unless the woman was already pregnant. The Society also provided each couple with a religious ceremony. Thus, the Society sought to strengthen the Christian family by helping people in consensual unions to marry, especially if they had children. It also strived to strengthen the bonds between parents and children by facilitating parental approval for marriage. If, however, parents refused their consent to marriage, the Society would help marry the young couple if they had been living together for several years and already had at least one child.

The Society facilitated only marriages between Catholics or, in a few cases, between Catholics and non-Catholics if the latter promised to raise the children as Catholics.

If the officers of the Society approved the couple for marriage, the Society then acted as intermediary between the couple and the authorities by assuring that the paperwork was completed correctly and paying for the official seals and notaries' fees for each document. It made sure that the birth, parental approval, and death certificates were in order, and it made special effort to secure the certificates of parents who lived in other departments of France, as well as the birth certificates of couples who had been born in other departments. In this task, the Société de Saint-François-Régis had the help and cooperation of other charitable societies in Paris and the provinces.

Of the poor couples receiving aid from the Society to legalize their union and legitimize their children between 1826 and 1841, most were employed and in long-term stable relationships; half of the couples had at least one child. Of the 6,867 couples for whom the duration of cohabitation was known, only 22 percent had been living together under one year; 24 percent had been together one to three years; 20 percent had been together for three to six years; and almost one-third had been living together more than six years. They were able-bodied poor—manual laborers and domestic servants, cooks, street vendors, and shop clerks. More than three-quarters of the women worked in the needle trades.[10] These couples could not afford the fees necessary to marry since their combined income was Fr 3 to Fr 6 a day.

Not everyone who sought assistance from the Society actually married. Over 8,500 couples applied between 1826 and 1841, of these 778 backed out during the period of "moral instruction" while waiting for the proper forms to be obtained and notarized. Fifteen percent of these could not obtain parental consent; 25 percent could not furnish all the required certificates; and in another 18 percent of such cases, one of the partners backed out, two-thirds of the time it was the man. Some who had already published official announcements never married; of these, Gossin hypothesized that indigence and lack of proper clothes was the main reason, although frequently one partner had disappeared or died. Approximately 75 percent of the couples actually married. Almost 30 percent of these couples lived in the populous working-class former twelfth arrondissement which was the Society's headquarters; most others lived in equally poor nearby arrondissements.[11] Charitable efforts of all kinds focused on the twelfth arrondissement, an area with high poverty, illegitimacy, and unrest.

An 1850 law on the marriage of indigents made the Society's work easier, less expensive, and less urgent. Since the 1840s, legislators and politicians such as Alexis de Tocqueville and René Villermé had encouraged legislation waiving some of the legal fees for marriage. In 1850, a law was enacted that was designed to preserve the family and diminish concubinage, especially in the cities, by facilitating the marriage of indigents and the legitimation of children. After a mayor or priest certified the couple's destitution, the police commissioner or appropriate local authority would deliver the "certificate of indigence" to the couple. Once equipped with that certificate, couples desiring to marry could have the cost of the birth and legitimation certificates waived and the notarial fees reduced to less than Fr 1 each.

No clear guidelines existed, however, to help authorities define indigence.[12] The difficulty of and accompanying shame in securing proof of indigence may have deterred couples from benefiting from this law. Couples still had to obtain, and pay for, written and notarized parental approval. This was a major stumbling block for migrant couples in Paris and other cities, and it was the way in which the Société de Saint-François-Régis helped them the most after 1850. To many legislators during the Third Republic, the law of 1850 did not go far enough, and they sought to include the certificates of parental approval among those furnished for free by the state.

The Société de Saint-François-Régis had even greater success assisting marriage toward the end of the century. From 1826 to 1875 it facilitated 53,936 marriages and legitimized 29,551 children in Paris alone. Of these marriages, 88 percent occurred after 1841. Between 1826 and 1841, the 7,165 couples receiving aid to legitimize their unions represented one-eighteenth of all marriages in Paris. Between 1856 and 1887, the Society funded one-ninth of all marriages in the department of the Seine.[13] This Society did not intend to alleviate poverty and gave no financial aid before or after the marriage. Only in rare exceptions of absolute indigence would it provide linens and diapers for the baby. It relieved the consciences of the donors (and perhaps the couples) more than it alleviated the economic suffering of the poor. Gossin, a devout Catholic, wanted to serve God more than the unmarried poor.[14] Nonetheless, the Société de Saint-François-Régis legitimized many children and secured women in marriage, thereby helping women achieve their marriage goals and possibly also securing paternal child support. By helping people marry, it also helped make them eligible for other forms of aid.

Shelter for the Pregnant

During the first three-quarters of the century only a few small private institutions assisted pregnant and parturient women. Most religious charities had an aversion to supporting homes for unwed mothers because they felt that such homes would reward the women for their behavior.

In the 1840s and 1850s some private religious charities opened protective homes (maisons de prevoyance) for domestic servants and other workers without jobs. Their goal was to provide shelter and work, and thereby prevent young, single women from falling into sexual activity and unwed motherhood. One patronage society helped pay for transportation and food en route to young women who would go back to their families in the provinces. It sought out young, single women who, having not been able to find work, were likely to fall into "disordered morals." It also assisted married women in Paris whose husbands disappeared or died and who had parents in the provinces willing to offer them shelter. Between 1844 and 1849 it returned 1,153 women to their hometowns.[15]

Only three institutions in Paris housed single pregnant women before the 1880s and even these opened only after midcentury, when attitudes had begun to change. The Hôpital Rothschild, which had only sixteen beds for indigent Jewish women, did not discriminate between the married and single. Two Catholic institutions accepted women in or beyond their sixth month of pregnancy if they wanted to conceal their first pregnancy. The Oeuvre de Saint-Raphaël, conveniently located in the center of a populous and poor working-class area of the city not too far from la Maternité, sheltered selected and recommended single pregnant women, "victims of a first fault." Some came directly from other departments in France.[16] Women spent their time in prayer and work. The poorest women were received without charge, others paid between Fr 1 and Fr 2 per day. Founded in 1866, the Asile Sainte-Madeleine housed unwed pregnant women prior to their delivery. This shelter charged Fr 30 per month but indigents were admitted free, according to space available, and contributed to their upkeep by sewing. The women lived in a dormitory-style room and delivered their babies a few blocks away at la Maternité. Most of the women in this shelter had been born in other departments of France; but more than half had been living in Paris two years or more. Thus, most came to Paris for reasons other than to hide their pregnancy. Only one-third of the women had been living in Paris fewer than six months before their babies were born.[17]

Other charities sought to rehabilitate young women but did not establish homes for unwed mothers, per se. For example, to save them from crime and prostitution, the dames de charité supported shelters for young repentant girls to provide them with religious instruction as well as training in an occupation such as needle work. Throughout the century the Refuges Bon-Pasteur sought to prevent poor young women, often orphaned or abandoned, from falling prey to "loose morals," pregnancy, and prostitution. The refuges endeavored to rehabilitate penitent poor girls who were sexually active. Some provided a type of halfway house for young women leaving prison, and some exploited the women's labor.[18]

For most of the nineteenth century, an unwed pregnant woman who did not qualify—by religion, poverty, or amenability to rehabilitation—for acceptance in any charitable institution was without shelter during her last months of pregnancy. Any provisions for her care devolved upon public assistance and the maternity hospital. It was not until the last decades of the century, when social action became motivated by the desire to save babies' lives, that private philanthropy and public welfare began to show more compassion for the pregnant poor. Charitable societies became secular, and they increased in number and scope. They even received subventions from the public treasuries, thus blurring the lines between private charity and public welfare.

Nonetheless, the first secular institution in Paris specifically for single pregnant women was public, not private. The Asile Michelet opened its doors in December 1893 to 100 pregnant, single, homeless women. It was established in response to the Academy of Medicine's 1891 proclamation that each department should establish a shelter to care for women in their last months of pregnancy regardless of their marital status. The Asile Michelet was designed to come to the aid of the "mother of tomorrow" who was exhausted, in great misery, and in danger of "succumbing to the distress of her situation," inflicting harm on herself or future baby either by fatigue, malnutrition, and overwork, or by attempts at abortion or infanticide.[19] This shelter hoped to prevent infant mortality by protecting the unborn child during the last month of gestation.

To be admitted, a woman had to appear at the doors of the Asile Michelet on Tuesday or Saturday afternoon, furnishing proof that she was French, that she had lived in Paris at least one year, and that she was at least seven months pregnant. Then she received a bath, a hair washing, and a uniform which she wore during her stay. The clothes she wore upon arrival were disinfected and returned to her when she left. A midwife and doctor examined her to confirm the stage of pregnancy and check her for infectious diseases. Then they assigned her a bed and some work according to her physical ability—mostly sewing and mending linens. Women received a small wage for this work, and when they left took their earnings, often enough to pay a wetnurse for their infant for a month. After her labor began, a vehicle took the woman to la Maternité; she did not have to walk the half-hour distance from the shelter.[20]

The demand for admission always exceeded the number of available beds, and just two years after the Asile Michelet opened, the municipal government voted the funds to double its size in order to accommodate 200 women. Between 1894 and 1900, the first six years of operation, it admitted 10,055 women who came from hospitals, municipal shelters for the homeless, or the streets. The great majority of its occupants were single migrant women in their twenties; 85 percent had never been married; 68 percent were in their 20s; 78 percent had been born in other departments. The high percentage (62 percent) of domestic servants at this shelter attests to their particular vulnerability. Another 18 percent were day laborers and seamstresses.[21] Although most doctors and philanthropists believed that the assistance was best given in the women's homes, they realized that the women who most needed the aid were those who wanted to hide their pregnancy and thus could not live at home. Domestic servants were particularly likely to lose their jobs, and their lodgings, as soon as their pregnancy became apparent.

The private, secular Philanthropic Society focused on homeless women, who were not necessarily pregnant. Starting in 1879, the Philanthropic Society established three shelters to serve women—regardless of their marital status, conditions of pregnancy, or number of children.[22] The vast majority of those temporarily housed in these shelters were homeless single mothers or married women who had been abandoned by their husbands. The Society tried to find women jobs, place their babies with a wetnurse if necessary, help them legitimize their children, and encourage them to reconcile with their families. Despite the intention of shelter directors to find work for the women upon their departure, during the initial decades of operation only about one-third were placed in jobs following their stay. From 1903 to 1906 this increased dramatically to five-sixths. From 1879 until 1906 the Philanthropic Society's shelters provided 237,115 women and 46,739 babies with room and board for an average stay of four nights, even though regulations stipulated that women spend a maximum of three nights. In 1906 alone, the Society's three shelters for women housed more than 9,000, many of whom were pregnant or new mothers.[23]

At the Asile Saint-Jacques, the only one of the Philanthropic Society's shelters that accepted pregnant women, a dormitory of twenty beds supplied shelter for women awaiting admission to la Maternité. Another room contained row upon row of beds and cribs for homeless women and their babies after they left the hospital.[24] The shelter provided clothing to needy women, and gowns, shirts, and diapers to their babies. One of the many thousands of homeless women who passed through that shelter was Marie Moran, an embroiderer earning what was a good salary of Fr 4 a day. She had been living with her parents and siblings, who helped care for her first child. At the age of twenty Marie became pregnant for the second time. She hid her condition from her family and in January 1881 secretly had her baby at home. The infant died. Frightened and bleeding, she ran to the nearest public hospital, la Pitié, but was refused admission because there was no available space. Afraid to return home, she wandered Paris for four days in the middle of January, cold, weak, and ill, before arriving at the Asile Saint-Jacques, almost three kilometers from la Pitié. Upon leaving the Asile after three days, she went back to work as a seamstress, only to be arrested for infanticide because her father had discovered suggestive evidence and reported her.[25]

Those who found shelter in the Asile Saint-Jacques before they delivered their babies at la Maternité typically were single. Between 30 percent and 50 percent were domestic servants and 75 percent had been born outside the department of the Seine. They ranged in age from seventeen to thirty-two. Between 2 and 5 percent of women giving birth in la Maternité gave the Asile Saint-Jacques as their address.[26] These women had no other home.

In 1886, Marie Béquet de Vienne combined her money, property, and political skills with that of the Philanthropic Society, Public Assistance, and the municipal government of Paris. With this broad base of support, she readied a building and opened a shelter for abandoned pregnant women and new mothers, regardless of marital status. Called the Asile Maternel, this shelter served homeless women who were without food or shelter, while protecting their anonymity. Marie Béquet de Vienne wanted to prevent abortion, infanticide, and child abandonment as much as shelter poor women and reconcile them with their families. By 1910 the number of beds in the Asile Maternel had doubled to forty and were always occupied. To be admitted women needed no birth certificate and could assume any name. They just had to be poor and homeless, pregnant or postpartum. Although the average length of stay was one month, pregnant women could stay as many as five or six months, during which time they would work in the laundry or the kitchen, or at sewing and mending. Their wages were saved for them so they would have some resources when they left.[27] They delivered their babies at la Maternité, and some returned after discharge from the hospital.

After childbirth, new mothers could remain in the Asile Maternel for up to fifteen days while learning about hygiene and infant care from physicians and receiving moral guidance from volunteer bourgeois women. The directors of this shelter would try to find the women jobs in which they could continue to keep and care for their babies. Failing that, they helped the mothers find good wetnurses. From its opening in November 1886 until 1906, a total of 12,314 women and 11,893 infants found shelter there for an average of twelve nights. This shelter found work for about half its clients.[28] One can only wonder what happened to women who did not have jobs when they left, because they were also without homes.

As the figures for the shelters attest, the number of homeless women in Paris was large and their need for shelter was urgent; charity and philanthropy could not provide enough assistance. Municipal and departmental governments also established several public shelters for women. They admitted the destitute homeless, married and single, pregnant or not, without apparent discrimination. When the authorities tried to send women in the shelters back to their home town, all expenses paid, fewer than 2 percent agreed to go. These shelters, not intended specifically for unwed mothers, nevertheless accepted them.

One of these, the Asile Pauline Roland, opened on July 14, 1890, on the rue Fessart in the Belleville section of the working-class nineteenth arrondissement. It was designed for able-bodied women temporarily without homes and work. Mothers with newborns and older children could stay there and work in the laundry or at needle work for up to three months then take the proceeds from their labor with them when they left. Pregnant women could begin a stay as early as their second month of pregnancy. Instruction in hygiene and morality accompanied the daily work routine, as it did in other public and private institutions for homeless women. This large shelter had beds for over 250 women and 40 infants or children, but only one-third of the women were pregnant. Among them appeared a young woman from Brittany, who had been fired as a domestic servant because she broke a vase. Ashamed to return home, she took a furnished room where, "defenseless," she had become pregnant. Desperate, she arrived at this shelter after living on the streets.[29]

The municipal Asile George Sand, inaugurated in 1894 and located in the populous, working-class twentieth arrondissement, had 97 beds and 20 cribs to shelter homeless women. It admitted more than 2,000 women per year between 1894 and 1900. The doors opened at 6 P.M. daily for admissions and no questions were asked of the women who sought to enter. Of the 17,466 women spending nights in this shelter during these years, about 70 percent were single and 75 percent had been born outside of Paris. Only one-fifth to one-third of the women in this shelter were pregnant, and fewer were domestic servants (only 36 percent) than at other institutions.[30] Thirty percent entered from other shelters.

The fact that women moved from shelter to shelter suggests that a culture of homeless people existed. This may indicate a welfare society, or a large group of dejected and desperate women, pushing the limits of public and private welfare systems. It also suggests that the women's informal and personal support systems failed to keep them out of these dismal institutions.

Fig. 5. Dining room of the Asile Pauline Roland on the rue Fessart. Reproduction courtesy of Centre de l'Image de l'Assistance publique.

These were women who came to Paris to work and live, not to hide a pregnancy. Although during the 1890s women born in the provinces outnumbered Parisian-born women by a ratio of about 5:1 in the shelters, between one-half and three-quarters had been in Paris more than one year. Only one-fifth had been in Paris less than nine months before poverty or pregnancy drove them into a shelter. Almost all were single; one-half were in their twenties, and of those who were pregnant, one-half had been domestic servants. For 56 percent of the women it was their first pregnancy; for another 25 percent it was their second, and for about 8 percent it was their third. Eleven percent, however, were experiencing their fourth, fifth, or sixth pregnancy.[31] Philanthropists and government officials no longer believed that sheltering unwed mothers would only encourage nonmarital sex. First and foremost they wanted to protect the future child; the enormous number of homeless pregnant women on the streets of Paris compelled a search for solutions. Providing rudimentary institutional shelters was just one solution.

Beginning in 1892, public assistance in Paris aided pregnant women by establishing prenatal consultations at the hospitals and welfare bureaus, and by supporting house calls by doctors and midwives to poor women.

Prenatal clinics for the poor and pregnant were first established in 1892 by Doctor Pierre Budin, professor of obstetrics at the Paris Medical School, chief obstetrician at la Maternité and Baudelocque, and a founding member of the League against Infant Mortality. Convinced that prenatal care and maternal rest before delivery were essential in reducing the numbers of premature babies and infant deaths, he established a free clinic at Baudelocque to provide such care. Women went to this clinic only if an emergency or abnormality sent a woman to a midwife who in turn referred the woman to the prenatal clinic. Usually a pregnant woman saw a midwife only once during her pregnancy before labor began. At that first visit, if the midwife determined that the pregnancy was progressing normally, she saw the woman again only at the time of delivery.

By 1910, at the urging of Dr. Budin and indefatigable city council member Paul Strauss, public assistance in Paris offered material aid to some working pregnant women so that they could rest from noxious or tiring employment. A woman had to appeal for such aid either to her local welfare bureau or to the offices of Public Assistance, with proof of indigence and residency in the department of at least one year, and with medical proof of the length of gestation. She would then be eligible for material aid, on the average of just Fr 15 a month, starting in her seventh month. Eligibility depended upon the difficulty of the pregnancy, the level of industrial danger, and the level of fatigue. A Fr 15 monthly allotment allowed a pregnant woman little rest since it was barely enough to live on for 10 days. Most of this pregnancy "protection" was awarded through the welfare bureaus to demonstrably needy married women during their last two months of pregnancy if they had other young children at home. Many women received the money for just one month before the baby was born.[32] By 1913, legislation permitted prenatal maternity leaves of up to four weeks for working women.

Childbirth

Childbirth itself presented a great hardship for poor women. Midwives charged between Fr 20 and Fr 200 for a delivery, depending on their degree of skill, whether they were trained and licensed, and whether the women boarded in the midwife's establishment, called a *maison d'accouchement*. Most of the approximately 700 governmentally licensed and supervised midwives in Paris at the end of the century charged more than poor, single women could pay.

It was not until 1901 that a private charity emerged to help poor women in childbirth, regardless of marital status and religious or political affiliation.[33] Founded by Dr. Blanche Edwards-Pilliet with private donations and public subsidies, the French League of Mothers of a Family (Ligue Française des Mères de Famille) tried to address the needs of women in childbirth. For women who gave birth at home, the league provided nurses to assist midwives and take care of parturient women before and after the birth. Women who gave birth in a maison d'accouchement or hospital necessarily were away temporarily from their families and so feared finding their husbands in a cabaret, their older children on the streets or abandoned to Public Assistance, and their homes deserted when they returned. For these women, members of the league looked after their home and family while they were away.

The women whom they aided were typically married women with many children. Their husbands were either dead or too sick to work. The league also assisted single mothers who wished to keep their children. To preserve ties between mother and child, league members helped women find work to do at home (usually sewing). Alternatively, they helped a single mother secure Public Assistance to enable her to send her infant to a wetnurse. Then they found her a job and helped her maintain contact with her baby until she could take care of her child herself. Bourgeois women donated used clothing and household goods to the league to distribute to the poor; its members discovered who was needy through a network that included Parisian midwives.[34]

The league started slowly, providing assistance to only 100 women during its first year of operation. By 1909, however, it had given childbirth and postpartum assistance to 3,699 women, most of whom were widowed or were married but whose husbands were sick or disabled. Dozens of volunteer nurses and female inspectors visited women's homes before, during, and after the childbirth to dispense advice on hygiene and deliver clean clothes, linens, and food. Volunteers came during the day, helped clean the house, make the dinner, and take care of the older children. They also notified other private charities and public welfare authorities if the family needed further assistance from another agency. They viewed themselves as an institution of solidarity, without religious or political affiliation, established to bring assistance in the form of jobs, money, linens, and cribs. Smaller organizations aided women during childbirth by supplying the linens for childbirth and even the midwife herself. One also supplied people to look after postpartum mothers during recovery just after home delivery.[35] In addition, married women could avail themselves of midwives provided by their local welfare bureau, bureau de bienfaisance.

The multipurpose bureaus de bienfaisance inherited their structure from the Ancien Régime and the First Republic. These welfare bureaus provided the earliest form of relief, although not specifically designed for the poor and pregnant. A July 1816 ordinance created one welfare bureau for each arrondissement of Paris in order to distribute goods and services to the needy at home.[36] To overcome inequalities in local resources, Paris's municipal council and Public Assistance subsidized welfare bureaus in proportion to the indigent population in each arrondissement.[37] The structure and purposes of the welfare bureaus changed little during the century except for the proliferation of substations and the infusion of more funds from Public Assistance after 1890.

The welfare bureaus provided some deserving indigents with temporary help and others with regular long-term aid. Short-term assistance was available to pregnant women and nursing mothers with at least two other children and no means of support, to the sick and wounded of both sexes, to orphans under 16, to male or female indigent heads of families with at least 3 children under 13, and to widows and widowers with at least 2 children under 13. The residency requirement changed over the course of the century: in the 1820s it was one year, by 1902 it was three years. Assistance took the form of finding work for the able bodied, providing food, clothing, and heating fuel, or paying for a midwife or other medical services.

The bureau routinely provided midwives only for married women with three or more children under age 13. The local bureau assigned a licensed midwife to each qualified poor woman in her ninth month of pregnancy, and the woman was to use the midwife to whom she was assigned. Some women, however, had greater confidence in one welfare-bureau midwife than another and went to the bureau midwife they preferred.[38]

In the 1890s, the local welfare bureaus were the organizations responsible for partial implementation of the Paris municipal council's policy of providing assistance to women from pregnancy through the end of lactation, in an effort to protect children from the fetal stage through weaning. In 1894 the council voted that poor pregnant women who had their own living quarters should have the same assistance in pregnancy as was accorded women staying at the municipal shelters. This implied that help with lodging, food, and clothes would be furnished to both married and single women for several weeks before the birth of their baby.[39] Yet, the records of the bureau de bienfaisance of one working-class arrondissement indicate that of 1,200 pregnant women who requested aid, only 857 received an average of Fr 10 each.[40]

The number of poor and pregnant women assisted by a bureau de bienfaisance midwife increased from 7,400 in 1865 to approximately 12,000 by the end of the century.[41] This 62 percent growth far exceeds the 2 percent increase in total births in Paris and the 20 percent increase in total births in the department of the Seine for the same time period.[42]

The figures represent the increasing poverty of women, the restrictive practices of the public hospitals from 1865 to 1893 and the increasing acceptability of welfare bureau services to the poor who may have felt that welfare was a stigma. The peak years, 1891–1894, were the years of widespread economic difficulties and exceptionally hard winters, years in which the number of indigents increased in Paris in general. After the turn of the century, the number of births assisted by a welfare bureau midwife declined from 35 percent of all welfare deliveries in 1899 to 21 percent in 1909.[43]

Single mothers had always been at the mercy of the public hospitals; the one central to their lives was la Maternité. Other major public hospitals, such as l'Hôtel-Dieu, la Charité, and la Clinique provided free childbirth care to indigent mothers but to far fewer than la Maternité.[44] Until late in the century la Maternité was the only hospital strictly for obstetrics, and it was always the largest, operating at capacity. Two to four thousand women delivered their babies there annually—an estimated total of 200,000 women between 1830 and 1900. Admissions procedures cut across the general population of the pregnant poor, provided that the women met the criteria of residency, indigence, or imminent childbirth.

Between 1800 and 1900 the proportion of Parisian women giving birth in la Maternité decreased in relation to area births, because the number of beds there remained constant while the number of new beds in other hospitals grew. At the beginning of the century, approximately 10 percent of all births and 33 percent of all illegitimate births in Paris took place at la Maternité. By the end of the century these figures had fallen to 5 percent and 20 percent, respectively. In 1900 there were 870 beds for maternity patients in Paris (of which 253 were at la Maternité).[45]

Public policy, which between 1870 and 1900 encouraged midwife-assisted births paid for by Public Assistance, further reduced the proportion of women using la Maternité. Moreover, the hospital restricted some admissions. Due to financial problems, puerperal fever epidemics, and over-crowding, maternity hospital authorities turned away 36,628 pregnant women who sought admission between 1865 and 1905. They did so by sending women to midwives and by strictly enforcing the one-year residency requirement. There was a loophole in the residency regulation, however, that benefited parturient women: a woman could be admitted to la Maternité once labor pains had become intense, no matter how long she had lived in Paris. Each year at least 250 pregnant women who had been in the city less than one year gave birth in la Maternité.[46]

Fig. 6.   La Maternité around 1900–1910. Reproduction courtesy of Centre de l'Image de l'Assistance publique.

Life and Death in the Welfare Hospital

When a pregnant woman sought admission to la Maternité she first entered the waiting room; from there she went to the consulting room where the midwife in charge would examine her to determine the term of gestation and whether the pregnant woman was to be admitted. Before 1869 the hospital admitted parturient women as long as it had beds. After 1869, if there were no apparent difficulties or if the hospital was crowded, la Maternité's officials often sent or escorted the pregnant woman to a nearby public-welfare midwife. This was to avoid contagion in the hospital from puerperal fever. The hospital administrators, not the pregnant woman, chose the welfare midwife. If the patient was admitted to the hospital, she was divested of her clothes, which the hospital laundered. The hospital staff then bathed her and provided her with a uniform. If childbirth was not imminent, she went to the thirty-bed ward for pregnant women. If there appeared to be medical complications, she went to a special ward with twelve beds. If the woman was about to have her baby, she went to one of two delivery rooms, where, if the presentation was normal, a midwife would conduct the delivery.

Complications usually brought a male physician to the scene. Since la Maternité was a teaching hospital that trained midwives, student midwives would observe and assist at the delivery, after which the patient went to one of two wards where she would stay the required week. These practices remained essentially the same from 1830 to 1900.[47]

Before 1855, the law required that a new mother notify the mayor's office of the birth within three days after delivery, which in principle required that regardless of the weather or her health she must leave her bed and take her tiny infant with her to register the birth. In 1855, the director of Public Assistance won approval for the midwives to file the birth certificate information. Still, sometimes the mayors took weeks in preparing the birth certificates, thereby delaying a woman's application for welfare, since a birth certificate was necessary before a mother could be considered for any public assistance.[48] When the new mother and baby left the hospital, authorities returned her clothes and provided a basic layette of diapers, shirts, and shawls for the infant. This procedure prevailed during the entire century with only one notable change: before 1852 if a mother wanted to abandon her baby she notified the hospital within 24 hours after birth and attendants took her infant to the foundling home; after 1852 she had to keep the infant with her in the hospital and take the baby when she left.

Before 1852, over half of all new mothers, both married and single, left the maternity hospital within the first seven days after birth. In 1852, legislation designed to promote maternal bonds with the baby and prevent infant abandonment stipulated that women and their babies must stay in the hospital for at least eight days. Both single and married mothers had to adapt. Thus, from 1852 to the end of the century, only 15 to 18 percent stayed fewer than eight days; 30 percent to 50 percent of the woman stayed the required eight days; the rest stayed longer. By 1900 almost 90 percent stayed in the hospital for eight days after childbirth. Staying in the hospital this long presented great difficulties for some women. One unfortunate mother in 1890 left after four days because she had five children at home whom she had to tend.[49] Others not only lost a week's wages but also lost their jobs and, unable to pay their rent, thus lost their rooms. Even if they nursed their babies for a week, at the end of that time circumstances forced many of them to send their infant to a wetnurse so they could resume work. Those first weeks became extremely difficult for the new mothers, who physically and emotionally suffered from newly nursing and then prematurely weaning their infants.

While in la Maternité, pregnant women had to contend with a variety of terrible conditions, such as infestations of rats and epidemics of puerperal fever and cholera.[50] Understandably, women feared giving birth at la Maternité and tried to avoid the place. Germinie Lacerteux, the pregnant domestic servant in the novel of the same name published by Edmond and Jules Goncourt in 1864, carefully saved money in order to pay a midwife and thereby avoid the hospital. She was forced to deliver her baby there only after her lover absconded with all her savings. A hospital worker urged her to leave soon after the baby was born to avoid dying of rampant disease.[51]

A poor woman's passage through the rooms of a nineteenth-century hospital was a terrifying experience, even if the delivery went smoothly. Visiting hours were only two afternoons a week, and most women never had a visitor. Women were given no prenatal preparation, no anesthesia, and no emotional support in what was a harsh and filthy environment. Women suffered greatly during childbirth, especially if the presentation and delivery offered any complications. Doctors' use of forceps and other instruments in delivery, or the performing of a Caesarean section without anesthesia or antiseptic procedures, not only caused unbearable pain but also led to almost certain death for the mother. Furthermore, methods of inducing labor could produce disastrous results, as in the case of one young woman who entered la Maternité on September 26, 1829. By September 30 she still was not in labor, so on October 1 the doctor administered ergot of rye. Since this produced only weak contractions, later that day the doctor delivered her baby with forceps. The mother died, as did four other women who delivered after her that day in the same room, and perhaps in the same bed.[52] In the Goncourts' tale, Germinie Lacerteux is terrorized by the sound of women screaming and the specter of women dying in the beds next to her; it was a response many would have had. As one doctor at la Maternité put it, "poor women would prefer to deliver in the streets than to step into our delivery rooms."[53]

The poor and pregnant also died in hospitals of what was termed peritonitis, metritis, or more generally, puerperal fever. Puerperal fever is a general term used to describe a highly contagious postdelivery bacterial infection, usually of the genital tract but often spreading throughout the body, that occurs within the first six weeks after childbirth. In nineteenth-century Parisian maternity hospitals, it spread when doctors went from performing autopsies or examining infected women to examining healthy ones without cleansing their hands and sterilizing bandages and instruments, and when healthy postpartum women were located next to those infected.[54]

The prevalence of puerperal fever in the hospitals concerned doctors, although until the 1860s they did not know its etiology. Some believed it was a result of various unhealthy conditions in the hospital: lack of fresh air, "miasmas," closed curtains around the beds, women lying too close together, inexperienced student midwives, failure to change the fetid and encrusted bed linens until the stench became unbearable, or "pernicious variations in the atmosphere." Others believed it resulted from the general debilitation of working-class women—their poverty, malnutrition, physical and moral weakness, and attempts at abortion that made them susceptible to a virus in the air, in dirty rooms, and on dirty linens.[55] Between 1843 and 1862 some doctors realized that they transmitted the disease themselves when they went from an autopsy to a delivery. Realizing that their hands smelled, they began to wash them before delivering a healthy woman. This was not enough to stop the bacteria's spread.[56]

The onset of puerperal fever usually began within three days after delivery; it rarely began after the sixth day. A fever, an elevated and weak pulse, vomiting, diarrhea, intense pain in the abdominal area, shivering, convulsions, delirium, and finally death within two to 49 days marked this disease. Treatment included induced vomiting, mercury medicines, bleeding, and feeding the woman sugared lemonade. Only drinking the lemonade, which would prevent rapid dehydration, had any effect.[57] An account from *Germinie Lacerteux* describes what it may have been like: "There was raging at la Maternité just then one of those horrible puerperal epidemics that breathe death upon human fecundity, one of those poisonous infestations which blow over rows of maternity beds and empty them . . . It was all round Germinie at the time, especially at night . . . deaths that seemed to go against nature, tormented deaths, raving and screaming, haunted with hallucinations and deliriums."[58]

Most women who died appeared to have been healthy, of a "good constitution," in their early twenties, and if they had had a previous delivery it had been an uncomplicated one.[59] Sylvain Témoin analyzed the deaths of women at la Maternité from 1856 through 1859 and concluded that puerperal fever killed women having a first baby twice as frequently as it did multiparous women. Single abandoned women without family or support, and especially those who had come from other departments of France and whose "morality was doubtful," had the highest mortality rate—10 percent.[60] His reasoning may be suspect, but single women alone and recent migrants were likely to be weak from malnutrition and poverty and least able to withstand the ravages of an untreated bacterial infection.

Between 1820 and 1850 maternal death in the hospital was less common than it was between 1850 and 1870, but this was not due to deteriorating hospital conditions per se. Before 1850 the mortality rate at the hospital was typically between 4 and 5 percent. At its worst before midcentury it was between 6 and 9 percent. Between 1850 and 1870 it more than doubled.[61] In part, this was because before midcentury women left the hospital within four or five days after delivery; so if they died, their deaths would often appear among the deaths in their arrondissement rather than on the records of the hospital. When, after 1852, mothers and their babies were required to spend a week in the institution, more were likely to die in the hospital rather than at home; of course, some also died at home. In 1856, 25 percent of the maternal deaths in the twelfth arrondissement occurred among women who had delivered in la Maternité.[62] Over the entire century, 60 percent of the women who died in la Maternité had stayed in the hospital more than one week after delivery, and almost half of them died between 16 and 49 days after delivery; fewer than 10 percent died during the first four days after delivery.[63]

Given the conditions in the hospital in the 1820s and 1830s it is remarkable that more women did not die. That any woman chose to deliver her baby there speaks to her destitution and desperation. One small stove was used to heat each thirty-bed ward. No one changed the bed sheets during a woman's stay, or even sometimes between patients. In the rooms for postpartum women, postpartum discharge penetrated mattresses which were changed less frequently than sheets. The stench was unbearable.[64]

Severe epidemics of puerperal fever occurred in 1854, 1856, and 1864. The most severe was in May of 1856, when all but one of the 32 patients died in a ten-day period. As a result, director Dr. Stéphane Tarnier closed the hospital for a thorough cleaning and directed parturient women to other public hospitals. Tarnier noted that maternal mortality in la Maternité was seventeen times greater than with home births assisted by a midwife in the nearby working-class areas. In 1856 one woman in nineteen had died in la Maternité, nearly all from puerperal fever. By comparison, one in 322 of the postpartum women in the twelfth arrondissement died that year, and of these, 29 percent delivered at la Maternité and died after they left the hospital. Women using the midwives of the welfare bureau died at the rate of 1 in 142.[65] Throughout the 1860s one in ten women at la Maternité died annually, except during 1864, when one in five women died. The hospital again closed for cleaning and some minor remodeling.[66] During that decade, 99 percent of la Maternité deaths resulted from puerperal fever; other deaths resulted from diseases such as scarlet fever, lung diseases, miscellaneous infections, or trauma and hemorrhaging surrounding delivery.[67]

No differences appeared between the women who died and those who did not in terms of ages, occupations, marital status, or place of origin.[68] Women who died spent a longer time in the hospital both before and after delivery than did the others; the average length of time was seventeen days before delivery, and fifteen days after. Survivors spent one to two days before delivery and seven to eight days after; one-third of those who died arrived in labor.[69] Though some who died arrived ill or with complications of pregnancy, it is clear that most acquired an infection there.

Since mothers seldom died within the first four days of delivery these data would support the theory that the increase in maternal mortality during the 1860s resulted directly from the mandated, increased length of stay in the hospital; but other interpretations are valid. The physical condition of the patients is an important variable. Women in the maternity hospital were predominantly destitute, single, and in poor physical condition; some may have tried to abort. Yet this alone could not account for the huge mortality rate. The conditions in the hospital itself are another variable. The hospital did attract difficult cases and emergencies, but the doctors' use of dirty instruments and their practice of going from autopsy to delivery without washing their hands greatly increased the likelihood of death from infection in the institution. Ignorant of the germ theory of disease and unaware of their own poor hygiene, the doctors concluded that mortality at la Maternité was aggravated by the terrible "moral and physical condition of the mothers" and by the frequency of difficult labors and surgical procedures. They were wrong; puerperal fever was the principal cause of death. Midwives in the city did not go from autopsy to delivery or immediately from a febrile patient to a healthy one, and as a result women who gave birth either at a midwife's place or in their own rooms were more likely to survive.[70]

After the last severe epidemics of 1864 to 1869, hospitals began to send women to welfare midwives, where the women were likely to survive, rather than admit them. From 1867 to 1875 fewer than 1 percent of the women who delivered with a welfare midwife died. By 1870 maternal mortality in the hospitals had declined to 2.3 percent, in part because the director of Public Assistance forbade all hospital personnel to enter the rooms of healthy patients either after visiting infected ones or after doing an autopsy.[71]

Advances in medicine and consequent changes in institutional practices during the late nineteenth century helped make la Maternité into a modern hospital. In 1846 Ignaz Semmelweiss had documented that puerperal fever could be spread by doctors; but it was not until after 1867, when Joseph Lister corroborated Semmelweiss's conclusions and proposed a germ theory of disease, that practicing physicians realized that diseases were contagious and could be spread by their own dirty hands and instruments. Under the orders of Stéphane Tarnier, the chair of Obstetrical Medicine on the Faculty of Medicine in Paris and head of obstetrics at la Maternité in the mid-1870s, medical practitioners in the

Paris hospitals began taking prophylactic antiseptic and aseptic measures. Tarnier mandated that doctors wash their hands and instruments with chloride of lime or carbolic soap. Such practices predictably reduced the incidence of uterine infection and puerperal fever. In 1876 a new wing was added to la Maternité, the Pavilion Tarnier, containing small rooms for the purpose of isolating infectious parturient and postpartum women.[72]

By the mid–1880s it was widely recognized that puerperal fever was contagious and could be spread by doctors, midwives, dirty bandages, instruments, and the air. Hospitals therefore had to be continually and thoroughly disinfected, women had to be isolated for six days after delivery, and each hospital was required to have two separate sets of personnel: one for sick women and one for the healthy.[73] The traditional curtains surrounding the beds, which had been washed only every six months, were eliminated. Antisepsis became customary in all hospitals, and the mortality rate dropped to 1 percent and never again rose to its earlier highs.[74]

In 1889, another new wing to la Maternité opened, the Clinique Baudelocque. This modern facility included a free prenatal clinic for mothers, and, after 1892, a free well-baby clinic for neonates. The revolution in Parisian obstetrics that began with the work of Tarnier and his antiseptic practices eliminated puerperal fever, but it also was an integral part of the medicalization of maternity. The poor and pregnant of Paris were the major beneficiaries of these modern medical practices, and women came to accept hospital intervention in childbirth and in other problems related to reproduction. Hospital beds in la Maternité, the Pavilion Tarnier, and the Clinique Baudelocque continued to be full.[75]

An 1892 law requiring that hospitals admit and deliver for free the babies of single and married destitute pregnant women helped change welfare for women in childbirth. This law became part of a national comprehensive free hospital plan for the indigent, enacted in 1893, which classed childbirth as an illness. This enabled women to obtain free hospital, medical, and pharmacological assistance for childbirth-related health needs and constituted a definitive step in the medicalization of maternity. It stipulated that any sick person (including pregnant women) deprived of resources and unable to be cared for at home must be admitted free to a hospital. As a corollary to the definition of childbirth as an illness, midwives working for the welfare bureaus or for Public Assistance were subject to inspections to ensure that they followed sterilization and antiseptic procedures.[76]

The combined effect of new medical knowledge, changes in hospital practices, and national health initiatives was improved care for the preg-

Fig. 7. The nursery at la Maternité. From *The Illustrated London News,* 8 March 1881.

10726

nant poor. More women sought hospital deliveries, and la Maternité became a hospital for the general population of women, not just for single, destitute pregnant women. It was no longer a place women shunned. Between 1870 and 1886, of all married women who gave birth in Paris, 2.5 percent chose a public hospital. Between 1893 and 1900, the percentage of women delivering in a public hospital tripled to 7.4 percent. The percentage of all Parisian out-of-wedlock births occurring at the public hospitals showed less of an increase: from 8 percent between 1870 and 1885 to 12 percent during the last seven years of the century. Between 1873 and 1900, the percentage of all babies in public hospitals that were born to married women doubled from 20 percent to 43 percent. Public hospitals and welfare midwives accounted for slightly more than one-third of Parisian births in 1878 and three-fifths of those births by 1896.[77]

The pregnant poor used a variety of public assistance personnel and institutions for help during the difficult months before and after childbirth.

In 1878, about 36 percent of the women who gave birth in the city were helped by public welfare. Of these women, one-half went to their local bureau de bienfaisance for a midwife in order to deliver at home; about one-fourth gave birth in a public hospital; and approximately another fourth went to a welfare midwife provided by a hospital and Public Assistance. Between 1878 and 1898 the annual number of women giving birth in all the public maternity hospitals of Paris increased 160 percent, that is almost tripled (from 5,442 to 14,096), the annual number of women sent from the hospital to a public welfare midwife increased 43 percent (4,104 to 5,876), and the annual number of births with a welfare bureau midwife increased by only 13 percent (from 10,630 to 12,025). In the 1890s the average annual number of pregnant women who received public assistance in childbirth increased to 34,181, representing almost half of all women who had babies in the city of Paris in a year. Only 35 percent of those who received public welfare delivered at home with the help of a midwife from their local welfare bureau, and only 17 percent went from the hospital to one of Public Assistance's midwives: fully 48 percent delivered their baby in one of the public hospitals.[78]

By 1909 more than 15,000 births occurred in the maternity hospitals, representing 45 percent of all public-welfare assisted births. The percentage of women choosing a bureau de bienfaisance midwife had declined to 21 percent of welfare-assisted births, and the number of births with public midwives increased to 34 percent of total welfare births.[79] The decline in the percentage of pregnant women seeking assistance from a midwife at a welfare bureau can be partially attributed to the relative prosperity France experienced, which left fewer women indigent and in need of aid from their welfare bureau. This decline is also partly attributable to the fact that more poor women were willing to be admitted to larger and safer hospitals than ever before. The hospitals would have sent women they could not accommodate to a public welfare midwife, increasing the number of births with those midwives.

Before the 1870s, assistance to the pregnant poor was rare. If women wished to marry, the Société de Saint-François-Régis could help. A married woman could receive assistance for the birthing itself from her welfare bureau or from the public hospitals; a single woman had only the maternity hospitals which may or may not have had room for her. Welfare and charity alike operated under the principle that giving assistance to unwed mothers, other than hospitalization for childbirth, would encourage immorality and single motherhood.

After 1870, social activists emphasized the production of healthy new citizens for the nation and developed more forms of charity and welfare for the pregnant poor, regardless of marital status. As a result, pregnant women had more options, even while their lives became increasingly regimented. They could find a place in one of the shelters for the homeless and could use one of the several improved hospitals for childbirth, or they could have public assistance pay a midwife. A few could have some prenatal care. Yet, along with institutional and medical care came medical surveillance of the women, not only for their own well-being but also and especially for the well-being of their fetuses and infants. In principle, after 1892, public and private welfare provided security through shelters, material aid, and medical advice. In fact, however, few women sought medical help, and those who did went late in their pregnancy; the material aid was woefully inadequate; the refuges were loathsome and served only as shelters of last resort. Charity remained a system based on personal referrals and contacts. Public welfare had become more institutionally structured; but nevertheless, charity and welfare still did little to alleviate the huge concerns of large numbers of pregnant women.

CHAPTER

6

Charity and Welfare for
New Mothers and Infants

When Victor Hugo published *Les Misérables* in 1862, he published a powerful account of life for France's poor in the first half of the nineteenth century. Fantine had few choices other than to carry her baby daughter, Cosette, about with her as she tried to find work. Private charities shunned women such as Fantine for whom there was no chance of marriage. She could not appeal to religious philanthropies because she had violated their norms of behavior. The only help Fantine could get, even from the state, was in childbirth at the public maternity hospital. After she had her baby, effectively only one form of welfare existed for her: the foundling home, the Hospice des Enfants Assistés, where she could abandon her infant to an almost certain death. To keep her beloved Cosette, Fantine needed money to pay a wetnurse, or a job and sufficient welfare to enable her to raise the baby herself. Fantine wandered from place to place trying to find work and a decent place to live. In the belief that only without her daughter in her arms would she find work, Fantine in desperation left Cosette with chance acquaintances whom she thought would properly love and care for her child. Then, because that foster family was greedy and evil, to support her daughter Fantine had to sell her hair, teeth, and eventually her body.[1]

If Fantine had lived toward the end of the nineteenth century, she would have had several other options. By that time philanthropists, legislators, and public officials had become sufficiently concerned with saving infant lives by aiding and protecting their mothers that they developed public and private programs, ones that had become increasingly overlapping and complex. These changes in charity and welfare for new mothers and their babies reflect the transformation in attitudes toward womanhood that occurred during the century. At the beginning of the century, private charity, usually religious, reflected the dominant view of a single mother as immoral and in need of redemption through religion or marriage. By the end of the century public welfare embodied the new focus on a child's right to life and the view of single mothers as not so much immoral as unfortunate. The change in attitudes resulted from increasing secularization of society and the political effects of depopulation concerns.

Charity and Motherhood

Before 1870, only a few charities existed for new mothers. One of the oldest devoted to assisting poor women during childbirth and for several months thereafter was the Société de Charité Maternelle. Founded in 1784 under the patronage of Marie Antoinette, it received subsidies from the royal family or from the state during most of the nineteenth century and continued as a private philanthropy into the twentieth century. Throughout the century, women of title or of the upper middle classes served as patrons, benefactresses, and administrators; the wife of the head of state, whether Queen, Empress, or President's wife usually served as chief benefactress. In the name of Christian love and charity, the Society devoted itself to helping poor women during childbirth and the postpartum period, but only if the women were married or would marry with a religious and civil ceremony.[2]

This Society provided these mothers with partial payment for the cost of a home delivery, including a midwife, a layette, and financial aid to encourage breastfeeding. They insisted on midwife-assisted home delivery because they thought it healthier both morally and physically than a stay at the maternity hospitals. The Society wanted to protect the "moral" married women from contagion by the "immorality" of single mothers who relied upon the hospital.[3] Its major efforts, however, helped poor married women after the birth of their baby. Like other religiously sponsored charities, the Société de Charité Maternelle confined its assistance to married women. Its members believed that one cause of social misery was the weakening of maternal feelings due to mercenary wetnursing. They subsidized maternal breastfeeding for married women, and eventually argued that maternal nursing would diminish infant mortality.

Religiously inspired bourgeois dames de charité, volunteering for the Society, visited aid recipients once a month. They would assess the mothers' behavior, inspect their surroundings, instruct them in proper religious behavior, and advise them in hygienic care of their babies. Financial aid was minimal, however, to encourage—or force—the husband to work to support his children. The Society paid nursing mothers less than Public Assistance paid wetnurses to raise abandoned children. In addition to a layette, diapers, and some clothes, financial aid ranged from Fr 4 to Fr 20 per month, up to twelve months, depending on perceived need and available funds.[4]

From 1810 to 1887, the criteria that established a need for maternal assistance from the Society barely changed. The women had to be in their last two months of pregnancy and furnish a certificate of indigence and good morals from their mayor or clergyman. They also had to have been married in a religious as well as civil ceremony, agreed to have the baby baptized immediately after birth, and promised to breastfeed their infant. If they were physically unable to nurse, upon the recommendation of the dames de charité, mothers could bottle-feed their baby and still receive the monthly allocation. If, however, a mother sent her infant to a wetnurse against the advice of the dame de charité and the Society's doctor, she forfeited all aid. Mothers who received assistance had to present their baby for inspection each time a dame de charité asked to see the child. In 1850 and after 1875 more stringent criteria were applied: if the husband were alive and living with the mother the couple had to have at least three children alive under thirteen years old, or the husband had to be chronically ill, or they themselves had to be infirm with at least two children living at home. Alternatively, if the woman "lost" her husband during her pregnancy she only had to have at least one other child at home to be entitled to aid. In principle, a woman living with her husband and benefiting from two incomes, or his higher wages, could support more children than could a single mother. In aiding only married women, members of the Society believed that they strengthened family bonds.[5]

The Société de Charité Maternelle worked with local municipal welfare bureaus and their midwives, operating both in the realm of private charity and public welfare. Starting in the 1860s, public funds in the form of subventions from the city of Paris, the department of the Seine, and the national Ministry of the Interior supplemented income derived from private donations and special fund-raising events. Even with these sources of support, the Society's officials complained of insufficient resources to provide for all needy mothers who requested help.

This Society may have been more interested in redeeming the morals of many women than in alleviating the poverty of a few; as the requests for aid increased, the amount of money given to each mother declined, with the reductions greatest during the last months of nursing. The amount of financial aid that each mother received over the course of her period of breastfeeding declined from Fr 100 at the beginning of the century to Fr 80 in the 1840s, to a meager Fr 54 in 1851.[6] At Fr 10 per month, this aid was hardly sufficient to enable a mother to nurse her infant without also working for wages. Still, it was better than nothing, especially if she could get by with working fewer hours or was able to supplement it with assistance from her welfare bureau or another charity.

Despite mandatory investigation of all charity recipients to determine their need and morality, the number of needy Parisian mothers receiving the aid increased from an average of 628 per year in the 1820s, to 912 in the 1840s. From 1861 through 1885 this Society aided an average of 1,500 women per year, and by the turn of the century it extended its coverage to about 2,600 women per year.[7] Most women who received aid from the Société de Charité Maternelle lived in the poorest areas of the city, as did the recipients of assistance for marriage from the Société de Saint-François-Régis. There is no indication that the charity recipients were the same for both societies, but a woman could first receive assistance from the Société de Saint-François-Régis for marriage and then receive aid for delivery and breastfeeding of her child from the Société de Charité Maternelle.

The Fr 20 (or even Fr 4) a month, plus baby clothes, that the Société de Charité Maternelle provided enabled some poor mothers to better manage the crisis of a birth and new infant. The relief saw them through some of the extra costs and loss of work that the birth of an infant entailed, and it enabled poor mothers to avoid the deplorable conditions of the public hospitals. The mothers, however, had to tolerate visits and inspections from charitable women.

Few shelters for mothers existed before the end of the century. One of the smallest yet oldest refuges that accepted homeless mothers, including the unwed, was the Asile-Ouvroir de Gérando, which housed young Catholic women from ages sixteen to twenty-four upon their discharge from a maternity hospital. In keeping with his philosophy, Gérando designed the refuge to rehabilitate those who had committed their first "fault," supervising their convalescence so they could return to virtue and legitimate employment. This shelter found the women work as domestic servants for religious families and exercised a benevolent patronage over them. In order to return to work and virtue, the mothers either placed their babies with wetnurses or abandoned them altogether. Protestants maintained their own shelters, such as the Refuge of the Protestant Convalescent House and the Temporary Shelter, both of which were for women and their children.

Several small charities also offered assistance to indigent mothers, usually in the form of food and clothing. For example, the Association of Mothers of Families (l'Oeuvre des Mères de Famille), founded in

1828 and in operation throughout the century, worked with the Société de Saint-François-Régis providing food, linens, clothing, and infant layettes to impoverished but worthy mothers unable to receive assistance from their local welfare bureau or from the Société de Charité Maternelle. It restricted its charity to women who were married in a church and having their first or second child, if they came to them during their pregnancy. Approximately 1,000 new mothers each year received food and clothing from this association.[8] Another private foundation, that of Bettina de Rothschild, gave an annual sum of over Fr 36,000 to Public Assistance to help poor mothers, regardless of their marital status or religion. Distributed through the hospital administrators or the bureaux de bienfaisance, it provided Fr 10 to Fr 15 total to needy women after childbirth; a related charity provided bandages and linens to Jewish women at childbirth.[9]

Institutions for New Mothers and Babies after 1870

After 1870, several interlocking institutions emerged in which secular private charities worked closely with municipal and departmental governments. Philanthropists and government officials alike designed organizations to serve their goal of preserving infant lives by reducing infant abandonment, combating mercenary wetnursing, and educating poor mothers about proper infant care. Institutions for new mothers multiplied, as did the numbers of poor women served. Most notably, the Philanthropic Society and like-minded reformers established shelters to care for mothers and babies immediately upon their discharge from la Maternité, when both mother and child were weak and the baby was in greatest danger of dying. Shelters extended their welcome to unwed mothers and to married women abandoned by their husbands.

The departmental and municipal government, in addition to providing subventions to secular private philanthropies, established two convalescent institutions in garden suburbs of Paris, with property donations from philanthropic individuals. The first institution, Vesinet, established in 1859, accepted single as well as married women after they left any of the public hospitals, including la Maternité. It provided them an average of three weeks' rest and nursing care. In only five years, the number of beds increased from 60 to 350. Life in Vesinet consisted of meager meals, chapel services, and either work, walks, or rest, as the women's health permitted. Residents were allowed visitors two afternoons a week. Women were on their own after leaving Vesinet until late in the century when other welfare was established.[10]

The public convalescent shelter Ledru Rollin in the suburb of Fontenay-aux-Roses was uniquely for women and newborns who left la Maternité. With a donation of property from the family of a former president of the Second Republic, Ledru Rollin, and with additional public support it opened in 1892. Twice a week, a bus brought women from la Maternité to this fifty-one-bed home, where they stayed up to one month and were taught how to clean, feed, and care for their babies. At the end of their allotted recuperation time, a bus returned them to Paris. If they had no place to go, they were left at the shelter Pauline Roland.[11] By 1910 both convalescent homes, Vesinet and Ledru Rollin, usually had empty beds. If new mothers had a home to go back to, they preferred it to a long stay in one of these two institutions with regulations, rigid schedules, and limited visitation allowed from family. Furthermore, women with families wanted to return to their other children.[12] Most mothers in these convalescent shelters, however, were single domestic servants, reflecting the population of la Maternité.

One particularly important philanthropy supplemented these public institutions. In 1906 two members of the Society for Maternal Breastfeeding (Société d'Allaitement Maternel), Paul Strauss and Marie Béquet de Vienne, with support from the president of the Republic, Emile Loubet, and his wife, founded the Society of Maternal Aid and its shelter, l'Aide Maternelle, to provide for new mothers devoid of resources and family support. On the outskirts of the eleventh arrondissement, l'Aide Maternelle welcomed desperate women who had recently had a baby. It sought to help mothers such as one young married woman who, on the advice of her neighbors, delivered her baby at la Maternité. Eight days later, she left the hospital and hastened home, never having received a visit from her husband. When she knocked on her door a stranger opened it. Her husband had sold everything and left with his mistress. This poor woman was found crying in the street and brought to l'Aide Maternelle.[13] This charity was also for unwed mothers who had been seduced and then abandoned and for poor country women who came to Paris to hide their pregnancies then decided not to return home.

Mothers stayed at l'Aide Maternelle for four weeks, during which time they nursed their babies. A convalescing mother's other children under five years of age could stay in the special child-care section of this institution. To ensure that when a mother left this shelter she did not abandon her baby, the Society of Maternal Aid found a job for the mother, a wetnurse (if necessary) for the baby, and the Society made the first payment to the wetnurse.[14] In addition, it organized services for mothers and their newborns after they left the shelter, including a free well-baby clinic, and a dispensary for free medicine, clothing and sterilized milk. This was thought to strengthen maternal ties and give the infants a better chance to survive. The Society of Maternal Aid worked in solidarity with its parent organization, the Society of Maternal Breast-feeding, in the struggle against infant mortality. They sheltered mother and child, teaching the mothers proper hygiene, cooking, sewing, and child care.

Several charities working together under the auspices of the Society for Maternal Breastfeeding helped women from the last stages of pregnancy through the first year of the infant's life, but concentrated their efforts on postpartum mothers and their babies. In one case a woman had been abandoned by her husband, who left her seven months pregnant and with two older children. She worked as a cook but could not manage the crisis of childbirth. Overcome with despair she thought of abandoning her baby. Hearing about the woman, volunteers went to help. After childbirth, the mother and her newborn were taken to the convalescent home, l'Aide Maternelle, until she regained her strength. When she left, the Society helped her find a wetnurse nearby and gave her fifteen francs a month for a year to help pay the wetnurse. The Society provided her with clothes and a layette, and it helped her find work. Whereas women entered the public convalescent homes directly from la Maternité, perhaps moving from one impersonal institution to another from their last stages of pregnancy through their convalescent period, those few admitted to l'Aide Maternelle had a more individual, if more restricted, route to assistance based on personal referral.[15]

Little was available to women once they left one of these shelters. One charity provided inexpensive meals to a limited number of nursing mothers who kept their infants and did not have a kitchen. Single workers in the needle trades, victims of the sweating system, day laborers, and married workers whose husbands were sick, alcoholic, or debauched could take some meals at one of the Cantines Maternelles for a cost ranging from 20 to 40 centimes for each hot meal.[16] The charitable couple who started these cantines believed that "in Paris, no mother and nursling should suffer from hunger." In 1905 they established two cantines, serving two meals a day, open to all nursing mothers. They asked nothing of a mother except proof of lactation. To gain admission, a woman had to uncover her breast and extract several drops of milk. The cantines also allowed pregnant women to take their meals there, provided they could attest that they were at least five months pregnant. This private charity eventually sponsored eight cantines, each feeding ten to fifteen women at a time.

In addition, poor working women, upon payment of Fr 45 a month, could find room and board at one of the thirty-seven homes run by the Sisters of Saint-Vincent-de-Paul. Women who had their own rooms could eat at one of the twenty restaurants in Paris that served only women and pay from 50 to 90 centimes for a meal.[17] For some of the poor, however, this amounted to half their daily wages.

By the turn of the century, a homeless pregnant woman could find refuge in the municipal Asile Michelet or in the private Asile Maternel, perhaps after first going to one of the shelters for the homeless, such as the one on the rue Saint-Jacques, or the municipal Asile Pauline Roland. She would have her baby in the state-run free maternity hospital, la Maternité, or she could use a midwife with the financial assistance of one of the private charities, Public Assistance, or her welfare bureau. Upon leaving the hospital or maison d'accouchement, she and her infant could be received at one of the private or public convalescent shelters. Alternatively, mothers who delivered at home or at a midwife's could receive some philanthropic home relief. None of these institutions existed before the 1880s. Mothers, however, needed aid for longer than a few weeks; they had to work in order to live and so faced the difficult problem of deciding how to combine their productive and reproductive lives.

Home Relief to Mothers and Infants

Some private philanthropies provided home relief to needy mothers and babies. For example, the League against Infant Mortality, an umbrella organization of private philanthropy, coordinated different private charities for children, and indirectly for their mothers. Its main agency, the Society for the Protection of Children, was founded in 1869 to encourage maternal breastfeeding and keep families intact. Often working with the Philanthropic Society, the League assisted the poor and pregnant of Paris with home relief before delivery, material and moral support during labor and delivery, and home relief after childbirth in order to facilitate breastfeeding. It provided coupons for free meat and bread to mothers who nursed their children. In 1908 it received 3,454 requests but could accommodate only 1,320 women.[18] The League's agencies did not discriminate based on religion or marital status; they worked with other private charities and public institutions with similar goals. Membership included the leaders in the battle against depopulation, such as Paul Strauss, Théophile Roussel, Georges Clemenceau, and numerous others. In keeping with this populationist stance, the League's concern for the mothers was only a means to preserve the infant's right to life and protect the baby against neglect and abandonment.[19]

Working with the League and augmenting its services was the Society of Maternal Breastfeeding, founded in 1876 by Marie Béquet de Vienne (receiving broad public support). The Society defined its goals as saving infants by providing mothers with moral and material sustenance, without regard to a woman's marital status or religion. Midwives played a crucial role in alerting Béquet de Vienne and other members of the Society when a particularly needy woman had just given birth. A member of the Society then visited the unfortunate mother to provide aid if they thought it justified. They brought used clothes for the family, food, a layette, and a crib (including mattress and sheets).

Starting in December 1892 Public Assistance and bureaux de bienfaisance helped implement the decision of the general council of the department of the Seine to provide relief for both married and single needy mothers during a baby's infancy. The council provided an additional subsidy of Fr 100,000 to welfare bureaus for use in providing relief for needy nursing mothers. The working-class eighteenth, nineteenth, and twentieth arrondissements spent more money to provide assistance to more women than did the other arrondissements. Reflecting official opinion of the 1890s, the council requested that the welfare bureaus provide relief to all married women and to all unmarried women living in a long-term relationship (ménage irrégulier).[20] Those living in consensual unions had to fulfill the same conditions of residency and number of children as did the married.

In 1898 the welfare bureaus began providing coupons redeemable at a milk dispensary for sterilized milk for each child under two years of age.[21] The bureaus also provided cribs for new infants and delivered the new, approved baby bottles to mothers unable to nurse. In the 1890s glass baby bottles with a short nipple replaced those with a tube. The milk had often soured and coagulated on the sides of the tube, sometimes up to two feet long, a breeding ground for bacteria. Mothers had preferred those bottles with a long tube because they could leave their infant unattended with the bottle for a long time as a type of pacifier.

Home relief and institutions for new mothers and their infants were rare before the 1870s. Existing institutions favored the married poor and tended to restrict single women's options rather than enhance them. After the birth of a baby, poor single mothers had little financial support available to them until after 1870.

Aid to Unwed Mothers

Antecedents of modern French public welfare programs for aid to mothers with dependent infants began in 1837 when Interior Minister A.-E. de Gasparin, along with some influential members of the general committee of public hospitals in Paris, advocated assistance to women

Fig. 8. Baby bottle with a moderately long tube, called "Biberon Robert," dating from the end of the nineteenth century. Reproduction courtesy of Centre de l'Image de l'Assistance publique.

who gave birth in these hospitals. In order to receive such aid, women had to display a determination to keep their babies or send them to a wetnurse but lack the resources to enable them to do so. At that time, the motivation behind the assistance was to reduce the number of abandoned children and the related expenses incurred by the public treasury.

As of January 1837, each mother who gave birth in a public hospital was given the right to know that if she wanted to keep her infant, she could (after investigation) receive a layette for the baby and money to cover the first month of feeding either by her or a wetnurse. This applied to single as well as married women.[22] Hospital and public assistance administrators were to visit the women in their hospital beds just after childbirth, and by means of a "paternal conversation" try to persuade them not to abandon their infants but rather to keep them and breast-feed them themselves. Believing that the child moralizes the mother, advocates of aid to unwed mothers held that a mother would "atone for her fault" and return to the path of virtue by being a good mother. Those women who were "vicious or perverted," indifferent to their infants, as determined by "paternal conversation," were encouraged to abandon the baby, since otherwise the child would become a victim of the mother's "hard heart."[23]

Most objections to the decree of 1837 were based on the adage that to aid unwed mothers was to condone their immoral activity. Some, however, objected that women who delivered their babies in the hospital would be submitted to undue persecution. Why, these critics demanded, should one impose the obligation to keep and nurse their babies on mothers dependent on hospital welfare? The administrators answered that it was in the interest of the mothers, the children, and society to do so, and furthermore, as administrators they had the right to decide who would be eligible for public welfare.[24]

At least one administrator, A. Boicervoise, was far ahead of his time in believing that "in the last month of pregnancy, women are often unable to work and it is impossible for them to save. . . . It is equally difficult for them to work during the initial time after their delivery; the birth of a child aggravates the economic condition of the family and is an extra burden. Aid to such families is always well placed and is sometimes indispensable. The question is how to determine who should get aid and who still has some resources to tide them over. To refuse someone needy may lead to her abandonment of the child." He argued that aid should be sufficient to deter child abandonment significantly and that public assistance should pay the mother just as it paid mercenary wetnurses for abandoned children. This system would even be economical for the government, since if the department paid the mother for the first two years it would then not have to pay for an abandoned child for the next ten years. He acknowledged, however, that the problems of preventing abuse of a system of such aid would be enormous. Boicervoise sounded like later reformers in insisting on aid in the interest of the child, but his main goal was the prevention of child abandonment and the subsequent care of the child at public expense. To that end, he and others believed that unwed mothers should have preference over married women in receiving aid. Married women, after all, could receive assistance from their welfare bureau and from the Société de Charité Maternelle.[25]

In the first years of aid to mothers to prevent abandonment (1838 through 1844), almost 17,000 women received a layette and money for the first month of feeding, usually the equivalent of the first month's payment to a wetnurse. Despite the stated preference for single mothers, slightly fewer than 65 percent of the mothers were single; 28 percent were married, and 8 percent were "living maritally;" the remainder were widows. Over 30 percent of the women had given birth in la Maternité. Only 25 percent of all women receiving this welfare breast-fed their infants themselves; about 38 percent sent their babies to a wetnurse. The funding for this program came out of general department funds with supplements from the Fondation Montyon for qualified women.[26] Established in 1819, this foundation donated a legacy to Paris hospitals to provide home relief to the needy. Starting in 1838 women leaving la Maternité were eligible, but the terms of the Montyon bequest favored married women and specifically excluded single mothers who abandoned their infants; it allowed aid to single mothers who kept their babies.

The possibility of financial aid to keep their babies may have affected women's decisions to enter la Maternité: the number of women giving birth there rose from 2,935 in 1837 to 3,388 in 1838. This represents a small increase in the percentage of total births in Paris (10 to 11 percent), but a larger increase in the percentage of out-of-wedlock births in that city (30 to 36 percent). The amount of aid, however, was too small and of too short a duration to greatly affect most women.[27] The aid ranged from 15 to 40 centimes a day which was sometimes distributed as Fr 5 a month for up to 4 months, or as a lump sum of between Fr 20 and Fr 30. To put this in perspective, in midcentury, the average monthly salary of a domestic servant was Fr 25 a month and that of a day worker was Fr 1 to Fr 2 a day, taking into account seasonal unemployment. A one-pound loaf of bread cost about 20 centimes, and first-quality white bread was 31 centimes a kilogram.[28] The money was insufficient to allow a mother to keep her baby more than a few weeks without working, or to pay a wetnurse for more than a month.

These programs had an undetermined effect on the number of infants abandoned at la Maternité during the early years. Hospital regulations, and possibly maternal welfare, led to a decrease in the percentage of babies born at la Maternité who were immediately abandoned: from 1816 to 1836 75 percent of all babies born at la Maternité were abandoned. In 1838 that figure fell to 46 percent; by 1844 it had dropped to 36 percent.[29]

In 1856 Public Assistance of Paris began providing some new mothers with one-month's payment for a wetnurse—usually Fr 30—for both legitimate and illegitimate babies who were in danger of being abandoned. Because of a lack of adequate funding and because of discrimination against single mothers, very few women received this assistance; most who did were married. A one-month payment for a wetnurse was virtually meaningless, in any case, because mothers could neither maintain the payments after the first month nor could they take their babies back and continue to work. Most often the babies were abandoned with their wetnurses, and such aid merely delayed abandonment. The percentage of mothers who left the maternity hospital with their babies but later abandoned them increased more than fifteen times from 1830 to 1869—from 2 percent in the 1830s to 31 percent in 1869.[30] Furthermore, there was nothing to prevent a mother from keeping the money and abandoning her baby. Maxime DuCamp, a critical observer of the Parisian scene, expressed hostility both to the women and to Public Assistance. He asserted that when women left la Maternité or the foundling home with the Fr 30 for the first month's payment to the wetnurse, they met their lovers who were waiting to take the money.[31]

Policy toward unmarried mothers changed with the beginning of the Third Republic when officials became more concerned with the related issues of depopulation and child welfare than they were with a mother's morality. Programs reflected the increasing influence of social scientists and the medical profession who saw the alleviation of social problems as one of their major functions. Doctors recognized that the mortality of newborns arose from the terrible conditions mothers faced, as well as from the mercenary wetnursing system, and so they advocated programs of aid to impoverished single mothers in attempts to ensure the health of their infants, alleviate their poverty, and reform their life-styles. Although unwed mothers might have been victims of moral, physical, and financial distress, most believed the children suffered much more. Public officials decided to aid the children while "moralizing" the mothers by increasing the number, scope, and financial resources of programs that their predecessors had begun decades earlier.[32]

In 1876 the administration of Public Assistance in the department of the Seine, under the auspices of the Ministry of the Interior, began a comprehensive program called "aid to unwed mothers to prevent abandonment" with the goal of providing for "children born outside of marriage" to enable mothers to keep and care for their babies. In response to critics who objected to giving aid to unwed mothers, in the next year Public Assistance dropped the phrase "to unwed mothers," calling the programs "aid to prevent abandonment" to underscore that they focused on the well-being of the children. The children who were aided were those infants who were in danger of being abandoned by their mothers and whose mothers, "despite their meager resources, agreed to keep and to raise." Since children of single mothers were abandoned at a far higher rate than children of married women, Public Assistance targeted all its abandonment prevention programs at them.[33]

These Public Assistance programs dispensed aid in a variety of forms that addressed specific problems of single mothers in Paris. Several targeted mothers who could not initially keep and nurse their babies themselves. In the beginning years of the program, officials frequently gave a voucher for Fr 35 (the first month's payment to a wetnurse) to mothers who, upon leaving the maternity hospital or a midwife's care, were too ill or too poor to keep and nurse their babies themselves. They also paid the cost of the infant's travel from Paris to the wetnurse in the countryside. In many cases this form of aid merely postponed abandonment. After the first month, if the mother failed to continue payments to the wetnurse or to take her infant back, Public Assistance would continue the payments to the wetnurse for up to ten months. In real terms, Fr 35 was the equivalent of one month's wages for a day laborer in Paris if she worked every day. Thus, if the mother had to pay the wetnurse herself, it would constitute her entire monthly wages. So it is not surprising that most single mothers depended on Public Assistance to pay the wetnurse for the full ten months. Both the administrators and the poor referred to this relief program as the "ten months." From 1888 through 1894, between 2,200 and 2,700 women each year in the department of the Seine received welfare assistance in the form of ten-months' wages for a wetnurse. Indeed, this ten months of wetnursing was tantamount to giving the child to Enfants Assistés because children receiving aid through their mothers became part of the program of Enfants Assistés.[34]

Another kind of assistance was a payment of Fr 10 to Fr 15 to sick and unemployed single mothers. This was renewable monthly, after investigation, for up to four months. Between 1,200 and 1,950 women in the department (or between 30 to 40 percent of those aided by these miscellaneous programs) received this aid annually. Given the usual wage of Fr 1 per day for working mothers, and an estimated minimum daily cost of living ranging from Fr 2 to Fr 4 a day, such an allotment of Fr 10–15 was insufficient subsistence. Women who threatened to abandon their babies at the maternity hospital or at the Hospice des Enfants Assistés could receive money immediately (usually Fr 35) if they agreed to keep their infants. This was known as "assistance for immediate need" and was never renewable, but fewer than 100 women per year (or less than 3 percent of the recipients of aid) received this payment. As early as 1874, Georges Clemenceau stated that "aid of one month is absolutely absurdly ridiculous" in preventing abandonment, and he advocated payments to the mothers or to the wetnurse for six to ten months.[35]

There were also forms of assistance that paid for the return of babies from wetnurses to mothers who wanted their infants back, that paid the expenses of seduced women who themselves had been abandoned children and wanted to keep their infants, and that paid for the return of mothers to their department of origin (secours de repatriement). Most of the women sent back home had been in Paris for a short time, were without permanent residence, and lived in shelters for the homeless. Administrators of Public Assistance believed that these women had become pregnant in the provinces and came to Paris to have their babies.[36]

The most important and influential program, offered regular, monthly aid to mothers to enable them to keep and breastfeed their babies. From 1880 to 1885 one-fourth of all recipients of aid to prevent abandonment received this form of aid: from 1885 to 1890 this increased to about one half. Initially, only single mothers were eligible for this assistance, since they were more likely than married mothers to abandon their babies. As the century progressed, especially after 1892, the distinction between married and single mothers became less important. In addition to monthly monetary payments, this plan of periodic aid to prevent abandonment provided the mothers with a layette for the infant (including a few diapers and baby clothes) and a crib. By 1890 Public Assistance was spending almost Fr 1 million combined annually on all of these programs to assist about 11,000 babies and their mothers.[37] This equaled the paltry sum of Fr 90 per baby per year.

The program of monthly aid to mothers to keep their infants was large in scope but small in terms of individual need. Initially, women were offered from Fr 10 to Fr 25 a month for up to three months, with continuation each month based on an assessment of need, hygiene, and morality. Despite constant enjoinders from the inspectors and the general council of the department of the Seine to increase the amount of money and give it to more women for a longer period of time, up until 1882 three months of aid was generally the maximum; by 1894 it had increased to six months. By the end of the century, in principle, women could receive up to Fr 30 a month for up to two years, but most still received Fr 20 a month for less than one year.[38]

Throughout the century, from two-thirds to three-fourths of the women receiving this form of aid received Fr 20 a month; the remainder generally received less.[39] Demand for aid was always more than double the number receiving it. During 1877, the first year in which this system operated, 26,370 women requested aid and 11,947 received it. The department's general council appropriated insufficient funds, and the average allocation per mother was only Fr 20 for the whole year. In the next year the budget more than doubled to Fr 772,000. It increased again in 1888 to Fr 972,000 per year; proportionately fewer women received assistance than a decade earlier, but they generally received it for longer periods. By 1899, of 50,388 women requesting assistance, only 14,301 received it.[40]

New mothers' need for financial assistance in the department of the Seine was enormous. In fact, in any given year aid was requested for between a quarter and two-thirds of all births in the department.[41] The increasing number of women who received aid is, of course, in part a result of the development of these new programs, but it also speaks poignantly to the overwhelming poverty of new mothers in the city. In the 1880s, for instance, about a third of all out-of-wedlock infants in the city of Paris received aid, and from 1891 to 1899 that percentage increased to 75 percent. By the end of the century fifteen percent of *all* children born in the department of the Seine received aid from Public Assistance.[42]

By 1885 Public Assistance had become more concerned with maternal feeding to enhance the survival of the infants than with the issue of child abandonment, although the problem of abandonment had not diminished. Accordingly, officials changed the name from "aid to prevent abandonment" to "aid for maternal infant feeding" (*secours d'allaitement*). In order to receive aid, mothers had to demonstrate need, an inclination to work (but not at prostitution), and a desire to keep and love their babies.

Public Assistance's policy was contradictory; it gave aid to mothers to breastfeed when these women were also supposed to work. It failed to recognize that not many available forms of work were compatible with breastfeeding. Nevertheless, policymakers at the end of the century erased the dichotomy that earlier social commentators had established between a woman-as-mother and a woman-as-worker. New, more sympathetic attitudes had supplanted the harshly judgmental and unrealistic old ones, relieving some of the hardships single mothers confronted; but other obstacles emerged. Even though both married and single mothers could now receive aid (for the well-being of their babies), policymakers presented mothers with a new set of constraints: mothers could receive aid if they found work and also could breastfeed.

Providing assistance to mothers with infants in order to prevent infant mortality received more support than did relief to women during pregnancy. Public assistance to support maternal breastfeeding were the most extensive welfare programs for new mothers. In the 1890s, in order to supplement those programs, public welfare developed measures to guard future citizens of the Republic from fetus through toddler. These included municipal support of infant day-care centers, medical welfare agencies such as assistance for pregnancy (secours de grossesse), and well-baby clinics.

Day Care and Well-Baby Clinics

Charity or welfare programs during the century rested on mothers working for wages. Many mothers could do piecework in their rooms, but most had to work outside the home as garment workers, day laborers, or maids. If they tried to keep their babies they faced the overwhelming task of finding someplace to leave them during their long hours of work. Day-care facilities for children of working mothers developed slowly.

The religiously inspired Société des Crèches opened the first crèche, or infant day-care facility, in Paris in 1844. Children of single mothers were especially needy, but they were excluded from these crèches until the last decades of the century. The Société des Crèches, by accepting only legitimate children, hoped to encourage single mothers to marry as well as to prevent abandonment and mercenary wetnursing of legitimate babies. The Society put great emphasis on piety and family ties; it aimed to make the mothers and children good workers, good citizens, and even good soldiers—under the influence of God. To Firman Marbeau, the social Catholic founding father of crèches, work and motherhood were not incompatible; work did not destroy female virtue. According to Marbeau, "Work is, after faith, the most powerful moralizing factor in the world. . . . Work makes a mother virtuous."[43] By putting her baby in a crèche, a mother could work and nurse her baby at least morning and night. At the same time, the crèches provided the child with appropriate food and allowed the mother to nurse during the day if and when she could. Mothers' alternatives to a crèche were leaving their babies alone all day, placing them with neighbors, sending them to wetnurses, or abandoning them. Marbeau argued that babies had a greater chance of survival in a crèche than they did under any of these other alternatives. His overwhelming desire to prevent married women from abandoning their babies and to see their babies survive gave him a different vision of the place of work in women's lives. He realized the necessity of work for many mothers, and his strong religious beliefs allowed work to become a virtue. His views marked the beginnings of a reconceptualization of the relationship between motherhood and work. His crèches were to save the innocent babies and maintain the families of poor mothers.

Each of the Society's crèches accommodated only about twenty infants at any one time, ranging in age from fifteen days to three years, at a cost to the parents of 20 centimes per day.[44] Marbeau and his affiliates considered 20 centimes affordable since it was equivalent to a loaf of bread. Private donations and bequests from numerous fund-raising events, as well as state, departmental, and municipal subventions, supported the few crèches that existed. In 1853 there were twenty-five

Fig. 9. Crèche for poor children opened in Chaillot in 1847, from *L'Illustration* of that year. Reproduction courtesy of Centre de l'Image de l'Assistance publique.

10727

crèches in Paris; in 1868 there were twenty-one, sheltering 880 babies; and in 1870 a total of twenty-three crèches accommodated 810 babies.

In December 1874, the city council approved a measure to encourage secular municipal crèches in order to protect infants from the danger of death with a wetnurse or from bottle feeding. Both single and married mothers would nurse their infants at a crèche, and the crèches would provide sanitary bottle feeding to supplement mothers' milk along with daily medical examinations of the babies. Volunteer women made sure that advice and moral assistance to the mothers accompanied custodial and nutritional care of their babies. The crèches were to serve as schools of hygiene and proper child care and allow women to fulfill their duties as mothers. In response to the priority of saving babies' lives, some private crèches began to admit children of select single mothers who by their "demonstrated good conduct deserved pardon." Even Marbeau changed his mind about excluding single mothers, admonishing members of the Society to "take the hand of the repentant as the divine Master has done."[45]

As a result of the development of municipal crèches after 1874, and increased state subvention of secular private ones, by the turn of the century sixty-seven public and private crèches in the department of the Seine provided for about 6,300 legitimate and illegitimate infants.[46] All were supported in large part as public utilities with public funds and were subject to Public Assistance regulations about cleanliness, health, and hygiene for the babies. Despite the increase in their number, their low cost, and an increasing acceptance of illegitimate children, the crèches were still too few, not open long enough hours, not in working-class neighborhoods, and unavailable to many single mothers.[47]

Mothers who put their babies into crèches differed markedly from those who used other charities. The Crèche Saint-Ambroise in the crowded working-class area of Popincourt in the eleventh arrondissement is emblematic. More than half of the women using this crèche (53 percent) were married. Only 5 percent of them were domestic servants. By far the greatest majority worked as laundresses (13 percent), seamstresses (10 percent), garment makers (17 percent), or day laborers (20 percent). A few of the mothers were semiskilled workers in gems and jewelry, reflecting the occupations of the arrondissement in which the crèche was located. The fathers were engaged in woodworking (17 percent), textiles (12 percent) and metal work (11 percent). Others worked in jewelry and gems, various forms of construction, or as general day laborers. A few were skilled workers or employees in commerce. People using the crèche belonged to a different socioeconomic group, with a higher family income, than did those who used charities. For example, Louise Rigoulot, a worker in crinolines, married to a clock maker, raised her son for eleven months and had him vaccinated and baptized before bringing him to the nearby crèche in good health. Alexandre Grouille's single mother, a skilled seamstress, could afford to send him first to a wetnurse for two years.[48]

Most of these parents did not use the crèche for their newborn infants; only one-fifth of the women put their babies into the crèche within the first two months. More than one-fourth (27 percent) had first sent their babies to a wetnurse, and after weaning, put them into the crèche. The mean age of entry into the crèche was 12 months. The crèches, therefore, did not serve as an encouragement to maternal breastfeeding or as an alternative to wetnursing for many mothers, but rather they shortened the length of stay with a wetnurse and served as an alternative to other forms of child care. Both single and married mothers, in equal proportion, followed similar strategies in rarely using the crèche immediately after birth, waiting until after weaning. Those who breastfed their infants themselves tended to put their children in the crèche at an earlier age than those who sent them to a wetnurse. The babies' health reflected the marital status of the mother; the babies of married mothers were in better health than those of single mothers, probably because these two-parent households would have had two incomes and so the mothers themselves would have had healthier diets for breastfeeding, and were able to afford nutritious food for these babies.[49]

Crèches, like maternal shelters, closely fit the aims of the Third Republic. In allowing for maternal nursing and medical care of the babies, crèches were expected to reduce infant mortality, to encourage maternal sentiment, and to further breastfeeding for working mothers. The crèches were supposed to save those 100,000 infants per year that France lost to the "angel-making" wetnurses.[50] Crèches became even more necessary with the application of the 1882 law on obligatory primary instruction for boys and girls; with the crèches, older sisters would be relieved of child-care duty, enabling them to go to public schools.[51]

Crèches, however, could not satisfy the child-care needs of many women. Some could not reclaim their children at night, and some still preferred to send their infants to a wetnurse. One charity continued to search for an acceptable alternative to wetnursing to preserve infant lives and family ties. The Société Maternelle Parisienne founded a Pouponnière in 1891 in the suburb of Porchefontaine near Versailles. Among its founding mothers were the wives of leading populationists like Paul Strauss and Emile Zola.[52] It operated in the following manner: a woman who worked outside her home as seamstress, tradeswoman, shopkeeper, or daily laborer could leave her baby at the Pouponnière all day and night and visit her baby on Thursdays and Sundays. Meanwhile, impoverished single mothers who lived in the Pouponnière each breast-fed their own babies and nursed but also bottle-fed two other children left at the facility. The single mother would thus trade her milk and her child-care services for food, lodging, and baby provisions. In addition, she would receive wages of Fr 10 per child, at most Fr 30 per month, which she could take with her when she left. The working mother would pay according to her income. A working woman could put her child in the Pouponnière from birth to three years of age, thus avoiding a wetnurse and obtaining the best nourishment and care available, assured by regular visits from doctors. This was an "Institute of Puériculture" to combat infantile mortality and the "terrible scourge of depopulation."[53]

Women who sought places for themselves and their new babies were all single, with nowhere else to go. Marie B., a child herself at fifteen years old with a two-month old infant but no job and housing, sought a place for herself and her infant at the Pouponnière. Laure D., a twenty-one-year-old orphan, gave birth at a maison d'accouchement and did not want to abandon her child. She had been earning Fr 1.50 per day and the father of the child abandoned her when she became pregnant; she could not manage on her own with an infant. Another woman, Marie R., had a little girl three months old before applying to the Pouponnière. She went from asile to asile so as not to have to sleep on the streets. She did not want to abandon her baby.[54] In general, the crèches and the Pouponnière were too small and too few to provide for the Parisian population at risk. Some mothers found publicly funded well-baby clinics, available after 1892, to be helpful in raising their infants, although the clinics did not supply child care.

The establishment of free well-baby consultation clinics furthered the power of doctors and Public Assistance in supervising and regulating working-class mothers' care and feeding of their infants. Dr. Pierre Budin took the lead in establishing the first well-baby clinic (consultation des nourrissons) at la Clinique, the hospital attached to the Paris Medical School. With the support of Paul Strauss and funds from Public Assistance, Budin soon thereafter established free consultation clinics at Baudelocque and la Maternité in 1892, open to all poor mothers and babies. The clinics also functioned as schools of motherhood in which doctors would teach mothers about hygiene and nursing schedules.[55] Regulations specified that mothers were to bring their babies to a well-baby clinic once a week until the child was two years old. An assistant would weigh the baby and record the weight on a "contrôle" card that the mother had to bring with her each time. Then the doctor would examine the baby and make sure that it was gaining enough weight and was generally healthy. If breast milk was insufficient, a mother regularly had to come back to obtain free sterilized milk. In this way, doctors exercised some control; the mother and baby had to come back every few days for advice and instruction in order to receive the free milk.[56]

In addition to the well-baby clinics, in 1894 Drs. Pierre Budin and Gaston Variot were instrumental in establishing dispensaries, called *gouttes de lait,* providing free sterilized milk for needy babies. In 1899 Dr. Henri de Rothschild, working with philanthropies and Public Assistance officials, created four additional milk dispensaries in working-class neighborhoods of Paris. Five years later that number increased to more than twenty. The milk dispensaries accepted milk vouchers that bureaux de bienfaisance distributed to needy mothers, and they also sold pasteurized, sterilized milk at prices of 10 to 25 centimes a liter (which were lower than milk prices in the stores) to any mother or other adult who came with a needy baby. At the first visit to a milk dispensary, the doctor provided a mother with a "contrôle" card for that particular baby which she, or someone else, had to present whenever they obtained more milk for that child. The staff of the milk dispensaries weighed the baby each time to assure proper uses of the milk, as evidenced by sufficient weight

Fig. 10. P. Sabattier, *The Consultation of Dr. Variot*. Reproduction courtesy of Centre de l'Image de l'Assistance publique.

gain and the absence of diarrhea that might have been caused by diluting the milk with unsafe water.

With the aim of educating the poor in proper childcare, physicians and their staff at these milk dispensaries, just as in the well-baby clinics, provided personal instruction in how to feed, clean, and care for a baby. If mothers were entirely incapable of breastfeeding, they taught them how to bottle feed properly, how often to feed, and which bottles to use. Although doctors stated that only two percent of women were unable to breastfeed because of physical problems, they realized that many poor working mothers found it necessary to bottle feed their babies at least once a day. Doctors denounced the use of bottles with a long tube because they were difficult to clean and as a result sour milk remained as a breeding ground for germs, leading to life-threatening infant diarrhea. Along with the clean milk, the doctors prescribed and sometimes provided glass bottles with small nipples.

While waiting in the crowded well-baby clinics or milk dispensaries for the staff to weigh their babies and to provide instruction, the mothers could chat with each other, comparing their experiences with their babies, with doctors, and with other public officials. These occasions could have been ones in which mothers provided each other with support and information. The well-baby clinics and the more numerous milk dispensaries had a dual role in poor women's lives: they functioned as places where they received instruction on childrearing, and they served as social centers.

By the dawn of the twentieth century, welfare officials and philanthropists had begun to realize that pre- and postnatal care could dramatically affect infants' health. This appreciation for the necessity of caring for pregnant and postpartum women—always for the sake of their children—led reformers to establish programs of maternity protection.

Maternity Protection

Legislators and philanthropists strived to protect a working mother during the last stages of her pregnancy, so she would have a healthy infant, and also, in part, to prevent abortion. Mutual maternity insurance programs began in 1891 when Félix Poussineau and several male leaders of clothing unions founded the first such maternity insurance program (*mutualité maternelle*) in Paris. As a solidarist concerned with infant mortality, Poussineau believed that a mutual association of women should pay into a maternity insurance program so that working mothers could take a four-week paid maternity leave from their jobs to stay home and nurse their babies for that month after childbirth. He envisioned that all working women would pay, but financial benefits would go only to only the poor and pregnant. Those who paid into the program but did not receive a paid maternity leave would benefit on another level—from a reduced national infant mortality rate and healthier women returning to work after childbirth.[57] Other politicians wanted to protect mothers from overwork that might lead to weak infants, while at the same time they wanted to save public funds. To them, mutual maternity insurance programs between workers and employers, with contributions from philanthropy and subsidies from the government, appeared to be one solution.

Originally, workers' unions in three garment trades whose work forces were largely comprised of women (lace and embroidery; trim, buttons, and haberdashery; and most important, needlework and dressmaking) organized the first mutual maternity insurance program under the patronage of a philanthropic woman, Madame Carnot. Each woman who was enrolled paid annual premiums of Fr 6 in return for benefits at childbirth. This mutual insurance fund was available to all women in these garment industries who were over sixteen years of age, but they had to be in the program at least nine months before they could collect the benefits of a postnatal maternity leave. In 1891, the first year of its existence, this program had only 607 members and by 1900 the membership had barely doubled to 1,335. It relied on state subsidies and private donations to survive. After a 50 percent reduction in premiums to Fr 3 a year starting in 1905, membership increased sharply; by 1909 it had 17,202 members and helped finance 2,667 births and postpartum leaves. Philanthropic donations, contributions from honorary members, union contributions, and large municipal and national subventions supplemented regular members' payments to maintain the insurance program. After 1906 external sources provided four-fifths of the total revenue. With the infusion of public money, the number of maternity insurance plans multiplied to 129 and included banks and manufacturers, as well as special cases like the fund for soldiers' wives.[58]

Members, usually married women with several children, received a payment of Fr 12 per week for four weeks after the birth of a baby, on the condition that they abstain from all work during that time and breastfeed their babies. Payment could be extended for another two weeks on the advice of a physician. The insurance program also provided for three prenatal visits after the third month of pregnancy, and compensation for lost wages if a doctor thought it necessary to rest during the last stages of pregnancy. To further ensure the survival of the baby, the mutual maternity insurance group established a well-baby clinic, staffed by doctors, where mothers were to bring their babies to be weighed and examined for weight gain problems and symptoms of illness. Although breastfeeding was preferred and encouraged, if absolutely necessary a mother could obtain sterilized milk for her baby. Occasionally, either from lack of planning or lack of resources, workers failed to enroll in this insurance plan for a long enough time before childbirth. In some of these cases, the society provided them Fr 15 for all four weeks, plus a bonus of Fr 10 for nursing. This matched the cost of the least expensive wetnurse and was comparable to what Public Assistance paid some of the mothers on welfare. The regular payments of Fr 12 a week for a total of Fr 48 more than doubled what Public Assistance paid its mothers to keep and breastfeed their babies. Along similar lines some companies and department stores such as the Bon Marché, Galeries Lafayette, and Printemps offered their employees a maternity leave up to three months after delivery.[59]

All of this mutual assistance had strings attached, not the least of it was enrollment for at least nine months prior to childbirth and the intention to breastfeed the infant. In addition, paid *dames visiteuses* (lower middle-class women who functioned as a type of social worker) came at least once a week with the money. They ostensibly also were to bring "a little joy and consolation" and ensure that the new mother had what she needed.[60] A dame visiteuse also inspected the premises, made sure that the mother was not working, that she was not supporting a man, and that she was tending the baby properly.

Despite its successes, politicians and scientists insisted that self-help such as the maternity program was inadequate. Young workers would not put away money for future pregnancies, the poorest workers could not afford even modest premiums, and women past childbearing age ceased to contribute. Too few women were paying into these plans, and many of the plans imposed moralistic conditions that excluded many needy women.[61] To these critics, new legislation supplied an important solution to the problems of ensuring the lives of future generations.

One major legislative achievement was the comprehensive national legislation of 1904 on protecting children. In many respects this law expanded nationally Paris's aid programs to prevent abandonment and encourage maternal breastfeeding. The first articles of this legislation specified that "any child, threatened with being abandoned, whose parents can not nurse or raise because of a lack of resources, can receive temporary aid in order to prevent abandonment."[62] Since infants could receive aid only through their mother, this law further stipulated that those eligible for assistance would include unwed mothers, as long as they were not living in an "irregular" household with the father of their baby. It also included abandoned married women, widows, divorced women, and those whose husbands were in an insane asylum or in military service. Single mothers received the same status in this law as did married mothers who had been abandoned by their husbands; in both cases the aid went to the children of mothers who were heads of families. Married women and those in consensual unions still were eligible for assistance from their local welfare bureaus. Fathers were given the same rights to public welfare if they and the child had been abandoned by the mother or if the child's mother had died.

By this law, mothers could receive monthly payments, never less than Fr 15 a month, when they raised and fed the child themselves. If they had at least two children and needed to place the youngest with a wetnurse they could receive welfare to pay her. In addition to monetary assistance, aid included clothes for the child, a crib, and sterilized milk in the well-baby clinics or milk dispensaries for mothers who could not nurse. Furthermore, if a mother wanted to return with her baby to her hometown outside of Paris, she could receive help for the cost of her journey. She could also receive money to send her infant to a wetnurse and reclaim the child later.

Two particularly important legislative acts in 1913 provided assistance toward poor mothers in the guise of protecting the children. The more well-known law, passed in July 1913, provided relief to poor families with three or more children under the age of thirteen years. The less familiar law, passed in June 1913, recognized postpartum maternity leaves as a way to save infant lives. To gain passage of the June 1913 law, advocates shifted the focus of the debates from the mothers' welfare to that of the babies as the principle beneficiaries of maternal rest.[63] After extensive debate, the June 1913 bill stipulated that any woman "in an apparent state of pregnancy" had the right to take a break from paid employment without penalties. This prenatal leave of up to four weeks was optional. The language "apparent state of pregnancy" was adopted because the legislators saw no accurate way of determining the duration of gestation. The postnatal leave of four weeks was obligatory for women in "all industrial and commercial establishments." This totaled a maximum leave of eight weeks for all French women who worked for wages outside the home, including domestic servants.[64]

By the beginning of the twentieth century the modern welfare state had begun to emerge in France, and a significant segment of Paris's poor became mothers on welfare.

7

Mothers on Welfare

Women faced terrible problems in keeping their child while still managing to work and earn their living. The fictional Fantine in *Les Misérables* had been abandoned by her lover. Eugène Légault not only failed to contribute to the support of his partner, Ernestine Pallet, or their son, but he took all of their money. A single mother could not encumber the wages of her lover to help with child support. Given women's limited job opportunities and derisory wages, often only the added income from a man could stave off destitution. New mothers with husbands, or with responsible mates in a consensual union, had three options that most desperately poor single women did not have: they could send their baby to a wetnurse and return to gainful employment; they could get welfare from their local welfare bureau if they had three or more children; or they could try to get by on their own by nursing their baby themselves.

Wetnursing

Throughout the century, women who did not breastfeed their infants themselves—either because they worked, had insufficient milk, or simply chose not to nurse—sent their newborns to a wetnurse. As many as 20,000 Parisian women a year sent their babies to wetnurses.[1] This figure represents approximately one-third of all births per year in the city. Before the widespread availability of pasteurized milk and the development of infant formulas in the late 1890s, sending a baby to a lactating woman in the countryside may have been safer than using bottled milk of dubious quality, if the wetnurse was truly lactating and so properly nurtured the infant. The wetnurse weaned her own baby or nursed both; but in some cases she nursed neither since she had ceased producing milk. Even if the wetnurse offered inferior infant care and fed the babies poor quality cow's milk, she still furnished necessary around-the-clock custody in her own home, thereby enabling an urban mother to work full time—often more than twelve hours a day.

Some mothers from the countryside left their babies to be bottle-fed by a relative at home, often with deadly results for the baby, while they took a relatively lucrative postpartum position as a live-in wetnurse for the bourgeoisie in Paris. Many of them got pregnant for a second time while in Paris and again sent their babies back to the countryside so that someone else could feed them. For example, Marguerite Verdier's aunt in the Cantal parented Verdier's daughter after she went to Paris to earn money as a wetnurse. Verdier sent her aunt some money to help with expenses.[2]

Wetnurses charged between Fr 15 and Fr 50 per month, with the majority charging between Fr 20 and Fr 40. This was exactly the range of wages for domestic servants or unskilled workers in the needle trades of Paris, so sending a baby to a wetnurse would absorb most of the income of these women. Yet, for domestic servants wetnursing was practically their only option; they could not keep both their child and their job.

The occupations of women who managed to send their babies directly from la Maternité to a wetnurse were indistinguishable from those of other women in that hospital, except twice as many married women as single used wetnurses. Few women sent their babies directly to a wetnurse, in part because the director of la Maternité thought it inadvisable to send babies to a wetnurse the first few days after birth. If a woman who delivered her baby in la Maternité wanted to send her infant to a wetnurse, the hospital would not help, except on rare occasions when authorities would seek aid for a woman before she left the hospital.[3] For example, Marie Descoust was a twenty-three-year-old single domestic servant who gave birth to triplets. In the hospital she nursed them herself, but she could not keep them because she had to work. Therefore the director of the hospital asked the director of Public Assistance to find three wetnurses for the infants and to give the mother extra assistance for ten months of wetnursing because of her extraordinary circumstances.[4]

In 1874 the French legislature enacted the Roussel Law to protect infants and nurslings, regulate the wetnursing industry, and oversee parental behavior. The law required that everyone who placed an infant with a wetnurse, with a foster parent, or with a custodian to whom they paid wages, make a declaration to that effect at their local mayor's office.[5] For just the mid-1880s, between 16,281 and 18,348 infants were registered each year at the mayors' offices of Paris, 95 percent of them placed outside of Paris.[6]

Wetnursing was more often the strategy of married lower-middle-class families than of single mothers; as many as two-thirds of the Parisian infants sent to wetnurses were sent there by married mothers or mothers living in consensual unions. They sent an equal number of boys and girls, and most infants came neither from the richest nor the poorest sections of town but from districts in which people worked predominantly in the retail trades, artisan crafts, garment trades, government and business bureaucracies, and domestic service. These were the central arrondissements (the first through sixth), as well as the tenth, eleventh, seventeenth, and eighteenth.[7] Women in the more affluent areas could afford a live-in wetnurse, and those in the poorest areas could not afford any, unless Public Assistance paid. During the 1880s, between one-third and two-thirds of the women in the first, third, and tenth arrondissements placed their infants with paid wetnurses outside of their homes. Of those babies going to a wetnurse, only 57 percent were newborns in the first month of life. Many mothers apparently kept and nursed their babies themselves for at least a month.[8] Married women paid higher wages to the wetnurse: of the single mothers, only 33 percent paid more than Fr 25 a month, compared with 60 percent of the cohabiting women and 70 percent of the married women.

The stated occupation of the women who sent their babies to a wetnurse resembled those who gave birth in la Maternité. About one-third were domestic servants and another third sewed in one of the garment industries. The remainder consisted of mostly skilled workers (in the jewelry, metallurgy, artificial flower, or paper and bookmaking industries in their arrondissements) and shopkeepers or employees in commerce, reflecting the population of their arrondissement. Relatively skilled female workers often worked alongside their husbands: one-third of the fathers worked in the skilled crafts of the arrondissement. One-quarter worked as accountants or clerks in government or business. Many fathers worked in the retail trade as shopkeepers or sales people, or as barbers, valets, and waiters. They earned a modest income, and their wives also worked so sending infants to a wetnurse became a practical solution to the problem of child care.

The wages a mother paid the wetnurse reflected her occupation, income, and marital status. The more skilled the mother the more she paid the wetnurse. Almost three-fourths of the domestic servants and other unskilled workers paid Fr 25 or less per month and none paid over Fr 40 a month—that would have been more than their wages. Only half of the skilled workers, such as those working in the gem and metal industries of their arrondissement paid Fr 25 or less to a wetnurse. Public Assistance's programs may have paid for some of the wetnurses, especially those used by domestic servants. The one-time only allotment of between Fr 25 and Fr 40 to pay a wetnurse would barely cover the cost of the wetnurse for a month and a trip to the wetnurse's town; the wetnurses domestic servants secured thus were the poorest—those willing to accept a lower than average payment.[9]

Not all of the women receiving the babies were lactating. Many women who called themselves wetnurses actually admitted to the authorities in the mayors' offices that they bottle-fed the infants. The more a wetnurse was paid per month, the greater the likelihood that she would breastfeed the infants entrusted to her; 63 percent of those who charged more than Fr 40 a month said they breastfed, compared with 20 percent of those who charged less than Fr 25 a month. This may indicate that the wetnurses who charged more gave better care, or simply that those who demanded more in wages felt more obliged to avow that they breastfed. The percentage of wetnurses who claimed to breastfeed declined toward the end of the decade. This decline may reflect the increased availability and acceptance of safe, sterilized milk, or merely that the increased regulation of wetnurses forced them to greater honesty in their claims. Specific mortality rates of infants placed with wetnurses are difficult to determine, but out-of-wedlock and bottle-fed children fared the worse. Infants placed with a wetnurse had a higher mortality rate than the general infant population of France, but not as high as abandoned children.[10]

If a poor single mother could not send her child to a wetnurse, and if she was deterred, for whatever reason, from abandoning her baby at the foundling home, she had no way to keep and raise her infant without help from her family, the father of the child, or from charity and welfare—assistance that was not readily forthcoming. Welfare for poor single mothers had begun on a small scale in 1837 and increased only gradually during the next forty years. It was not until after 1876, and the development of specific public welfare programs for women and children that welfare had any impact on alleviating the hardships confronted by poor women. Toward the end of the century, for political as well as humanitarian reasons, public welfare programs furnished a woman with more options, enabling (or forcing) her to keep her child. Welfare programs designed to prevent infanticide and child abandonmment also served as a means whereby male administrators hoped to encourage, or force, women to exercise their maternal duties. By encouraging breastfeeding, they made the mother the paid wetnurse of her own infant.[11]

Applications for Welfare

In order to receive any form of aid from Public Assistance, a woman had to have requested it at the offices of Public Assistance with the baby in her arms, to have given birth in a free, public hospital and then threatened to abandon her baby, or to have gone to the Hospice des Enfants Assistés with the avowed intention of abandoning her child. A postpartum mother could not even request any aid until she left the hospital. Some officials argued that a mother should be allowed to file the initial application for aid to prevent abandonment while she was still in the hospital or with a midwife, then she might not be devoid of resources when she left. If the mother had been a domestic servant, her problems became acute the moment she left the hospital because she no longer had a job or housing. She needed temporary shelter and help with her baby. Still, shelters, available only since the 1890s, merely provided a temporary solution.

At the time of the request, the mother had to have the child's birth certificate as well as a certificate of indigence. She obtained both at the mayor's office of her arrondissement through a process that sometimes was agonizingly slow.[12] In lieu of going to the Public Assistance offices, a woman could appeal for aid directly at the mayor's office. Letters from these women to their mayors requesting aid reveal both contrition and threats. A single mother asked pardon for her "fault which I committed involuntarily" and asked for "grace for the infant and herself from God, the police," and the mayor—in that order. A mother of five children asked for aid in the name of Jesus, but added that if the mayor refused her such aid she would have no choice but to steal in order to raise her family.[13]

After a mother made her written and oral request for welfare, officials then interrogated her about her family, her morality, and her need. They also investigated her living quarters and place of employment, and sought evidence that despite her so-called fault of having a baby even though single, she was essentially moral. This they did by asking questions of her concierge, neighbors, and parents, and even shopkeepers in her neighborhood.[14] She was dependent on the good words of kin and neighborhood acquaintances. By the 1890s, an elaborate procedure for requesting aid had developed. Women made their requests either by letter or in person, and if they were refused, they could make further applications. In the meantime, a mother and her infant had to wait, often without any resources, for a response to her request.

Authorities said that they treated initial requests the same day and tried to reach a decision within twenty-four to forty-eight hours; but they often took four or five days, and sometimes as long as two weeks.[15]

When the need was extremely urgent, such as when a mother was threatening suicide or child abandonment, her request for assistance was supposedly handled immediately with a small amount of temporary aid.[16] Public welfare, with the goal of discouraging abandonment, forced women to threaten child abandonment in order to obtain the aid they needed.

The bureaucrats realized that most abandoned children had been born out-of-wedlock and therefore gave preference to single mothers. There was a problem in determining whom to aid since some women did not want to admit that they needed to abandon an infant because of their poverty, while others pled poverty and threatened to abandon their babies just to get the aid. Bureaucrats often turned away deserving women, sometimes rudely and insensitively.[17] Securing aid was a difficult process. The central office of Public Assistance, where mothers had to apply for aid, was on the Avenue Victoria near the Hôtel-de-Ville and the hospital l'Hôtel-Dieu. The walk from la Maternité could take an hour, and was particularly terrible during the heat of summer and the rain and cold of winter, especially when still weak from childbirth and also carrying her infant. There, a woman often had to wait several hours, complete the necessary forms, and submit to an interrogation.

In 1881 Ernestine Pallet testified that when she entered the main offices of Public Assistance and told an employee that she needed "some small assistance because I had nothing to give my child to eat, he treated me very badly. He told me to go away and come back in several days; he did not take my name. I left in tears. . . . [Employees] then led me to another office. There I sat from 10 A.M. until 1 P.M., but when I saw that no one would pay attention to me, I left." The director of Public Assistance, Michel Moring, denied such treatment of Pallet, alleging that she probably went neither to the central offices of Public Assistance nor to the Hospice des Enfants Assistés, since she was unclear about where she went. He insisted that Public Assistance never, "in ordinary circumstances" made a person wait eight days, but reached a decision in forty-eight hours. If it was urgent, he said, they gave the aid immediately and made the inquiries later.[18]

Pallet was not alone in complaining that she encountered particularly insensitive bureaucrats. In 1899 a twenty-six-year-old domestic servant applied for aid to prevent abandonment and was kept waiting several days for the formalities and investigation to be completed. In the meantime she had no resources and no place to live. In desperation, holding her baby in her arms, she jumped into the Seine where two bargemen saved them. After later receiving some charity, she suffocated her infant.[19] Sometimes the bureaucrats at Public Assistance simply found a mother morally unworthy of aid. Such may have been the case with

L. Jouannet, who lived near la Maternité. She had three children, including eight-month-old twins. She was refused aid and posted a complaint. Following a police inquiry, she was found to have been living with another woman and two men in an apartment and had been at that address only two months. The police reported that she did not spend time with her children but came and went at her discretion all day long.[20] Denied public assistance, she nevertheless had some help from friends.

On at least one occasion, it took a concerted effort on the part of several people to secure assistance. An abandoned single mother who gave birth at Clinique Tarnier was without any resources when she left the hospital. She went to Public Assistance to apply for aid but several days later was refused all welfare. She returned at different times, with her infant whom she nursed, and each time was refused and sent away. After five weeks she could not pay her rent and was out on the streets, with no shelter or bread. A passerby took her to Jeanne Leroy, a charitable woman, who contacted Marie Béquet de Vienne, who admitted the young mother to a temporary shelter run by her philanthropy. Leroy instructed the young mother about how to go to Public Assistance to obtain immediate assistance, but when the mother tried again she was sent away and told she would have an answer within three days. Finally, forty-nine days after the mother left the hospital, she received Fr 20. Leroy wrote an open letter to the director of Public Assistance, complaining about this treatment of the young mother, at the same time praising the care and solicitude that private philanthropists showed young mothers. The director responded that "our resources are a mere drop of water in an ocean of misery that assails us" and that occasionally there are negligent employees. Besides, he added, the young mother did not have to wait very long for her welfare.[21]

Rather than merely demonstrating actual need, the key to obtaining assistance was to threaten child abandonment.[22] With this manipulation of the system, poor mothers gained some control and could maximize their chances of receiving help; but not all were successful. Pallet was one of more than 20,000 women that year, or two-thirds of the applicants, who were turned away.[23]

Though it usually went unreported, occasionally a mother abused the system. A mother of twins went to the offices of Public Assistance and received monthly assistance for maternal nursing. She later went to the Hospice des Enfants Assistés and threatened to abandon her twins in order to receive payments for a wetnurse. Another mother received the initial wetnurse's payments from the hospital, and then also an additional Fr 56 from Public Assistance to nurse her child herself. Several women reputedly received aid for maternal nursing when they already had abandoned their infants. Finally, an untold number had lovers who took the money as soon as they picked it up at the mayor's office.[24]

In order to improve the efficacy of Public Assistance's program to support newborn babies and supervise their mothers' behavior, starting in 1877 the administration of Public Assistance used an inspection system analogous to the ones for the inspection of babies sent to wetnurses. Authorities argued that since mothers were paid by public welfare to nurse their babies, they required inspection in the same way that wetnurses did. As a result, public assistance officials, rarely physicians, annually visited each child and mother receiving aid. They determined whether the mother was indigent and deserving, and thus whether the aid should be continued. They based their judgment on one visit, and the word of *dames visiteuses,* who inspected the aid recipients once a month. They were also expected to exercise a moralizing influence on the mothers and instruct them in proper infant care and hygiene. At best, they were friendly intruders into working-class women's homes and lives. These dames visiteuses submitted reports to the paid male inspectors, who in turn reported to their superiors.[25] The state invaded women's private lives with agents, inspectors, and dames visiteuses, all of whom frequently talked about surveilling and controlling women's behavior.

The inspectors themselves were responsible to the director of Public Assistance and to the general council of the department of the Seine (*conseil général de la Seine*), whose main concern was the budget. Inspectors had insufficient sums of money to allocate and had to choose between giving more women less money or fewer women more money. They decided whose aid would be stopped but not to whom aid was initially awarded. Dames visiteuses had to serve two masters: the inspectors and the general council of the department of the Seine. Many may have been more sympathetic to the mothers than the inspectors liked. Inspectors often complained that the dames visiteuses did not notify them when the mother was cohabiting and did not always suggest termination of aid when appropriate, that they acted like charity women rather than state employees, and that they were too sympathetic to the mothers who worried about how they were going to survive when their aid was stopped.

Marriage and Morality

The welfare programs of the late nineteenth century rested upon changed concepts of morality and poverty in which a single mother, no matter how many out-of-wedlock children she bore, could receive assistance in the interests of her children. Public Assistance inspectors did not castigate mothers who had several illegitimate children; rather, they asked for more than the maximum aid of Fr 30 per month for mothers of several children who had tried to take good care of them.[26] The key was no longer the matrimonial status of the mother, but her morality in caring for her children in a hygienic environment.

Morality of the mothers was secondary to the welfare of the children. As a result of this focus, officials did not always refuse a woman aid if she was found with a man in her apartment, or even if they viewed her morality questionable. Even women living in a consensual union sometimes received aid because "it is really the infant who is the victim."[27] Inspectors saw their role, and that of the dames visiteuses, as trying

> to lead the women to a more regular conduct by advice or even sometimes by threats. But one must not forget that it is the child, and not the mother, whom we aid and that the morality of the mother must only be a small part in the motives for giving aid. Her exact use of the money is difficult to ascertain. One does not doubt that often the money profits those other than the infant, but it is only through surveillance by surprise visits that one can put the mothers who fear surprises on their guard. If they use the money for anything other than the aid of their children, aid should be terminated. Dames visiteuses should visit the mother the day after the delivery of the money to determine misuse.[28]

Some inspectors still sought to eliminate the aid if the mother was obviously cohabiting or entertaining several men by purchasing liquor with her monthly payments. One, echoing the sentiments of reformers of the early part of the century, called the aid a "subsidy of debauchery." He added that "it is not rare, especially in the first days of the month, at the time that the woman gets her welfare, to find men in her apartment, often eating and drinking."[29] Most inspectors, however, did not eliminate the aid even when they found men drinking and eating with the mother in her room, if they judged the mother needy and the child benefiting from the assistance.[30] They did not preach that women should marry but sometimes encouraged them to do so. Inspectors had some power to interpret the rules and decide on the continuation or termination of aid. Despite their varying understandings of these women, they shared an outlook that the women should be assisted unless they deprived their infants of aid.

The mothers did not necessarily behave as officials would have liked, even though the dames visiteuses claimed that "mothers are generally docile and observe the instructions they are given."[31] Dames visiteuses came once a month at a prearranged time to ensure that the mothers would be home. Since the mothers knew in advance of the visits, it was a simple matter for them to hide traces of a lover or cohabitant and appear to be doing what the dames visiteuses had asked them to do. Women also knew of impending visits by inspectors and could scurry to get a cohabitant out of their rooms (and to hide the wine) if they suspected that one of the "stricter" inspectors was visiting their area.[32] True surprise visits were rare because the inspectors and dames visiteuses did not want to make a visit if there was some danger of the mother and baby not being there.

Living Arrangements

In nineteenth-century Paris many poor mothers did not marry. Living with a man did not necessarily imply a casual relationship. The relationship may have been a long-term consensual union of two people who saw no need to legalize the arrangement or could not afford to do so. Furthermore, some of Public Assistance's policies may have provided a further incentive not to marry.

Late in the century, these policies recognized and accommodated the very type of lifestyle earlier reformers had sought to eliminate. From 1875 to 1892 women had to remain single (or at least claim that they were) as a condition for aid. The purpose of aid to single mothers was less to improve their morality than to alleviate poverty so that their young children would have a better chance to live, but the program contained inherent contradictions. Many inspectors believed that people in consensual relationships ought to legally marry. At the same time, many women feared that if they married they could lose their aid. Inspectors, dames visiteuses, and Public Assistance officials assumed that a husband's income would alleviate poverty and enable an infant's needs to be met without public welfare.[33] As a result there was widespread, and somewhat justified, reluctance among mothers to marry.[34] The name of the program had been changed from "aid to unwed mothers" to "aid for maternal feeding" in part to remove this fear.

Most inspectors criticized the practice of routinely terminating welfare to married women; they believed that the department should subsidize needy couples who married, if for no other reason than to exercise some control over their child care practices. One inspector during the late 1880s, Antonin Mulé, argued in favor of continuing aid to married mothers in order to maintain some supervision of their lives. He reminded the administrators of Public Assistance that they could best achieve the social order that so concerned them by means of the inspection and "contrôle" that accompanied aid. He added, on a more sympathetic note, that continued aid would benefit all mothers because life was especially difficult for them, whether married or not, and for their infants during the first few months after childbirth.[35] Another outspoken inspector concurred: "It is necessary that all those in *ménages irréguliers* know that the administration [of Public Assistance] does not consider the marriage of unwed mothers as necessarily and incontestably leading to the cessation of aid. The women should not conclude that they should not legitimize the infant."[36]

The dames visiteuses saw their role as determining whether or not any given marriage would reduce the needs of mother and child. They supported the view that indigence, rather than marital status, should be the major criterion for aid. As one dame visiteuse reported:[37]

> Sometimes the unwed mothers . . . postpone marriage until after expiration of their welfare because they fear that marriage would lead to a termination of aid. I have encouraged them to marry as soon as possible, affirming that the Administration [of Public Assistance] never makes marriage a cause for the suppression of aid. If the husband is a good worker and by his work earns a living, then it is only natural that he contribute to the needs of his family and aid terminate; but in many cases, there are two destitute people who marry, and I have proposed maintaining the welfare at least during the first months of marriage.

The process for determining whether a woman lost her aid if she married began with the dames visiteuses, who reported the mothers' needs to the inspectors. These officials then made the final decision. Inspectors and dames visiteuses made it clear that if a woman did lose aid, it was because her husband worked and earned an income judged sufficient to provide for the child, without help from Public Assistance.

After 1892, Public Assistance made no distinction in the marital status of recipients of "aid for maternal feeding" except that married women (regardless of the number of their children) might have to go to their local bureau de bienfaisance for aid. From 1892 through 1895, apparently believing that their husbands' presence would not deprive their children of relief, many mothers openly acknowledged the fathers of their children. For many women, being a single parent was without stigma, especially since it enabled them to get the much needed welfare money. They apparently knew how the system worked, and that knowledge gave them power to maximize their aid. With seeming cruelty, however, in the years after 1892, unlike previous years, almost one-fourth of the terminations of aid from Public Assistance were because the "father returned."[38] Termination of aid to these married women indicates that either the income from the father disqualified the women and children, or that in the interest of fiscal responsibility, Public Assistance told them to seek continuation of their assistance from their local welfare bureau.

Any glimpse of the women's lives comes through the eyes of dames visiteuses and inspectors. Because women would hide their husbands or cohabitants, the marital and household status of welfare recipients is difficult to determine accurately. One inspector stated in his annual report, "I have brought to your attention a goodly number of single mothers indicated [by the dames visiteuses] as living alone and having made a declaration to that extent. In fact, they live in a consensual union and aid should cease because of the daily wages of the father of the infant or of her lover."[39] From 1888 to 1891, between 65 and 90 percent of recipients of Public Assistance's programs of aid to mothers and children (including both women who kept their babies and those who sent them to wetnurses) were single mothers. Roughly one-fifth of the single mothers lived with their families, and the rest lived alone with their baby. Among just those mothers receiving periodic aid for maternal nursing (in 1890) only 2 percent were married, while 6 percent were single and living in consensual unions. The overwhelming majority—92 percent—were single mothers claiming to live without a partner.[40]

After 1892 slightly more of the mothers receiving monthly aid for maternal nursing were married. Still, married women living with their husbands, and women in consensual unions, did not commonly receive Public Assistance for maternal feeding. Between 2 and 7 percent of those receiving aid were in consensual unions, and about the same numbers received aid while living with their husbands. Fewer than 10 percent were married women abandoned by their husbands or whose husbands were permanently incapacitated and could not work. At least 70 percent of women receiving aid were single mothers, and half of them were living with their families.[41]

News of the inspectors' visits spread through the districts and buildings in which the mothers lived, suggesting that a women's street culture and information network existed. Women living alone may have belonged to a network of kin and friends providing help to one another with food and child care, forming a supportive family or neighborhood community.[42] They may have met each other regularly at the well-baby clinics or milk dispensaries. Through a domestic web of information, people would learn when a mother received her welfare money and could get paid back for money and services lent during leaner times. The network also could warn mothers of inspectors' arrivals or spread the news that a certain mother had lost her welfare because she lived with a man. Such news might have inspired a fear in some single mothers that the same might happen to them, encouraging them to forego marriage or overt cohabitation. Furthermore, inspectors contacted concierges for information about aid recipients. Concierges played an important role in female networks and the exercise of power among working-class women. Inspectors, reluctant to climb six flights of stairs to the mothers' rooms, would ask the concierge for information. A kindly concierge could help ensure a mother's continued aid; a hostile one might cause it to be terminated.[43]

By the end of the century, the desire to save infant lives by preventing abandonment and encouraging maternal nursing was so strong that public authorities accepted the single status of many poor mothers.[44] They modified the bourgeois family ideal to meet the practices of the working classes. New questions were thus introduced toward the end of the century to determine a woman's morality: Was her general conduct morally trustworthy? Did she have one or several lovers? Did she neglect or abuse her infant? What were her personal hygiene and domestic cleanliness standards and her work habits? Most important, did she breastfeed her baby?

Work and Welfare

Mothers had to work for wages both as an economic necessity (since Fr 20 per month in welfare was inadequate to cover costs) and as a condition of receiving aid. Administrators expected that single mothers who received aid would earn between Fr 1 and Fr 2 a day, if possible by sewing or doing other piecework in their rooms so they could remain at home and breastfeed their babies.

About one-third of the mothers requesting welfare noted their occupation as domestic servant. This is somewhat misleading, since that was undoubtedly the occupation of the women *before* childbirth, not after, as domestic servants were predominantly single and childless. After childbirth, in order to retain employment as a domestic servant, a mother typically had to send her baby to a wetnurse, give the infant to a parent, or abandon the child. Those who kept and nursed their babies were deprived of their customary employment and so took whatever menial work they could find. Many probably became daily maids (femmes de ménage).

Other frequently listed occupations of women receiving welfare were day laborer, seamstress, and laundress. It is likely that needle and garment trade workers and laundresses could continue their work after childbirth, but most needle workers probably left the workshops to do piecework in their rooms. Other occupations, for example machine operators and metal polishers (such as Ernestine Pallet), were incompatible with full-time maternal nursing, and the women in these jobs probably took lesser jobs that allowed them to work and nurse, or they sent their babies out to a wetnurse or found other means of child care.[45]

After childbirth, mothers who worked in a semiskilled trade at home could earn more than Fr 2 or Fr 3 per day when they worked. On days when there was sufficient work to be had they worked about fifteen hours per day in order to live and to feed their children. They labored during the night and at other times when their infants slept. Still, during the slow season they often did not have enough work to earn a sufficient wage, no matter how many hours they were willing to spend at their tasks. These women usually somehow managed to nurse their infants, and the inspectors generally believed that their babies were cared for adequately.[46] Most mothers, however, found it necessary to work outside the home. Their salaries averaged about Fr 1.25 a day, with a range from Fr .90 to Fr 2 a day, according to their trade, not counting seasonal unemployment; but there was great variation in the nature of their work and in their wages.[47]

Some mothers were essentially unemployed. When they did find work, they earned between Fr .25 and Fr .30 a day as daily maids or by doing menial piecework in their rooms. Many made carton boxes, strung beads, punched holes in leather or "pearls" (at Fr .05 for 6,000 holes), or made nails at the rate of Fr .05 for two gross. In order to earn the Fr .20 to Fr .25 a day, they had to work while their babies slept, until midnight or one o'clock in the morning. Even the inspectors noted that women's seasonal unemployment, lack of sufficient work to be done even during periods of employment, and especially the employers' refusal of finished work led to discouragement and a sense of hopelessness. At least one inspector concluded that the customary aid was insufficient and ought to be increased to Fr 30 per month and continued for three years.[48] Yet even he did not understand how difficult it was to find time to do piece work, tend a baby, and sleep. Many mothers could not find any work at all. They tried to care for their babies but were too sick or too poor, and too malnourished to nurse them.[49]

With both regular work and the aid from Public Assistance the single mother still had an annual income of only about Fr 600 to Fr 675 while her cost of living ranged from Fr 850 to Fr 1200 a year. Making ends meet without family support or a cohabitant was thus a virtual impossibility, and where and how they lived were constant negotiations with poverty.

Housing and Hygiene

Mothers on welfare lived in the poorest working-class arrondissements of Paris. Of the women receiving assistance to keep their babies,

14 percent lived in the twentieth arrondissement, closely followed by the eleventh, thirteenth, eighteenth, and nineteenth arrondissements, with from 10 to 12 percent in each. These were the arrondissements with the most severe overcrowding, and the lowest rents. In the thirteenth and twentieth arrondissements, 75 percent of the apartments rented for less than Fr 300 a year, but these areas experienced significant rent increases during the 1880s. Most workers, and these included working men, could not afford rents in excess of Fr 300 to Fr 350 per year.[50] These minimal rents exceeded the annual income of many of the poorest mothers, unless they had welfare or shared their room and apartments with others. The thirteenth, nineteenth, and twentieth arrondissements contributed proportionately the most mothers receiving aid when compared with the female population of these arrondissements.[51]

A single mother faced a complicated situation because landlords frequently refused to rent an unfurnished place to a single woman, even if she had the necessary bed and chest of drawers to indicate a modest level of respectability. If, however, the same woman came back with a man and implied that they were going to live together, the landlord would rent it to them. Landlords elected to rent to couples, preferably those without children, since a couple (even unmarried) signified respectability, and perhaps ability to pay the rent; a single woman implied prostitution.[52] Yet, until 1892 those who received aid had to live without a man sharing their room as a condition of receiving aid—at least when the inspectors made their predictable annual visits.

The eligibility requirements for recipients of periodic aid for maternal nursing also influenced the women's housing choices. Women living in furnished rooms (*garni*) were likely to be refused aid because officials believed that such residences indicated immorality. In 1899, half of the refusals of aid were based on the fact that the women were "logeant en garni."[53] Occupants of furnished rooms were generally recent migrants, those too poor to afford even the minimal furniture, and people of questionable virtue, especially prostitutes.[54] Although inspectors were willing to ignore some evidence of a mother's so-called "immorality," such as the presence of a male drinking partner, they did not condone evident, or even suspected, prostitution.

Women generally found housing in old, dirty buildings, frequently on the sixth floor or in the mansard attic. The top floors of the city, the *sixièmes* where small rooms were rented by workers or inhabited by servants, were notoriously unhealthy, uncomfortable, and sexually dangerous, yet they provided housing and community for residents who sometimes sewed for each other and cared for each other when ill. A repairman reported that an entire street of Montparnasse had a single top floor that functioned as a street suspended in midair, because residents had removed the stones of the joint walls between the buildings.[55] Women and their babies often lived in one narrow room, "sometimes even in a small room isolated in a rear corner of a building that is even more dilapidated and dirty on the inside than outside. Dark, without sunlight or air, the small room frequently served as the only lodging for a family of several persons."[56] Whether in one or two rooms, furnished or not, their housing was in the words of several inspectors, "deplorable," "unhealthy," and very damp; it often had blackened walls, was too small for the number of persons living there, was unlit except by one small window or skylight, had garbage and debris all about, and was invariably either too cold or too hot. Latrines were frequently in a corner under the stairs, shared by more than a dozen people, and the buildings reeked of feces and urine. Such housing cost Fr 100 to Fr 150 a year. Sometimes the stench and filth was so unbearable that the dames visiteuses and inspectors insisted the mothers meet them in the concierge's lodgings; and sometimes they requested more money for the woman so she could afford to move.[57]

In such surroundings, an infant usually did not sleep in a crib but shared the mother's bed or slept on the floor. Public Assistance gave cribs to welfare recipients who nursed their infants, but a mother had to ask for one, and then pick it up at the offices on Avenue Victoria in the center of the city and lug it back to her room on the outskirts. Many mothers did not make this effort and even if they did, Public Assistance did not provide the mattresses and bedding. In any case, there usually was no space in the small rooms. Some mothers who picked up their cribs, lacking the bedding and space, were so needy that they sold the cribs. Inspectors argued that if women received a crib, mattress, and linens with their first welfare payment, or if the dames visiteuses would deliver these at their first visit, fewer babies would sleep with their mothers, and by implication, fewer infants would die from asphyxiation.[58]

Inspectors often criticized women for not keeping their rooms clean. Midafternoon inspections revealed that beds were not made, remnants of vegetables were crammed into cracks in the wood floor, clumps of dust abounded, linens and clothing of doubtful cleanliness were scattered about, and windows remained closed. Many of the inspectors complained that the women had time to clean while the infant slept and implored the dames visiteuses to be more diligent in teaching single mothers cleanliness and hygiene.[59] Inspectors and Public Assistance administrators agreed that cleanliness helped to prevent disease and death. Proper hygiene was part of middle-class culture, but it was not generally an aspect of poor women's lives, because in their struggle for survival they had no time to clean in addition to working and caring for their babies.

Care and Feeding of the Infants

Public Assistance's emphasis on preventing infant mortality to combat depopulation stressed breastfeeding. Officials believed that breastfed infants had a far greater chance of surviving their first year than did those who were bottle-fed. Furthermore, breastfeeding was a sign of maternal love, and authorities wanted to foster such sentiments in the hope of discouraging infant abandonment, which often led to infant death. Dames visiteuses were to support and encourage maternal breastfeeding.

Even without such pressure, mothers usually breastfed their babies if they could; this may have been both a product of love and a function of economics. Nursing mothers received Fr 5 more aid per month than did nonnursing mothers, despite the equal need of both. Nonnursing mothers had to buy milk and bottles, but nursing mothers had greater physical demands for food and sleep to produce enough milk for a healthy baby. One inspector, expressing sentiments shared by many late nineteenth-century reformers, argued that maternal nursing was a national duty. He intoned that "military service for all able-bodied men was compulsory. Therefore, maternal nursing should be obligatory for all robust and healthy mothers. This would be a way for her to give her blood to the nation."[60] Mothers on welfare, however, were far from healthy and robust; they often lacked proper nourishment for breastfeeding and their milk reputedly was poor in quantity and quality. Nevertheless, between two-thirds and three-fourths nursed their newborns.[61]

In the 1890s, most inspectors believed that nonnursing mothers were unfairly penalized. Mothers bottle-fed their babies, they said, because they lost their milk either out of sickness or malnourishment, or because they had to work outside the home. Mothers who worked outside the home usually nursed their infants in the morning and at night, and the child-care provider gave the infant a bottle during the day. Those who mixed breastfeeding with bottle-feeding showed the same solicitude for their children as did nursing mothers.[62] Infants who were bottle-fed suffered ill effects from poor quality cow's milk and the unhygienic baby bottles with long rubber tubes that inspectors and doctors discouraged. A working mother left the bottle of milk near the baby, who drank until it was empty and then continued to suck on the tube. Owing to the constant surveillance and advice of the dames visiteuses and inspectors, by the end of the 1890s the "bottle with the long tube" virtually disappeared from use.[63]

Clean and high quality milk was expensive and mothers on welfare could not afford it for their babies. Because many mothers nonetheless needed to feed their babies from a bottle, Public Assistance developed dispensaries for sterilized milk similar to the *gouttes de lait*. In June 1895 the first distribution center for sterilized milk for infants of mothers on welfare opened in the eleventh arrondissement, and there were at least six in Paris by 1900. The distribution of free sterilized milk became so important that the Commission on Enfants Assistés voted in 1909 to begin home distribution of free sterilized milk to all welfare mothers who lived far from the dispensaries.

A woman would come to a dispensary with her baby and "contrôlle" card every few days, but it cost her half a day of wages to do so. As in the other milk depots, doctors and nurses who staffed the dispensaries measured and weighed the baby each time to assure that it was gaining weight, and they regulated how much milk the mother would get. They also insisted that she use the new glass bottles with rubber nipples. To get this free sterilized milk, mothers had to submit to rules and regulations established by the attending physicians and their approved medical personnel.[64]

Infant feeding was just one area in which the dames visiteuses and other officials tried to educate the women. Keeping the baby clean was almost as important. Mothers on welfare listened to the suggestions on hygiene and cleanliness that the dames visiteuses and inspectors offered, but many clung to their mothers' advice on how to raise a baby. Inspectors often complained that the babies were tightly swaddled and had dirty heads and hair, a crusty rash on the scalp, and very long fingernails.[65] Yet what the inspectors viewed as a lack of hygiene was really the persistence of rural culture and folklore.[66] Mothers of these children were not negligent, just ignorant; they believed that to wash a baby's head or cut her nails would lead to idiocy. In addition, poverty and exhaustion from work made cleanliness difficult. It was hard to wash a baby in cold rooms when there was no running water; unless the dames visiteuses supplied the oil to clean the baby's scalp the mother did not spend the time or money to get the oil. One can only wonder how mothers washed the diapers and baby clothes, unless they had money to take them to a laundry. Most mothers did not have the money for a layette or numerous diapers: unless a woman delivered her baby in one of the public hospitals or with a welfare midwife, and received a free layette, her baby went without diapers, blankets, shirts, and shawls.

Despite the best of intentions babies became sick, and getting a doctor was no easy matter. The mother had to recognize when the baby needed a doctor, and she had to care enough about the baby to seek medical help. Mothers did not always know when to see a doctor, and a mistrust of doctors, so common in earlier decades, lingered on. If a mother decided that a doctor was necessary, she had to leave work and walk to either the bureau de bienfaisance or the mayor's office in her arrondissement to request the doctor on the Public Assistance staff. Sometimes she brought her sick child with her, regardless of the weather. Other times she went without her baby, and if the doctor demanded, she had to go home to get the baby and bring it to him. Some mothers could not make this effort, and some of the inspectors sought to change the system so that doctors visited automatically. Inspectors complained that many doctors employed by Public Assistance did not make house calls, and that those who did arrived after several days. Moreover, doctors frequently failed to furnish the free medicines available to these welfare recipients.[67] Inspectors typically castigated not the mother but the doctor and the system for inadequate infant medical care. Both attending to hygiene and cleanliness as demanded by the inspector and taking the baby to a doctor required losing time from work.

Whether mothers worked in their rooms or outside the home, they resorted to a variety of strategies to provide child care. Single mothers had limited help from friends and relatives. The lucky few lived with their mothers or sisters, who shared the care of their infants.[68] In Emile Zola's novel, *Fécondité,* Norine Moinaud and her child received public assistance and lived with her sister. They both folded boxes at home while caring for each other and Norine's baby.[69] Norine's situation parallels that of actual mothers on welfare. Of these women who did not live with their families, some could leave their babies with an aunt or with their own mother while they worked; sometimes an older child watched the younger ones; every so often a mother could place her infant with a neighbor typically who charged between 0.75 and 1.25 francs a day. Thus, child care absorbed most of the mother's salary and left her in continual financial uncertainty with little more than the 20 francs a month from Public Assistance on which to live.

Only 2 percent of mothers receiving welfare placed their babies in crèches. Crèches for illegitimate infants were insufficient and inadequate.[70] They were usually open from 7 a.m. to 7 p.m., but the mothers worked longer or different hours. Few crèches were located in the working-class districts where the poor single mothers lived. Since crèches charged Fr .20 a day while a caretaker cost four times as much, mothers were not deterred from using the crèches on grounds of relative cost. Many mothers did not use them because they did not know of the existence of inexpensive municipal crèches or, if they knew about them, the women thought the infants were poorly supervised, badly cared for, mistreated, given infusions of poppies or other narcotics, were in danger of epidemics, or received insufficient and spoiled milk. Some mothers may not have placed their babies in a crèche because it " 'would be to take the bread out of the old peoples' mouths.' "[71]

Frequently, a mother was too exhausted to dress a baby and take it some distance to a crèche. She may also not have had enough money to purchase sufficient clothing for the child to take it outside. It was easiest, and cheapest, to leave a baby alone in a room all day with a pacifier consisting of a rag soaked in a mixture of wine, water, and flour. Some may also have had a general fear of institutions; as late as 1898 the dames visiteuses reported that mothers have a "veritable antipathy" to the crèches.[72]

In a continual effort to urge and enable women to breastfeed their infants as the best means to avoid infant gastrointestinal disorders and weanling diarrhea, some public officials advocated that factories and workshops provide crèches for infants of employees receiving public assistance. Mothers could then conveniently nurse their infants during the day.[73]

Administrators of Public Assistance in the latter decades of the century had come to believe that the nurturing conditions promoting infant survival would more likely be met when mothers nursed their own infants instead of abandoning the babies outright or sending them directly to wetnurses. Accordingly, Public Assistance designed its programs to protect the children's lives by enabling thousands of poor mothers to keep and nurse their babies themselves.

Evaluation of the Programs

Administrators of Public Assistance believed that some mothers, even with welfare, were unable to provide for their children's well-being. From the outset, poverty was both a reason to grant aid and a reason to deny it. Public Assistance officials screened all applicants for aid and denied it to mothers whom they thought were not needy, as well as to those they thought were too poor to care for their babies adequately, even with assistance. They also denied relief to mothers suspected of debauchery and prostitution or whom they thought might flagrantly mistreat or neglect their babies, encouraging those women to place their babies with Enfants Assistés.[74] In cases where welfare was denied, Public Assistance officials did not force mothers to give up their children; rather the officials decided to give up on those mothers and children. Thousands annually may have slipped through this safety net, Ernestine Pallet and her baby among them.

Fewer than 5 percent of the mothers lost aid because of mistreatment of their children or because of suspected prostitution.[75] Child abuse may have occurred but was rarely an issue, unless the child was left in filth and unfed while the mother squandered her monthly welfare payments on drinks with many men. The child-saving movement of late nineteenth-century France was committed to keeping babies with their mothers, under surveillance by inspectors and dames visiteuses. Aid to unwed mothers cost the public treasuries less than raising an abandoned child and it increased infants' chances of survival.

Inspectors rarely accused unwed mothers of a lack of maternal love for their children, although the mothers may not have actively demonstrated affection. Single mothers' lives were distorted by destitution. One inspector commented that much maternal affection existed, but sometimes it was *"dénaturée"* owing to *"misère."* He added that "misère paralyzes maternal sentiments."[76] Other inspectors, in their descriptions of health, hygiene, and infant feeding gave evidence of what we would consider maternal love.

When dames visiteuses and inspectors decided to terminate the welfare to the mothers and children they most frequently cited as the reasons for the suppression of aid that the baby was too old (42 percent of the cases) or the mother was no longer needy (18 percent of the cases). In the latter cases it was either because the mother had found sufficiently remunerative work or the father of the child had begun to contribute to the family income. In 7 percent of the cases the mother lost welfare because she had placed the child with a wetnurse; another 7 percent of the women were removed from the welfare roles when they left Paris or moved with no forwarding address. In just 3 percent of the cases did mothers abandon the infant. Another 3 percent lost their welfare because of "bad conduct" or the "bad care" that they gave their child. In 19 percent of the cases, when aid had been stopped it was because the child had died.[77]

A comparison of the mortality rates for those babies who received aid from Public Assistance with the departmental and national infant mortality rates suggests that Public Assistance's programs had some success. Mortality rates for the babies whose mothers received aid for maternal feeding fluctuated from 14 to 20 percent during the 1880s and 1890s, depending on epidemics and other factors.[78] Mortality rates for all infants in Paris declined from 16 percent in the period 1881–1885 to 10 percent in the period 1906–1910.[79] Infant mortality among those receiving welfare was equal to or greater than infant mortality in Paris as a whole, but never greater than among abandoned babies or those sent to a wetnurse. Furthermore, the figures on infant mortality in Paris include babies of more affluent families and not just the poor. During the same twenty-year period, the infant mortality rate of babies abandoned in Paris was around 30 percent—much higher than the national average, and higher than among those whose mothers received aid for maternal nursing. These figures support the premise that abandoned babies had a greater likelihood of death than those kept by the mother. The program to some extent prevented infant mortality because it prevented abandonment; only 3 percent of the women who received welfare abandoned their babies. Yet drawing conclusions from the abandonment figures is difficult since they were influenced by many variables, including restrictive legislation. If it is assumed that these poor mothers without aid would have abandoned their children as they claimed, then the aid was effective since they did not do so in large numbers, either directly or by first sending them to a wetnurse. After the period of aid expired, however, there was little to stop them from abandoning their babies—except the maternal ties that may have developed. If maternal ties prevented abandonment, then welfare realized one of its major goals.

The destitute women and children of France needed help in order to survive, and an enormous proportion of all mothers depended on public assistance. In 1878 one out of every three women giving birth in the city of Paris did so with the aid of public assistance.[80] By the end of the century that proportion had increased to one out of two. In the last years of the century, the number of mothers requesting public assistance after childbirth, either for a wetnurse or to breastfeed their baby themselves, increased from 20,000 in 1886 to over 50,000 in 1899, an increase from one-fourth to two-thirds of all births in the department of the Seine. Some of the mothers, however, may have made multiple requests, thereby inflating the relationship to all births. The proportion of single mothers who received some form of public assistance more than doubled, from one out of three in the early 1880s to three out of four in 1900, and as many as 15 percent annually of all mothers (married and single) in the department of the Seine received public welfare in the period between the mid 1880s and 1900. The data speak eloquently of the overwhelming poverty of new parents in the city, and of the relative success of the welfare system in attempting to address some of the needs of single mothers.[81] These figures indicate clearly that women knew about the welfare programs. Needy women sought out and used welfare, even though the assistance was meager and they would have to sacrifice some independence. Nevertheless, they made a choice to seek the assistance.

Public Assistance's welfare programs to aid maternal nursing accepted the very behavior that earlier philanthropists and reformers had tried to discourage. The leading bourgeois officials redefined the social concerns, which earlier had focused on the depravity of the working classes, to ones they could work toward solving—infant mortality and depopulation. Rather than defining single motherhood as a moral problem, officials of Public Assistance transformed the problems surrounding poor single mothers and their babies into social and national concerns. Questions of hygiene replaced questions of morality, and this concern with hygiene coincided with the broader rhetoric of depopulation. Immorality was not easily amenable to government policies; reducing infant mortality was. Public Assistance officials joined step with other social reform agendas of the time: agendas concerned about infant hygiene, pediatric care, and proper infant feeding, about educating mothers in healthful child-care practices, and about reducing the frequency of infant abandonment. A "scientific" understanding of childrearing and of motherhood, along with the availability of safe, sterilized, and inexpensive milk, prompted officials to teach, moralize, and perhaps control the recipients in order to save infants' lives.

This shift away from a policy directed at the single mother's morality and toward subsidies for her child suggests a possible underlying change in the concept of motherhood. The entire construction of motherhood seems to have moved away from a cultural, nurturing, Rousseauean one toward a more instrumental one in which the mother produced babies. After producing the child, the mother served as a vehicle through which the government provided aid to the infant to reduce the child's likelihood of death. It is not a clear-cut substitution of one for the other, however; while producing babies for the nation, mothers were expected to follow Rousseau's child-nurturing model. Saving the children through family preservation (even in a single-parent family) was a way of maintaining the ideology of female domesticity and the notion of women in a domestic role. Though the women's domestic role was extolled and encouraged, they also had to work. The inspectors preferred that a mother work for wages at home; but this was seldom possible, and aid was invariably insufficient to allow a woman to perform a purely domestic role. Moreover, the legal position of the single mother remained unchanged: she had sole responsibility for her child. Public Assistance assumed child support in the absence of the father and became a surrogate patriarch in the single mother's household.

CHAPTER

8

Birth Control and Abortion

Some poor and pregnant women never appeared in public maternity hospitals, at any of the public shelters, or among the mothers receiving welfare. They nevertheless appeared in the criminal court records because they opted for abortion. Birth control, including abortion, was an attempt on the part of these women to exert some control over their own lives and maintain whatever modicum of independence they had. They could thereby avoid both the destitution engendered by childbirth and the intervention in their lives imposed by public assistance or private charity. Many women had the network of contacts to secure an abortion but not the protective network to avoid suspicion or discovery. Although abortion was a criminal offense throughout the nineteenth century, many women risked death, arrest, and imprisonment by taking this desperate measure. What circumstances led women to seek abortions and how did they go about securing one?

In one court case, charges were brought against twenty-eight-year-old Marie Madeleine Ditte. Ditte worked as a cook, and in March 1873, when she first feared she might be pregnant, she asked the concierge what to do to get back her menstrual periods. She was dismissed soon thereafter for "bad conduct." She moved to a garni and immediately found another job in a tapestry workshop. In June she confided to a woman who came from her hometown that she had not had her periods for three months. Marie Ditte then sought help from a fresh produce peddler who told her that she needed to drink a beverage including extracts of the plants rue or savin. When she asked her pharmacist for these herbs, or for something to bring on her periods, he replied that he did not know the right ingredients. Finally, Marie Ditte asked a woman whom she met on the stairs of her building to recommend a midwife. At the end of June, Ditte went to this unlicensed midwife who injected something into her uterus that led to severe stomach pains and the restoration of her menstrual periods. Her boyfriend later testified that he had never had sexual intercourse with her and that he had promised to marry her. The reasons for her seeking an abortion are obscure. Ditte, her boyfriend, and the midwife were all acquitted.[1]

In the court case involving Euphrasie Aimée Blazy the woman's motives for seeking an abortion are easier to discern. A twenty-three-year-old seamstress, she was dependent upon her lover, a thirty-one-year-old clock maker, with whom she had already had one son when she was nineteen. She placed this child with a wetnurse, whom her lover paid. When she became pregnant a second time, he threatened to abandon her and the infant she was carrying. He complained that "we already have one boy . . . it is not necessary for us to have two. . . . I will return to Paris in a week; if you have not found someone who will relieve you of this, I will arrange for it myself. I know a pharmacist who will get me the remedies." Euphrasie Blazy went to the same midwife who delivered her first child, but she refused to perform the abortion, even for the Fr 200 offered her. Blazy then went to a fortune-teller who sent her to a midwife who aborted her fetus. Blazy later denied that her lover had forced her to have the abortion, and when confronted with her conflicting testimony responded, "What do you want me to do? If he goes to prison, who is going to support me? I can not go back home because everyone will scorn me." Blazy was acquitted, her lover received two years in prison, and the midwife had to spend six years in prison doing hard labor.[2]

Constance Fauquet had her first baby in June 1883 when she was twenty years old. The baby, whom she placed with a wetnurse so she could work, died one month later. In November 1885 she had her second baby delivered by a welfare midwife to whom the public hospital had sent her. That baby went to a wetnurse recommended by her neighbors. Fauquet paid Fr 25 a month regularly to the wetnurse, possibly with some initial help from Public Assistance. Neighbors testified that Fauquet loved her daughter, and that only her long workday made it impossible for her to care for the child herself. In 1886, having never married, she thought she was pregnant again and cried when informing her new lover of the pregnancy. He, a twenty-five-year-old messenger who she recently met in a restaurant, soon left Paris to return to his home in Montpellier to marry someone else. Although he acknowledged having sexual relations with Fauquet, he said that he would do nothing to help her. He testified that "I did not take any precautions . . . and did what I could for her [by giving her some money], but as for marrying her, that is another matter and she should act as if I no longer existed on this earth." Under interrogation, Fauquet argued that based on her wages of Fr 3.25 a day as a button maker, from which she also had to pay the wetnurse, she had no resources, and "overcome with the burden which would result from the pregnancy . . . resolved to abort."

The first midwife that Fauquet visited refused to perform the abortion and told her that "Public Assistance would come to her aid in raising her child if she was indigent." Desperately seeking an abortion, Fauquet then found a laundry worker who was willing to perform the task for Fr 15. She clearly stated her reason for the abortion: "I said to myself that if the infant came at term, I would be forced [because of extreme poverty] to abandon it to Enfants Assistés; I believed that it would be unhappy and that I would have remorse all my life; I thought that in having an abortion I would risk hurting no one but myself, and furthermore, the pregnancy was so little advanced that one could extract it when it is not yet truly a child." She was acquitted and the abortionist received a prison sentence of one year.[3]

Given that abortion was dangerous and illegal, these three women, and others like them who sought abortions, faced a grim choice between bearing a child and thereby becoming poorer than ever or getting an abortion and thereby perhaps going to jail, or even dying as a result of an unsafe abortion. There were no reliable methods of contraception.[4]

Contraception

Safe and effective contraception was unavailable to poor women until the twentieth century. The three women whose stories briefly appear above all entered into sexual relationships knowing that pregnancy might result. Others, however, may not have had a choice. Germinie Lacerteux was raped when she first came to Paris. Some were victims of incest. For example, August Fuye raped and then had continued sexual relations with his teenage legitimate daughter, Louise. His wife, Caroline, turned a blind eye to his actions but took Louise to an abortionist when the young girl become pregnant.[5]

Male politicians manipulated the birth control and abortion issue, and it became inextricably intertwined with the diverse issues of morality, social reform, national strength, economic growth, and protection of the two-parent nuclear family.[6] Thus, the French government kept abortion illegal and hindered the dissemination of birth control information. Opposition to contraception came from all bands of the political and social spectrum. Men of various political and religious persuasions, especially conservative Catholics, linked contraception with "sexual excesses," and equated contraceptive literature and devices with pornography. Even otherwise moderate republicans, such as Ferdinand Buisson and members of the League of the Rights of Man, opposed selling contraceptive devices and pharmaceutical products to young women on the grounds that this would encourage their debauchery.

These worries over public morality, which had always been a factor in public policy directed at women, coexisted with concern for national population strength. When the Commission on Depopulation, first convened in 1902, issued its 1911 report the members urged prohibition of the dissemination of birth control information and literature.[7] French populationists differed from their British counterparts in their approach to contraception among the poor. The British eugenicist movement wanted to discourage the high fertility rates of the working classes while encouraging the fertility of the upper classes. In France, populationists did not want anyone to control fertility, even the workers. Most socialists also opposed contraception. They believed that the state should provide the support facilities and women should welcome each pregnancy. In France, as in England, the birth control debate emerged as part of a discussion about the rights of the state and the state's responsibility to address the plight of poor mothers and their children. The rights of the mothers were not an issue.[8]

Birth control, including abortion, can best be understood in the context of class, occupation, and locality.[9] In nineteenth-century Paris, poor working women, whether single or married, lived in a world where motherhood could present great hardship. Infant and child mortality, the value of female labor, the economic utility of children, charity and welfare options, a woman's level of poverty, and her social and religious values all had a bearing on whether and how a woman would seek to limit her fertility.

Women enjoyed several benefits from limiting fertility. It increased a woman's control over her own sexuality. It would also reduce the health problems associated with repeated pregnancies, childbirth, abortions, and miscarriages, as well as possible prison terms associated with abortions and infanticide. Control over her own childbearing provided a woman with greater hope for her own and her family's economic survival. Her ability to work steadily made it possible for her to contribute to her family economy and provide for those children she already had. This became increasingly important at a time when the economic value of child labor was decreasing as a result of compulsory primary education and child protection labor legislation. Limiting fertility was not, however, easily accomplished. Abstention and coitus interruptus, herbs and folk remedies, backed up with abortion, were almost the only options until barrier contraceptives became more widely available in the twentieth century.

Paul Robin, with the support of anarchists and syndicalists, launched the French birth-control movement in 1878 as an offshoot of the British Malthusian league. He and his colleagues believed that by limiting births, the proletariat could relieve some of their misery. Few others shared his enthusiasm. Robin's birth-control movement came precisely at the height of support for populationist ideas among powerful politicians and doctors. When, almost twenty years later, Robin started the League of Human Regeneration in 1896, doctors and politicians responded with hostility, in part because Robin was associated with anarchists, but also because in France the birth rate was already declining. It had fallen from 33 per thousand around 1800 to 27 per thousand in the decade of the 1840s and by the end of the century was at 22 per thousand.[10]

The most widely used method of contraception was coitus interruptus. European working-class people had practiced it for ages, and even peasants in isolated villages knew of this method of "cheating nature."[11] Voluntary male withdrawal might work for a married couple, or a couple in a stable consensual union, but it was hardly a method practiced by the men who seduced and abandoned domestic servants.

Even after the vulcanization of rubber in 1843–44, people still associated condoms with prostitutes and with protection against venereal disease. Brothel keepers and tobacconists sold them for about 50 centimes, more than twice the price of a loaf of bread, and almost half a day's wages for a poor working woman.[12] Only after the First World War did they become inexpensive and generally available to the working-class population. The use of condoms and coitus interruptus were entirely dependent upon the cooperation of the male. Not all men were willing to try to prevent conception; for instance, Constance Fauquet's lover admitted to not taking precautions.

Women who wanted to avoid pregnancy, knowing they could not rely on men, tried several means of contraception. Some doctors, and perhaps some working-class women, knew of a rhythm method, but they had the timing wrong. They believed that a woman's fertile time surrounded her menstrual periods. Other methods were just as useless. Herbal concoctions and a range of potions containing teas, rue, and sassafras were largely ineffective as oral contraceptives. A cervical sponge, however, especially when soaked with lemon juice, proved more effective. Douching as a contraceptive practice began in Britain and America in the early nineteenth century and made its way quickly to France. Tampons, the vaginal diaphragm, and the cervical cap were not unknown during the nineteenth century in Europe, but they became more available only well after the First World War.[13]

When these methods of birth control proved ineffective, married couples, as well as single women, used abortion to control fertility. In fact, in nineteenth-century France almost half of those accused of having an abortion were married. In France, as in parts of England, it was marital birth control, including abortion, that was responsible for reduced national birth rates.[14] Given the absence of safe and efficacious contraceptive methods for poor women, abortion—although illegal and therefore accessible only through interpersonal information and communication networks—became an important back-up method of birth control.

Abortion

Abortion became a "veritable industry" in nineteenth-century France.[15] Voluntary abortion in France was a criminal offense and the law was harsh, especially toward the doctors and other health professionals who performed them. The laws treated the women who had abortions in a milder manner. Article 317 of the 1810 Napoleonic Penal Code, in effect until after World War I, specified that any woman who self-aborted or had another person perform an abortion on her was guilty of the crime of abortion and liable to imprisonment. Doctors, surgeons, other health officers, and pharmacists who performed abortions were subject to a heavier penalty—longer-term imprisonment, with forced labor.

The law did not penalize unsuccessful attempts at abortion. Because the law was broad and only vaguely defined abortion, failed to distinguish between the stages of the embryo, and did not specifically mention midwives, it was rarely invoked in the first decades after its promulgation. Beginning in 1855, Ambroise Tardieu, in his capacity as professor of forensic medicine at the Faculty of Medicine in Paris, launched a crusade against abortion. He strove to clarify the issues in order to get more arrests and convictions. In 1862, legal experts sought to change the law by arguing that it was inconsistent with Article 2 of the Penal Code which stated that all attempts at a crime, whether the crime had actually been completed or not, were to be considered as criminal. Commentators may have been divided on whether an unsuccessful attempt at abortion was a crime, but judges tended to keep to the letter of Article 317 and not punish attempted, but failed, abortions.[16]

Outlawing abortion undermined women's reproductive rights prohibiting the only effective means of fertility control available to them.[17] The maintenance of this restrictive legislation throughout the nineteenth century was generally motivated by populationist and religious concerns; but the professionalization of doctors and their desire to eliminate rival medical practitioners, such as midwives, also contributed to the campaigns against abortions.[18] Doctors, especially those in forensic medicine, played a central role in deciding if an abortion had taken place and if it was a criminal, spontaneous, or therapeutic abortion.

Therapeutic and Spontaneous Abortions

By the letter of the law, abortions performed by doctors for therapeutic reasons, such as saving a woman's life, constituted criminal acts. In mid-nineteenth century, however, some doctors claimed that "induced abortions" were medically justified when the mother's life was in peril; but they should wait as long as possible to try to assure fetal viability.[19] Doctors who opposed therapeutic abortion, including Ambroise Tardieu, argued that therapeutic abortion would be abused as camouflage for criminal abortion, and its practice would increase and spread. In the midst of much controversy and discussion, in 1852 the Academy of Medicine reinterpreted the law by ruling that abortion was permissible if it was to save a mother's life, but only at the doctor's discretion. Doctors opposed any other form of induced abortion.[20]

Spontaneous abortions, or involuntary miscarriages, were difficult to differentiate from criminal ones, and it was one of the major tasks of forensic doctors to make this differentiation. Most social commentators from 1830 to 1914 agreed that women could spontaneously abort and the terms *avortement* and *fausse couche* have virtually the same medical meaning, with *avortement* most frequently used to denote both spontaneous miscarriage and induced abortion.[21] Both terms refer to the expulsion of the fetus prior to 180 days of gestation. Doctors in the mid-nineteenth century estimated that one pregnancy in every four or five resulted in a spontaneous miscarriage. Toward the end of the nineteenth century doctors thought the rate of spontaneous miscarriage was higher, especially among working-class women.

Dr. Paul Brouardel was professor of legal medicine, dean of the Faculty of Medicine of the University of Paris, and the leading professor and practitioner of forensic medicine at the end the century. According to Brouardel, among working-class women "the number of miscarriages [*fausses couches*] is appreciably greater than that of pregnancies normally brought to term." He concluded that certain women miscarry with an extraordinary facility, despite all precautions taken. He admitted that owing to the number of possible causes of spontaneous miscarriage, it was difficult for a doctor to determine exactly what caused a pregnancy to be interrupted.[22]

Doctors acknowledged that several problems associated with the health of the woman and her pregnancy could cause a spontaneous abortion. According to the social commentator Louis Villermé, since famine among animals leads to spontaneous abortion, extreme malnutrition might also lead a woman to abort. While not denying famine as a cause of abortion, medical men of the time believed that syphilis among women was the foremost cause of spontaneous miscarriage. In addition, they suggested that insufficient nourishment for the mother, fatigue, an "excess of sexual intercourse," a woman's age (either too young or too old), or problems of the egg and placenta could lead to a spontaneous miscarriage.[23] Doctors denied that uterine diseases caused by bacteria or traumas to the uterus, such as falls or blows, could provoke an abortion. By 1900, Paul Brouardel and other doctors were aware that certain infectious diseases in addition to syphilis (such as smallpox, typhoid fever, scarlet fever, measles, cholera, and pneumonia) contracted during pregnancy could lead to a spontaneous miscarriage. They recognized that chronic illness, such as pulmonary tuberculosis, cancer, or heart and kidney disease, could also cause a woman to miscarry, and that uterine growths such as tumors, polyps, and cancers could affect the development of the uterus and cause abortions. The only acknowledged way in which the male seed could have contributed to a woman's spontaneous abortion was if the man had syphilis.[24]

Certain environmental toxins were also known to cause an involuntary miscarriage. Phosphorus was a known abortifacient, and match makers who worked with phosphorus frequently aborted. Many of those who did not abort had sickly and weak infants who did not live long.[25] Tobacco could cause miscarriages among women who worked in factories processing this plant, although doctors employed by the government tobacco monopoly were quick to declare that women working in the tobacco industry did not abort more frequently than women in other industries. Women working with arsenic, antimony, mercury, lead, and carbon disulfide also had a higher probability of miscarrying. Women working with lead had a greater than fifty percent probability of miscarrying, and of those pregnancies lasting until fetal viability, one-third of the babies died during the first year and only one-fourth lived more than three years. Illness and miscarriages from these chemicals was so great that certain industries using them did not employ married women.[26] In these cases the economics of production and reproduction took precedence over married women's right to work.

Women who entered the hospitals of Paris for *avortement* usually needed treatment for spontaneous miscarriages or follow-up for severe complications of criminal abortions that had taken place outside the institution. Sometimes, in addition to the word *avortement* the hospital records recorded "torn uterus," metritis, or in at least one case, *accouchement incomplet*. There is no indication in the records as to whether an abortion was spontaneous or induced. Nonetheless, despite what appears to be the hospital staff's difficulty and apparent lack of interest in determining if a criminal abortion had taken place, Tardieu, Brouardel, and other doctors during the entire century spent much time and effort trying to figure out ways to differentiate between criminal abortions and spontaneous miscarriages. They usually based their decisions on fetal autopsies or examinations of the women.[27]

At the major public hospitals in Paris the percentage of all patients there for reasons related to abortion doubled from an average of 9 percent in 1890 to 18 percent in 1904. It is impossible to determine if this was an increase in provoked abortions or spontaneous miscarriages, although a survey at the time estimated that half had been spontaneous.[28] Half of the women were single and in their third month of pregnancy. Of the 327 abortions at Hospital Saint-Antoine from May of 1897 to January 1900, 41 percent had transpired in the first three months of the pregnancy, 39 percent in the fourth or fifth month, and 19 percent in the fifth or sixth month. None of the abortions were recorded as follow-up cases of women who had criminal abortions in the city, but it was possible that botched abortion attempts sent women to the hospital for medical attention—especially if the abortion attempt occurred after the first trimester, when the complications are more apt to have been serious. Quite likely, hospital officials, either acting in support of their patients or simply protecting their privacy, did not officially acknowledge admitting women for follow-up care after criminal abortions. As Dr. Henri Roulland of the Hospital Saint-Antoine reported: "Many times I have interrogated women who came to ask us to finish an abortion which has begun or to cure the uterine infection caused by criminal acts. As soon as they are sure that we are bound by professional discretion they are all quite open; some even are proud of their action and declare themselves ready to do it again, not wanting, or not wanting any more, children." Most doctors maintained their professional pledge of doctor-patient confidentiality.[29]

Since this confidentiality rule led doctors to label almost all abortions outside the hospital as spontaneous, it is difficult to determine precisely what percentage was not. One 1902 estimate reckons that 7 percent of all women hospital patients were recovering from abortions induced outside the hospital. Other estimates of hospitalized women recovering from induced abortions were higher—from 18 percent around the turn of the century to 30 percent of all female hospital patients in 1913.[30] If the patient died, doctors tended to link her death in the hospital with an abortion begun by a midwife in the city. In 1906 the chief of obstetrics at la Maternité estimated that in that hospital maternal deaths resulting from abortion were most often criminal abortions.[31]

The Crime of Abortion

The number of women who sought abortions in France and in Paris in the nineteenth century is impossible to determine. The only figures that have any degree of accuracy pertain to criminal accusations and court trials, and these figures suggest that legal sanctions against abortion were seldom enforced. Throughout the century, the number accused was almost two-thirds greater than the number of those actually arraigned. From 1826 to 1880 the total number of people accused of abortion in all of France was 2,581 (an average of 48 per year) of whom 41 percent were brought to trial. Toward the end of the century, the numbers of those accused of abortion increased from under 80 per year between 1879 and 1884 to an average of about 200 per year from 1885 to 1888.[32] Almost 10 percent of all arrests for abortion occurred in the department of the Seine. That percentage is particularly striking because in the 1850s the department of the Seine had only 3 percent of the total population of the country, and even by 1901 it contained only 7 percent of the nation's people. Between 1851 and 1865, in that department alone, authorities accused 111 people but found enough evidence only to bring 40 percent of them to trial, the same percentage as in the nation as a whole.[33]

The number of women using Paris's hospitals for one type of abortion or another, and the number of people accused of that crime, is undoubtedly far below the number of women who actually tried to induce their own abortion or who sought the assistance of a midwife or abortionist. In one estimate for 1884, there were as many abortions in the country as there were live births. Others conjectured that there were 600,000 abortions in France in 1890 and 900,000 per year on the eve of World War I. Dr. Robert Monin estimated that in 1909 there had been between 100,000 and 150,000 abortions in Paris alone. If his figures were approximately correct, they would indicate that there were at least 20,000 more abortions in that city than there were live births per year.[34]

These astonishingly high estimates of criminal abortions were probably exaggerations. Doctors who made the crude estimates had reasons to err on the side of higher numbers. They gathered these figures to support their political, pronatalist positions and tried to blame the depopulation of France on extensive abortion practices. They also resented midwives, and used these figures as evidence of the necessity to license, supervise, and curtail midwives' practices. According to Angus McLaren, "proabortionists cited the same data but for quite different reasons. Their argument was that since abortion was so widespread it had to be legalized and made medically safe. One can only assume that the actual number of abortions carried out lies somewhere between the few dozens noted by the police and the hundreds of thousands claimed by physicians. Even if the figure is placed at 100,000—an extremely low estimation in the eyes of many commentators in the 1890s—one is still faced with a major social issue."[35] Those obsessed with depopulation, not surprisingly, complained about how many abortions occurred and escaped detection completely. What was even more horrifying to many men was that not only the unwed but also married women had recourse to this practice.[36]

Abortion served as a back-up form of birth control, a second line of defense against having unwanted children if the male method (coitus interruptus) had failed. Economic constraints, as well as the cultural and legal position of women, established disproportionate burdens of child care on the mother, leading her to desperate measures. Women knew about abortifacients and abortionists not because midwives pushed them, but because women wanted to know. This information seems to have been transmitted within class from one working-class woman to another, rather than across class from the elite to the masses.

Some women had abortions despite the objections of their male partners, even when the men promised to support them and the baby.[37] Alternately, many abortions were forced on single women by their lovers or seducers. For example, twenty-year-old Madeleine Dolens had moved to Paris from the Nièvre. She had just taken a job as a domestic servant for café owners when she met Pierre Labat, who had the reputation of being "violent and debauched." Six months after she met him, she left domestic service and moved in with him. When she became pregnant, Labat told her she must abort and forced her to drink doses of absinthe and white wine boiled together. When these did not work he tried to abort her himself with his fingers. When this failed, he chased her out. After several days on the streets without resources she finally went to live with her cousin, a concierge. In desperation, she soon found a midwife who charged Fr 100 for an abortion, which Labat paid.[38]

Married women sometimes chose an abortion, or submitted to one, at their husband's insistence. Two cases serve as examples. Madame Caran entered l'Hôtel-Dieu in 1876 suffering from acute peritonitis as a consequence of an abortion that her husband practiced on her. They already had four children, two born before they were married. Before she died in the hospital she said that her husband had borrowed the abortion instruments and that she had agreed to the abortion. She feared her husband because he was furious at the news of a fifth child and the burden it would put on their already strained family resources. After she died, he went to prison, and their four children were placed among the abandoned children of Enfants Assistés.[39] Isidorine Lanen, a twenty-two-year-old sewing machine operator, had a daughter one month after she married Jean Lanen in May 1878 and she left the baby with a wetnurse so she could work. She and her husband, a shoemaker, managed to obtain a "little home." When she became pregnant again, in 1880, he accused her of infidelity and urged her to abort. He prepared a drink of rue, absinthe, and white wine and obtained the address of a midwife/abortionist from some of the women working in the neighborhood. When Isidorine cried from the pain of contractions brought on by her visit to the midwife, he stifled her cries by stuffing a bed sheet in her mouth. At her trial she complained of his brutality and said that because of it she took her daughter and left him to live with her mother, a daily maid. In retaliation, her husband went to the police to claim he was a model husband, denouncing her for having an abortion.[40]

Very few abortions actually took place within the first trimester. Only married women who had already experienced several pregnancies were likely to realize within the first two months that they were pregnant. Single women, especially those for whom it was their first pregnancy, might be slower to realize their condition either because of psychological denial or because in their undernourished condition their menses might already have been irregular. Even after they suspected that they were pregnant, they might delay an abortion for several reasons. They might have hoped that their periods would return and they would spontaneously abort; or, they might have hoped for marriage or that the "author of the pregnancy" would support them and the child, thus obviating the need for an abortion. Some doctors believed that women could not really be sure enough of pregnancy to risk abortion techniques before the third month.[41] Eventually, however, a woman would realize that she had an unwanted pregnancy and try to end it herself, using available information and folklore about home remedies and abortifacients that she gathered from friends and neighbors. Most women induced abortion in the fifth month of pregnancy, because at that stage fetal movement had convinced them that they were pregnant and earlier attempted solutions to the problem of pregnancy would have failed.[42]

The most widespread first attempt at self-induced abortion was drinking a beverage of absinthe, rue, and white wine. This mixture could not produce an abortion, but Parisian folklore nevertheless ascribed abortive powers to it. Women also tried various recipes of relatively harmless substances such as saffron, borax, sassafras, aloes, and chamomile.[43] These beverages contained no abortifacient qualities and when taken in excess caused only intestinal upset.

Women with access to an herbalist or pharmacist then added other ingredients to their potion. Their mixtures included white wine, absinthe, and any other drug or plant they could obtain.[44] Sometimes a pharmacist or herbalist who worked as an abortionist administered a mixture of savin, rue, absinthe, and saffron in a drink formed of a solution of bicarbonate of soda and tartaric acid. The properties of the drugs varied widely according to their freshness and dosage. Potassium iodide, sometimes sold by pharmacists, has the properties of an emmenagogue when taken by spoon. According to Brouardel, the sap or ground leaves of the yew might bring on a woman's periods, but this plant is also a poison that could produce a coma or even death.[45] Savin, a variety of juniper, had a universal reputation as an abortifacient, but this highly toxic plant causes vomiting and intense intestinal cramps. Contractions of the uterus are only part of the body's response to this herb. Savin could make a woman abort, but it might kill her first.[46]

Rue and ergot of rye were the two most prevalent drugs women took to abort. Rue, a plant whose leaves contain a volatile oil that was considered an abortifacient, could work better than savin in provoking the expulsion of the embryonic material, but only when made into a concoction of the sap of fresh leaves or roots and in women predisposed to miscarry. Women who took rue to abort suffered weakness, heavy vomiting, and horrible stomach pains—all symptoms of poisoning.[47] Ergot, a well-known oxytocic mold that helps contract the smooth muscles of the uterus, occasionally had been used by doctors and midwives since before the eighteenth century to induce abortions or births. In the nineteenth century it was widely employed by doctors and midwives to hasten uterine contractions and to stop hemorrhaging after an abortion or a normal delivery.[48]

Doctors such as Tardieu and Brouardel recognized that none of these herbal drugs worked as an effective agent in bringing about an abortion, unless the woman was about to abort anyway; they only served as powerfully overwhelming purgatives and poisons.[49] Savin, ergot, and other herbs could produce muscle contractions or dilation of the cervix that might bring about an abortion, but a dose large enough to do this might also poison and kill the woman. Only if the liquid were injected into the womb could it effectively cause an abortion—not because of the qualities of the herbs, but because the physical intrusion of the foreign substance could provoke the detachment of the embryo from the wall of the womb.

Some measures were risky, others just uncomfortable, but women tried whatever was in their folklore arsenal. They took hot or cold baths, especially foot baths with mustard, and wore tight constricting garments. These almost never work, neither would violent exercise, jumping, falling down stairs, or blows to the stomach—unless a woman had a predisposition to abort and was about to do so anyway. Direct external pressure on the uterus would not cause an abortion unless it dislodged the fetus from the uterine wall, an unlikely event.[50]

Some women were not beyond using their own fingers or instruments to try to dislodge the contents of the uterus, and sometimes their husbands or lovers tried to help. Direct manipulations of the vagina, cervix, and uterus were the most successful methods used to induce abortions and these were the easiest for doctors of forensic medicine to detect. If a woman tried these methods on herself, she had to have some knowledge of anatomy—information that may not have been part of the knowledge system of a young, isolated, primiparous woman. Furthermore, she ran a dangerous risk of perforating her uterus and introducing infection.[51] When all of these measures failed, as most of them usually did, a desperate woman sought an abortionist, frequently a midwife. By then she was in at least her third or fourth month of pregnancy, and the search for an abortionist could take several weeks.

Women relied on an informal information network to find an abortionist. Herbalists and pharmacists kept their shops or stands in the neighborhood where poor women would find them in their daily routines, but finding an abortionist was more difficult. Some actually advertised in the Paris newspapers that they could resolve menstrual problems and bring on a woman's period, discretely and infallibly. Some abortionists were clustered near the train stations and the large department stores to provide for women coming into Paris from the country, but most were found by word of mouth.[52]

In nineteenth-century France, as in America, "securing abortion and contraception made up a shared female experience." Indeed, the difficulties of securing contraception and abortion necessitated women working together; it required a network, a community of women.[53] Women like Marie Ditte, living in a garni and employed in a workshop with other women, had access to an information network that often included women from their home villages. They also used networks among merchants and neighbors. Some herbalists ran a regular referral system to their favorite midwife/abortionist.[54] Domestic servants, who usually lived in isolation, had a more difficult time getting information. When possible, they consulted other domestic servants, usually the cook. Cooks went about the neighborhood in the course of their daily grocery shopping, knew the community, and had access to all kinds of information. They were central to the working woman's and the domestic servant's network.[55] Neighborhood networks could be problematic; the more people who knew that a woman was concerned about her missed periods, the more people who could point an incriminating finger at that woman.

Relatives also formed an information network that could refer the poor and pregnant to abortionists. For example, Claire Bouton had lived with her parents in the Meuse. At the age of twenty she had her first child, a boy who lived about three weeks. At twenty-three she became pregnant again but went to Paris to conceal this second pregnancy from her parents. They had forgiven her first "fault" but said that they would show her the door if she became pregnant again. Her lover, a married man, paid the cost of the trip, the midwife, and the wetnurse. When he stopped paying the wetnurse, the wetnurse abandoned the baby at Enfants Assistés. When the same married man made her pregnant for the third time she went to another Parisian midwife who aborted her. Meanwhile, her brother, Eugène, had planned to marry Maria Forney when he completed his military service. When Forney became pregnant a second time she asked Claire Bouton (her lover's sister) for advice. Bouton recommended the same midwife/abortionist she had hired.[56]

Abortionists and Their Methods

Doctors, midwives, pharmacists, herbalists, veterinarians, and a variety of charlatans and quacks performed illegal abortions on the poor and pregnant of Paris. By far the greatest number were midwives practicing without education or formal training and without a license. Of the 75 people arrested in Paris for performing an abortion between 1846 and 1850, three-fourths were women. Of those 75 people arrested, 63 percent were midwives and 16 percent were male doctors; older women in general (but not midwives) constituted almost 7 percent, and charlatans, pharmacists-herbalists, women acting alone, and husbands provoking abortions on their wives constituted about 3 percent each.[57] This prevalence of midwives among those tried for criminal abortion gave them the eponym of "angel makers." One particularly notorious woman was called *Mère Tiremonde*.[58] Doctors so closely associated midwives with abortions that they called the midwives' private maisons d'accouchement *ateliers d'avortement* (abortion workshops). Doctors who performed criminal abortions were the *déclassé* who, driven by their desire for money, "damage not only their reputations, but that of the profession as well." Doctors were also known to have practiced abortions on domestic servants whom they impregnated.[59]

Abortionists fees ranged from Fr 10 to Fr 500, often on a sliding scale according to a person's ability to pay, with an average at the end of the century of Fr 100. This was about three months' salary for the poorest of needle workers and domestic servants in Paris. The less skilled abortionists, and those whom the poor sought, usually charged less than Fr 50.[60] Most abortionists, especially those who were skilled, could avoid detection because women who had successful abortions would be unlikely to tell. Abortionists most often came to the attention of authorities when the attempted or actual abortion resulted in hemorrhaging, peritonitis, and death for the mother. For example, Amelie Roche, the midwife of Joinville, was sentenced to five years in prison for three abortions; all of those patients had died.[61]

A midwife or other abortionist often employed the same methods as the women tried on themselves. She would first give her patient some herbal or chemical beverage to drink. If and when this failed, she would then physically try to dislodge the embryo from the womb, often with a finger and instrument, so that the woman could expel the contents of her uterus. Ordinarily, the finger alone could not penetrate the womb to disloged its contents; therefore, midwives used instruments such as pointed probes or sounds (sonde à dard) to dilate the cervix, knitting needles, curtain rods, or even porcupine quills and goose feathers. In rare cases, more frequent toward the end of the century, the abortionist first would introduce a medically prepared sponge into the cervix to dilate it.

The most common, and successful, method of inducing an abortion was to inject a liquid, usually hot or cold water, into the interior of the uterus with the help of a syringe, and possibly a probe to first dilate the cervix. Sometimes irritants such as soap, or reputed abortifacients such as ergot, were added to the liquid. Introduction of a liquid, even just water, into the uterus with a syringe could effectively cause an abortion as early as the third week of pregnancy. The problem was dilating the cervix sufficiently to insert the syringe without damaging the uterus or cervix. Pregnant women either lay on a table, squatted, or leaned against a wall. The midwife then placed a syringe with a long nozzle and rubber tube inside the pregnant woman, using her fingers to guide her. She also had a jar of liquid, usually of a whitish appearance, which she injected into the woman with the syringe. After one injection the midwife looked to see if any liquid or blood flowed out, indicating to her that the method was successful. If there were no signs of success, a few minutes later the midwife would repeat the procedure. Several hours later, the woman would have her abortion, accompanied by blood loss.[62] Irritating the uterus would cause it to contract, and this would usually be enough to produce the abortion. A surer method involved first using a probe to dilate the cervix so an instrument could dislodge the fetus.

Many women experienced a sharp pain at the time of the abortive maneuver, followed by painful uterine cramping sometimes accompanied by loss of consciousness, and then a loss of blood and amniotic fluid. Occasionally more severe hemorrhaging followed, and in those cases the abortionist sometimes administered ergot. In almost all cases the woman walked home after the midwife's procedure. Within several hours, but sometimes as much as several days later, the woman experienced extreme pains from uterine contractions. Sometimes nothing happened and the whole interventionist procedure had to be repeated before the uterus expelled its contents. The actual uterine expulsion most frequently occurred in the woman's own room. She then disposed of the material in her night chamber pot, in the toilet room or water closet, or in a sewer, canal, river, or cemetery. Then, presumably most of the time, the woman resumed her usual activities without any damage other than slight temporary weakness. Even among the poor and pregnant, a high number of women survived abortions and their possible complications. Others had some hemorrhaging, and a few had an infection from which they soon recovered.

An unknown number suffered the long-term effects of an illegal abortion at the hands of an unskilled abortionist. Such consequences were metritis and peritonitis, irregular periods, inflammation and perforation of the uterus, kidney troubles and urinary tract infections, and nonfatal mutilations or ruptures of reproductive and intestinal organs. Occasionally the placenta was not expelled and the midwife or doctor had to pull it out, frequently resulting in hemorrhage and septicemia, usually followed by death.[63] Infections and ruptures of the uterus were complications of both criminal abortions and spontaneous miscarriages as well as of a regular delivery at term, but Brouardel asserted that infections were more common among women who had had an unclean and unsterile instrument and finger inserted inside her, and that uterine ruptures prevailed among poor women who had abortions by unskilled abortionists. By the turn of the century, because childbirth became safer, abortion was more dangerous for the woman than a normal delivery.[64] This may not have been true earlier in the century when women suffered and died in childbirth at alarming rates.

Untold numbers of women may have died as a result of abortion. Tardieu estimated that half of the known cases of criminal abortion in Paris resulted in death from metritis, peritonitis, and especially from hemorrhaging.[65] This mortality rate is much higher than the average probability of death from an abortion, since it is based on known criminal cases. The police, courts, and forensic doctors were more likely to find out about a provoked abortion if the woman died. If she died in a hospital, doctors, who otherwise probably would have ignored the possibility of a criminal abortion, might seek her abortionist and try to bring her to trial, and the poor woman's survivors would likely be more anxious to indict the abortionist. In one way or another, her death in a hospital called attention to the abortion and usually led to an investigation and search for the culpable abortionist, but other events could also lead to arrests and investigations.

Criminal Procedures, Courts, and Convictions

Abortion required an information network and support, but that very network could also lead to a woman's arrest. Women helped one another but also went to the police when provoked to protect themselves from suspicion as an accomplice. Sometimes sewer cleaners or canal workers found an aborted fetus. In other cases neighborhood gossip about an abortion reached the ears of the police. These scenarios led to a criminal procedure against the woman who had the alleged abortion and those who helped her.

All prosecutions of women suspected of abortion or infanticide proceeded in a similar manner. They began with the police arresting and placing the suspects in detention. Usually within one day of the arrest the pretrial investigation began; this could take many months. Women suspects being investigated to determine if their case could be brought to trial were incarcerated in the prison Saint-Lazare. There they mingled with other prisoners, sometimes others involved in the same case. Typically, an abortion case involved one midwife or abortionist and several women on whom she allegedly performed the abortions. All could have been in Saint-Lazare at the same time.

Under the nineteenth-century French legal system, public prosecutors (procureurs) ordered the investigation of the case and the gathering of evidence before the case was actually brought to trial. Only if there was sufficient incriminating evidence would the case be heard in the Assize Court. The courtroom scene, therefore, represents the culmination of months of investigation. Although defendants could choose their attorney, or have the court name one for them, the juge d'instruction (a magistrate appointed by the President of the Republic upon the advice of the public prosecutor) conducted the investigation. He had enormous powers to search premises, read suspects' mail, and determine whom to question as witnesses. He tried, often successfully, to uncover the entire past life of the accused to ascertain her and her family's economic and moral circumstances. Hearsay testimony was admitted, and rules of evidence were lax.

The juge d'instruction questioned suspects and witnesses, individually and secretly, in his chambers where the defendant was without counsel. Only in 1897 was the law modified to allow the defendant the right to have her lawyer present at the interrogations. Cross-examination was not allowed, and the suspect had no protection against self-incrimination. A court secretary recorded each question and response.[66] The juge d'instruction ordered a specified doctor of forensic medicine, a medical-legal expert, to examine the woman and any product of conception that might have been found. Occasionally the court-appointed doctor also questioned the defendant when and where he examined her, while she was under arrest in a hospital or prison. This occurred most frequently in cases where the woman had been in the hospital; doctors apparently did not question the women in the magistrate's chambers.

Forensic doctors designated by the juge d'instruction played pivotal roles in determining if there was sufficient evidence to bring a case to trial. Their reports became part of the official body of evidence. If a case went to the courts, their testimony was crucial in getting juries to convict the women who had the alleged abortions and the people accused of having performed them. Ambroise Tardieu and Paul Brouardel dominated the Paris criminal courts in cases of suspected abortion or infanticide from the 1850s until into the twentieth century; they exerted great influence, both through their books and by their testimony at criminal proceedings.

First forensic doctors had to determine if an abortion had occurred, and then whether it had been a spontaneous one or a criminally provoked one. To do this, they analyzed the economic and social circumstances, the stage of pregnancy, and the age of the women "who did not recoil from this crime." They also gave pelvic exams to all women accused of having an abortion to ascertain if she had recently been pregnant, but this was difficult to establish, especially in multiparous women. The doctors searched for cuts and scratches on the reproductive organs for evidence of wounds resulting from direct manipulation of the uterus and cervix. The doctors also examined her breasts for signs of swelling and milk. If the pregnancy had terminated some weeks before the examination, as was often the case, a woman's body might bear no trace of a recent pregnancy. In the absence of all signs, the doctors then interrogated the women about beverages they drank, manipulations made on them, whether instruments were used, and possible other attempts at abortion. Forensic doctors asserted that the women often confessed after "intensive questioning," that sometimes bordered on intimidation.[67] In case of maternal death, doctors performed autopsies to look for inflammation, evidence of peritonitis or metritis, perforations of the uterus, and other wounds that could have resulted from an abortion. Brouardel admitted that it was often difficult to prove the crime.

Although Tardieu, writing in the middle of the century, severely censured both the women who had the abortions and those who performed them, Brouardel, writing at the century's end, found a way to "excuse, in part, the poor young girls seduced and abandoned." They could have acted in a moment of dread and terror or in a momentary loss of mind caused by "their sad situation." He spared no sympathy, however, for the married women who had abortions for what he termed "egotistic" reasons.[68] Brouardel was not as anxious as Tardieu to indict midwives. He cautioned others to recognize the difficulty of proving that a criminal abortion had been performed. For example, the presence of uterine probes or speculums in the rooms of a midwife was not incriminating evidence, since midwives needed them in the practice of their trade.[69]

Public prosecutors and forensic doctors found it difficult to obtain convictions from the twelve-man juries, even though it required only a majority to return a verdict. In France, juries acquitted 40 percent of those tried for abortion from 1830 to 1880 and granted extenuating circumstances in 78 percent of the convictions. From 1880 to 1910 the number of acquittals rose to 66 percent, and 80 percent of those convicted were with extenuating circumstances, "which caused a well-known publicist to remark that the 'French jury is Malthusian.' "[70]

Juries acquitted women because proving an abortion was extremely difficult and because they may not have regarded abortion as a crime necessitating the severe penalty that the law dictated. Many people viewed abortion more as a "pardonable sin" than a crime. After 1832 juries had the power to convict with extenuating circumstances, but they did not have to specify what those circumstances were or provide any reasons for finding extenuating circumstances. Juries could not determine the penalty, but may have pressured the judges to be lenient because they thought that the punishment mandated by the Penal Code was too harsh. If juries wished the defendants to have a reduced or lenient sentence based on extenuating circumstances, they invited the judge into the room in which they were sequestered to discuss the penalty. Often the judge was not willing to guarantee a reduced or lenient sentence, something he frequently could not do because he could not speak for the other magistrates who also had a voice in the sentencing; then the jury would vote to acquit. Parisian juries were especially noted for leniency in cases of abortion and infanticide, although they were more severe with married women and more indulgent with young single women.[71] If a woman cried and showed remorse, and character witnesses and neighbors testified to a record of otherwise good conduct and exemplary moral behavior, the juries were prone to acquit or grant extenuating circumstances. Judges, juries, and legislators agreed that the most guilty were the persons who actually performed the abortions.

The sensational 1891 trial in Paris of Constance Thomas, "the cold-blooded killer of infants," and the investigation of the women on whom she reputedly performed abortions, sheds light on who had abortions and what happened to them. This "angel maker," who was accused of performing more than 200 abortions, came to the attention of the doctors and the police when one of her patients died. Thomas's arrest triggered the interrogation of 118 people who purportedly had secured an abortion from her. Of these 118, only 53 were detained for trial; 47 were women (the men were tried as accomplices). Generally, in both France and the department of the Seine, women comprised 75 percent of those brought to trial for abortion. Of those women on trial for having Thomas perform abortions on them, half had never been married. The occupations of Thomas's patients were similar to those of women in the maternity hospitals: almost 25 percent were domestic servants and 20 percent were seamstresses; cooks, day laborers, and concierges constituted the majority of the remaining 45 percent. About 43 percent had no children; 30 percent had 2 children and 25 percent had one child. In general, they came from the same departments as did women in la Maternité at that time.[72]

Parisian newspapers and politicians believed that the courts should show no leniency to Thomas and to abortionists like her who contributed to the depopulation of France. Yet the same critics said that the juries "should be indulgent toward the seduced and abandoned unwed mother, toward the poor mother of a family abandoned by her husband. [Juries should] have pity on all the unfortunates whom misery and the fear of dishonor leads to crime, but be inexorable toward all the Thomases who come."[73] Of the 53 people accused of having an abortion (including the 7 accomplices), 49 were acquitted. Thomas received twelve years of forced labor.

For most, the odds of actually going to prison were slim, and those who were convicted for having an abortion usually served under three years. Moreover, the chances of an abortion never being discovered must have been considerable. Consequently, the benefits of an abortion to many women outweighed the risks, the danger, and the pain. Dr. André-Théodore Brochard lamented that women did not consider abortion the crime it really was: "Who has not seen married women regretting a pregnancy, for them undesired, and bitterly complaining of it? From the regret to the abortion is only a step, and this step is often taken by married women. How can it not be taken by unfortunate young girls who see on one side shame, on the other safety?"[74]

Reasons for Abortions

Many nineteenth-century doctors agreed with Tardieu's contention that unwed mothers had abortions out of fear of dishonor, to hide the shame of the "fault" and to protect their reputations. For almost all the women who were tried for abortion, however, it was poverty, not shame, that compelled them to limit the number of children they had. A woman who was abandoned by her seducer, prohibited by law from pursuing the father of the child for support, with few resources at her disposal, and without sufficient protection from society, might well ask herself, What would become of me if I had the child? Such women opted for an abortion because they realized that they would not have sufficient resources to raise their child. Some, like Constance Fauquet, believed that abortion was more humane than having a child and then abandoning it.

Married women also had abortions for reasons of poverty. The social critic and commentator Maxime DuCamp observed that "abortion is the savings plan of poor families."[75] Sometimes it was the husband who refused to feed another mouth and insisted on the abortion. For example Marie Robert testified that her husband told her that he would leave her if she had the child. He admitted saying, "You can not force me to raise your fifth child, but do what you want." He then gave her Fr 50 to give to the abortionist.[76] A married woman could be just as desperate as the unwed poor and pregnant young girl if her husband left her with yet another child. Her honor may not have been at stake, but she was just as poor. Some doctors who were unsympathetic to married women who had abortions argued that these women sought abortions because they lost their husbands, but also because of their "avarice, . . . fear of childbirth pains," and a "weakness of the spirit of sacrifice."[77] In fact, for some married women, it was the fear of poverty and the fear of seeing their infants suffer hunger that pushed them into an abortion.[78]

It is difficult to determine if any of these women accused of abortion were prostitutes. Some worked at respectable trades yet admitted taking money in exchange for "favors." Some men made economic arrangements with these women. For example, Marie Dhury worked as a *fille de brasserie* and had one lover, a law student who paid for her room. Englantine Piallat was a domestic servant who had one lover, but he was a married man and paid her Fr 2 each time. Constance Froment's lover said he paid her Fr 8 per week.[79] Their acceptance of some money indicates not only the sale of sex but also their dire economic straits. Under interrogation, these women never admitted that they might have chosen an abortion out of a desire to return to prostitution; their avowed motive was always destitution and hopelessness. Most prostitutes probably had networks that allowed them access to safe and discrete abortions.

Attempts at Abortion Reform

The acquittal of most of the defendants in the trial of Constance Thomas and some of her clients, the high percentage of suspected women never brought to trial, and an acquittal rate of over 50 percent persuaded some politicians to seek to change the law.

It was the increasingly powerful male-dominated medical profession that brought the issue of abortion to the attention of nineteenth-century moralists, legislators, and criminologists. By 1907, the same men who espoused "right-to-life" for infants and helped to establish social welfare for mothers and babies extended their "right-to-life" argument to the issue of abortion. Dr. Gustave Drouineau, an influential member of the League against Infant Mortality, referred to the "right to life for infants not yet born." Drouineau and others were primarily motivated by a nationalistic desire to prevent the depopulation of the nation. His colleague Paul Strauss declared, "France must not permit criminal abortion to decimate her natality" and lead to the "degeneracy of the population."[80] Doctors' desire to eliminate midwives, or to put them under male medical supervision, also spurred their drive to curtail and punish abortion.

The subcommittee on infant mortality of the 1902 Commission on Depopulation studied the issue of "criminal abortions" intermittently for nine years. Its final report, issued in 1911, called for shutting down all unauthorized private midwives and recommended the licensing and regulating of all maisons d'accouchement; opening a maison d'accouchement without authorization should result in a fine and a prison term.[81] Furthermore, licensed midwives were to be under administrative surveillance at all times and only admit women who were at least six months pregnant. The subcommittee, reflecting the wishes of the doctors and pronatalist politicians, also proposed laws prohibiting midwives from advertising that they restore menstrual regularity. They wanted a law stipulating that midwives could advertise only their names, addresses, titles, price, and whether or not they accepted pregnant women as boarders.

By 1911, politicians also sought to obtain more convictions of midwives. None of the midwives tried between 1903 and 1908 for performing abortions was convicted without extenuating circumstances and none was sentenced to forced labor. Juries had acquitted between two-thirds and four-fifths of accused midwives. Reacting against such leniency, legislators called for changing the law to require a fine of Fr 200 to Fr 10,000 and imprisonment of one to five years for all persons who performed abortions. By reducing the penalty for inducing an abortion they hoped to gain more convictions. Legislators believed that to assure convictions the penalty should be punitive but not excessive.[82] In 1922 the French legislature, by making abortion a misdemeanor, moved abortion cases out of the hands of lenient juries and into the hands of reputedly sterner judges.

Few raised their voices or lifted their pens to give poor women the choice as to whether or not they wished to have children, although a few proposed assistance to pregnant women and mothers of infants as a means of providing alternatives to women propelled to an abortion by poverty.[83] E. Adolph Spiral's critique of the abortion law in 1882 was one of the first attempts to decriminalize abortion. Spiral considered the law counterproductive, illogical, class biased, and inequitable, with serious consequences for mothers in misery; although based on maintaining morality, it really fostered immorality. As a consequence of the law, many poor single women, victims of seduction, unwillingly bore their children. As a result they fell into dishonor, further poverty, and perhaps even prostitution. Those who chose abortion did so to save themselves from the double danger of dishonor and misery. The desperate who could not abort would turn to infanticide.[84] Spiral noted that the bourgeoisie had their own methods of marital contraception which were not punished by law. The law was aimed simply at the methods of the poor. Many women were forced toward abortion by public policies that restricted anonymous child abandonment and forbade recherche de la paternité. Spiral's solution to the plight of the poor was to permit abortions to those who were desperate, allow anonymous child abandonment, and to permit recherche de la paternité.[85] The seduced young woman was Spiral's first concern. To Spiral, legalizing abortion would eliminate some of the worst evils, namely fatal operations and criminal prosecution suffered by the poor and unlucky.

Dr. Madeleine Pelletier led the feminist argument for a woman's right to choose whether or not to bear a child. Abortion was particularly important for working-class women, she argued. They could not afford the contraceptives of the upper classes and often had to deal with indifferent or brutal men who refused coitus interruptus. If abortions were legal, the rates of suicide, infanticide, and prostitution would decrease.[86] If its criminality were repealed, abortion would be available from doctors or licensed midwives, making the procedure safer. The danger in abortion, Pelletier argued, was in the ignorance, negligence, and lack of cleanliness among those who performed them. She concluded that abortions should be legal during the first trimester, before the fetus shows signs of life.[87] Claire Galichon and Marie Béquet de Vienne argued along lines similar to Spiral and Pelletier. Galichon urged legalization of abortion during the first four months of gestation, and for any woman or girl who was victimized by rape, or by seduction and abandonment.[88] Rather than viewing abortion as a female crime, Marie Béquet de Vienne asserted that "the man is the only one guilty." He seduced and abandoned the woman and then abandoned all responsibility.[89]

Inherent in the debate were issues of class and gender, because by the end of the century many recognized that abortion was the last resort of poor women; the rich could exercise their choice to limit family size by contraception. Poor women had only abortion and infanticide. They could not even force paternal responsibility on the father of their child.

By the end of the nineteenth century, debate on abortion had become linked to the debate on paternal irresponsibility, infanticide, and child abandonment. By the twentieth century, many influential legislators and reformers equated abortion with infanticide, and complained that both led to the depopulation of the country. To prevent both, they argued, child abandonment should become easier.[90]

Abortion was not for everyone. Some may have believed it wrong. One had to have access to an information network and to money to pay for the drugs and the abortionist. Proportionately more women were arrested and tried for having an abortion in nineteenth-century Paris and the department of the Seine than in any other area of France. This speaks not only to the power of the doctors in that metropolis and to the efficiency of the police system but also to the strength of that city's abortion information network. The relatively large number of abortions in Paris led social commentators to believe that abortion was an urban crime while infanticide was a rural one. Domestic servants in Paris, however, could be just as isolated as women in rural villages.

Infanticide
and Child Abandonment

Isabelle Caze was just nine years old when her mother died. She continued to live with her father, who farmed in the Pas-de-Calais. At the age of seventeen, Isabelle had her first child, whom her father helped raise; but when she became pregnant for the second time at the age of nineteen, she left for Paris in the hope of keeping this pregnancy secret from her father. A Catholic charity found Caze a position in domestic service, but she lost that job because of her obvious pregnancy. When her labor pains began on August 2, 1885, her new employer took her to la Maternité, where Caze gave birth to a son whom she named Henri. During the night of August 11, Henri was found dead in his crib beside his mother's bed. Midwives at the hospital suspected that Caze had killed the baby, because she had kept asking what she could do with her infant to hide him from her father. Another midwife testified that the infant might have died naturally because occasionally he had convulsions and turned blue. A student midwife reported that during the night Henri died, she had given him some milk from a bottle because Caze seemed too tired to nurse. This same student commented that Isabelle was not a model mother, since when Henri's hands and feet were cold she refused to take the infant into bed with her, saying it was against hospital rules.

Caze confessed to strangling Henri, and her testimony during the trial indicated her emotional confusion. She professed that she had given her son all the care she could, and in despair, without thinking, wrapped her scarf around his neck. She had held him in her arms another moment and then placed him in his crib. Under interrogation, she cried that she feared the reproaches of her family if she had a second child, and yet she dreaded abandoning him to Enfants Assistés. She preferred to see her infant dead rather than placed in the foundling home, where she would condemn him to suffer a miserable existence. She pleaded temporary insanity and added, "if the blood did not mount into my head, all this would not have happened." The doctor's autopsy report indicated that Henri was a tiny infant of about five pounds who died of pulmonary congestion; the body bore no trace of violence, and he thought the pulmonary congestion could have occurred spontaneously. The jury acquitted Caze.[1]

Anna Bordot was less lucky. The daughter of a poor, pious family in the Auvergne in central France, Bordot had been working as a domestic since the age of fourteen. In 1875, in her mid-twenties, an Alsatian brewery worker residing in her home town courted her. He did not inspire her parents' trust, but after eight months they gave their approval for marriage. This permission achieved, Bordot testified that she had "abandoned" herself to him six weeks before the wedding. The Saturday before the nuptials, her fiancé disappeared, taking the trunk which contained her hard-earned trousseau. This humiliation was followed by her realization that she was pregnant. Bordot had one thought: to hide her condition. She took the train to Paris where she found work as a domestic. Her employers, pleased with her services, noticed she was pregnant and offered to help. Too ashamed to admit she was pregnant, she denied her condition and refused their help. She made no preparations to receive the child and said that she had intended to go to a midwife when she was ready to deliver. The baby came sooner than she expected, and she gave birth to the infant alone in her room during the night. She wrapped the baby, still attached to the placenta, in her skirt and suffocated it. Her employers noticed the next morning that she did not look well, but Bordot did not want to see the doctor they summoned for her. Soon, the body of her baby was dicovered in an unused stove. Bordot was convicted and sentenced to six years of forced labor.[2] Bordot and Caze typified those in nineteenth-century Paris who committed infanticide: female, single domestic servants, in their early twenties, abandoned by their lovers, and afraid to dishonor themselves and their hardworking families.

Infanticide in nineteenth-century France often functioned as a form of delayed abortion. Both abortion and infanticide involved concealment of the pregnancy, were easy to commit and difficult to prove, and enabled women to avoid motherhood in an era before reliable contraception. Some anthropologists hypothesize that infanticide is not pathological but rather a form of adaptive behavior; it is less a desperate response to extreme stress and more a reproductive strategy, a form of birth control especially in times of economic need. Other scholars look for a relationship between poverty and crimes against infants.[3] Whatever the cause, infanticide has served a variety of functions in various societies—from family limitation, to gender selection, to improving the chances of survival for the parent or other family members. It has been practiced for centuries by women who had no contraceptive methods or access to abortion, yet wished to avoid motherhood.

Infanticide remained a major issue in nineteenth-century France. Its incidence apparently contradicts Philippe Ariès's conclusions that by the nineteenth century a new concern with the lives and well-being of children had replaced traditional indifference to infants. Infanticide, however, need not be taken as evidence of a lack of maternal love for infants.[4] Among women who thought they had no acceptable alternative, infanticide was a back-up measure when contraception and abortion were unavailable or had failed. Infanticide was a desperate strategy among destitute and isolated women.

Infanticide and the Law

Nineteenth-century law about infanticide hearkens back to the Edict of Henry II in 1556, which made it a capital offense. It declared that any woman who hid her pregnancy, delivered clandestinely, and whose baby died without baptism could be guilty of infanticide. Henry II also advocated a declaration of pregnancy from unwed women, although the Edict did not explicitly mandate such a declaration. In practice, by making such a declaration, the neighborhood and local authorities would know that this woman was pregnant, making it more difficult to hide the birth and subsequent infanticide. A pregnant single woman was to name the father of the child, and he might be subject to sharing responsibility as well as shame. Henry II believed the public shame of the declaration would discourage nonmarital sexual behavior in both women and men, contribute to marital stability, and decrease the abandonment and murder of infants, the overwhelming number of whom were illegitimate.[5] Later, the 1791 Penal Code made infanticide part of the common law and equated it with murder. It removed the special status accorded to an unbaptized newborn and required an examination of the corpse as evidence that the infant had met a violent death.

The Penal Code in effect throughout the nineteenth century still required evidence that the infant had been killed, but it in effect reversed the 1791 legislation by differentiating between intentional infanticide and other murder. Article 300 of the 1791 Code defined infanticide as the premeditated murder of the newborn child, and article 302 made that crime punishable by death.[6] Article 319 of the nineteenth-century

Code delineated a lesser crime of nondeliberate infanticide by omission and neglect. Inattention, negligence, or imprudence that resulted in an infant's death was punishable by up to two years in prison and a fine ranging from Fr 50 to Fr 600.

In practice, some of the spirit of the Edict of 1556 still remained. One way of proving premeditation was to demonstrate that a woman had kept her pregnancy a secret and delivered clandestinely. In the nineteenth century, a woman customarily still was supposed to make her pregnancy known, but to her employer and community, not the local authority. At least one of the poor and pregnant in nineteenth-century Paris had been aware of the desirability of making a declaration of pregnancy. In 1878, when Marie Blanchard realized she was pregnant she went to her mayor's office to make the declaration, but he refused to receive such a deposition.[7] There was no regulation requiring that he receive such a statement and he had no legal authority to do so. Trying to inform the mayor may have been Blanchard's alternative to telling a priest or a doctor that she was pregnant. A priest may have severely criticized Blanchard, and a doctor cost money. Not concealing her pregnancy may have led to Blanchard's later acquittal of infanticide charges.

According to the law, and the courts' interpretation of it, in cases of infanticide and abortion the juries could only convict or acquit. Since in cases of infanticide the penalty for conviction was death, juries were reluctant to convict. To gain convictions, in 1824 the courts admitted extenuating circumstances for the mothers, but not for other guilty parties. In 1832 the possibility of extenuating circumstances was admitted for all crimes, including infanticide and abortion.[8] In 1863, *suppression d'enfant,* keeping the birth of an infant secret so it could not be determined how the infant died, was made a simple misdemeanor. The category of a misdemeanor for suppression d'enfant allowed some cases of suspected infanticide to be deferred to lesser courts and thereby liable to a lesser charge and punishment. In order to obtain more convictions the French parliament in 1901 formally abolished the death penalty for infanticide.[9]

Rates of Arrests and Acquittals

The first suspicion of infanticide usually emerged when cesspool cleaners or sewer workers, canal and river dredgers, or household members or employees found an infant's body and turned it over to the police. Then the police and the public prosecutor would order a forensic doctor to perform an autopsy. If they thought the infant had been murdered, the police looked for a suspect. Women suspected and tried for infanticide had usually given birth alone and silently in their rooms. They believed that they then could easily and without detection dispose of their newborn. The number of cases is legion in which the infant's body, dead or alive, had been thrown down the latrines into the open sewers and then found by the cleaners and brought to the police.[10] The police traced those bodies back to the specific building whose latrines emptied into the particular area of the cesspool in which workers had found the bodies.

Less frequently, such as in the case of Anna Bordot, an employer informed the police that her domestic servant had had a suspicious loss of blood and sudden decrease in size, and that she suspected infanticide. Sometimes, when suspicion of infanticide preceded the discovery of an infant's corpse, the tiny body was found in a fireplace or stove, or occasionally in a trunk or under the bed in the mother's room.[11] Once there was a suspect, the case was turned over to the juge d'instruction, who ordered a forensic doctor to examine the woman, just as in cases of suspected abortion.

Although women found it harder to conceal nine months of pregnancy than a shorter term of gestation and an abortion, an unknown number managed to keep their pregnancy a secret. Concealing a pregnancy for nine months may not always have been difficult. Women layered loose-fitting clothing, and domestics often wore aprons. If a woman was normally heavy, observers could confuse a pregnancy with weight gain. Even in la Maternité, in the midst of doctors and midwives, at least one student-midwife managed to conceal her pregnancy until labor pains began.[12] If she could conceal a pregnancy among trained specialists, it must have been relatively easy for a domestic servant to hide a pregnancy from unobservant employers. Some employers noticed that their domestic servant was increasing in size, but attributed the gain to their nourishing food.[13]

Infanticide was almost as hard as abortion to detect and prove, even among postpartum women in a maternity hospital or maison d'accouchement. On occasion nurses or midwives at la Maternité found babies who had seemed healthy in the evening inexplicably dead in their cribs the next morning. In these cases, they always called the police, who ordered autopsies. Sometimes the police decided that the death had been accidental; the conclusion depended on the doctor's autopsy report and on whether or not the mother had spoken of hiding or abandoning the baby.[14] Sudden Infant Death Syndrome as a cause of death was not part of nineteenth-century medical knowledge, and hospital regulations forbade an infant from spending the night in the mother's bed in order to prevent death from suffocation if a mother rolled over on the child.

Given the difficulty in detecting and proving infanticide, the estimated rates of people accused of infanticide in France differ widely and un-

doubtedly underestimate the actual incidence. On the average, 30 percent of those accused were brought to trial, although during the fourteen
years from 1851 to 1865 that percentage was much higher.[15] All data
reveal a doubling of the rate of infanticide crimes in France from an
average of about 100 per year in the decades of the 1820s and 1830s to an
average of 210 per year the decades of the 1850s and 1860s. By 1900 the
rate declined to 108, just below its 1825 level.[16]

Ambroise Tardieu tried to show a high number of murdered infants in
Paris alone. Between 1837 and 1866 he recorded that a total of 1,244
dead newborn babies arrived at the Paris morgue. The prosecutor's
office suspected murder in 81 percent of these cases and ordered autopsies on them. Of those he autopsied, Tardieu believed that 72 percent
had been murdered.[17] Other figures for infanticide in Paris reveal an
average of forty-four women prosecuted for that crime per year from
1866 to 1885 with only minor fluctuations in individual years. From 1886
to 1900, the average annual number of prosecutions for infanticides
increased to forty-eight rather than declining as the figures did in the rest
of France.[18] This could reflect population growth or prosecutions in
Paris but it may also indicate the continued isolation and poverty of
women in that city.

Whatever the actual figures are, it is clear that the raw rate of arrests
or prosecutions for infanticide in France rose during the 1860s and 1870s
and then declined. The rate of arrests for infanticide in relation to live
births also declined sharply from an all-century high of 127.6 per 100,000
births in the period from 1856–60 to an average of 56.5 per 100,000
live births in the first decade of the twentieth century. Contemporary
social commentators (as well as modern historians) sought to explain the
change in the infanticide rate by examining which environmental factors
might correlate with the crime. While there may have been a relationship between economic misery and infanticide on a personal level, at the
aggregate level economic deprivation (as measured by the price of
wheat) does not predict the level of infanticide. The changing rate of
infanticide fails to correlate with the average annual price of wheat, even
with a time lag.[19]

Intangible reasons, such as greater affection for children, may have
contributed to the decline in infanticide in the decades before the First
World War. Perhaps, as some have suggested, poor working-class mothers in the last quarter of the century made the "discovery of childhood"
and showed a new attachment to their babies, thereby leading to a reduced infanticide rate.[20] A low infanticide rate, however, even if one
could be determined, may be unrelated to the value placed on infant life.
It could indicate simply a change in police activity or the increased availability of contraception. It could also reflect changes in bureaucratic

record-keeping procedures, definitions of the crime, attitudes of doctors investigating the possible infanticides, changing administrative and medical efficiency in ferreting out the crime, as well as changes in women's maternity strategies. Even Tardieu believed that the increase in the numbers of infant corpses and the reputed rise in infanticide was due to increased police efforts in suspecting infanticide and ordering autopsies during the Second Empire.[21] It is clearly impossible to determine if the reported infanticide rate reflects incidence.

Statistics on reported cases of infanticide represent just part of the picture. Once arrested and brought to trial for the crime, women were frequently acquitted although the rate of acquittals was never as high as that for abortion (one-half to two-thirds). Between 1826 and 1862 the acquittal rate averaged 26 percent, and between 1862 and 1880 the rate averaged 38 percent. When juries convicted, 99 percent of the time it was with extenuating circumstances. Of the fifty-five women sentenced to death, forty had their sentence commuted.[22] By the turn of the century, half of all women tried for infanticide were acquitted. In the department of the Seine, juries showed leniency by granting extenuating circumstances to all whom they convicted.

Judges as well as juries became increasingly lenient toward women convicted of infanticide. In the 1820s, judges sentenced 27 percent of those convicted to hard labor in perpetuity; by 1890 that percentage had fallen to just under 2 percent, and after 1890 no woman was sentenced to hard labor in perpetuity for killing her newborn. Prior to 1890, judges sentenced 75 percent of all those convicted to a five- to twenty-year term of hard labor; that declined to 50 percent in the last decade of the century, and then to just 2 percent in the first decade of the twentieth century. Correspondingly, those sentenced to a prison term increased; women sentenced to a term of five years or more increased from 3 percent in midcentury to 8 percent by 1913. The number convicted of infanticide who received a prison sentence of less than five years increased from 17 percent in the mid-nineteenth century to about 90 percent in the first decade of the twentieth century.[23] Juries granted extenuating circumstances, and judges meted out increasingly mild sentences. In both abortion and infanticide cases the judicial system became more lenient, which flies in the face of growing concern over depopulation, the putative increase in control over female reproduction, and the growing influence of the medical profession. Judges and juries were not as ardently nationalistic and populationist as the leading politicians and doctors. Nonetheless, women were taken to court and, throughout the nineteenth and into the twentieth century, a key aspect of the prosecution's case against a woman remained the doctor's testimony.

Witnesses for the Prosecution

As soon as the police found an infant's corpse and the suspicion of murder had been raised, the *procureur* (public prosecutor) of the department of the Seine or the juge d'instruction requested that a doctor of forensic medicine perform an autopsy on the cadaver and conduct a physical examination of the woman suspected of killing that infant. These doctors claimed to have specialized knowledge and the courts relied heavily on them in criminal proceedings. It was their job to demonstrate, not just assert, that a particular person had committed infanticide. Although they maintained that they were not determined to convict and that what they provided was "expert" scientific testimony, they really served the prosecution.

From the time of Ambroise Tardieu, who served as the major medical witness at the investigations of infanticide in Paris from the 1850s through most of the 1870s, to Paul Brouardel, who held a similar position throughout the 1880s and 1890s, medical expertise changed. Brouardel, with more medical knowledge at his disposal, expressed less certainty than Tardieu that an infant had been killed. Although still effectively a witness for the prosecution, when there was any major medical doubt about whether an infant had been murdered, Brouardel demonstrated to judge and jury the various interpretations of his clinical findings. Of the 804 cadavers of newborns on which Tardieu performed autopsies, he found that 69 percent were infanticides. Brouardel, in comparison, found that only 43 percent of the 531 newborn corpses that he examined were infanticide victims.[24]

Forensic doctors had several basic tasks. They had to establish the age and identity of the newborn and ascertain that the infant had lived and breathed outside the womb. This was indispensable to establishing infanticide. The age of the infant was also important in determining if the woman would be tried for murder or infanticide. Until 1835, murder of a baby of up to three months old constituted infanticide. But in that year an appeals court ruled that infanticide occurred only within the first three days of an infant's life, before the declaration of birth had been made.[25] Having determined the infant's identity and that it had lived, doctors then had to establish the cause of death—whether the infant had died from natural causes or as a victim of murder. This they did by demonstrating that the "physical and moral conditions" surrounding the woman accused of infanticide indicated that she had killed her infant.[26]

To determine that an infant had lived and breathed, and then was killed, required several steps. First, doctors had to establish that the infant was born at term and viable; this usually meant a birth weight of seven pounds, although it could be as low as five pounds.[27] For an infant of this low weight to survive under the adverse environment into which it had been born would have been extraordinary. After determining the viability of the infant, the forensic doctor then had to establish whether or not it had breathed. To do this he visually examined the lungs and placed them in water to see if they contained any air. According to Tardieu, if the lungs floated, the infant had breathed; if they sank, the infant was stillborn and had not breathed. By the end of the century there was some controversy as to what the sinking or floating of the lungs really signified.[28] After deducing that the infant had been born at term and viable, forensic doctors then ascertained the cause of death.

Doctors carefully examined the cadaver for traces of violence. Usually they looked for a flattened nose and lips indicating the infant had been suffocated by pressure to stop its breathing. If a woman wanted to conceal the birth, the first thing she had to do was stifle any cries by placing her hand, bedding, or clothing over the baby's nose and mouth. Tardieu maintained that the deformation occasioned by such suffocation remained after death and appeared on the cadaver. Brouardel noted that in trying to hush the infant's cries an exhausted young mother could have unintentionally suffocated the infant.[29]

To counter women's most common defense that the infant suffocated accidentally either during birth or in the short time thereafter when she temporarily lost consciousness, doctors tried to show how improbable that actually was. They acknowledged that sometimes when a woman delivered her baby alone she rested, or even fainted, after the infant was expelled. If the infant remained facedown, it could accidentally die on the mattress with its nose and mouth obstructed; but for death to occur, the infant needed to be in that position for some time. That, Tardieu averred, was unlikely because infants have an instinct to live and to move in such a manner as to cry and breathe. Brouardel added that to prove death from suffocation this way there would have to be evidence in the infant's respiratory system. Furthermore, the woman would have to demonstrate that she really passed out after a long and tiring labor, or from excessive blood loss, and did not just let the infant lie there and perish for lack of care. In the rare cases in which the mother suffocated the baby by rolling over him, Tardieu argued that sometimes this happened by accident, but more often it was with criminal intent.[30] According to Brouardel, there were natural causes of sudden infant death that looked like suffocation and that Tardieu had attributed to infanticide.[31]

Suffocation, which Tardieu cited as the cause of death in half of the cases and Brouardel said occurred only about one-tenth of the time, rarely left any marks. The absence of signs of violence on the body and the presence of air in the lungs led Tardieu to conclude suffocation. By the

1880s, Brouardel testified that it was entirely possible to find lung problems and similar autopsy indications in an infant who had died naturally as well as in one who had been suffocated.[32] Strangulation of an infant was often combined with suffocation. Some women testified that in trying to hasten the birth they pulled the infant from themselves and inadvertently strangled it. Although Tardieu argued that this was "extremely difficult, if not impossible," for a woman whose abdomen was greatly distended, he admitted that it was not rare for an infant to be accidentally strangled by the umbilical cord around the neck.[33] Brouardel found external evidence of strangulation in one-fifth of the infanticides he autopsied.[34] Generally, however, the infant bore no traces of violence.

Doctors and prosecutors went to inordinate lengths to try to negate the most common, somewhat formulaic, defense in Paris. Women said they mistook the pressure of the descending fetus for an overwhelming need to defecate and went to the toilet and did not know they were near the time of delivery. They testified, "While I was on the seat the infant emerged, fell in the toilet and slid down to the sewer; I could not retrieve it."[35] Although Tardieu and Brouardel admitted that confusing labor pains with intestinal cramps was possible, and that a woman in an exceptional circumstance could deliver rapidly, such events happened only rarely. The doctors' task involved proving that the mother intended to kill the baby and that the infant had not accidentally fallen down to the sewers. To supplement the doctors' testimony, the juge d'instruction often summoned an "expert" plumber to visit the location and examine the dimensions and angles of the latrine, the holes, and the pipes. Usually the angles were wrong or the holes were too small to allow for a free fall.[36] By 1882, however, some toilets in Paris were large enough for an infant to fall through.[37] In most cases, doctors maintained that the infant had been pushed.[38] Immersion in the sewer system was one of the commonest means of disposing of an unwanted infant at birth.

When a forensic pathologist saw skull fractures (these occurred in about 10 percent of the cases), he had to prove that they were intentional and not the result of the infant accidentally falling on its head during a delivery in which the mother was standing, as she might have claimed. Tardieu had maintained that although it was not impossible for a woman to deliver a baby from a standing position, obstetricians (as well as common sense) argued that when women are seized with labor pains, they "instinctively protect the infant from falling" by crouching. Furthermore, at the moment the infant is expelled, it is still suspended from the eighteen-inch umbilical cord. For the infant to fall and damage its head on the floor the placenta would have to tear first, and it was unlikely that the force of the fall would rupture the cord. According to forensic doctors, the skull was usually broken by a brutal blow and not by hitting the floor. Generally, a woman did not mutilate or dismember her infant to kill it, but to better hide the evidence.[39]

Few women went to trial for killing their newborns by neglect, in part because it was extremely difficult to prove premeditated murder under the terms of article 319 of the Penal Code. Doctors tried to prove infanticide by negligence when the mother failed to cut the umbilical cord and the infant died as a result. It seems likely that women having their first baby would not have known that the cord must be cut, or would not have had the knowledge, means, and strength to do so. Some women contested Tardieu's accusation that they willfully killed the baby by failing to cut the cord. Marguerite Vibert exclaimed, "The doctor [Tardieu] can say what he wants. Not having killed my first [child], I did not kill the second."[40] Brouardel disputed Tardieu's assertion that a mother's neglect to cut or tear the cord would lead to infant death by hemorrhaging; infant death from an uncut umbilical cord would be rare. In cases of infanticide the infant was suffocated or strangled long before it had time to die of umbilical hemorrhaging, because the mother wanted to quell the cries.[41]

The story of Marie Toulouse provides a typical case of infanticide by negligence. She claimed ignorance of being pregnant and asserted that the delivery had taken place during an act of defecation. She cut the cord; then feeling very weak, she left her five-pound daughter on the floor and went to bed for two hours. When she rose, she found the baby dead and threw it down the latrine. A worker found the baby, and suspicion rested on Toulouse. Upon examination, the forensic doctor found no evidence of violence on the infant, but he concluded that the baby had lived and breathed and then died of exposure. After examining Toulouse, the doctor concluded that it was not possible for her to have been unconscious for two hours as she had claimed, and that the newborn had therefore died of neglect. Toulouse was condemned to two years in prison.[42]

The prosecutors and doctors also had to prove that it was the suspect who had committed the crime, and that it was premeditated. They based their conclusions on a physical examination of the mother, while she was under arrest, to find out if she really had delivered a baby and if her date of delivery corresponded to the date of birth of the infant whose cadaver they autopsied. The woman had a right to refuse this examination, but such a refusal would not have been well received. Doctors first looked for external signs of a recent pregnancy. They then proceeded to an internal pelvic examination for indication of a recent pregnancy. In their examination of the women, retold in explicit detail, doctors also reported on their inspection of the women's breasts for stretch marks, color, and presence of milk or colostrum.[43]

One of the key ways of proving premeditation was demonstrating that a woman told no one about the pregnancy, that she made no preparations for the arrival of the baby, and that she had no plans for childbirth assistance and had prepared no layette. The prosecution also tried to demonstrate the woman's immorality—that she had several lovers and "bad conduct," that this was not her first pregnancy, that she was not desperately poor, and that she was cold hearted and calculating.[44]

The Defense

A woman's defense rested on repudiating the prosecutor's and doctor's charges, and demonstrating her good conduct, hard work, and victimization. The defense tried to show that it was a nightmare and overwhelming responsibility for a destitute single woman to be pregnant and then take care of a child. Convincing judge and jury that she worked hard, was of good morals, and came from a good though poor family— but had become a victim of social, economic, and legal circumstances beyond her control—formed the crux of a woman's defense. In testimony and in court, it was advantageous for her to appear as an innocent, inexperienced, docile, meek-demeanored victim of social misery, unaware that her baby was due. The law prohibiting paternal responsibility for an out-of-wedlock child could also make her the pitied victim of seduction and abandonment.

By the later decades of the century, the defense often added the argument that the aberrant physiological and mental condition that accompanied pregnancy and childbirth might have led a woman to an infanticidal act. In the latter decades of the nineteenth century, some medical, criminal, and legal authorities associated deviant behavior with physiological origins.[45] Through the normal biological function of pregnancy and childbirth a woman could become pathological, exhibiting mental instability and deviant behavior. The belief in "folie puerpéral," though not new, achieved greater prominence and was an early recognition of postpartum depression with psychosis. A woman who committed infanticide was possibly a victim of society; but she might also have been a victim of her body—of her biology and sex. Such views both reflected and created greater roles for doctors as well as forensic pathologists.

Starting as early as 1876, women occasionally added to their defense the excuse that they had acted under the influence of "temporary insanity," in a "maniacal furor" or without a conscious knowledge or any memory of what had happened at the time of delivery. In these cases, the women did not deny infanticide but claimed lack of responsibility and innocence by virtue of "postpartum insanity." Mothers frequently repeated the phrase, "I lost my head." Ernestine Pallet in 1881 repeated that "I was desolate. . . . I was like a maniac. . . . I no longer knew what I was doing."[46]

To try to prove premeditation and willful intent to murder, doctors made certain assumptions about a woman's physical and moral state during and after delivery. They addressed the question posed by the juge d'instruction: "Could the acts of violence committed by a woman on her infant be the result of a perversion of her affective mental faculties or of puerperal delirium?" To this question and to the defense of temporary insanity, Tardieu replied:

> One must limit the discussion of insanity of a newly delivered mother to the first moments which follow delivery. These hapless women, in their defense, claim to have been temporarily insane when they killed their infant. They claimed that the atrocious pains of childbirth led to feverish over excitement, a type of maniacal furor which transports them and under which they kill their infant, without any awareness or conscience. One must coldly judge the facts. It is undeniable that if the labor of childbirth is prolonged and aggravated that women are incoherent, speak violently, and even have outbursts against their newborn infant. But from that state to madness, to the perversion of a homicidal furor, to a lack of conscience and responsibility for her acts is an impassable abyss. It is not insanity, it is not even a transitory perversion of her faculties; it is an over excitation of her sensitivities that leaves intact her reason and instincts. These facts, demonstrate only one thing, that is the falseness of the interpretation [of temporary insanity].[47]

Brouardel acknowledged "childbirth insanity," but believed that it lasted longer than a few moments after birth and could last for many months. He alleged, however, that the excuse of mental aberration was valid only when the women were also otherwise insane. He may have been more equivocal than Tardieu in ascribing infanticide based on his autopsies, but he was just as adamant in his disbelief that a woman who hid her pregnancy, delivered the baby all alone in her room, and made no provisions for the child could be suddenly seized by a momentary, temporary insanity which led her to kill her baby and not realize that she was committing that crime.[48]

Doctors did not start excusing women for "folie puerpéral" until the turn of the century. In 1897 Félix Martin proposed that the Senate initiate changes in the legislation regarding infanticide. Martin wanted the law to consider that a mother may not have premeditated her act, but that she acted under a fit of temporary insanity owing to her allegedly weakened and troubled mental state during pregnancy and childbirth. This provision failed to pass Parliament, but by 1900 some doctors were writing that a woman could be mentally deranged by virtue of having given birth and so might understandably commit infanticide.[49]

Another defense women adopted when doctors accused them of concealing pregnancy was to deny knowing that they had been pregnant.[50] Tardieu and Brouardel both addressed the question as to whether a woman could be unaware that she was pregnant. Both believed that for a multiparous woman it was not possible to be unaware, except in circumstances such as obesity or mental derangement. They agreed that a woman experiencing her first pregnancy may not have realized her condition during the first three or four months, especially if her periods had been irregular. It would have been hard, however, for any woman not to consider pregnancy when the fetus began to move at around five months of gestation. Even an innocent young woman experiencing such bodily changes would ask advice of someone.[51]

When confronted with a lack of preparation for the infant as a sign of premeditated murder, mothers usually said that the infant came suddenly and they thought they still had another two weeks to go before their due date, time enough to get the layette together. Some maintained that they had planned on delivering their baby at one of the public hospitals which supplied a baby's layette.[52] Other women, such as Elise Verney and Louise Mornet, refused to believe that their pregnancy was at term. Verney, a domestic servant, did not go to a maternity hospital despite the advice of a doctor whom she visited one month before her delivery. At her trial she claimed that she believed that she still had two weeks to go and the labor pains surprised her. She had been living in Paris for three years, and so she would have qualified for hospital admission. Mornet, another who was surprised by early labor, delivered in the stairwell of her building.[53] The women had no prenatal care and appeared naive and ignorant of their body and insisted they confused labor pains with intestinal cramps.[54]

A common line of defense was for the woman to maintain that she fainted at the time of delivery, lost consciousness, could not attend to the newborn, remembered nothing, and when she awoke the baby was lying dead between her legs. She underscored her deep remorse. Tardieu asserted that most women who claimed that they lost consciousness were lying.[55] Brouardel, a bit more sensitive to the women, reluctantly conceded that a woman delivering all alone in her room could pass out from an excessive loss of blood, or from the pain of labor, the isolation, and the emotional stress. This could make her unable to save her infant. Usually, however, only a great loss of blood would cause her to pass out long enough so that her infant would die from lack of care.[56]

Faced with the evidence of an infant's corpse and a doctor's testimony that they had recently had a baby, many women insisted that their babies had died accidentally or were stillborn.[57] It was up to the doctors and prosecutors to prove premeditated murder, and often they could not do so to the juries' satisfaction.

Reasons for Acquittal

Doctors might have been the self-proclaimed experts, but juries could ignore the doctors, acting according to the dictates of their consciences. When juries acquitted or acknowledged extenuating circumstances, they in essence forgave a woman her crime because of her victimization, ignorance, or misery.

Since neither the law nor the judges required juries to explain their decisions, all reasons for acquittal must remain speculative. Nevertheless, several patterns emerge in the case histories from the Assize Courts. Based upon the juge d'instruction's extensive investigation into the woman's prior morality, juries formed opinions about the suspect. For a woman to be acquitted employers and neighbors needed to attest that the suspect had demonstrated "good conduct," had only one lover, worked hard to support herself and perhaps some family members, and was from a hardworking family of "honest artisans" or "honest cultivators." If rumors abounded that called her morality into question—such as her laziness, or having many lovers, or general "bad conduct" and "loose morality," and perhaps several prior children whom she had abandoned—then she was likely to be convicted, but with extenuating circumstances to avoid the death penalty.[58] If good morality was supplemented by the promise of marriage, seduction, and then abandonment this was in her favor, especially toward the end of the century.

An increasing acquittal rate and the universal granting of extenuating circumstances in cases of convictions reveal juror sympathy for the poor young mothers. In a way, women had committed a crime to preserve their honor and that of their family; juries acquitted to help protect the sanctity of the family and the honor of individuals. Sentiments of pity or sympathy for the poor seduced, abandoned, and desperately lonely woman outweighed jurors' sentiments for the newborn infant and the national concern with depopulation and saving babies' lives.[59] Jurors did not feel the horror that police, doctors, and prosecutors felt when hearing about (or seeing) the atrocities committed against the infant. Brouardel believed that juries were sympathetic to the women because they did not see the infant's corpse; they only saw the poor young girl with a good reputation who had been seduced and abandoned by someone from whom justice demanded nothing. It is at this point, said Brouardel, that the forensic doctor must intervene to describe the cadaver.[60]

In acquitting women of infanticide, jurors may have shared the concern of some reformers about the lack of alternatives for these desperate women. There was no easy, anonymous infant abandonment and the prohibition against recherche de la paternité placed all of the responsibility on the mother and may have led many to infanticide. The jurors even may have held a particularly sympathetic view of the woman on trial by adhering to the idea that even in infanticide cases, there is one more guilty than the poor unwed mother—the man who promised marriage and then seduced and abandoned her.[61]

In one case jurors recognized a mother's difficult situation and the father's irresponsibility. Marie Girard had already left her small-town home in northern France when a pregnancy forced her to Paris. In 1880 Girard was in her mid-twenties and working as a domestic servant when she had a sexual relationship with another worker in her employer's house. When she became pregnant she asked her lover to fulfill his promise of marriage to her, but three months later he married someone else. Shame prevented her from returning to her family and motivated her to hide her pregnancy from them. When the juge d'instruction indicated that the father might have some responsibility and asked her if she had implored the father of the child to help her raise their child she shrugged, "What was his responsibility?" Interrogated neighbors and employers only had good things to say about her conduct, morality, and her work. The jurors acquitted her.[62]

When juries convicted, usually violence to the child was too severe to ignore. Yet no matter how bad the morality of the women or how heinous the crime, juries never called for the death penalty, even in cases of a second arrest for the same crime. If the doctor could prove brutality or mutilations, a conviction certainly followed, but juries still voted extenuating circumstances. Judges reserved the severest penalty for women who mutilated, dismembered, or violently treated their infants.[63] Sometimes a woman, such as Anna Bordot, actually admitted that she killed her infant. It was difficult to acquit someone who admitted the crime unless she pled temporary insanity; that plea, however, did not appear frequently until the 1880s.

Reasons for Infanticide

The search for individual motivation is complicated and marred by the problems of deducing motivations from behavior. If poverty and fear of shame led women to kill their newborns, why was infanticide so rare? Any assessment of the women's motives should distinguish between excuses provided to the jury to try to obtain an acquittal and women's real motives, uncovered only with the aid of women's trial testimony and informed speculation. An examination of the age, occupation, and marital status of the women accused of infanticide sheds some light on their motives.

Infanticide was a crime of the young, the isolated, and the poor. In the seventy-six cases of infanticide existing and available in the Paris archives of the Assize Courts between 1867 and 1891 all of those tried were the mothers; almost 90 percent were single, proportionately more than had delivered their babies at any of the public hospitals in Paris. One-third had come to Paris pregnant. For only about half of the women brought to trial was this their first pregnancy. Two-thirds of the women tried for infanticide were domestic servants. Domestic servants were poor, isolated, and could not keep both an infant and their jobs.[64] Still, most domestic servants who became pregnant did not kill their infants. What motivated the few to do so?

In almost all cases the women gave birth by themselves, alone in their rooms, without the knowledge or support of family, friends, lovers, employers, or landlords. Homes for unwed mothers were nonexistent until the 1890s and many women could not afford to pay a midwife or become a boarder at one of the maisons d'accouchement. They had to try to keep their jobs, especially if they were domestic servants, because their jobs also supplied their food and lodging. If a woman could time things right, she could work up to the onset of labor pains and then go to a free hospital to deliver the baby. After staying the required week in the hospital she could then abandon the infant at the foundling home and try to find a new job since her former employer probably would not take her back. It was not easy, however, for a poor isolated domestic servant to get to a public hospital while in labor. Many lived and worked far from a hospital. Furthermore, many of the women who were tried for infanticide had been in Paris less than the one year required for hospital admission or were not in "peril of immediate delivery." For example, Esther Dupont claimed that she never intended to kill her baby. She had gone to the hospital but they told her that she had not been in Paris long enough to be admitted. When refused admission she "lost [her] head."[65]

Marie Blanchard knew the hospital's admissions procedures quite well. Before setting out for the hospital she had tried to see a doctor to obtain a certificate that she was at term. She tried two neighborhood doctors, neither of whom was available. She waited until she was in active labor before going to the hospital, but she waited too long. After several hours of contractions she got up to go to the hospital but the baby arrived unexpectedly. She claimed that she then lost her head and suffocated her infant; she did not know what else to do.[66]

Even some women who used public assistance for childbirth killed their babies. Marie Bresselle and Marie Chebeault, both nineteen-year-old domestic servants, went to la Maternité. They were taken from there to a nearby welfare midwife. Both mothers and their newborn girls stayed the required week and nursed their babies with difficulty. When each woman left the midwife, instead of giving her baby to a wetnurse and going back to work, as she had promised, Bresselle went to the canal and threw her infant into the water and Chebeault threw her infant into the Seine. Both testified that they had intended to drown themselves as well.[67]

Bresselle and Chebeault may not have known about Public Assistance's program of money to pay a wetnurse, or of any programs of aid to unwed mothers to encourage them to keep their babies. As domestic servants, without hope of any other type of job, keeping a baby was impossible. They simply could not afford the Fr 15–25 per month that even the least expensive wetnurses charged. Moreover, they may have heard stories about being denied aid. These poor women saw themselves in a hopeless position. How much easier, the women may have thought, just to dispose of the problem.

Infanticide may have been an act of desperate self-defense in a male-dominated society where many women had low status, low self-esteem, and few options and where they tended to be economically vulnerable. For those who suffocated their infants as soon as they were born it may have been a deliberate form of delayed abortion. For many others the onset of labor could have brought about the final realization that they were about to have a baby, something they had been denying to themselves and others. They acted in the confusion of the moment, with improvised behavior in response to the events rather than with careful plans.

The sanctity of the infant's life may not have been important to the mother who was struggling to survive, with limited options and possibilities. One said that she destroyed her infant, "a being incapable of sensing the loss of life," in order to avoid subjecting herself and her unfortunate child to shame and misery.[68] Such a choice is hardly specific to nineteenth-century Paris. Famine, poverty, and hopelessness have led people everywhere to put their survival above that of their children.[69]

Fear of dishonor might have led many single women to hide the pregnancy. Then, the fear that the out-of-wedlock child would bring dishonor to herself and her family might have led several women to commit infanticide. Having already been abandoned by their lovers, women may have feared abandonment by their families, by society, and by their employers if they did not conceal the pregnancy and the baby. Ironically, a criminal act became the moral safeguard of a woman's honor and that of her family.[70] After arrest some women appealed to the juge d'instruction to pardon "this poor unhappy person" [speaking of herself] because their conviction would bring great hardship, dishonor, and unhappiness on their family. So pleaded Anna Bordot, who left her provincial home for Paris to save her family's honor when she realized that she was pregnant.[71]

It was not only a first pregnancy which would lead to dishonor. Henriette Setier, a twenty-two-year-old domestic servant first became pregnant at the age of twenty in her hometown in the Indre by a man who soon married another; her mother raised the little girl. Setier came to Paris, supposedly as a wetnurse, to earn more money. She sent her mother half of her monthly wages of Fr 20. While in Paris she had a relationship with a forty-year-old man who never promised to marry her but had agreed to help raise the child. Instead, he left her for another. She said that she hid the pregnancy and childbirth because she was ashamed.[72]

In many court cases, the women tearfully claimed that their families would tolerate and help support a first out-of-wedlock child, born of a mistake, but to err again and have a second child was an unbearable shame and economic burden. Women scrimped and saved enough money to send about Fr 20 a month back to a relative in the country who took care of their first child, but they could not afford to pay the expenses of a second. Twenty-six-year-old Félicité Nauget had her first child when she was only twenty and immediately came to Paris as a wetnurse for a bourgeois family. She had been sending between Fr 20 and Fr 30 a month to her aunt who had been caring for her son, and she had frequently visited them and brought him clothes. She testified: "I gave in to an evil thought. I did not dare tell my parents that I had a new infant, and I had no more aunts in my home town."[73]

Women who killed their neonates claimed to have been filled with shame, guilt, and confusion. They may have been unable to deal with the problems that recognizing a pregnancy and caring for an infant posed. They often may have psychologically denied the pregnancy throughout the entire gestation and may have repressed what they did during the delivery and killing of the child. Women may have been telling the truth when they said that they did not remember the delivery and what happened afterward.[74] Their actions could be diagnosed as exhaustive psychosis, postpartum depression, or post-traumatic shock syndrome. Some women who killed their babies may really have been pathologically criminal, impulsive, hostile, and evil, with no sense of moral values. Some rid themselves of an infant because they could not stand to hear it cry, or for another pathological reason; others beat and starved their infant for no apparent reason at all.[75]

Abandonment

For a woman who killed her infant, either child abandonment was not a considered option or she thought such an act would be impossible. From the mid 1860s to mid 1880s, regulations governing child abandonment became restrictive and anonymous child abandonment became virtually impossible. These regulations may have deterred some women, or the women may have thought that killing the baby was better than subjecting the child to a lifetime as an abandoned child under the tutelage of Public Assistance. Isabelle Caze, who committed infanticide, and Constance Fauquet, who had an abortion, preferred to risk criminal prosecution rather than subject a child to a lifetime of misery as an abandoned child.[76]

To many mothers and to society in general, child abandonment was an alternative strategy to abortion or infanticide. Much social policy concerning child abandonment was designed to prevent these crimes. Even during the July Monarchy, many critics of public programs supporting the free foundling homes and their *tours* (those turnstiles in the foundling home permitting anonymous infant abandonment) grudgingly admitted that child abandonment was a necessary evil in protecting infant lives and preventing a worse evil—infanticide of legitimate children.[77] Defenders of the *tours* and of child abandonment argued that when foundling homes were closed, infanticide went up and, in effect, it was better to find an infant alive in a *tour* than dead in a ditch.[78]

In 1846, François Vidal, a Fourier socialist, stated:

> The [*tours*] have been closed and the poor mother, the working-class girl, has been left no other option than abortion or infanticide. In our bleak society many mothers have cursed their fecundity, and more than one, in thinking of the future which awaits her newborn child, has broken its head on the cobbles or strangled it with maternal hands in order to *deliver it from life,* to spare it misery, suffering, to save it from prostitution. Happy those children of the working-class who die in the cradle![79]

With the intention of saving infant lives, from the 1860s to the end of the century doctors such as Ambroise Tardieu, André-Théodore Brochard, and Gaston Variot continued the argument that infanticide rates rose wherever and whenever the *tours* were closed. Without the possibility of open and secret abandonment, they contended, the number of abortions and infanticides was immense and growing, thereby contributing enormously to the depopulation of France. Without a *tour* or another system of incognito abandonment, a woman had to go to the foundling home with her baby and provide information about herself and her infant at the admissions office. Many mothers, especially domestic servants, may have been afraid to enter that huge, somewhat forbidding foundling institution with its numerous corridors and personnel. These pathetic women who wanted to keep their pregnancy and childbirth a secret either committed infanticide or abandoned their babies to death on the roads or in obscure places rather than submit to the interrogation that surrounded child abandonment.[80] According to Brochard, the *tours* not only would decrease the number of infanticides, but they would also decrease the acquittal rate. If women had the option of anonymously abandoning their infant to save their honor, those who killed their infants for the same motive would be less leniently treated by the juries.[81]

Some ardent populationists opposed the *tours* and sought other means to reduce the infanticides. They proposed the opening of offices in each hospital where a mother could bring her baby and abandon it with total anonymity. They also insisted that women should be admitted to la Maternité under a veil of secrecy if they so wished.[82] In essence, however, their argument resembled that of the proponents of the *tours*.

Giving a baby up for adoption was not a legal option for the poor and pregnant in nineteenth-century France. People did, however, try illegal adoption. For example, one morning a nurse from la Maternité accompanied a mother and her newborn to Enfants Assistés, the foundling home where the mother was going to abandon her baby. They met an elegantly dressed couple who proposed that the mother give her baby to them for adoption, in return for a payment to the mother and to the nurse. When the mother refused, they said that they would wait for another mother coming from la Maternité who might be more amenable to their proposition.[83] How many times people offered to purchase a baby from the new mothers who walked out of la Maternité is unknown.

The only legal options available to a mother of a newborn were abandoning the baby at a foundling home, sending the infant to a wetnurse, or keeping the child. Mothers for whom keeping their infant was an impossibility frequently chose to abandon their baby at the state-supported foundling home in the major city of their area. Leaving a baby on a doorstep or in an alley was a crime drawing a heavy punishment. Women rarely chose this alternative, and police and priests brought those babies left on streets or in churches to the foundling home.

Abandonment of an infant at the foundling home was a free and socially approved strategy of survival for mothers during most of the century. In Paris in the 1830s, 45 percent of all illegitimate children born in the department of the Seine were abandoned at the Hospice des Enfants Assistés—the only state-run founding home and legal depository for abandoned children in that department. It was conveniently located around the corner and across the street from la Maternité. Starting around midcentury, however, proportionately fewer women abandoned their children. The trend reversed in the 1880s, but the rate of abandonment of legitimate and illegitimate children never returned to its pre–1852 high. Why did women change their strategy of coping with their newborn infants? What were the political, economic, and demographic factors affecting child abandonment?[84]

Legislative changes affected women's decisions to abandon their infants, including regulations restricting abandonment and programs of aid to unwed mothers to prevent it. As a result of hospital regulations, the percentage of women who abandoned their babies directly from la Maternité to the Hospice des Enfants Assistés fell precipitously from an average of 73 percent in the years from 1830 to 1834 to 47 percent in 1838.[85] Then, in 1852 a regulation effectively curtailed child abandonment *directly* from la Maternité and limited it to those women who were close to death or died soon after delivery. As a result, the percentage of mothers who left la Maternité with their babies, and whom the authorities (sometimes erroneously) believed kept their babies, almost doubled to about 90 percent after the 1852 regulation. Furthermore, from midcentury to the mid-1880s, foundling home authorities made anonymous abandonment almost impossible by requiring that the mother supply a birth certificate for her baby before abandoning it. Although the *tour* remained open until 1862, starting in 1852 it operated only during the night, and a watchman (often a policeman) was posted there. At any other times the mother had to go to the admissions office.[86] At first glance it appears that public policy changes, which effectively were implemented in July 1852, forced more women to keep their babies.

What is apparent is not always real. In many cases, the mother left la Maternité with her baby, and the hospital records indicate that she kept the baby, but the records of the Hospice des Enfants Assistés indicate that many of these mothers abandoned their babies after departure from the hospital (usually within a day). The percentage of mothers who left la Maternité with their babies but who later abandoned them at the Hospice des Enfants Assistés multiplied more than fifteen times from 1830 to 1869—from 2 percent in the 1830s to 31 percent in 1869. Thus, the overall rate of child abandonment to the Hospice des Enfants Assistés decreased from the mid 1850s to the mid 1880s; only the proportion of mothers who abandoned their children days, weeks, or even months after they left la Maternité increased in relation to women who abandoned their babies directly from la Maternité. Public policy did affect women's abandonment strategies. More mothers kept their babies; others merely delayed abandonment or struggled along.[87]

To abandon her child legally in Paris from the closing of the *tours* in 1862 to the establishment of open and secret admissions in 1886, a mother had to complete numerous forms and provide her name and a birth certificate for the baby. This might have deterred many from abandonment and led them to infanticide or child murder instead. When Ernestine Pallet tried to abandon her son in 1880 she had to answer a multitude of questions and supply a birth certificate.

Starting in 1886, programs to prevent abandonment became significantly less restrictive. Departmental policy still tried to prevent abandonment, but legislators and officials developed a more positive approach and offered aid to women to keep their babies. In keeping with the expressed concern for the welfare of the mothers and children, authorities eased admission to the foundling home: they eliminated a birth certificate as a prerequisite for abandonment.

Despite the relatively unrestricted child abandonment practices that emerged late in the century, an "ogre" at the admissions office, such as the one Mme Barré met, could make abandonment difficult. A journalist reported the story of Mme Barré, who approached an admissions officer at the Hospice des Enfants Assistés in 1899 saying, "Monsieur, I wish to entrust my infant to you because he is going to die of hunger." He responded, "You abandon him! Another one without any heart! You have no shame!" To that she replied, "Monsieur, I do not want to abandon him. I beg you, save him. . . . Give him something to eat just until the time when I can do so myself." Her son was admitted, whisked away, and joined the ranks of abandoned children. Mme Barré left in tears. According to the rules, only once every three months could she receive word about whether or not her abandoned son lived. She could never see him. When ten months had passed and Mme Barré had a job and earned her living, she rushed to the offices of Public Assistance to reclaim him and was told, "That is not in the regulations." The official told her to write to the director of Public Assistance. She wrote and received no response. She wrote again two weeks later and even enclosed a stamp. Still no response. She wrote a third time, again without a response. Finally she went to the editorial offices of a newspaper which later published her story under the title "L'Assistance Ogresse."[88]

For some women, policy changes and harsh bureaucrats made matters more inconvenient and decidedly unpleasant, but they had no alternative to abandonment. Abandoning their infants was a difficult and painful decision for many. Barré may have thought she was giving her baby to Public Assistance for the ten months of wetnursing and so had not

Fig. 11.   Jean Geoffroy, *At the Hospice des Enfants Assistés*. The abandonment of an infant. From *L'illustration,* 1882. Reproduction courtesy of Centre de l'Image de l'Assistance publique.

10728

intended to abandon him. Other women who abandoned their infants left notes pinned onto their infant's clothing indicated that they could not at the present time keep their baby but hoped to reclaim him or her. Some mothers put ribbons, bracelets, or half a medal around their baby's wrist or neck so that they could later identify and reclaim their child. In principle, women could get their babies back if they had a job and could repay Public Assistance for the money the agency had paid the wetnurse. It would also help her petition to reclaim her child if she was married, preferably to the father of the child.

Public welfare programs had little obvious effect on the abandonment rate. During midcentury, the programs of aid to prevent abandonment applied to few women, and the amount of aid was too small and of too short duration to change most women's behavior. The effects of public aid in preventing abandonment after 1880 are uncertain because at the same time that the government implemented programs of welfare enabling some women to keep their babies, the foundling home eased restrictions on abandonment. Although the rate of abandonment increased somewhat, scarcely any mothers who received welfare abandoned their children within a year after birth.[89]

The demographic profiles of the mothers themselves provide some clues about why some women decided to abandon their newborn. The mother's age and the baby's sex were not related to a woman's decision to abandon her infant. Marital status is a strong indicator, however; single women abandoned their babies twice as frequently as married women at the beginning of the century and almost five times as often at the end. Decreasing percentages of married women who had given birth at la Maternité abandoned their babies: from 36 percent in 1837 to zero in 1869. Single women giving birth at la Maternité abandoned their babies in far higher percentages, decreasing from 68 percent in 1837 to 42 percent in 1869. This pattern contrasts with the poignant picture of eighteenth-century France painted by Olwen Hufton and with the histories of Madrid, Milan, and Moscow in the eighteenth and nineteenth centuries, in which destitute married women did abandon their babies.[90]

What caused the decline in child abandonment by married women? It is possible that in the nineteenth century children became more important in two-parent families. Whether this was because of an increase in affection or an increase in the economic value of the children is difficult to say. It is also possible that the acute poverty of the eighteenth century that may have led married women to abandon their babies declined in the nineteenth. Possibly, by the later decades of the nineteenth century more married women had recourse to contraception and abortion and therefore had fewer unwanted children. Furthermore, charities designed for married women helped them raise the ones they had. A more likely explanation for married women keeping their babies are the regulations that made it much more difficult for married women to abandon them. Also, they could not easily reclaim their children, as could women in Madrid and Milan, and therefore they were unlikely to use child abandonment as a temporary survival strategy in times of crisis.

Conditions of employment, as much as poverty per se, interfered with single and married women's ability to keep their children. Domestic servants abandoned their babies with greater frequency than did women in other occupations. From 1830 to 1869, more than 50 percent of the domestic servants abandoned their babies compared with 40 percent of seamstresses and laundresses. Even correcting for the overwhelmingly high correlation between domestic service and single marital status, domestic servants were still the most inclined to abandon their babies, and laundresses were more apt to keep theirs. The reason seems simple: domestic servants could not keep their jobs and their babies. Laundresses had a community of similar workers and could keep their children around. Moreover, laundresses usually earned higher wages than did seamstresses or day-laborers. They also had a shorter and less severe period of seasonal unemployment than other female workers (including domestic servants) in Paris; during July and August, the customary months of unemployment, some laundresses may have continued to work in hotels for the already existing tourist trade. If better-paid workers with less seasonal unemployment were more likely to keep their babies, then poverty played an important role in a woman's decision to abandon her child.

Certain economic variables correlated with child abandonment. Until 1886, the wages of domestic servants correlated consistently with abandonment rates: as they rose, the rate of abandonment declined. During the first half of the century, which included the agricultural crisis of the 1840s, the price of grain and potatoes in the department of the Seine and the price of bread in Paris did not have significant effects on the rate of abandonment. However, from 1853 to 1885 (including the years of economic crisis 1853–55), the price of bread was a strong indicator of abandonment. For the period from 1886 to 1900, no economic causes of child abandonment stand out. Throughout the entire century, despite the various correlations with economic indices, conditions of employment, and female poverty, the rate of illegitimacy consistently was the best predictor of child abandonment.[91]

In initial efforts to decrease the numbers of abandoned babies, authors of public policy believed that an extended stay in the hospital would increase the chances of mothers keeping their babies, and in effect it did. From 1830 to 1869, fewer than one-third of the mothers who stayed in the hospital over eight days abandoned their infants, whereas one half of those who stayed under eight days did so. Length of stay in the hospital was not associated with age, occupation, or marital status of the mother. Reformers were correct in assuming that if women and their babies stayed in the hospital together for a week the likelihood of child abandonment would be reduced. Yet those women who stayed longer may already have been inclined to keep their babies and simply needed the encouragement. Those who left early may have been those who were determined, for whatever reason, to leave the hospital as soon as they could in order to abandon their infants and go back to work.

The years 1886 to 1900 were ones of change in public programs and policies. On the one hand, the elimination of the birth-certificate requirement for abandonment (in effect since the 1850s) made it easier for some mothers to leave their babies. On the other hand, public programs during the last decades of the century helped other mothers to keep their babies. The establishment of municipal day care centers (crèches) that accepted illegitimate children, important programs of aid to unwed mothers, free medical aid to the poor, and other regulations and legislation enacted during the Third Republic made it easier for women to care for their babies. Not all women were to benefit from the public welfare; some such as Ernestine Pallet were not offered aid. Desperate isolated women continued to take desperate measures. Nevertheless, public policy, by the establishment of the welfare programs, did influence women's choices by increasing the number of available options.

Conclusion

Changes in the religious and political convictions of French society profoundly affected the lives of poor women because these changes promoted and shaped the development of charity and welfare programs. During the first three-quarters of the nineteenth century, charity differed from welfare in rationale, in sources of funding, and in attitudes toward single women. Private charities, almost all under religious auspices, dominated. Impelled by the perception of the unwed mother as immoral and by the desire to encourage religious values, most charities focused on helping married women, or those who would marry, though some aid was granted to unmarried pregnant young women and new mothers in the hope of redeeming them. Until the 1870s charitable organizations saw themselves as defenders of the conservative trinity: family, property, and religion. During the 1870s, although charities continued to select their recipients and control their resources, the major charities operated with public subsidies as public utilities, with some government regulation.

During the Third Republic, saving infant lives was of such primary importance that leading administrators worked to combine public and private efforts to achieve that goal. Once philanthropists had started programs, the national and local governments often gave subventions. By 1900, public welfare came to dominate assistance programs to mothers and infants, but private charity helped to implement them. Private charity and public welfare initiatives sought to save infant lives in order to preserve the future of France; and they wanted to mold that future according to modern views of health and hygiene and less according to views of morality that had so preoccupied aid programs in the past.

Charity and welfare during the Third Republic continued to emphasize maternal love and maternal feeding, but less in the name of God and the religious sanctity of the family, and more in the name of decreasing infant mortality and promoting republican ideals. The depopulation issue engendered new attitudes toward women, poverty, crime, and morality, and led to philanthropic and public efforts to aid illegitimate children (and indirectly their mothers) during the Third Republic. The crucial difference between charity and welfare was the more maternal or paternal nature of charity versus the more rational, bureaucratic nature of welfare based on a person's rights and the nation's duties. By the twentieth century state paternalism had displaced bourgeois maternalism. State welfare took some of the personal, sometimes whimsical, nature out of charity and made assistance more impersonal, and perhaps more available.

The concept of social reform was a concept of "reform from above" based on the idea of the social responsibility of the middle class, on the idea of humanity and solidarity, and on the legislative and administrative power of the government and its bureaucracies. Underlying the middle-class concept of humanity and solidarity were assumptions about class and gender. Relatively rich men designed and implemented programs for poor women that they believed were in the best interest of their children. They created a "welfare patriarchy" which replaced the patriarch of a family—the absent, inadequate, or incapacitated father of the child. Charity and welfare policies that had been based on the idea that female-headed households would promote immorality and irresponsibility were eclipsed by the idea that single female-headed households were a necessary evil to beget children as long as such households were supervised. By the end of the century the ideal couple could consist of the mother and child, and not just a huband and wife.

Many women slipped through the gaping holes in the welfare net of nineteenth-century France. A few delivered their babies all by themselves in their rooms and were accused of infanticide if the baby died. They were the ones who lived alone, without support networks. For them, isolation and lack of information was pernicious. Public assistance denied welfare to tens of thousands of other women annually; others received too little and for too short a period to ensure their relative well-being. They had to manage, and an unknown number relied on family and friends.

Since there was never sufficient assistance for all, there may have been competition for welfare and some women may have refused to share information. Still, the evidence suggests relations of mutual support among women in securing what they could from the authorities, or helping one another with child care. If a midwife or hospital authority failed to inform a needy mother about public assistance for maternal nursing, the monthly rounds of the dames visiteuses were hardly a neighborhood secret. A pregnant seamstress undoubtedly noticed when her neighbor received assistance and visits. She had only to ask for details. Women chatted about "giving the baby to Enfants Assistés for the ten months." Ernestine Pallet, whose story opened this book, knew enough to make the trip to the offices of Public Assistance, or at least to allege that she had. Reports from Lille and Mulhouse in the 1830s testify that women brought their infants to the mills with them and cooperated in hiring someone to watch the babies in a corner of their workplace.[1] There is little reason to believe that women behaved differently in Paris than in other cities. When Parisian legislators at the turn of the century advocated the establishment of day-care facilities in industries employing large numbers of women, they may have been acknowledging women's practice of bringing their babies with them to work. Reports from Public Assistance's inspectors indicate that women who worked outside the home often gave their babies to willing neighbors to watch.[2] Working women who relied on family and neighborhood to help them care for their children were not abdicating their responsibilities as mothers; they were trying to live up to them.

The father of the child was usually absent from poor women's support systems. Some men doubtless supported their out-of-wedlock child but are absent from the historical record because the combined family income would have excluded the women and children from charity or welfare aid, and thus the records of these programs. Even if the father's support was so small that aid could be granted, administrative records failed to note the unwed father's contribution. Ironically, fathers appear in the administrative records only when Public Assistance recorded that their support for their child disqualified that child for welfare. Florence LeLong's brief statement at the infanticide trial of her cousin is one of the few pieces of direct evidence of a father supporting his out-of-wedlock child. LeLong testified that "my cousin was pushed by despair because her lover abandoned her while mine surrounds me with care and helps me raise my child."[3] Such stories reveal the wide range of family relations.

Poor mothers had to struggle to find ways to survive, especially if they were single. Even with support from family and friends, it was difficult for them to gain control over their lives. Powerful politicians and doctors tended to view them as pathological captives of their bodies—especially in terms of sexuality and childbirth—and sought to regulate their behavior by restricting access to contraception, abortion, and child abandonment options. Nevertheless, the most critical danger facing female-headed households was poverty, and the French government began to do something about that through welfare programs designed to aid the children.

Nobody likes welfare, neither those who pay for it, those who administer it, nor those who depend on it for survival. Yet, public policy in late nineteenth-century France attempted to address a social problem of enormous magnitude, poor women and their children, in a comprehensive way. As social problems became increasingly severe, as urban unrest and homelessness escalated, attitudes toward single mothers and their children born out of wedlock changed. Reluctant as legislators were to admit not only that the poor were a permanent aspect of the economy but also that they would increase and multiply without the aid or approval of Church or State, they turned their attention from moralistic warnings to practical action. Some legislators were moved by humanitarian concern with the welfare of innocent children, no less needy for being born out of wedlock; but what inspired them, above all, was a pervasive sense of national crisis. Concerned by the threat of depopulation and racial degeneration, dismayed by the relatively weak position of France vis-à-vis its international competitors, the legislators decided to help children by aiding their mothers. Welfare they would rather not dispense, for doing so might only encourage laziness and vice. Instead they implemented a form of workfare. Manners and morals did not change, but a realistic concern with the state of the nation led legislators to realize that child assistance was paramount. Nationalism inspired legislators to provide aid, rather than sermons, for the poor and pregnant, not to please God, but to save France.

Different countries had different ways of dealing with similar problems. In England as in France, middle-class charity did not generally extend to all needy unwed mothers; rather, only those who could return to a respectable life could benefit from private charity. Charitable rescue homes aided worthy single mothers and their children. In England, local parish workhouses and rescue homes provided the only regularized assistance to poor single mothers and their infants, and many passed through the workhouse at some point. Some sought the workhouse because they needed shelter and help during childbirth. Others sought it because they needed temporary asylum. For married or unmarried women who had been deserted by the father of their child, the workhouse and parish relief offered some help. There was little home relief, such as aid for maternal breastfeeding, that would enable single mothers to live in their own surroundings. In England, as in France, a single mother with children was expected to work.[4]

The welfare programs that emerged in France around the turn of the century were not unique to France, even though the French government may have begun them sooner and granted them an unprecedented level of support. In Britain, Germany, and the United States, the charitable programs for poor women and children, often initiated by maternalistic middle-class women, laid the groundwork for public welfare policies. By 1914 most major western European countries and the United States had well-baby clinics and infant milk depots, and some had legislated maternity leaves. Russia had no paid maternity leaves but programs to encourage mothers to keep their babies appeared in Moscow in 1891. In an effort to deter child abandonment and limit expenses at the foundling home, Moscow authorities offered a "subsidy to the mothers for child care at their own residence until the baby reached one year of age." As in Paris, some objected that the "subsidy was a reward for fornication," and "proposed to limit participation to one time for any woman and thus avoid the possible emergence of unwed motherhood as a means of subsistence. . . . [But] members of the governing board were not concerned about the perception of the subsidy as a reward for sexual immorality, so long as the child benefited."[5] This program bore a remarkable resemblance to the one in Paris to encourage maternal nursing.

In nineteenth-century Paris, complicated requirements to qualify for charity or welfare impelled women to act in certain ways. Poverty made their lives so precarious that they had to know what help was available to them in order to survive, and they had to know how to work within the system. If they wanted to marry, they went to the Société Saint-François-Régis. If they were pregnant and wanted to marry, they received benefits from the Société de Charité Maternelle for help in crisis management during pregnancy and for a few months after birth. If they were married and had several children, their local bureau de bienfaisance could supply some assistance. If marriage was not a possibility, they had little recourse to charity or welfare until late in the century. They gave birth in la Maternité if they could not afford a midwife, many abandoned their infants, and a very few received a short-term payment to a wetnurse for their baby. After 1875, remaining single entitled mothers to the same, or more, relief than married women. Some found temporary shelter in institutions although these may have been places of profound squalor and misery. Many more single mothers received public welfare to enable them to keep their babies. A single mother's economic situation was so desperate that her survival often depended on the availability of charity or welfare.

In a small but important way, working-class mothers influenced the development of programs and manipulated the system to their benefit. To a limited extent, women could make choices and alter the actual way charity and welfare functioned by threatening to abandon their babies— a threat that may have forced the hand of welfare officials. By the end of the century, philanthropists and public assistance leaders recognized that single motherhood was an unfortunate but necessary fact of life for many in Paris. They no longer predicated maternity benefits upon marital status. Still, no activity of the mothers would have succeeded without the nationalistic and humanitarian desire to prevent depopulation and save babies' lives. By 1900, the preoccupation with saving infant lives was so great that charity and welfare officials accepted women's non-marital behavior patterns and accommodated their programs to the behavior of the mothers.

Even though their avowed goal was population growth and moralization of the poor, organized charity and welfare addressed real needs: marriage, help in childbirth, and financial aid in the months after the birth of a child. Women took advantage of whatever program was available to them. Neither charities nor welfare ever had enough money or facilities to meet the demand. However onerous and demeaning the task of applying for assistance and submitting to interrogation and inspection, many women managed to marry, to keep their babies, and to see them safely through infancy. Nonetheless, throughout the century and even considering the improvements, assistance was available to too few women, and it was too minimal to enable those few who received it to avoid a life of poverty.

Nineteenth-century charity and welfare was designed to imbue the working classes with bourgeois values, and this required that public officials, the bourgeoisie, and the state intrude into private lives. The moral and political agendas of politicians, philanthropists, and welfare officials took precedence over the rights and independence of poor women. Yet, Jacques Donzelot's view of middle-class intervention in the working-class family as a form of social control is a simplified picture of the nineteenth-century Parisian world.[6] Intervention by middle-class reformers and the state may have been designed to "moralize," and thereby control, a part of the population, but such intervention ultimately improved living conditions and saved people's lives. Many of the recipients tried to maximize charity and welfare to their advantage, and women were not always compelled to accept the aid nor to change behavior in order to receive it.

There was a tradeoff as far as women were concerned: an end to discrimination against poor women, especially if they were single, and a nominal entitlement to assistance, were gains accompanied by women's loss of freedom of choice in how to raise their children and a loss of individual liberty. The state became involved in attempting to control mothers' life styles, their living arrangements, their working situation, and their marital relationships. Though the state may have failed in this attempt, by the dawn of the twentieth century it had become an intimate companion in women's lives. In nineteenth-century France a contest raged between individual rights and social welfare reform. For women and children, social welfare reform prevailed—but sometimes so did the women.

Organized society requires a code of accepted behavior, allowing some deviation. According to most social reformers during the century, young women might engage in nonmarital sex, but only if they had a promise of marriage or had been seduced and abandoned. Living in a long-term consensual union received less social opprobrium than did having more than one sexual partner. If a single woman became pregnant, her family and much of society might forgive that first slip, but they would judge subsequent pregnancies more harshly. Judges and juries even ruled that infant murder—one of the most unacceptable forms of behavior in the twentieth century—could be tolerated under certain circumstances. Pressure to conform came from the policies of social reformers, legislative authorities, judges and juries, and frequently from the woman's own family. A poor pregnant woman's peer group, other poor working women in the city, exerted less pressure on her and at times could offer a network of support for options that violated bourgeois norms.

Everyone had opinions about women's proper moral behavior. Writers, politicians, and reformers of the first two-thirds of the century believed misery was the result of moral weakness, lack of religion, decline of family ties, and relaxation of personal hygiene—all because women failed their responsibilities. At the beginning of the century the greater goals were economic productivity, religious morality, and the sanctity of a nuclear family. Toward the end of the century the national mood had shifted; the new goals became national strength, secular social peace, and protection of the race and the children. Reformers and politicians, including leading physicians, believed that national economic and military weakness resulted from women's improper child-care practices; so principles of hygiene replaced those of religious morality. The poor and pregnant remained pawns in political and nationalistic games.

A single mother had the sole right and responsibility for her child. With new ideologies and welfare programs of the last decades of the nineteenth century, single mothers began to gain some resources at the expense of that unique control. Paul Strauss spoke for many mainstream politicians when he declared: "The child has rights over which the society is the responsible guardian; society has duties [to the child] and the liberty of the mothers themselves will not become an obstacle [to the fulfillment of those duties]."[7] Women had to struggle to maintain some control over their lives and their babies at a time when politicians considered the mothers unable to make wise decisions on their own. Women, they thought, needed to be corrected, reprimanded, and assisted by those who knew better than they—doctors, inspectors, and politicians.

The debates about the poor and pregnant, and the successes and failures of many of the programs in the nineteenth century, set the stage for the development of the welfare state in the twentieth century. Twentieth-century ideas such as the medicalization of maternity, the emphasis on social hygiene, prenatal and postnatal education of mothers, maternity leave policies, and subsidies to large families took root in the late nineteenth century.[8]

By the decade before the First World War, France was becoming what François Ewald accurately describes as the "provident state."[9] The French phrase "l'état providence," referring to the welfare state, indicates the secular appropriation of a religious term, and underscores the merging of private Christian charity ideals with secular public welfare goals, where the prior is subsumed under the latter. The secular, anticlerical French state assumed the paternalistic charity which had been the hallmark of Christianity. Welfare at the turn of the century was more rationalized and inclusive than the earlier Christian charity. Despite these changes, women continued to be victims of the economy, of male power, and of public attempts to control the autonomy of their private reproductive lives. Despite the hardships, and perhaps because of them, poor women were nonetheless instrumental in the reformulation of programs, even while their efforts were directed not at reforming institutions, but at their own survival.

Notes

Introduction

1. For a few examples of recent scholarship on this theme see the following: Elinor Accampo, *Industrialization, Family Life, and Class Relations: Saint Chamond, 1815–1914* (Berkeley: University of California Press, 1989); George Alter, *Family and the Female Life Course: The Women of Verviers, Belgium, 1849–1880* (Madison: University of Wisconsin Press, 1988); Lenard R. Berlanstein, *The Working People of Paris: 1871–1914* (Baltimore: Johns Hopkins University Press, 1984); Gay L. Gullickson, *Spinners and Weavers of Auffay: Rural Industry and Sexual Division of Labor in a French Village, 1750–1850,* (Cambridge: Cambridge University Press, 1986); Katherine A. Lynch, *Family, Class, and Ideology in Early Industrial France* (Madison: University of Wisconsin Press, 1988); Mary Lynn Stewart, *Women, Work, and the French State* (Montreal: McGill-Queens University Press, 1989). Many of us are indebted to the earlier pathbreaking works on this theme: for example, Theresa McBride, *The Domestic Revolution and the Modernization of Household Service in England and France, 1820–1920* (New York: Holmes and Meier, 1976); and Louise A. Tilly and Joan W. Scott, *Women, Work, and Family* (New York: Holt, Rinehart & Winston, 1978).

2. Joan W. Scott, *Gender and the Politics of History* (New York: Columbia University Press, 1988), chap 7, esp. 141–143, 154–158.

3. This chapter, in part, builds upon Bonnie Smith's insightful work on the department of the Nord; Bonnie G. Smith, *Ladies of the Leisure Class: The Bourgeoises of Northern France in the Nineteenth Century* (Princeton, N.J.: Princeton University Press, 1981).

4. For discussions of prostitution in France, and especially in Paris, see Alain Corbin, *Les filles de noce: Misère sexuelle et prostitution aux XIXe et XXe siècles* (Paris: Aubier Montaigne, 1978); and Jill Harsin, *Policing Prostitution in Nineteenth-Century Paris* (Princeton, N.J.: Princeton University Press, 1985).

5. Scott, *Gender and the Politics of History,* chap. 7.

6. Peter Laslett, "The Bastardy-Prone Sub-Society," in *Bastardy and Its Comparative History,* ed. Peter Laslett, Karla Oosterveen, and Richard M. Smith, 217–246 (Cambridge, Mass: Harvard University Press, 1980).

7. Michel Foucault, *Discipline and Punish: The Birth of the Prison,* trans. Alan Sheridan (New York: Pantheon, 1977); and Jacques Donzelot, *The Policing of Families,* trans. Robert Hurley (New York: Pantheon, 1979).

1. *The Poor and Pregnant*

1. Archives de la Ville de Paris et Département de la Seine, (ADS), Dossiers Cour d'Assises, D2 U8 (120) Dossier 27 September 1881. She lived on the rue de l'Orillon close to both the tenth and twentieth arrondissements. See also *Gazette des Tribunaux* (Paris) 28 September 1881. The confidentiality of the cases cited from the Cour d'Assises must be maintained, although in some instances, the women's names and circumstances were made public. Unless there had been press coverage of the trial, I have changed all names. For a detailed description of life in this working-class area of Paris see Gérard Jacquemet, *Belleville au XIXe siècle* (Paris: Editions de l'Ecole des Hautes Etudes en Sciences Sociales, 1984).

2. ADS V bis 6I³1 Certificates of morality, November 1846.

3. See for example, ADS, Dossiers Cour d'Assises, D2 U8 (51) Dossier 19 August 1876. Court cases are used here for their illustrative value. They are cases of abortion and infanticide brought before the Assize Courts. All court cases reveal selection by the police and the doctors. Even women's testimonies, ostensibly in their own words, are actually filtered through the records of others, such as court reporters. I attempted to identify and eliminate outright lies or strategies that women employed in an attempt to secure an acquittal or conviction with extenuating circumstances. The stories used are all corroborated by witnesses and letters. While the cases of infanticide and abortion brought before the courts do not present a broad picture of the poor and pregnant in Paris, without letters, memoirs, and autobiographies, they offer valuable glimpses into the lives of individual women. A careful reading of the interrogations, depositions, witness reports, character investigations, and letters that some of the women wrote to their parents or lover should correct for possible distortions in the documents themselves. Surnames are fictitious.

4. ADS, Dossiers Cour d'Assises, D2 U8 (37) Dossier 13 April 1875.

5. ADS, Dossiers Cour d'Assises, D2 U8 (75) Dossier 7 August 1878.

6. ADS, Dossiers Cour d'Assises, D2 U8 (21) Dossier 13 September 1873; (146) Dossier 22 May 1883; (169) Dossier 22 September 1884.

7. ADS, Dossiers Cour d'Assises, D2 U8 (88) Dossier 22 August 1879.

8. ADS, Dossiers Cour d'Assises, D2 U8 (114) Dossier 23 March 1881. For another example of maternal support see ADS D2 U8 (108) Dossier 8 December 1880.

9. ADS, Dossiers Cour d'Assises, D2 U8 (88) Dossier 4 August 1879.

10. ADS, Dossiers Cour d'Assises, D2 U8 (109) Dossier 28 April 1881; (192) Dossier 17 November 1885.

11. ADS, Dossiers Cour d'Assises, D2 U8 (32) Dossier 14 October 1874. For another example see D2 U8 (48) Dossier 20 May 1876.

12. For an example of a bourgeois family's attempt to conceal the out-of-wedlock pregnancy and birth see *Marthe* (Paris: Editions du Seuil, 1982).

13. ADS, Dossiers Cour d'Assises, D2 U8 (109) Dossier 7 January 1881. Her newborn had been dredged from the Seine and she was convicted of infanticide.

14. ADS, Dossiers Cour d'Assises, D2 U8 (53) Dossier 29 September 1876; ADS D2 U8 (4) Dossier 29 May 1867; ADS D2 U8 (166) Dossier 26 July 1884.

15. ADS, Dossiers Cour d'Assises, D2 U8 (128) Dossier 3 March 1882.

16. ADS, Dossiers Cour d'Assises, D2 U8 (137) Dossier 28 September 1882; (139) Dossier 9 November 1882. Not all the dossiers supplied the parents' marital status for women accused of infanticide or abortion.

17. Laslett, "The Bastardy-Prone Sub-Society," 217–246.

18. For several examples see ADS, Dossiers Cour d'Assises D2 U8 (5) Dossier 5 June 1867; (137) Dossier 28 September 1882; (37) Dossier 14 April 1875; (55) Dossier 13 December 1876; (139) Dossier 9 November 1882.

19. Administration générale de l'Assistance publique, *Statistique médicale des hôpitaux de Paris*, 4 vols. (Paris, 1867), 2:275, 3:471, 4:295. Data on the women's housing exist only for 1862–1864.

20. Theresa McBride, *The Domestic Revolution: The Modernization of Household Service in England and France, 1820–1920*, (New York: Holmes & Meier, 1976), chaps. 3 and 6; Anne Martin-Fugier, *La place des bonnes: La domesticité féminine en 1900* (Paris: Grasset, 1979), 125–147, 287–328; and John R. Gillis, "Servants, Sexual Relations, and the Risks of Illegitimacy in London, 1801–1900," *Feminist Studies* 5 (1979):142–173. Anna Clark details the vulnerability of domestic servants in *Women's Silence, Men's Violence: Sexual Assault in England, 1770–1845* (London: Pandora Press, 1987), 28, 90–109.

21. The picture provided by Cissie Fairchilds for the eighteenth century remained prevalent in nineteenth-century Paris. Cissie Fairchilds, "Female Sexual Attitudes and the Rise of Illegitimacy: A Case Study," *Journal of Interdisciplinary History* 8 (Spring 1978): 627–667. ADS, Dossiers Cour d'Assises, D2 U8 (189) Dossier 4 September 1885 (case of employer seducing his domestic).

22. ADS, Dossiers Cour d'Assises, D2 U8 (192) Dossier 17 November 1885; (146) Dossier 22 May 1883; (153) Dossier 23 October 1883; (139) Dossier 10 November 1882; (48) Dossier 9 June 1876.

23. See, for example, ADS, Dossiers Cour d'Assises, D2 U8 (47) Dossier 10 May 1876.

24. Michel Frey, "Du mariage et du concubinage dans les classes populaires à Paris (1846–1847)," *Annales: Economies, sociétés, civilisations* 33 (1978): 803–829, esp. 817; Othenin d'Haussonville, *Salaires et misères de femmes* (Paris, 1900), 14–36; Maria Vérone in *La Fronde,* 14 January 1903.

25. Frey, "Du mariage et du concubinage," 829. Emphasis in the original.

26. Emile Levasseur, *La population française*, 3 vols. (Paris, 1889–1892), 2:34; quote is from Adna Weber, *The Growth of Cities in the Nineteenth Century* (rpt., Ithaca, N.Y.: Cornell University Press, 1965), 405. The actual estimated percentages of consensual unions varied between 27 and 33 percent.

27. For further discussion of the vulnerability of female migrants in Paris, see Rachel G. Fuchs and Leslie Page Moch, "Pregnant, Single, and Far From Home: Migrant Women in the Metropolis," *American Historical Review* 95 (1990):1007–1031. Hospital records and most other sources are silent on whether women lived in consensual unions, noting only if they were married. Sometimes hospital doctors assisted in marriage *in extremis* of a woman in a consensual union if a woman died, and they facilitated the marriage of terminally ill postpartum women to legitimize the child. See Archives de l'Assistance Publique (AAP), l'Hôpital Port-

Royal, Registres des correspondances, 31 January 1881; 12 March 1885; 28 December 1892, and 7 November 1894.

28. Data on where migrant women stayed between their arrival in Paris and delivery is based on information for the 563 women who delivered in Paris less than one year after arrival in 1894 and 1895 and who were offered a free trip back home to their native department. Administration générale de l'Assistance publique à Paris, Service des Enfants assistés de la Seine, *Rapport présenté par le directeur de l'Administration générale de l'Assistance publique à M. le Préfet de la Seine* (Montevrain, 1877–1904), 1894:23–24; 1895:3–4.

29. Alain Corbin, *Les Filles de noce: Misère sexuelle et prostitution aux XIXe et XXe siècles* (Paris: Aubier Montaigne, 1978), 75–76, 109; ADS, Dossiers Cour D'Assises, D2 U8 cases of "Détournement d'une mineur" and infanticide 1867–1889; D2 U8 (62) Dossier 3 July 1877; (48) Dossier 20 June 1876; (55) Dossier 11 December 1876; Martin-Fugier, *La place des bonnes,* 43–101.

30. ADS, Dossiers Cour d'Assises, D2 U8 (37) Dossier 13 April 1875.

31. Administration générale de l'Assistance publique à Paris, *Rapport,* 1888: 15–16; 1889:41; 1892:6–8; 1893:27–28; 1894:22–24; 1895:2–4.

32. Only one in twenty women arrived in Paris so late in her pregnancy that she went directly to the hospital to deliver. AAP, l'Hôpital Port-Royal, Registres des femmes en couches envoyées chez les sage-femmes, 1869–1880. Data are based on a random sample of 300 women sent to a welfare midwife for the years 1869 through 1880. These are the only years in which records exist for the length of stay in Paris prior to childbirth. See also Levasseur, *La population française,* 2:34.

33. Administration générale de l'Assistance publique à Paris, *Rapport,* 1888: 15–16; 1889:41; 1892:6–8; 1893:27–28; 1894:22–24; 1895:2–4.

34. To reconstruct the population of the hospital la Maternité, a random sample was collected of approximately 100 women per year from those admitted to that hospital for the following years: 1837, 1838, 1840, 1852, 1855, 1860, 1869, 1875, 1880, 1885, 1890, 1895, and 1900. The years 1837, 1838, and 1852 were selected to pinpoint the effects of legislative changes and public policy on women's strategies. The year 1869 was chosen instead of 1870 because the data for 1870 (a war year) were incomplete. A smaller sample of fifty women admitted during the years 1830, 1847, and 1848 was gathered to see the effects of political and economic crises.

35. Préfecture de la Seine, Service de la statistique municipale, *Annuaire statistique de la ville de Paris* (Paris, 1880–1914), 1880:200; 1881:230; 1882:162; 1883:214; 1884:170. For a detailed analysis of demographic variables of women at la Maternité, and for statistical tables, see Rachel G. Fuchs and Paul E. Knepper, "Women in the Paris Maternity Hospital: Public Policy in the Nineteenth Century," *Social Science History* 13, no. 2 (Summer 1989): 187–209.

36. Administration générale de l'Assistance publique, *Statistique médicale des hôpitaux de Paris,* 4 vols. (Paris, 1867), 2:278, 3:475, 4:299. *Annuaire statistique de la ville de Paris,* 1880:200; 1881:230; 1882:162; 1883:214; 1884:170. These are the only years for which such data are available. In 1880 most multiparous women delivering in la Maternité were between the ages of twenty-two and

twenty-nine, while most of those there for their first baby were between nineteen and twenty-five. In 1860 la Maternité's records noted all the women who came with their older children because they were desperate and had no alternative place to leave those children during their confinement and no one to care for them. About half were married and over 60 percent worked as seamstresses, day laborers, and garment workers in various needle trades. On women with no place to leave their older children see AAP, l'Hôpital Port-Royal, Registres des correspondances, 7 May 1867, and Armand Husson, *Etude sur les hôpitaux* (Paris, 1862), 137.

37. Only 2 percent of the total had been widows. See Fuchs and Knepper, "Women in the Paris Maternity Hospital," 195, table 5. A survey conducted in 1862 revealed that half the married women admitted to la Maternité that year had been abandoned by their husbands or legally separated from them. Paul Delaunay, *La Maternité de Paris* (Paris, 1909), 121.

38. At the beginning of the nineteenth century almost 40 percent of all births in Paris and the surrounding area were illegitimate. By just after midcentury, that figure declined to approximately one-fourth of the total births, where it remained until the end of the century. The index for illegitimacy in nineteenth-century Paris is the percentage of illegitimate births of all live births. This figure, although imprecise, is the only computation possible because of the lack of accurate age-specific data on single women. See Etienne van de Walle, "Illegitimacy in France during the Nineteenth Century," in *Bastardy,* ed. Laslett, Oosterveen and Smith, 264–277; Levasseur, *La population française,* 2:400–401. The percentage of marriages in Paris and the department of the Seine did not increase at the end of the nineteenth century. The best data available are the number of marriages per year in Paris compared with the population of Paris. Data on the population and number of marriages in Paris come from: Bureau de la statistique générale, Statistique de la France, *Statistique annuelle,* 1871–1906; and the *Annuaire statistique de la ville de Paris* (Paris, 1899), 197 (Documents rétrospectifs). Etienne van de Walle, in *The Female Population of France in the Nineteenth Century: A Reconstruction of 82 Départements* (Princeton, N.J.: Princeton University Press, 1974), does not include the department of the Seine because the available data are of dubious accuracy.

39. Between 1870 and 1900, 23 percent of married women admitted to la Maternité were there for problems other than actual childbirth, compared with 15 percent of the single women, and 2 percent of the married women before 1870. These women needed medical or surgical care for problems such as miscarriage, ovarian and uterine growths or infections, metritis, perforations of the uterus, general pelvic inflammation, or complications of pregnancy. The likelihood of these women arriving as a result of botched abortions will be discussed in a subsequent chapter.

40. About one-third entered when they were six or seven months pregnant, when a pregnancy became increasingly difficult to hide. Another 16 percent entered in their eighth month. AAP, l'Hôpital Port-Royal, Registres des entrées, 1830, 1837, and 1838.

41. The mean number of hospital days before delivery for single women was

20.8; for married women it was 12.9. This is a statistically significant difference. On inducing labor in the hospital see AAP, Fosseyeux 707[2], "Rapport sur le Service de Santé de la Maison d'Accouchement [la Maternité] fait à M. Jourdan, Administrateur à MM Cruveilhier et Moreau, Médecins-en-chef et adjoint Paul Dubois, Professeur d'Accouchement et Alizat, Agent de Surveillance, par J. A. Frigerio, pharmacien, (1831), 37–38. This manuscript is unpaginated. On the needle work performed by women before delivery in the hospital in the early years of the century see Delaunay, *La Maternité de Paris*, 123.

42. The remainder were at least in their seventh month of pregnancy since the hospital authorities at that time admitted women starting in their seventh month if they were either in imminent danger of labor or else in extreme indigence and devoid of all means of existence outside the hospital. Delaunay, *La Maternité de Paris*, 117–118.

43. Statistical tests all indicate a significance at better than .01 that hospital stays before delivery were greater before 1870 than after. See Fuchs and Knepper, "Women in the Paris Maternity Hospital," 192, table 1. All data were derived from the random sample collected from AAP, l'Hôpital Port-Royal, Registres des entrées.

44. AAP, l'Hôpital Port-Royal, Registres des correspondances, 16 November 1857. Because names of hospital patients in Paris cannot be revealed within 150 years of admission, this patient has been assigned a pseudonym.

45. For further discussion of domestic servants see Fairchilds, "Female Sexual Attitudes and the Rise of Illegitimacy"; McBride, *The Domestic Revolution;* Martin-Fugier, *La place des bonnes;* Gillis, "Servants, Sexual Relations, and the Risks of Illegitimacy in London"; Ann R. Higginbotham, "The Unmarried Mother and Her Child in Victorian London," (Ph.D. diss., Indiana University, 1986).

46. Theresa McBride, "The Modernization of Women's Work," *Journal of Modern History* 49 (June 1977):231–245, esp. 242, and *The Domestic Revolution,* 103. Data from la Maternité reveal that of all domestic servants at that hospital, only 5 percent were married before 1870; that percentage doubled after 1870. The increase in the percentage of married domestic servants coincided with the increase in the percentage of domestic servants in the Parisian population who were married during the 1880s.

47. McBride, "The Modernization of Women's Work," 242, and *The Domestic Revolution,* 103. Of the *femmes de ménages,* or daily maids, in la Maternité, 75 percent were single, with no change in their marital status during the century.

48. Jules Simon, *L'ouvrière* (Paris, 1862), 227.

49. ADS, Dossiers Cour d'Assises, D2 U8 (83) Dossier 24 March 1879.

50. Fuchs and Knepper, "Women in the Paris Maternity Hospital," 194, table 4.

51. Ménagères were likely to have been married, or in long-term consensual unions. These probably were women who stayed home after the birth of their first or second children. For a discussion of ménagères and the life styles of bourgeois women see Marguerite Perrot, *Le mode de vie des familles bourgeoises* (Paris: Presses de la Fondation nationale des Sciences politiques, 1982),

79; Yvonne Knibiehler and Catherine Fouquet, *Histoire des mères* (Paris: Editions Montalba, 1977), 236–241.

52. During the 1840s, the highest proportion of women in la Maternité had been born outside the department of the Seine: 89 percent of the total and 93 percent of the single mothers. Then at the end of the century the proportion born outside the department decreased from 81 percent of both married and single in the 1870s and 1880s to 75 percent of the total and 82 percent of single women in the decade of the 1890s.

53. Louis Chevalier, *La formation de la population parisienne au XIXe siècle* (Paris: Presses Universitaires de France, 1950), 285.

54. Fuchs and Moch, "Pregnant, Single and Far From Home." All data were computed from a series of cross-tabulations from AAP, l'Hôpital Port-Royal, Registres des entrées.

55. For details on l'Hôtel-Dieu, see AAP, Fosseyeux 151, Service d'Accouchement de l'Hôtel-Dieu. Notes relatives au service des accouchements de l'Hôtel-Dieu. No author. Handwritten manuscript dated November 16, 1853. The number of women seeking admission tripled between the average of 300 per year admitted before 1852 to an average of 900 per year between 1853 and 1862. From the late 1860s until the late 1880s the obstetrical service of this hospital was closed because of uncontrollable maternal mortality.

56. A sample of 400 women who delivered their babies at l'Hôtel-Dieu from the years 1850 through 1865 was taken to enable a generalization from the patients at la Maternité to the poor and pregnant of Paris. The number of deliveries at l'Hôtel-Dieu was 641 in 1850. It then doubled to 1,289 in 1853 and rose to almost 2,000 in the 1860s.

57. Of the over 7,000 women giving birth in the hospitals of Paris each year for the years 1861 to 1864, three-fourths were single, compared with 85 percent single in la Maternité alone. Administration générale de l'Assistance publique, *Statistique médicale des hôpitaux de Paris,* 1:90, 2:266, 3:400, 4:284. Of the 29,163 women giving birth in the hospitals of Paris from 1881–1885, 20,353, 70 percent, were single. *Annuaire statistique de la ville de Paris,* 1881:231; 1882:163; 1883:215; 1884:171; 1885:191.

58. Twenty-two percent were domestics, 37 percent were needle workers, and another 25 percent were day workers in diverse trades. Laundresses were another 10 percent. Administration générale de l'Assistance publique, *Statistique médicale des hôpitaux de Paris,* 1:94, 2:274.

59. Administration générale de l'Assistance publique, *Statistique médicale des hôpitaux de Paris,* 1:95, 2:276, 3:472, 4:296.

60. AAP, Fosseyeux 151, Service d'Accouchement de l'Hôtel-Dieu. Notes relatives au service des accouchements. Handwritten MSS, no author, dated November 16, 1853. Unpaginated. During times of overcrowding, such as between 1853 and 1865, hospital administrators placed maternity patients in the same rooms with sick women, and the babies in the same beds with their mothers.

61. AAP, Fosseyeux 151, Service d'Accouchement de l'Hôtel-Dieu.

62. Gabriel Ancelet, *Essai historique et critique sur la création et transformation des maternités à Paris,* Thèse pour le doctorat en Médecine (Paris, 1896),

11–33; Delaunay, *La Maternité de Paris,* 118, 157–170; Léon LeFort, *Des maternités: Etude sur les maternités et les institutions charitables et d'accouchement à
domicile dans les principaux états de l'Europe* (Paris, 1866), 51–53; Stéphane
Tarnier, *Memoire sur l'hygiène des hôpitaux de femmes en couches* (Paris, 1864),
3–4, 11; and *De la fièvre puerpérale observée à l'hospice de la Maternité* (Paris,
1858), 74–81.

63. AAP, l'Hôpital Port-Royal, Registres des femmes en couches envoyées
chez les sage-femmes, 1869–1900.

64. Adolphe Pinard, *Du fonctionnement de la maternité de Lariboisière et des
résultats obtenus depuis 1882 jusqu'en 1889* (Paris, 1889), 10–14; AAP, l'Hôpital
Port-Royal, Registres des correspondances. See, for example, 15 April 1880, 3
March 1882, 7 March 1895, and 8 May 1881 on the reputation of an abusive
midwife. If a woman's labor was progressing normally, it was a matter of chance
(and crowded conditions at la Maternité) which women were sent to welfare
midwives.

65. Corbin, *Les filles de noce,* 203.

66. Elizabeth A. Weston, "Prostitution in Paris in the Later Nineteenth Cen-
tury: A Study of Political and Social Ideology," Ph.D. diss., State University of
New York-Buffalo, 1979, 52–56; O. Commenge, *La prostitution clandestine à
Paris* (Paris, 1894, rev. ed. 1904), 1–108, 301–324, 332–356.

67. The only set of data on these women comes from département de la Seine.
Administration générale de l'Assistance publique à Paris, *Rapport sur le traitement des malades à domicile pendant les années 1890, 1891 et 1892 présenté au
Conseil de surveillance de l'Assistance publique par le directeur de cette administration* (Paris, 1894), 50, table 2. This report was also issued for the years 1896–1901.

68. Compare this to the only slightly larger percentage (20 percent) who used
midwives and who worked as seamstresses or in the needle trades. Laundresses
and general workers (*ouvrières*) also appeared to be similarly distributed between hospital patients and those who chose a welfare midwife. Computed from
tables in Administration générale de l'Assistance publique, *Rapport sur le
traitement des malades à domicile,* 1894:50; 1900:86; 1903:54. These cover the
years 1890–96, 1896–1901. Comparisons were made from data sampled in AAP,
l'Hôpital Port-Royal, Registres des entrées. See Fuchs and Knepper, "Women in
the Paris Maternity Hospital," 194, table 4.

69. Othenin d'Haussonville, *Misère et remèdes* (Paris, 1892), 214; Lenard R.
Berlanstein, *The Working People of Paris, 1871–1914* (Baltimore: Johns Hopkins University Press, 1984) 39–52, 201.

70. Just Sicard de Plauzoles, *La maternité et la défense nationale contre la
dépopulation* (Paris, 1909), 156.

2. *Immorality and Motherhood:
1830–1870*

1. Victor Hugo, *Les Misérables,* trans. Norman Denny (London: Penguin
Classics, 1976), 125, 137, 143.

2. The data are for the department of the Seine. See Rachel G. Fuchs, *Abandoned Children: Foundlings and Child Welfare in Nineteenth-Century France* (Albany: State University of New York Press, 1984), 72–76.

3. Chevalier, *La formation de la population parisienne au XIXe siècle*, 39–43, and *Laboring Classes and Dangerous Classes in Paris during the First Half of the Nineteenth Century,* trans. Frank Jellinek (New York: Howard Fertig, 1973), 181–185; Scott, *Gender and the Politics of History*, 119.

4. The discussions of culture in the works of Clifford Geertz and Peter Burke prove relevant. Clifford Geertz, "Ideology as a Cultural System," in *Ideology and Discontent,* ed. David E. Apter (New York: Free Press, 1964), 64; Peter Burke, *Popular Culture in Early Modern Europe* (London: Wildwood House, 1988), prologue; Katherine A. Lynch, *Family, Class, and Ideology in Early Industrial France: Social Policy and the Working-Class Family, 1825–1848* (Madison: University of Wisconsin Press, 1988), 25.

5. John Boswell, *The Kindness of Strangers: The Abandonment of Children in Western Europe from Late Antiquity to the Renaissance* (New York: Pantheon, 1988), 345. In the Ancien Régime, if a woman determined paternity, then she could bring suit to try to force the putative father to pay financial damages. See James R. Farr, *The Wages of Sin: Sexuality, Law and Religion in Burgundy during the Catholic Reformation (1550–1730)* (New York: Oxford University Press, forthcoming), chap. 4.

6. Susan Moller Okin, *Justice, Gender, and the Family* (New York: Basic Books, 1989), 33; Carol Pateman, *The Sexual Contract* (Stanford, Calif.: Stanford University Press, 1988), 98–100.

7. H. A. Frégier, *Des classes dangereuses de la population dans les grandes villes, et des moyens de les rendre meilleures,* 2 vols. (Paris, 1840), 1:9, 2:201. In his translation of Chevalier, Frank Jellinek translates Frégier's phrase as "productive breeding ground" (*Laboring Classes and Dangerous Classes,* 141). The female reproductive imagery remains. Frégier's study, awarded a prize by the Institut de France in 1838, became a key work of the nineteenth century.

8. Scott, *Gender and the Politics of History*, 121.

9. William Coleman, *Death Is a Social Disease: Public Health and Political Economy in Early Industrial France* (Madison: University of Wisconsin Press, 1982), 69–70. The terms social economy and political economy are often used interchangeably, but when analyzing the political economists' views of social and familial issues, the term social economy is more precise and will be employed in this chapter as synonymous with political economy.

10. Social economists held local and national government offices and had prominent representation in the important body of public authority, the Academy of Moral and Political Sciences. Society members studied social questions, the most important of which was the causes of misère and then made policy recommendations. See Scott, *Gender and the Politics of History*, 117; and Coleman, *Death Is a Social Disease,* 8. The Academy itself contained two major divisions: that of political economy and that of moral science. Therefore, it may be convenient to think of the ideologies of political economists as following two close paths, sometimes converging and sometimes diverging: that of social (political) economy and that of moral economy. Louis René Villermé, himself, started

in political economy, but in 1851 moved to moral science. See Coleman, *Death Is a Social Disease*, 8. Coleman refers to Villermé as a political or social economist; Lynch refers to him as a moral economist. Not only did Villermé change his affiliation over time, but this somewhat confusing labeling illustrates the overlap between ideologies. See Lynch, *Family, Class, and Ideology*, chap. 2.

11. *Journal des débats,* December 7, 1837; *Journal du commerce,* 1835; B.-B. Remacle, *Des hospices d'enfants trouvés en Europe, et principalement en France* (Paris, 1838) 164; Jean-François Terme and J.-B. Monfalcon, *Histoire des enfants trouvés,* Nouvelle édition (Paris, 1840), 196; Thomas J. Duesterberg, "Criminology and the Social Order in Nineteenth-Century France" (Ph.D. diss., Indiana University, 1979), chap. 2; William M. Reddy, *The Rise of Market Culture: The Textile Trade and French Society, 1750–1900* (Cambridge: Cambridge University Press, 1984), 235.

12. Reddy, *The Rise of Market Culture,* 235; Louis René Villermé, "De la distribution par mois des conceptions et des naissances de l'homme, considéré dans ses rapports avec les saisons, avec les climats, avec le retour périodique annuel des époques de travail et de repos, d'abondance et de rareté des vivres, et avec quelques institutions et coutumes sociales," *Annales d'hygiène publique et de médecine légale* 5 (1831): 55–155. Cited in Coleman, *Death Is a Social Disease,* 218, 193.

13. Louis René Villermé, *Tableau de l'état physique et moral des ouvriers employés dans les manufactures de coton, de laine et de soie,* 2 vols. (Paris, 1840), 1:122. See also 1:31, 122, 363, and 2:13, 51–53, 324; Terme and Monfalcon, *Histoire des enfants trouvés,* 196.

14. Villermé, *Tableau,* 1:31, 122, 363; 2:13, 51–53, 324. Political and moral economists used the French word *moeurs* excessively. They usually used it pejoratively, with the adjectives *désordre* or *dépravation,* and usually meant sexual morality. *Moeurs* defined a complex relationship of behavior patterns—including sexuality, family and economic planning, hygiene, and alcoholic consumption. In the interests of simplicity, I have translated *moeurs* as "morals" or "morality"; those terms signify the whole gamut of behavior that the nineteenth-century moral reformers implied by *moeurs.*

15. Villermé, *Tableau,* 1:56, 123; 2:49–54.

16. Charles-Marie Tanneguy Duchâtel, *De la charité dans ses rapports avec l'état moral et le bien-être des classes inférieures de la société* (Paris, 1829), 37–57, 153, 191–194, 207. Duchâtel joined the government in 1830, served as Minister of Commerce from 1834–1836, then as Minister of Finance and Minister of the Interior from 1840–1848 when he retired from government with the fall of the monarchy and his mentor, Guizot. For the 1836 edition he changed the title of his work; the content remained exactly the same. The 1836 title was *Considérations d'économie politique sur la bienfaisance, ou de la charité dans ses rapports avec l'état moral et le bien être des classes inférieures de la société.* In 1829 he wrote the book for the contest sponsored by the Academy, and the title was according to the terms of the contest. In the preface to the 1836 edition he added that the title on charity did not express the character of his book with sufficient precision.

17. Villermé, *Tableau,* 1:65, 246–7; 2:11–15. For a similar sentiment see Duchâtel, *De la charité,* 29. In 1836, François Naville, a devout Protestant social economist, invoked the Gospels in saying that "Providence rested social order on marriage and good morality. *Charité légale* would invert this sacred law" and sanction "libertinage and disorder." François-Marc-Louis Naville, *De la charité légale, de ses effets, de ses causes, et spécialement des maisons de travail et de la proscription de la mendicité,* 2 vols. (Paris, 1836), 2:34, 36.

18. Duchâtel, *De la charité,* 49–57, 153, 197, 243.

19. Scott, *Gender and the Politics of History,* 147; Lynch, *Family, Class, and Ideology,* 48–64.

20. They, too, were members of the Academy of Moral and Political Sciences and were the authors of numerous works, all dealing with their perceptions of the causes and remedies of poverty, which they submitted to competitions sponsored by the Academy.

21. See, for example, Simonde de Sismondi, *Nouveaux principes d'économie politique; ou, De la richesse dans ses rapports avec la population,* 2 vols. (Paris, 1819), 2:307–309, as cited in Coleman, *Death Is a Social Disease,* 88; and Charles Dupin, *Des forces productives et commerciales de la France* (Paris, 1827), 1:101–102, as cited in Lynch, *Family, Class, and Ideology,* 78–79.

22. Joseph Marie de Gérando, *De la bienfaisance publique,* 4 vols. (Paris, 1839), 1:lxv, lxxvij–lxxxij, 265, 312–318, 501; 3:377. In 1838 Gérando served on the conseil général des hospices sur le service des enfants trouvés dans le département de la Seine. According to Gérando, of all places of employment, only domestic service would assure good morals because young women, born to serve others, would be under the patronage of another family. His comment is ironic given how many domestic servants became pregnant or prostitutes. Although mentioning conditions of inequality between the sexes, he failed to recognize the consequences of male sexual advances.

23. Gérando, *De la bienfaisance publique,* 3:408, 417–419.

24. Ibid., 1:lxv, lxxvij–lxxxij; 3:380–382.

25. Ibid., 3:409. Gérando described scenarios similar to that of another reformer, Louis Desloges, who blamed naive young women who came to the capital from the provinces for succumbing to a seduction; both advocated refuges and attempts at moralization before inscribing these women as prostitutes. Louis Desloges, *Des enfants trouvés, des femmes publiques et des moyens à employer pour en diminuer leur nombre* (Paris, 1836), 42.

26. Gérando, *De la bienfaisance publique,* 3:410–412. There is no mention of what these women did with their infants, but given Gérando's acceptance of child abandonment, it is likely that these women abandoned their newborns at the Paris foundling home. P. A. Dufau, *Lettres à une dame sur la charité* (Paris, 1847), 53, 281.

27. Joseph Marie de Gérando, *Le visiteur du pauvre* (Paris, 1820), 86–87. Alphonse Esquiros also advocated home relief for unwed mothers but to combat poverty as a motive for abandonment. See Alphonse Esquiros, *Paris, ou les sciences, les institutions et les moeurs au XIXe siècle,* 2 vols. (Paris, 1847), 2:377.

28. For an analysis of Social Catholicism during this period (1830–1870) see

Jean-Baptiste Duroselle, *Les débuts du catholicisme social en France, 1822–1870* (Paris: Presses Universitaires de France, 1951); quote on 598. For a discussion of Social Catholicism and its relationships to class structure see Lynch, *Family, Class, and Ideology,* 36–39.

29. The philosophy of Social Catholicism is well expressed in the words of La Rochefoucauld-Liancourt: "il doit exister une classe pauvre vivant des libéralités du riche. La réciprocité des services est la base et la vie de toute société. . . . Il faut que la prévoyance sociale qui ne place nul homme dans la dépendance d'un autre homme, mais chacun sous la protection de tous, s'attache à ne laisser aucun citoyen inutile dans l'Etat, aucun sans les moyens de se créer à soi-même un avenir." See La Rochefoucauld-Liancourt, Discours du 17 avril 1837 sur la Société de Morale Chrétienne, as quoted by Ferdinand Dreyfus, *L'assistance sous la Seconde République, 1848–1851* (Paris, 1907), 11. Two strands of Social Catholicism existed before 1851: the conservative and the democratic Christian (which was somewhat tinged with socialist ideals). After the Coup of 1851, the only branch left was the conservative.

30. Duroselle, *Les débuts de catholicisme social en France,* 598.

31. Alban de Villeneuve-Bargemont, *Economie politique chrétienne, ou recherches sur la nature et les causes du paupérisme en France et en Europe, et sur les moyens de le soulager et de le prévenir,* 3 vols. (Paris, 1834), 1:25, 235, 254; 2:259, 353. Ferdinand Dreyfus refers to him as a "socialiste chrétien," but that is strictly a matter of terminology. See Dreyfus, *L'assistance sous la Seconde République,* 13, 17. Before 1860 there was a fine line between Christian Socialists and Social Catholics. Moreover, the title of Villeneuve-Bargemont's book bears witness to a confusion between Social Catholics and political economists. There were, indeed, some parallel beliefs. See also Gérando, *Le visiteur de pauvre.*

32. Villeneuve-Bargemont, *Economie politique,* 1:116, 2:259, 353; 3:2, 8–9.

33. Ibid., 1:254; 3:34, 68–69.

34. Ibid., 3:106–107.

35. Ibid., 1:235.

36. Adolphe-Henri Gaillard (Abbé), *Recherches administratives, statistiques et morales sur les enfants trouvés, les enfants naturels et les orphelins en France et dans plusieurs autres pays de l'Europe* (Paris, 1837), 50–54, 319, 323, 352. From his pulpit and publisher in Poitiers, from the late 1830s through the 1850s, he actively campaigned against aid to unwed mothers and in favor of facilitating child abandonment at a foundling home. All social reformers preached celibacy prior to marriage, some more explicitly than others. See also, for example, Jules Gossin, *Manuel de la Société de Saint-Régis de Paris* (Paris, 1851), 93.

37. Gaillard, *Recherches administratives . . . sur les enfants naturels,* 324, 329, and *Examen du rapport de M. le Baron de Watteville sur les tours, les infanticides, etc.* (Paris, 1856), 9.

38. Jules Gossin, Société charitable de Saint-Régis de Paris, *Recherches statistiques* (Paris, 1844), 3, and *Circulaire du président de cette société de charité à toutes les sociétés de Saint-Régis* (Paris, 1844), 86–87, 102.

39. Gossin, *Circulaire du président de cette société de charité,* introduction.

40. Statement from Institut de France, February 23, 1846. Cited and discussed in Jules Gossin, *Note ayant pour objet d'obtenir une addition à l'article 9 du projet relatif au droit d'assistance* (Paris, 1848), 13.

41. Alphonse de Lamartine, *Discours sur les enfants trouvés,* Prononcé le 30 avril 1838 à la Société de Morale Chrétienne (Paris, 1838). For the Protestant view on the family see Agénor-E. de Gasparin, *La famille, ses devoirs, ses joies et ses douleurs,* 2 vols. (Paris, 1863), 1:4–5.

42. Duroselle, *Les débuts du catholicisme social en France,* 27. The Société Saint-Vincent-de-Paul was the more active and stronger right arm of social Catholicism. The Société Saint-Vincent-de-Paul, however, gave almost exclusively to male deserving poor. Their records are devoid of women, and they did not admit female members. See Duroselle, *Les débuts du catholicisme social en France,* 154–197.

43. Other women members included the Mesdames de Lafayette, Say, and Belloc. Dreyfus, *L'assistance sous la Seconde République,* 24.

44. Edward R. Tannenbaum, "The Beginnings of Bleeding-Heart Liberalism: Eugène Sue's *Les Mystères de Paris,*" *Comparative Studies in Society and History* 23 (1981): 491–507, see esp. 498. Membership included: the duc d'Orléans, the duc de Chartres, duc de Broglie, François Guizot, Benjamin Constant, Alexis de Tocqueville and Alphonse de Lamartine.

45. Dreyfus, *L'assistance sous la Seconde République,* 11.

46. Eugène Sue, *The Mysteries of Paris,* n.t. (Philadelphia, 1912), 13. For a discussion of the theme of the virtuous heroine see Smith, *Ladies of the Leisure Class.*

47. Sue, *Mysteries,* 179.

48. Sue, *Mysteries,* 346. Emphasis in the original.

49. For another romantic image of a virtuous single mother who loved her child see Eugène Sue, *Martin, the Foundling: A Romance* (London, 1927), 62–63, 79.

50. Sue, *Mysteries,* 430. For a discussion of the moral philosophy of Eugène Sue, see Tannenbaum, "The Beginnings of Bleeding-Heart Liberalism," 491–507.

51. As quoted in Christopher H. Johnson, *Utopian Communism in France: Cabet and the Icarians, 1839–1851* (Ithaca, N.Y.: Cornell University Press, 1974), 90.

52. As quoted in Claire Goldberg Moses, *French Feminism in the Nineteenth Century* (Albany: State University of New York Press, 1984), 230–231, 94–95.

53. Eugène Buret, *De la misère des classes laborieuses en Angleterre et en France. De la nature de la misère, de son existence, de ses effets, de ses causes, et de l'insuffisance des remèdes qu'on lui a opposés jusqu'ici; avec l'indication des moyens propres à en affranchir les sociétés,* 2 vols. (Paris, 1840), 1:74, 78–82; 2:231, 235. Buret proclaimed that he was in the tradition of Adam Smith, Ricardo and J.-B. Say. His critiques of the industrial system, however, place him more among the Social Catholics or pre-Marxian socialists. In essence, he

borrowed some tenets from the moral and social economists and some from the Social Catholics in seeking to understand the nature and causes of what he termed "the plague of pauperism." See Hilde Rigaudias-Weiss, *Les enquêtes ouvrières en France entre 1830 et 1848* (Paris: F. Alcan and Presses Universitaires de France, 1936), *passim*.

54. Buret, *De la misère*, 1:267; 2:13, 243, and 278.

55. Ibid., 2:12, 256–258.

56. Ibid., 2:71, 247–248, 276–277.

57. Duroselle, *Les débuts du catholicisme social*, 80–90.

58. Archives Nationales (AN) C1039, especially the discourse of Montalembert and of Alphonse de Lamartine, March 1853. See also Alphonse de Lamartine, *Résumé de la discussion sur les enfants trouvés et observations sur la loi proposée au corps législatif* (Paris, 1853).

59. Scott, *Gender and the Politics of History*, 153.

60. Dreyfus, *L'assistance sous la Seconde Republique*, 102, 170–171.

61. Scott, *Gender and the Politics of History*, 153, 157–158; Jules Simon, *L'ouvrière*, 4th ed. (Paris, 1862), 3–16, 79–89. Simon is difficult to categorize. A liberal Catholic, his views are sometimes associated with social Catholicism and sometimes with those of the moral economists. He was always a moderate Republican who sometimes asserted his brand of liberal, social Catholicism during the many years he shared power.

62. Duroselle, *Les débuts du catholicisme social*, 666.

63. Armand de Melun, *Rapport fait au nom de la commission d'assistance chargée d'examiner le projet de loi sur l'assistance publique*. Séance Assemblée nationale législative, 26 mars 1851.

64. P. A. Dufau, *Essai sur la science de la misère sociale* (Paris, 1857), xx, 17, 39. Dufau was member of the governing boards of several charitable organizations, and an Administrator of the Bureau de Bienfaisance of the Xth arrondissement of Paris. Dufau's causes of misère resemble those of most other social analysts of his era and earlier.

65. Ibid., 17–19, 21.

66. Ibid., 141, 49, 204, 146–147.

67. Ibid., 145. See also H. E. Dutouquet, *Enfants trouvés. Création de la Société de Notre-Dame de Refuge et de ses asiles* (Paris, 1858).

68. Dufau, *Essai sur la science de la misère sociale*, 211–213. Many of these ideas, especially those of child abandonment, were also part of official ideology. See A. Valdruche, *Rapport au conseil général des hospices sur le service des enfants trouvés dans le département de la Seine* (Paris, 1838).

69. Dufau, *Essai sur la science de la misère sociale*, 115–117. On the idea of the necessity of assuring liberty to all at the same time as security for society, see, Ambroise Clement, *Essai sur la science sociale: Economie politique, morale expérimentale, politique théorique*, 2 vols. (Paris, 1867), 1:80, 92. Dufau argued against Duchâtel and the political economists who maintained that the state should not intervene in charity.

70. For an example of this argument see Gaillard, *Recherches administratives . . . sur les enfants naturels*, 296–300.

3. Depopulation and Motherhood: 1870–1914

1. The phrases *droit de vivre* or *droit à la vie* (right to life) appeared in almost every reformist tract discussing mothers and children. *La revue philanthropique* 1 (1897):901; Paul Strauss, *Dépopulation et puériculture*, (Paris, 1901), 245. Archives de la Ville de Paris et Département de la Seine (ADS), "Rapports d'inspection sur le service des Enfants assistés de Paris", Manuscrits, M. Brindejont, 1888. (Hereafter cited as ADS, "Rapports", manuscript, author, and date.) For a discussion of degeneracy and depopulation see Robert A. Nye, *Crime, Madness, and Politics in Modern France: The Medical Concept of National Decline* (Princeton, N.J.: Princeton University Press, 1984).

2. Emile Zola, *L'Assommoir*, trans. Atwood H. Townsend (New York: Penguin, 1962) 7–30; *Nana*, trans. George Holden (London: Penguin, 1972), *Fécondité*, (Paris, 1957). See *Fruitfulness*, trans. Ernest Vizetelly (New York: Doubleday, 1900), 91–99, 216–233, 360–383. This strongly repopulationist novel features a couple, Matthieu and Marianne, who bear many children in the countryside. Both the family and the land prosper from fertility. Those couples who limit their number of children fail to prosper as they had hoped and suffer from the economy and hands of the abortionists. For a discussion of the images of women in Zola's *Fécondité* see Catherine Toubin-Malinas, *Heurs et malheurs de la femme au XIXe siècle: "Fécondité" d'Emile Zola* (Paris: Méridiens Klincksieck, 1986).

3. For example, see Paul Strauss, *L'enfance malheureuse* (Paris, 1896), 46, 51–53, 59, 60; Jacques Mornet, *La protection de la maternité en France (Etude d'hygiène sociale)*. Thèse pour le doctorat en médecine, Faculté de Médecine de Paris (Paris, 1909), 111–112. The French terms are: "mères misérables, mères delaissées, mères clandestines, mères défaillantes par misère," or "les pauvres filles séduites."

4. Dr. Gustave Drouineau, "Maternité," *La revue philanthropique* 14 (1903–1904):557–558, and *De l'assistance aux filles-mères et aux enfants abandonnés* (Paris, 1878), 15–16; Othenin d'Haussonville, *Salaires et misères de femmes* (Paris, 1900).

5. Mornet, *La protection de la maternité*, 82.

6. Théophile Roussel as quoted by Edouard David, *La fille Bazentin: Pièce sociale en quatre actes sur l'Assistance publique* (Amiens, 1908), xi. No citation to Roussel given. I am indebted to Sylvia Schafer for providing me with David's relatively unknown play.

7. Mornet, *La protection de la maternité*, 112.

8. For an important discussion of this theme see François Ewald, *L'état providence* (Paris: Grasset, 1986).

9. Paul Nourrisson, *La question des enfants martyrs et la protection des femmes à Londres* (Paris, 1897); George K. Behlmer, *Child Abuse and Moral Reform in England, 1870–1908* (Stanford, Calif.: Stanford University Press, 1982).

10. David L. Ransel, *Mothers of Misery: Child Abandonment in Russia* (Princeton, N.J.: Princeton University Press, 1988), 102.

11. Kaiser Wilhelm II even had come out publicly on behalf of the three k's— kinder, kirche, küche—for women. See Karen Offen, "What Price Citizenship? The Sexual Politics of French Nationalism from 1905 to the First World War," paper prepared for the Conference on Aspects of Nationalism in France, April 1989, unpublished MSS. See also Anna Davin, "Imperialism and Motherhood," *History Workshop,* no. 5 (Spring 1978), 9–65; Jane Lewis, *The Politics of Motherhood: Child and Maternal Welfare in England, 1900–1939* (London: Croom Helm, 1980); Linda Gordon, *Woman's Body, Woman's Right: A Social History of Birth Control in America* (New York: Penguin, 1977), chap. 7; Richard J. Evans, *The Feminist Movement in Germany, 1894–1933* (Beverly Hills, Calif.: Sage Publications, 1976), 145–173. Even George Bernard Shaw, in his introduction to *Three Plays by Brieux* (New York: Brentano, 1911), xxxix, declared that the population of England was threatened by "actual retrogression" and that "the appointment of a Royal Commission to enquire into the decline of the birthrate . . . is probably not very far off."

12. Henri Hatzfeld, *Du pauperisme à la sécurité sociale, 1850–1940* (Paris: Armand Colin, 1971), 276–277.

13. Othenin d'Haussonville, *Socialisme d'état et socialisme chrétien* (Paris, 1890), 9, 18, 28, and *Socialisme et charité* (Paris, 1895), 491. Haussonville was permanent senator, a member of the Académie française and of the Academy of Moral and Political Sciences, and a prolific writer. In addition to his other works cited above see, e.g., Othenin d'Haussonville, *La vie et les salaires à Paris* (Paris, 1883), and *Misère et remèdes* (Paris, 1892).

14. Alain Becchia, "Les milieux parlementaires et la dépopulation de 1900 à 1914," *Communications,* no. 44 (Seuil, 1986), 201–241.

15. Hatzfeld, *Du paupérisme à la sécurité sociale,* 193.

16. Paul Strauss, *Assistance aux vieillards ou infirmes privés de ressources* (Paris, 1897), 5.

17. Jules Simon, *De l'initiative privée et de l'état, en matière de réformes sociales.* Conférence faite au Grand-Théatre de Bordeaux, 7 November 1891 (Bordeaux, 1892), 19–20.

18. Writers primarily sought to establish causes of the low natality and sought ways in which to remedy it. The most widely heralded and reprinted book, Jacques Bertillon, *La dépopulation de la France: Ses conséquences, ses causes, mesures à prendre pour la combattre* (Paris, 1911), analyzes both low natality and high infant mortality. Arsène Dumont, *Dépopulation et civilisation, étude démographique* (Paris, 1890), attributes low natality to *capilarité sociale,* the theory of social mobility whereby an individual seeks to better his social position, usually by having only one child, preferably a son. His argument bears remarkable similarity to that of a modern British historian describing the situation in England during the end of the century. See Joseph A. Banks, *Prosperity and Parenthood* (London: Routledge & Kegan Paul, 1954). Others such as Paul Leroy-Beaulieu believed that a decline in religious beliefs, the rise of compulsory schooling, and factory labor legislation making children less profitable workers contributed to a lower fertility rate. See Paul Leroy-Beaulieu, *Le travail des femmes au XIXe siècle* (Paris, 1873), 73. Frédéric LePlay, *L'organisation de la*

famille selon le vrai modèle signalé par l'histoire de toutes les races et de tous les temps, 3rd ed. (Tours, 1884), blamed the individualism of the French and the system of partitative inheritance. Devout Catholics blamed anti-Christian laws such as divorce and general anticlericalism of education for degeneracy and a low birth rate. See D. M. Couturier, *Demain. La dépopulation de la France, craintes et espérances* (Paris, 1901), 57–59. Social commentators hypothesized a myriad of contributing factors to the depopulation of France including atheism, secular education without moral principles, lack of surveillance of wetnurses, lack of punishment for abortion and infanticide, lack of virility, and lack of hygiene. See also Dr. Picon, *Aperçu sur les principales causes de la dépopulation et de l'affaiblissement progressif de la France* (Paris, 1888), 6–12, and Dr. André-Théodore Brochard, *Des causes de la dépopulation en France et des moyens d'y remédier* (Lyon, 1873). This chapter attempts only to show how the preoccupation with depopulation affected attitudes toward the poor and pregnant in Paris and the survival strategies of those women. For current works on the subject see Joseph Spengler, *France Faces Depopulation* (Durham, N.C.: Duke University Press, 1979), chap. 10; Karen Offen, "Depopulation, Nationalism, and Feminism in Fin-de-Siècle France," *American Historical Review* 89 (June 1984):649–653, 658–659; Catherine Rollet-Echalier, *La politique à l'égard de la petite enfance sous la IIIᵉ République* (Paris: Presses Universitaires de France, 1990); and Joshua H. Cole, "The Power of Large Numbers: Population and Politics in Nineteenth-Century France," Ph.D. diss., University of California, Berkeley, 1991.

19. See, e.g., Picon, *Aperçu sur les principales causes de la dépopulation,* 6–7. This concern led to the passage of the 1874 Roussel Law that regulated and inspected the system of wetnursing. See George D. Sussman, *Selling Mothers' Milk: The Wet-nursing Business in France* (Urbana: University of Illinois Press, 1982), chaps. 5–7; and Fuchs, chaps. 5–6.

20. Paul Cère, *Les populations dangereuses et les misères sociales* (Paris, 1872), introduction, 1–4, 300–301.

21. From 1881 to 1901 the population of France increased by less than 3 percent while that of Germany increased by almost 20 percent; from 1890 to 1896 twenty-two Germans were born for every ten French babies. André Armengaud shows a decrease in the population of France by 124,289 from 1886 to 1891: André Armengaud, *La population française au XIXe siècle* (Paris, 1971), 12, 25. B. R. Mitchell shows a total population increase of 339,000 between 1886 and 1896, with a net population growth of 136,000 people between 1891 and 1896. According to Mitchell's statistics, only in 1890, 1891, 1892, and 1895 did France have an excess of deaths over births. In Germany, however, births exceeded deaths by over 12 per 1,000 per year. See B. R. Mitchell, *European Historical Statistics, 1750–1974* (New York: Columbia University Press, 1981), 30, 95. See also Spengler, *France Faces Depopulation,* 53; Paul Ponsolle, *La dépopulation. Introduction à l'étude sur la recherche de la paternité* (Paris, 1893), 1–21 (Ponsolle refers to babies as "human capital"); and Dr. A.-T. Brochard, *Des causes de la dépopulation en France,* 8–9.

22. Dr. Just Sicard de Plauzoles, *La maternité et la défense nationale contre*

la dépopulation (Paris, 1909), 93–94; Jean Frollo, *Le petit Parisien,* 24 June 1899.

23. See, e.g., Dr. A. Balestre and A. Giletta de Saint-Joseph, *Etude sur la mortalité de première enfance dans la population urbaine de la France* (Paris, 1901). A pamphlet by Camille Rabaud, *Le péril national ou la dépopulation croissante de la France. Le péril, les causes, les moyens* (Paris, 1891), 13, is an especially striking example of the use of military metaphors in referring to the national peril of France, menaced by a war which could break out at any instant.

24. For example, Doctors Théophile Roussel, Jacques Bertillon, Henri Napias, Gustave Drouineau, Paul Brouardel, Henri Thulié, Emile Combes, and Georges Clemenceau were prominent either as deputies, senators, or prime ministers, or active members of the Conseil supérieur de l'Assistance publique—a national parliamentary committee. Dr. Pierre Budin and his pupil Dr. Henri de Rothschild were especially prominent in Paris politics. In the Chamber of Deputies of the Third Republic the number of doctors was large and increased from 33 in the period 1871–76 to an average of 57 in the period 1877–1893. They were predominantly opportunist Republicans or Radicals. For detailed analysis and discussion of the increased power of the medical profession, see Jacques Donzelot, *The Policing of Families,* trans. Robert Hurley (New York: Pantheon, 1979); Jacques Léonard, *La médecine entre les savoirs et les pouvoirs* (Paris: Aubier Montaigne, 1981), and *La vie quotidienne du médecin de province au XIXe siècle* (Paris: Hachette, 1977), 224–226, 231; Robert A. Nye, *Crime, Madness and Politics in Modern France: The Medical Concept of National Decline* (Princeton, N.J.: Princeton University Press, 1984); Jack D. Ellis, *The Physician-legislators of France: Medicine and Politics in the Early Third Republic* (Cambridge: Cambridge University Press, 1990).

25. Anson Rabinbach, "The European Science of Work: The Economy of the Body at the End of the Nineteenth Century," in *Work in France: Representations, Meaning, Organization, and Practice,* ed. Steven Laurence Kaplan and Cynthia J. Koepp (Ithaca, N.Y.: Cornell University Press, 1986), 476, 481; Robert A. Nye, "Degeneration and the Medical Model of Cultural Crisis in the French *Belle Epoque,*" in *Political Symbolism in Modern Europe: Essays in Honor of George L. Mosse,* ed. S. Drescher, D. Sabean, and A. Sharlin (New Brunswick, N.J.: Rutgers University Press, 1982).

26. Quoted by Sicard de Plauzoles, *La maternité,* 202–203. Even earlier, Dr. Gaston Variot iterated the same sentiments in his "Instructions aux mères pour allaiter leurs enfants," *La revue philanthropique* 9 (1901):630, when he said: "The first task of a mother is to nourish her child. The milk of the mother belongs to the child. It is a law of nature that must be respected."

27. *Bulletin de l'Académie de Médecine* (12 November 1907), 331, as quoted by Sicard de Plauzoles, *La maternité,* 252–264.

28. A.-T. Brochard, *L'ouvrière, mère de famille* (Lyon, 1874), vii; Discours de Dr. le professeur Lannelongue at the Ligue contre la mortalité infantile, in "Variétés," *La revue philanthropique* 30 (1911–1912):203. The quotation is found in A.-T. Brochard, *Education du premier âge. Utilité des crèches et des sociétés de charité maternelle.* Conférence faite par M. le Dr. Brochard, Cheva-

lier de la Legion d'honneur, Lauréat de l'Institut, Rédacteur en chef de *La jeune mère,* en faveur de la Société de Charité maternelle de Saint-Etienne (Saint-Etienne, 1876), 2.

29. Léonard, *La vie quotidienne du médecin,* 193.

30. D. M. Couturier, *Demain. La dépopulation de la France,* 13; Charles Gide, *La France sans enfants* (Paris: Chez M. Léon Peyric, 1914), 13; see also de Nadaillac, *La dépopulation de la France* (Paris, 1891).

31. Rabaud, *Le péril national,* 19, 40, 42.

32. Othenin d'Haussonville, *Misère et remèdes,* esp. pp. 303–371.

33. Francis Ronsin, *La grève des ventres: Progagande néo-Malthusienne et baisse de la natalité en France 19e–20e siècles* (Paris: Aubier Montaigne, 1980), 57, 160–170.

34. Eugène Brieux, *Maternity,* in *Three Plays by Brieux,* ed. and intro. George Bernard Shaw, trans. Mrs. Bernard Shaw (New York and London, 1911), 40, 73. This is a reference to the strike of the wombs, *la grève des ventres,* advocated by neo-Malthusians.

35. Robert Hertz, *Socialisme et dépopulation. Les cahiers du Socialiste,* no. 10 (Paris, 1901), 8. In 1911, *La revue socialiste* endorsed Hertz's stance. For the neo-Malthusian views of so-called depopulation, see Ronsin, *La grève des ventres,* 175–177.

36. Hertz, *Socialisme et dépopulation,* 28–29.

37. Sicard de Plauzoles, *La maternité,* 58–59, 249.

38. Ibid., 30, 73, 97–103, 108, 21–22.

39. Ibid., 75, 245, 280, 117–118, 160, 250, 279.

40. Léon Bourgeois, *Solidarité* (Paris, 1896), 6, 36, 63, 98–99, 115–116.

41. Léon Bourgeois, *Discours en faveur de l'assistance à l'enfance,* à l'assemblée-générale de la maison maternelle, 7 November 1897, 9–10; Amédée Bondé, *Etude sur l'infanticide, l'exposition et la condition des enfants exposés en droit romain. De la condition civile des enfants abandonnés et des orphelins recueillis par la charité privée ou par la charité publique et du projet de loi sur la protection des enfants abandonnés, délaissés ou maltraités en droit français* (Paris, 1883), 89.

42. Emile Cheysson, *La question de la population en France et à l'étranger* (Paris, 1885), 1, 22–24. For an analysis of Cheysson's life and programs see Sanford Elwitt, *The Third Republic Defended: Bourgeois Reform in France, 1880–1914* (Baton Rouge: Louisiana State University Press, 1986), 13, 52, and chap. 2.

43. Paul Strauss, "Bulletin," *La revue philanthropique* 1 (1897):950. See also, "Variétés," *La revue philanthropique* 30 (1911–1912):303–305; Commission de la dépopulation: Sous-commission de la mortalité, *Rapport géneral sur les causes de la mortalité,* présenté par Paul Strauss (Melun, 1911), 11, 13, 18, 21–22. The commission issued its report in 1911 after almost a decade of discussion. Edme Piot, *La dépopulation. Enquête personnelle sur la dépopulation en France* (Paris, 1902), 75–81; Sicard de Plauzoles, *La maternité,* 133. For an analysis of the debates surrounding paid maternity leaves see Mary Lynn [Stewart] McDougall, "Protecting Infants: The French Campaign for Maternity Leaves, 1890–1913," *French Historical Studies* 13 (Spring 1983): 47–78.

44. "Variétés," *La revue philanthropique* 30 (1911–1912):303–305; Commission de la dépopulation: Sous-commission de la mortalité, *Rapport géneral sur les causes de la mortalité*, 11, 13, 18, 21–22.

45. Emile Laurent, *L'état actuel de la question des enfants assistés* (Paris, 1876) quoted by Pierre Fleury, *Des causes de la dépopulation française et de la nécessité de réorganiser les services d'assistance et d'hygiène* (Paris, 1888), 83. Dr. A.-T. Brochard argued forcibly that child abandonment was preferable to an indigent woman trying to keep and nurse her baby herself when she would have preferred otherwise. If an unwilling mother kept her baby, it would likely die of neglect. Dr. André-Théodore Brochard, *La vérité sur les enfants trouvés* (Paris, 1876).

46. Brieux, *Maternity*, in *Three Plays by Brieux*, 54–57, 328. For a critique of Brieux's play, see Dr. Gaston Variot, "Les nourrices mercenaires et la stérilisation du lait," *La revue philanthropique* 8 (1900–1901):513–520.

47. Building upon the work of the Waldeck-Rousseau Commission, a similar commission convened in 1912 to propose legislative changes which would encourage marriage (and numerous children within marriage) and discourage abortion, infanticide, and out-of-wedlock births. Commission extraparlementaire chargée d'étudier les questions relatives à la dépopulation en France et de rechercher les moyens d'y remédier (Instituée par décret du 5 novembre 1912), Sous-commission administrative et juridique, *Procès-verbaux des séances* (Paris: Impr. Nationale, 1913), 7–8; Député T. Steeg, "Assistance aux familles nombreuses," *La revue philanthropique* 26 (1909–1910):5–24; de Nadaillac, *La dépopulation de la France*, 20–21; Piot, *La dépopulation*, 45–52.

48. Piot, *La dépopulation*, 46–58.

49. Mornet, *La protection de la maternité en France*, 19, 30; Piot, *La dépopulation*, 75.

50. Dr. Gaston Variot, "Conférence sur l'allaitement," *La revue philanthropique* 12 (1902):134.

51. See, e.g., Commission de la dépopulation, Sous-commission de la mortalité, *Rapport général sur les causes de la mortalité*, 9; Report in the *Gazette des tribunaux* (5–7 December 1883), 1165, 1169, 1173 of the debate in the Senate on the proposal of Berenger; Report of the Chambre des députés, sixième législature, session extraordinaire de 1897, Rapport fait au nom de la commission relative à la recherche de la paternité, in BMD, DOS 347 ENF; 2e Congrès international des oeuvres et institutions féminines, 1900 (Paris: Charles Blot, 1902), 1:270–287. Othenin d'Haussonville, *Socialisme et charité*, 82–87; Sicard de Plauzoles, *La maternité;* Ponsolle, *La dépopulation*, 29–30.

52. Strauss, *L'enfance malheureuse*, 34. For a similar argument see Dr. Gustave Drouineau, "Maternité," *La revue philanthropique* 14 (1903–1904):557–558.

53. Commission de la dépopulation, Sous-commission de la mortalité, *Rapport général sur les causes de la mortalité*, 9.

54. Pierre Fleury, *Des causes de la dépopulation françaises et de la nécessité de réorganiser les services d'assistance et d'hygiène* (Paris, 1888), 22–23; Haussonville, *Salaires et misères de femmes*, xx, xxxii, and *Socialisme et charité*, 86–87.

55. *La revue philanthropique* 1 (1897):950. He repeated the exact words in *La*

revue philanthropique 2 (1897–1898):112. On the solidarists and solidarism, see Judith F. Stone, *The Search for Social Peace: Reform Legislation in France, 1890–1914* (Albany: State University of New York Press, 1985); and Elwitt, *The Third Republic Defended.*

56. Paul Feillet, *De l'Assistance publique à Paris. Avec une préface par M. Paul Strauss* (Paris, 1888), vii; Strauss, *Dépopulation et puériculture,* 245.

57. Paul Strauss, "Bulletin," *La revue philanthropique* 9 (1901):654, *Assistance sociale: Pauvres et mendiants* (Paris, 1901), 3, and *L'enfance malheureuse,* 19, 206.

58. Strauss, *Dépopulation et puériculture,* 2, 6, *L'enfance malheureuse,* iii, *La croisade sanitaire* (Paris, 1902), 41, 234, 267, and *La revue philanthropique* 1 (1897):2.

59. Strauss, *Dépopulation et puériculture,* 36–37, 40–41, and *L'enfance malheureuse,* 162–163, 184–186, 189.

60. *La revue philanthropique* 1 (1897):3; Strauss, *L'enfance malheureuse,* vi, 46, *Assistance sociale,* 3, 152, and *La croisade sanitaire,* 340.

61. Strauss, *Assistance sociale,* 264, 271, Commission de la dépopulation, *Rapport général sur les causes de la mortalité,* 17.

62. Steven C. Hause, "Anti-Protestant Rhetoric in the Early Third Republic," *French Historical Studies* 16 (Spring 1989):195, and "Protestant Radicalism and the Making of the Third Republic, 1861–1885," paper presented at the 103rd annual meeting of the American Historical Association, Cincinnati, Ohio, December 1988. Protestants such as Henri Monod, Charles Gide, and Camille Rabaud condemned the atheism, vanity, pride, and love of luxury that led to voluntary family limitation among the bourgeoisie. They believed that the main way to increase population was by sacrificing individual interests to the general interests, and that the state must encourage parents to have several children. See Charles Gide, *La France sans enfants,* 10, 14; Rabaud, *Le péril national ou la dépopulation croissante de la France,* 21, 28–29, 32, 42–43, 54–55.

63. Agénor-Etienne de Gasparin, *La famille. Ses devoirs, ses joies et ses douleurs,* 2 vols. (Paris, 1865), 1:220; Feillet, *De l'Assistance publique à Paris,* 111–112.

64. The Protestant notion of *devoirs* and charity differed in a fundamental way from a similar notion of Catholics. See Smith, *Ladies of the Leisure Class,* 103. The hierarchical Catholic notion of charity flowing downward differed from the more egalitarian notion of solidarity. See Maxime DuCamp, *Paris bienfaisant* (Paris, 1888), 161–290.

65. Henri Monod, *Ma mise à la retraite (Pour ma famille et quelques amis)* (Paris, 1907), 55. For an elaboration on Henri Monod's importance as a Protestant and politician, see Rachel G. Fuchs, "From the Private to the Public *Devoir:* Henri Monod and Public Assistance," *Proceedings of the Annual Meeting of the Western Society for French History* 17 (1990):373–382.

66. Henri Monod, *L'Assistance publique en France en 1889 et en 1900* (Paris, 1900), 15, 47, 133–134.

67. "Conseil supérieur de l'Assistance publique," report of meeting of 1900, *La revue philanthropique* 7 (1900):164–165. Protestants opposed contraceptive

measures and their religious beliefs in the right to life fueled much of the depopulationist movement. See Ronsin, *La grève des ventres*, 122.

68. *Compte Rendu* du IV Congrès international de l'association catholique internationale des oeuvres de protection de la jeune fille, 1906, 58, 75; Eugène de Margerie, *La société de Saint-Vincent-de-Paul* 2 vols. (Paris, 1874), 1:16, 107–108, 123.

69. Haussonville, *La vie et les salaires à Paris*, 7–13, 16.

70. Haussonville, *Salaires et misères de femmes*, 15.

71. Haussonville, *La vie et les salaires à Paris*, 24–31, 41–49; on language and on criticism of men's seduction of women and their love of liberty that made marriage repugnant to them, see his *Socialisme et charité*, 61–65, 67–73, and *Salaires et misères de femmes*, xx. Haussonville did not use the word "concubinage," but rather referred to such living arrangements as an "irregular household," a "Parisian marriage," or a "free union."

72. Othenin d'Haussonville, *Assistance publique et bienfaisance privée* (Paris, 1901), 49–52, and *Misères et remèdes*, iv.

73. Ernest Semichon, *Histoire des enfants abandonnés depuis l'antiquité jusqu'à nos jours* (Paris, 1880), 2.

74. For an elegant discussion of "l'ouvrière as the antithesis of la mère" see Scott, *Gender and the Politics of History*, chap. 7.

75. Ewald, *L'état providence;* Simon, *De l'initiative privée et de l'état*, 17.

76. Sicard de Plauzoles, *La maternité*, 265.

4. *Morality and Motherhood: Women's Voices*

1. The term "elite" is employed in this context to mean upper class, from nonaffluent bourgeois women, to women of title, to the occasional empress or wife of head of state. Some were religious women, others were feminists, still others were relatively wealthy bourgeoisie who contributed money, and sometimes time, to philanthropy and charity.

2. Even Jules Michelet wrote that "woman has a language apart": Jules Michelet, *L'amour*, 3d ed. (Paris, 1859), 1–3. Quoted in Claire Goldberg Moses, *French Feminism in the Nineteenth Century*, 159. See also Carol Gilligan, *In a Different Voice* (Cambridge, Mass.: Harvard University Press, 1982). Gilligan's interpretation of women's "different voice" informed some of the interpretation in this chapter. It is dangerous to base an analysis of literature of over one hundred years ago upon contemporary American feminist, psychological interpretations of women's thought processes. Nevertheless, an awareness that women stress relationships, as Gilligan has analyzed, can be a useful tool in understanding the differences in the male and female discourse about the poor and pregnant of the last century. For an analysis of the many aspects of feminism see Karen Offen, "Defining Feminism: A Comparative Historical Approach," *Signs: Journal of Women in Culture and Society* 14, no. 1 (1988):119–157.

3. For an elaboration see Smith, *Ladies of the Leisure Class,* chap. 6.

4. Empress Eugenie supported orphanages and donated money to facilitate parental reclamation of abandoned children. Madame de Lamartine, in 1848, distressed by troubles in the street, wanted to use public funds for poor women without work.

5. *La revue philanthropique* 28 (1910–1911):120.

6. Smith, *Ladies of the Leisure Class,* chap. 6.

7. P. A. Dufau, *Lettres à une dame sur la charité,* 14.

8. Comte Agénor-Etienne de Gasparin, *Les réclamations des femmes* (Paris, 1872), 66, 69. Even though the date of publication was 1872, this source is typical of those of the July Monarchy, the government in which he served in the 1830s.

9. Comtesse A.-E. de Gasparin, *Il y a des pauvres à Paris . . .* (Paris, 1846), 8, 15, 23, 26.

10. Ibid., 36, 79, 86.

11. Comtesse A.-E. de Gasparin, *Mariage au point de vue chrétien,* 3 vols. (Paris, 1843), 2:246.

12. See, for example, Mathilde Froment Bourdon, *La charité en action* (Lille, 1859). See also Smith, *Ladies of the Leisure Class,* chap. 6.

13. Bourdon, *La charité en action,* 42. This tale bears remarkable similarity to Haussonville's of about thirty years later. Their tellings of the tale differ in motive and tone. Bourdon was more moralistic and advocated charity; Haussonville wanted charity only until the laws were changed.

14. Mathilde Froment Bourdon, *Antoinette Lemire, ou l'ouvrière de Paris* (Paris, 1861), 138.

15. Smith, *Ladies of the Leisure Class,* 10–14. Such a typology of the "cult of the virtuous heroine" was not unique to women writers of the time, as the depiction of Rigolette by Eugène Sue illustrates.

16. Gasparin (Comtesse), *Mariage au point de vue chrétien,* 253–254, 257.

17. Comtesse A.-E. de Gasparin, *Un livre pour les femmes mariées* (Paris, 1845), 144–158, 162, 224–225 and *passim.*

18. Smith, *Ladies of the Leisure Class,* 103.

19. Mathilde Froment Bourdon, *Charité, légendes,* 3rd ed. (Paris, 1864), vi, 71, 138, 182, and *passim.* This book was reprinted ten times from 1864 through 1902 as a manual for Catholic charity.

20. Eugène Gossin, *Vie de M. Jules Gossin, 1789–1855* (Paris, 1907), 53; Jules Gossin, *Notice sur Madame Dalbanne* (Paris, 1851), 34.

21. Smith, *Ladies of the Leisure Class,* 139–140.

22. P. A. Dufau, *Lettres à une dame sur la charité,* introduction, 5, 277.

23. Moses, *French Feminism,* 133.

24. Moses, *French Feminism,* 85–86, citing Suzanne Voilquin, *Souvenirs d'une fille du peuple; Ou la Saint-simonienne en Egypte* (Paris, 1978), 94, 97–98, 82, 83, 112.

25. Zoé Charlotte Gatti de Gamond, *Fourier et son système* 5th ed. (Paris, 1841–1842), 250–251. Quoted in Moses, *French Feminism,* 96–97.

26. Julie-Victoire Daubié, *La femme pauvre au dix-neuvième siècle,* 2d ed.

(Paris, 1870), 130–131, 136; quotation from Daubié, "Travail manuel des femmes, deuxième partie. Industries diverses," *Journal des économistes,* 2d ser., 38 (15 May 1863), 211.

27. Daubié, *La femme pauvre,* 150.

28. Daubié, "Travail manuel des femmes," 199, 207. Daubié also focused on the prostitution problem related to women's conditions of poverty and inequality.

29. Daubié, *La femme pauvre,* 51, 123, 148.

30. Ibid., 145–146, 156.

31. Smith, *Ladies of the Leisure Class,* 158.

32. Henri Rollet, *L'action sociale des catholiques en France (1871–1914)* 2 vols. (Paris and Bruges: Desclée de Brouwer, 1958), 2:155.

33. Comtesse d'Haussonville (née Pauline d'Harcourt), *La charité à travers la vie* (Paris, 1912), 186–187, 199–200, 208.

34. Mlle. Marguerite Jules Simon, *La vie de l'ouvrière* (Paris, 1911), 51–52.

35. *La femme* (15 August 1900), 1; quotation from *La femme* 13 (1 August 1899), 113.

36. *La revue philanthropique* 4 (1898–1899):402, 404; Mme Lydie Martial, founder of *l'Ecole de la Pensée* and of *l'Education humaine,* writing in *Le solidariste,* September 1908. Clipping in Bibliothèque Marguerite Durand (BMD), DOS 362 MUT; Madame Hervieu, *Appel aux mères de France: Reconstitution de la famille* (Sedan, 1891), 5, 7, 22.

37. Karen Offen, "What Price Admission: The Sexual Politics of French Nationalism from 1905 to the First World War," paper presented at St. John's College, Cambridge, England, 10–12 April 1989. For a translation of a relevant document see Blanche Edwards-Pilliet, "Rapport de Mme le docteur Edwards-Pilliet, rapporteur," *Congrès international de la condition et des droits des femmes, Paris . . . 1900* (Paris, 1901), 66–68, cited in Susan Groag Bell and Karen M. Offen, eds., *Women, the Family, and Freedom,* 2 vols. (Stanford, Calif.: Stanford University Press, 1983), 2:145.

38. Association "Le Dû aux Mères," in BMD, DOS 362 DU, 18–19. Emphasis added.

39. Vicomtesse de Lysle de Lys, [no first name given], "Le Dû aux Mères," (May 1902), 18–19, in BMD, DOS 362 DU.

40. Letter from Vve de Lysle de Lys to Madame et illustre collègue [no name given], 19 June 1902, in BMD, DOS 362 DU.

41. Louise Georges Renard, *L'aide maternelle* (Paris, 1909), 4–5, 8–9.

42. *La revue philanthropique* 1 (1897):243. It is not at all clear what good it would do for a mother to know her rights unless the charitable women were organized to help the mother achieve her rights.

43. Claire Galichon, *Amour et maternité* (Paris, 1907), 282.

44. Marie Béquet de Vienne, "A Monsieur Paul Strauss," *La revue philanthropique* 2 (November 1897–April 1898):12.

45. Ibid., 12–13.

46. Ibid., 14–15; Mme Léon Béquet, née de Vienne, *Dépopulation de la France,* Allocution prononcée au congrès général des institutions féministes (Tenu à la mairie du VIe arrondissement le 14 mai 1892), 1–2.

47. Béquet, *Dépopulation de la France,* 3; Mme Béquet de Vienne, quoted by Victor Margueritte, *Journal* (16 December, 1907), in BMD, DOS 362 SOC.

48. Mme Béquet de Vienne, "Causerie" à l'assemblée générale de l'oeuvre de l'allaitement maternel, 2 June 1908. Quoted by Just Sicard de Plauzoles, *La maternité et la défense nationale contre la dépopulation* (Paris, 1909), 86–90.

49. Maria Vérone, article in *La fronde,* 14 January 1903. Contained in Archives de l'Assistance Publique (AAP), Fosseyeux 688[1]. See also Offen, "The Sexual Politics of French Nationalism."

50. See for example, "l'Asile Michelet, Hospitalisation des femmes enceintes," Rapport de Mme Léo Caubet, directrice, séance du mardi 19 juin, in *2e Congrès international des oeuvres et des institutions féminines, 1900,* 4 vols. (Paris, 1902), 1:68, 69.

51. Prior to the nineteenth century and in some rare court cases in mid-nineteenth century, a mother could bring suit to secure financial damages from the father of her out-of-wedlock child. Bonzon was evidently unaware of the law of 1670 and French customs before the Napoleonic Code which, with the *déclarations de grossesse,* permitted and encouraged *recherche de la paternité.* See Fairchilds, "Female Sexual Attitudes and the Rise of Illegitimacy," 627–667; and Farr, *The Wages of Sin,* chap. 4.

52. *2e Congrès international des oeuvres et des institutions féminines,* 1:263, 271, 274.

53. *2e Congrès international des oeuvres et des institutions féminines,* 1:269, 270.

54. Mme d'Abbadie d'Arrast, "2e Congrès international des oeuvres et des institutions féminines," *La femme* (15 August 1900), 124.

55. *2e Congrès international des oeuvres et des institutions féminines,* 1: 276–277.

56. Ibid., 485–486, 289.

57. Sicard de Plauzoles, *La maternité,* 241; Marie Georges-Martin, "Le conseil national des femmes françaises," *La revue philanthropique* 13 (1903): 695–701.

58. Renée Rambaud, *La fronde,* 14 May 1901.

59. Clotilde Dissard, "Chronique Féministe," *La fronde,* 24 January 1900.

60. *La femme affranchie,* October 1904. Francis Ronsin has described this journal as "revolutionary feminist, violently antimilitaristic, and neo-Malthusian." Francis Ronsin, *La grève des ventres: Propagande néo-Malthusienne et baisse de la natalité en France 19e–20e siècles* (Paris: Aubier Montaigne, 1980), 159.

61. Gabrielle Petit, *La femme affranchie,* September 1904. This was an editorial signed by Gabrielle Petit, the editor.

62. Raphaël Duffouic, "Filles mères," *La femme affranchie* 2 (August 1905). I wish to thank Mary Lynn Stewart for bringing this poem to my attention. Although Petit believed in birth control, she did not disseminate contraceptive information in her journal, probably because that would further risk the shutting down of the publication. She referred her readers to the neo-Malthusian publication, *Régéneration.* See Ronsin, *La grève des ventres,* 159.

63. Hubertine Auclert, "Le féminisme, l'éxemption du bâtard," *Le radical* (9 January 1899), in BMD, DOS 360 Ass.

64. Galichon, *Amour et maternité*, 243–318, 99, 244, 254.

65. Ibid., 246–253, 263–264, 269–270, 273, 137, 147, 225–230.

66. Ibid., 137, 147–164, 256.

67. Ibid., 316–317.

68. Ibid., 316–318, 99, 271.

69. Madeleine Pelletier, *Le droit à l'avortement* (Paris, 1913), 6.

70. Pelletier, *Le droit à l'avortement,* 18.

71. *La femme affranchie,* August 1904. As an ardent neo-Malthusian, Nelly Roussel spoke at rallies and argued that overpopulation was responsible for misery and war. See Ronsin, *La grève des ventres,* 161.

72. Nelly Roussel, speech given at the women's meeting called to protest the centennial of the Civil Code, 29 October 1904. First published in *La fronde,* 1 November 1904, and translated by Karen Offen, in Bell and Offen, eds., *Women, the Family, and Freedom,* 2:135.

73. Lucie Delarue-Mardrus, *Marie, fille-mère* (Paris, 1908). See especially 12, 34, 83, 100, 165, 180, and 195 for references to attitudes of Delarue-Mardrus.

5. Charity and Welfare for the Pregnant Poor

1. For discussions of poverty, charity, and welfare in the eighteenth century see: Cissie C. Fairchilds, *Poverty and Charity in Aix-en-Provence, 1540–1789* (Baltimore: Johns Hopkins University Press, 1976); Olwen H. Hufton, *The Poor of Eighteenth-Century France, 1750–1789* (Oxford: Clarendon Press, 1974), especially chap. 12 for women and children; and Robert M. Schwartz, *Policing the Poor in Eighteenth-Century France* (Chapel Hill: University of North Carolina Press, 1988). For discussion of welfare and the poor in the First Republic, see Alan Forrest, *The French Revolution and the Poor* (New York: St. Martin's Press, 1981), 27.

2. The topic of abandoned children has been discussed at great length elsewhere. See Janet Ruth Potash, "The Foundling Problem in France, 1800–1869: Child Abandonment in Lille and Lyon," (Ph.D. diss., Yale University, 1979); and Fuchs, *Abandoned Children.*

3. Joseph Marie de Gérando, *De la bienfaisance publique,* 4 vols. (Paris, 1839), 1:lxv, lxxvij–lxxxij [sic], 317–318, 417–418; Archives Nationales (AN), Firman Marbeau, Société des Crèches, septième séance publique annuelle, 1853, 8; F. Gille, *La Société de charité maternelle de Paris* (Paris, 1887); Ferdinand Dreyfus, *L'assistance sous la Seconde République,* 8–9, 102, 170–171.

4. Oeuvre des mariages des pauvres, *Rapports et compte rendu* (Paris: Au secrétariat de la Société de Saint-Vincent-de-Paul, 1876), 13; Archives de la Préfecture de Police (APP) D/B 90, proposals to amend the law of 1850 on the marriage of indigents, 1876, 1890.

5. Michel Frey, "Du mariage et du concubinage dans les classes populaires à

Paris (1846–1847)," *Annales: Economies, sociétés, civilisations* 33 (1978):803–829. For an assessment of the value of clothing and the shame that indigents felt when they lacked special clothes for a wedding see Archives de la Ville de Paris et Département de la Seine (ADS), VD4/4989. *Compte rendu, pour l'année 1845, des résultats obtenus par la Société charitable de Saint-François-Régis de Paris, pour le mariage civil et religieux des pauvres du département de la Seine qui vivent dans le désordre.* ADS, Dossiers Cour d'Assises, D2 U8 (88) Dossier 22 August 1879, (103) Dossier 20 August 1880; (139) Dossier 23 October 1882.

6. Jules Gossin, Société charitable de Saint-Régis de Paris, *Recherches statistiques sur les 17,176 pauvres dont la société charitable de St.-Régis, établie à Paris pour faciliter le mariage civil et religieux des indigents du département de la Seine, s'est occupée depuis le 1er mars 1826 jusqu'au 31 décembre 1841 inclusivement et résultats obtenus par la société sur les 8,588 couples inscrits entre ces deux époques* (Paris, 1844), 3, and Société charitable de Saint-Régis de Paris, *Circulaire du président de cette société de charité à toutes les sociétés de Saint-Régis* (Paris, 1844), 86–87, 102.

7. ADS VD4/4989. La Société charitable de Saint-François-Régis de Paris, *Compte rendu pour l'année 1845.* It received the bulk of its funds from private benefactors, although the state provided some subventions until 1877, when the Minister of Interior and the conseil général de la Seine (general council of the department of the Seine) found it too exclusively religiously Catholic and stopped all financial allocations. In 1858 the Protestant Oeuvre evangélique des mariages (Evangelical Organization of Marriages) was established along lines similar to those of the Société de Saint-François-Régis in order to foster and assist Protestant and mixed marriages in Paris. ADS, VD6/1909 no. 3, Oeuvre evangélique des mariages. See also ADS, VD6/1909, no. 3, Oeuvre des mariages des pauvres, *Rapports et compte rendu,* 3–5; Jules Gossin, *Manuel de la Société charitable de Saint-Régis de Paris* (Paris, 1851), 6, 53, 60, 67, 134–136. For further discussion of this Society and different examples of cases brought before them, see Katherine A. Lynch, *Family, Class, and Ideology in Early Industrial France* (Madison: University of Wisconsin Press, 1988), 88–100.

8. See ADS VD4/4989, La Société charitable de Saint-François-Régis de Paris, *Compte rendu pour l'année 1845;* VD6/1909, no. 3, Oeuvre du mariage des pauvres, *Rapports et compte rendu,* 4.

9. Gossin, *Manuel de la Société charitable de Saint-Régis de Paris,* 68–70, 90.

10. Of the men, 27 percent were *menu peuple;* 64 percent were manual laborers, and 6 percent were marginally indigent; of the women, 78 percent were in the needle trades; 8 percent were "without profession," and 13 percent worked at heavy labor. This society was in existence throughout the century, but such data were available only for this early period. Jules Gossin, Société charitable de Saint-Régis de Paris, *Recherches statistiques,* 7.

11. In 1845 slightly more than 85 percent of those who applied for this assistance got married. Gossin, *Recherches statistiques,* 10, 24–25; ADS VD4/4989, *Compte rendu pour l'année 1845.* See also Archives de l'Assistance Publique (AAP), Fosseyeux Collection (Foss.) 708[19]. In 1860 Paris was administratively enlarged and the surrounding suburbs brought into the city proper. The number

of arrondissements increased from 12 to 20. The old, or former, twelfth arrondissement roughly consisted of the present fifth and sixth arrondissements.

12. Adolphe de Watteville, *Législation charitable* (Paris, 1863), 2:145–147; Gossin, *Manuel de la Société charitable de Saint-Régis de Paris*, 50–52. APP, D/B 90. Circular from préfet de police to commissaire de police, 22 May 1847.

13. Computed from the number of marriages in the department of the Seine for each year. See Préfecture de la Seine, Service de la statistique municipale, *Annuaire statistique de la ville de Paris* (Paris, 1880–1900). The year 1900 contained retrospective data. For data on the number of marriages this Society performed see Oeuvre du mariage des pauvres, *Rapports et compte rendu*, 5. See also Angus McLaren, *Sexuality and Social Order: The Debate over the Fertility of Women and Workers in France, 1790–1920* (New York: Holmes and Meier, 1983) 174.

14. Eugène Gossin, *Vie de M. Jules Gossin, 1789–1855* (Paris, 1907), 119, 248, 295.

15. ADS, VD6/1909, no. 3 Oeuvre de Notre-dame de la persévérance, Oeuvre de St.-Antoine, Maisons de prévoyance pour les femmes sans place et les ouvrières sans travail. The former was affiliated with Saint-Vincent-de-Paul. For the patronage society see ADS, VD4/4993 and APP, DB/90, Société de patronage pour le renvoi dans les familles des jeunes filles sans place et des femmes délaissées. See also *Recueil des oeuvres, associations et sociétés reconnues comme établissements d'utilité publique jusqu'au 1er juillet 1906* (Paris, 1906), and Dufau, *Lettres à une dame sur la charité*, 281.

16. One family's efforts to hide their daughter's out-of-wedlock pregnancy in the Asile Saint-Raphaël can be found in *Marthe. A Woman and a Family: A Fin-de-Siècle Correspondence*, trans. Donald Frame (New York: Harcourt, Brace, Jovanovich, 1984), 10, 16–18, 48–51; See also Jacques Mornet, *La protection de la maternité en France (Etude d'hygiène sociale)*, Thèse pour le doctorat en médecine, 1909, Faculté de Médecine de Paris (Paris, 1909), 91–92; R. P. Dauphin, *Une plaie sociale, Un remède* (Paris, 1900).

17. Mornet, *La protection de la maternité*, 91–92. Data in AAP, l'Hôpital Port-Royal, Registres des entrées (1869–1900), and Registres des femmes en couches envoyées chez les sage-femmes (1869–1898).

18. Mathilde Froment Bourdon, *La charité en action* (Lille, 1859), 88–92; Dufau, *Lettres à une dame sur la charité*, 276. Some unscrupulous women ran bogus orphanages, seeking only to exploit the labor of unfortunate young girls. Correspondance asking for state subvention to this private charity found in Archives Nationales (AN) F17 12529. See also *L'oeuvre libératrice, Société de réhabilitation* (Paris, 1903).

19. Mornet, *La protection de la maternité en France*, 83.

20. *La revue philanthropique* 8 (1900–1901):86–87. If a woman wished, she could be admitted incognito.

21. *Annuaire statistique de la ville de Paris* (1894, 1895, 1900), see especially 1894:576–579; 1895:614–619; 1900:582; *La revue philanthropique* 8 (1900–1901):86–87.

22. These were the asiles of the Philanthropic Society at 253 rue Saint-Jacques with 100 beds in the fifth arrondissement near la Maternité, another one with 53

beds at 44 rue Labat across the river in the working-class eighteenth arrondisse-ment, and the third one with 41 beds at 166 rue de la Crimée in the nineteenth arrondissement.

23. Société philanthropique de Paris, *Rapports et comptes rendus, Annuaire de 1906–1907* (Paris, 1906), 142–146.

24. Ernest Legouvé, article in *Au jour le jour* in APP, D/B 90.

25. ADS, Dossiers Cour d'Assises, D2 U8 (114) Dossier 23 March 1881. She was tried and acquitted.

26. AAP, l'Hôpital Port-Royal, Registres des entrées, 1885–1900. See also *La revue philanthropique* 1 (1897):907–914; Société philanthropique, *Annuaire de 1906–1907,* 142–146.

27. During the first year of operation 302 women, mostly unwed mothers, came there after delivery. In the second year this shelter admitted 493 women. By 1902 it received 900 women each year. Société philanthropique, *Annuaire de 1906–1907,* 150. See also *La revue philanthropique* 28 (1910–1911):90, 402; Mornet, *La protection de la maternité,* 88.

28. Société philanthropique, *Annuaire de 1906–1907,* 150. See also *La revue philanthropique* 28 (1910–1911):90; by 1909 the number of women admitted increased to 14,617.

29. APP, D/B 90, article from *Le journal,* 22 June 1906. On this shelter, see also *Annuaire statistique de la ville de Paris,* 1892–1895; A. D'Echérac (G. Dargenty), *L'assistance publique: Ce qu'elle fut; ce qu'elle est* (Paris, 1909), 245; *La revue philanthropique* 8 (1900–1901):84–85.

30. These are the few years for which we have data. Préfecture de la Seine, Service de la statistique municipale, *Annuaire statistique de la ville de Paris,* 576–579; Seine (département), Administration générale de l'Assistance publique, *Rapport général sur le fonctionnement des vingt bureaux de bienfaisance* (Paris, 1899), alternatively titled *Rapports des bureaux de bienfaisance des vingt arron-dissements de Paris sur leur fonctionnement pendant l'année 1898* (Paris, 1900), 270; *La revue philanthropique* 8 (1900–1901):82–83; Mornet, *La protection de la maternité,* 86.

31. "L'Asile Michelet, Hospitalisation des femmes enceintes," Rapport de Mme Léo Caubet, directrice, séance du mardi 19 juin 1900, in *2e congrès interna-tional des oeuvres et institutions féminine* (Paris, 1902), 1:68–69; *Annuaire statistique de la ville de Paris,* 1894, 1895, 1900.

32. Em Arnoux, "L'assistance aux femmes enceintes," *La revue philanthro-pique* 30 (1911–1912):502; "Revue d'assistance," *La revue philanthropique* 27 (1910):55; Mornet, *La protection de la maternité,* 96.

33. Bibliothèque Marguerite Durand (BMD) DOS 362 LIG.

34. Ligue française des mères de famille, *Bulletin,* no. 1 (Paris, 1903), 15, 29.

35. "La Société de l'allaitement maternel et des refuges-ouvroirs. Compte rendu moral par Madame Béquet de Vienne, fondatrice, *La revue philanthro-pique* 26 (1909–1910):472–473; Ligue française des mères de famille, *Bulletin trimestrier* (Paris, 1906), n.p.; Mornet, *La protection de la maternité,* 124–126; Henri Rollet, *L'action sociale des catholiques en France (1871–1914),* 2 vols. (Paris and Bruges: Desclée de Brouwer, 1958), 2:155.

36. Forrest, *The French Revolution and the Poor,* 76.

37. *Rapport général sur le fonctionnement des vingt bureaux de bienfaisance;* John H. Weiss, "Origins of the French Welfare State: Poor Relief in the Third Republic, 1871–1914," *French Historical Studies* 13 (Spring 1983):49–50.

38. AAP, Fosseyeux 96, Procès verbaux, bureau de bienfaisance, VI arrondissement, 23 January 1852. By the 1890s women were examined starting in their seventh month of pregnancy by a welfare bureau midwife of their own choosing from a list of about seven or eight approved midwives. See *Rapports des bureaux de bienfaisance des vingt arrondissements de Paris,* 64, and *Rapport général sur le fonctionnement des vingt bureaux de bienfaisance,* 50.

39. AAP, Fosseyeux 94, Procès verbaux 3ème arrondissement, bureau de bienfaisance, séance 20 avril 1894. See Mornet, *La protection de la maternité,* 122.

40. *Rapports des bureaux de bienfaisance des vingt arrondissements de Paris sur leur fonctionnement pendant l'année 1898,* 270–271; see also Ville de Paris, bureau de bienfaisance du Ve arrondissement, Antonin Papet, *Manuel de l'administrateur du bureau de bienfaisance, ses fonctions, ses devoirs* (Paris, 1902), 91–95.

41. *Rapport général sur le fonctionnement des vingt bureaux de bienfaisance,* Appendix no. 10.

42. Data collected from the *Annuaire statistique de la France* and the *Annuaire statistique de la ville de Paris* for 1865–1900.

43. Dr. Em. Arnoux, "L'assistance aux femmes enceintes, indigentes ou nécessiteuses," Rapport présénté à la société médicale des bureaux de bienfaisance de Paris, *La revue philanthropique* 30 (1911–1912):505.

44. During the years from 1802 through 1862, the total number of childbirths at the major Parisian public hospitals was 224,145: 69 percent of these were in la Maternité; 10 percent each occurred in each l'Hôtel-Dieu and la Clinique; 7 percent were in l'Hôpital St.-Louis; and 2 percent each took place in Lariboisière and l'Hôpital Saint-Antoine. See Stéphane Tarnier, *Mémoire sur l'hygiène des hôpitaux de femmes en couches* (Paris, 1864). Lariboisière only opened in August 1854 and the maternity wing expanded and became significant as late as 1882. As with la Maternité, all beds were usually occupied. See Dr. Adolphe Pinard, *Du fonctionnement de la maternité de Lariboisière et des résultats obtenus depuis 1882 jusqu'en 1889* (Paris, 1889), 10, 12, 18.

45. Toward the end of the century, when la Maternité added two semiautonomous units, Clinique Tarnier and Baudelocque, the data become ambiguous as to which combination of hospital units are included. Combined births at all units of la Maternité were 8.25 percent of all births in Paris and 30.8 percent of all illegitimate births. See Paul Delaunay, *La Maternité de Paris* (Paris, 1909), 127. Data on the number of births in Paris are found in Préfecture de la Seine, Service de la statistique municipale, *Annuaire statistique de la ville de Paris, 1880–1914* (Paris, 1800–1902), (several volumes contain retrospective data for the century). See also France, Bureau de la statistique générale (1871–1906), *Statistique annuelle* and France, *Annuaire statistique de la France, 1842–1865* (Paris, 1842–1865); L'Assistance publique à Paris, *L'Assistance publique à Paris en 1900* (Paris, 1900), 500, 506.

46. Administration générale de l'Assistance publique à Paris. Service des Enfants assistés de la Seine, *Rapport présenté par le directeur de l'administration générale de l'Assistance publique à M. le préfet de la Seine* (Montevrain, 1888–1895), 1888:15–16; 1889:41; 1892:6–8; 1893:27–28; 1895:2–4.

47. Gabriel Paul Ancelet, *Essai historique et critique sur la création et transformation des maternités à Paris,* Thèse pour le doctorat en médecine (Paris, 1896), 39–43.

48. ADS, D2X4(1), Letter to the préfet de la Seine from Henri Davenne, Administration générale de l'Assistance publique à Paris, 5 November 1855; AAP, l'Hôpital Port-Royal, Registres des correspondances, 22 November 1880, 17 October 1882.

49. For a more detailed discussion of this regulation and its effects see Fuchs, "Legislation, Poverty, and Child Abandonment in Nineteenth-Century Paris;" Fuchs and Knepper, "Women in the Paris Maternity Hospital," 193, table 2; ADS, D1X4(26–27) "Rapports d'inspection sur le service des Enfants assistés de Paris," MSS, M. Raoult, 1892 (hereafter cited as ADS, "Rapports d'inspection," MSS, author, and date).

50. AAP, l'Hôpital Port-Royal, L.2, Registres des correspondances. Rats seemed to be a severe problem in May of 1860, and cholera was bad in 1865.

51. Edmond Goncourt and Jules Goncourt, *Germinie Lacerteux* (Paris: Société des Beaux Arts, 1910), chap. 20.

52. AAP, Fosseyeux 707[2], Frigerio, "Rapport sur le service de santé de la maison d'accouchement," handwritten and unpaginated manuscript, approximately pages 37–38. Ergot had been known to cause uterine contractions. Frigerio attributes her death to infection, but adds in defense of the procedure, that the woman was scrofulous, showed signs of having been treated with mercury, and was probably syphilitic. He added that the four other women died as a result of "absorption of the miasmas in the room."

53. Paul Dubois, quoted in "Des services d'accouchement dans les hôpitaux; ce qu'ils sont; ce qu'ils devraient être par un Privat-Docent, extrait du journal *Le médecin practicien* (Paris, 1882), 3; Goncourt and Goncourt, *Germinie Lacerteux,* 77–78. The Goncourt brothers refer to the hospital as "la Bourbe," which was the colloquial name for la Maternité near midcentury because it was located on the street then called rue de la Bourbe.

54. Puerperal fever can be caused by any number of bacteria—streptococci and staphylococci (found on the skin), or clostridia or coliform bacteria from the stool or in a urinary tract infection. In 1879 Louis Pasteur isolated streptococcus bacteria as responsible. The incidence of puerperal fever in the United States today is 10 percent. It can occur with a premature breakage of water not followed by sanitary conditions, or it can also come from a vaginal or cervical laceration. It is acquired from hospital personnel when scrupulous aseptic technique is not observed. Ralph C. Benson, *Handbook of Obstetrics and Gynecology* (Los Altos, Calif.: Lange Medical Publications, 1983), 300–301.

55. Husson, *Etude sur les hôpitaux,* 137; AAP, Fosseyeux 708[2], Recherches tendant à découvrir la cause de la maladie qui s'y produit sous le nom de fièvre

puerpérale," undated but probably 1833; AAP, Fosseyeux 707[2], Frigerio, "Rapport sur le service de santé de la maison d'accouchement," 13–14. The quoted phrase is from Frigerio. On the influence of atmospheric conditions and the "moral state" of the women, see Sylvain Témoin, *La Maternité de Paris pendant l'année 1859*, Thèse pour le doctorat en médecine, 1859 (Paris, 1859), 43, 46–47. See also Antoine Corre, *Manuel d'accouchement et de pathologie puerpérale* (Paris, 1885), 402; Hippolyte Bourdon, *Des maternités* (Paris, 1870), 2.

56. Léon LeFort, *Des maternités. Etude sur les maternités et les institutions charitables d'accouchement à domicile dans les principaux états de l'Europe* (Paris, 1866), 62–96, 101–124.

57. AAP, 3Q2(3, 4), l'Hôpital Port-Royal, Registres de décès des femmes enceintes et en couche; Archives générales de Médecine, *Journal*, 22 (1830), 456–505; Témoin, *La Maternité de Paris pendant l'année 1859*, 62–96. Stéphane Tarnier, *Mémoire sur l'hygiène des hôpitaux de femmes en couches* (Paris, 1864), 11–12; Edward Shorter, *A History of Women's Bodies* (New York: Basic Books, 1982), 129.

58. Goncourt and Goncourt, *Germinie Lacerteux*, 78; Témoin, *La Maternité de Paris pendant 1859*, 30.

59. Tonnellé, "Des fièvres puerpérales observées à la Maternité de Paris, pendant l'année 1829, des diverses méthodes thérapeutic employées pour les combattre, et spécialement des mercuriaux, des vomitifs, et des évacuations sanguines," Archives générales de Médecine, *Journal* 22 (1830):345–371, 456–505.

60. Domestic servants had a higher mortality rate than women in any other occupation at 5 percent; among needle workers it was 4 percent and among day laborers 3 percent. Témoin, *La Maternité de Paris pendant 1859*, 47, 50, 53.

61. Delaunay, *La Maternité de Paris*, 146, 160; AAP, Fosseyeux 707[2] Frigerio, "Rapport sur le service de santé de la maison d'accouchement," Appendix; just from 1860 to 1864 the mortality rate was 12.4 percent. The mortality rate at other hospitals was between 4 and 8 percent. Tarnier, *Mémoire sur l'hygiène des hôpitaux de femmes en couches*, 5; LeFort, *Des maternités*, 24–29. LeFort, as others who presented comparative morality rates, failed to specify length of time after delivery in which deaths occurred, to correct for number of days after delivery that the women died, and to consider only women with comparable economic and social backgrounds. They just concluded that puerperal fever was rare among women who give birth outside of hospitals.

62. Delaunay, *La Maternité de Paris*, 157.

63. These figures are based on the random sample from AAP, l'Hôpital Port-Royal, Registres des entrées and Registres de décès.

64. AAP, Fosseyeux 707[2] Frigerio, "Rapport sur le service de santé de la maison d'accouchement," 20–24, 33.

65. Delaunay, *La Maternité de Paris*, 157, citing Tarnier; Tarnier, *Mémoire sur l'hygiène des hôpitaux de femmes en couches*, 6; AAP, l'Hôpital Port-Royal, Registres des correspondance, February and March 1857 and April 22, 1863.

66. AAP, l'Hôpital Port-Royal, Registres des entrées, 1860, 1865, and 1869. During just 1861 and 1862, the maternal death rate of women in all the hospitals of Paris was 1 in 13; in comparison, among those delivered by welfare bureau

midwives and among women delivered by midwives in the city it was about 1 in 175. Tarnier, *Mémoire sur l'hygiène des hôpitaux de femmes en couches*, 4, 6; LeFort, *Des maternités*, 51.

67. Administration générale de l'Assistance publique, *Statistique médicale des hôpitaux de Paris*, 1:93, 2:269, 3:463, 4:287.

68. Administration générale de l'Assistance publique, *Statistique médicale des hôpitaux de Paris*, 3:478, 4:362.

69. AAP, l'Hôpital Port-Royal, Registres des entrées, 1860, 1865 and 1869.

70. LeFort, *Des maternités*, 52–53, 60–61, 226.

71. AAP, Stéphane Tarnier, "Hygiène des femmes en couches. Chambres d'isolement destinées à prevenir la propagation des épidemies puerpérales. Système du docteur Tarnier de l'Académie de Médecine. Professeur en chef de la clinique d'accouchement à la Maternité de Paris," MSS, 1880. In the sample collected of women who delivered with a welfare midwife between 1869 and 1900 fewer than one-fourth of 1 percent died. That is partially because the women who posed difficult deliveries stayed at la Maternité. Tarnier, *Mémoire sur l'hygiène des hôpitaux de femmes en couches*, 15–24; Delaunay, *La Maternité de Paris*, 174.

72. AAP, Tarnier, "Hygiène des femmes en couches"; Ancelet, *Essai . . . sur la création et transformation des maternités à Paris*, 11–33, 39–73, 110–122; Delaunay, *La Maternité de Paris*, 136–185; Jean Imbert, *Hôpitaux en France* (Paris: Editions Privat, 1982), 390–391; Jacques Léonard, *La médecine entre les savoirs et les pouvoirs* (Paris: Aubier Montaigne, 1981), 148, 155–170, 242–262, 302–324; Henri Napias and A.-J. Martin, *L'Etude et les progrès de l'hygiène en France* (Paris, 1883), 291.

73. Ancelet, *Essai historique et critique sur la création et transformation des Maternités*, 25, 31.

74. All of this did not seem to keep down the population of rats, which were still a problem in the 1880s. See AAP, l'Hôpital Port-Royal, Registres des correspondances, 1884–1888. The situation at the hospital Lariboisière paralleled that at la Maternité. After the modernization of the maternity service at this hospital, mortality declined to under 1 percent. Adolphe Pinard, *Du fonctionnement de la maternité de Lariboisière et des résultats obtenus depuis 1882 jusqu'en 1889* (Paris, 1889), 10–21.

75. *L'Assistance publique à Paris en 1900*, 500, 506. Yvonne Knibiehler and Catherine Fouquet, *La femme et les médecins* (Paris: Hachette, 1983), 239–241; Knibiehler and Fouquet, *Histoire des mères* (Paris: Editions Montalba, 1977), 276–277; Mireille Laget, *Naissances: L'accouchement avant l'âge de la clinique* (Paris: Editions du Seuil, 1982).

76. G. Drouineau, "L'assistance maternelle," Rapport présenté à la ligue contre la mortalité infantile, *La revue philanthropique* 12 (1902):279; *Rapport général sur le fonctionnement des vingt bureaux de bienfaisance pendant l'année 1898*, 106.

77. Computed from data in Préfecture de la Seine, *Annuaire statistique de la ville de Paris, 1880–1914* (especially 1880:190); France, Bureau de la statistique générale, *Statistique annuelle, 1871–1906*.

78. All data on women's use of Public Assistance for childbirth are derived from Paul Strauss, *L'enfance malheureuse* (Paris, 1896), 108–109; Budin, "Variétés: Les accouchements dans la ville de Paris," *La revue philanthropique* 8 (1900–1901):455–462.

79. Data for 1909 come from Arnoux, "L'assistance aux femmes enceintes," 505.

6. Charity and Welfare for New Mothers and Infants

1. Victor Hugo, *Les Misérables,* trans. Norman Denny (London: Penguin, 1976).

2. In 1876 the national government gave it a subvention of 40,000 francs, one of the largest amounts of money given to any private charity in that year. In 1911, however, that subvention had been reduced to 22,000 francs. The Banque de France was always one of the largest financial contributors to this society. F. Gille, *La Société de charité maternelle de Paris* (Paris, 1887), title page, 12, 186, and Liste alphabétique des dames protectrices, des dames administrantes et des trésoriers de 1784 à 1885, 283–298. For a statement about the Society's moralising goals see Archives Nationales (AN) F15 3799–3805, Société de charité maternelle, *Compte rendu pour l'année* 1876. Branches existed in most of the major cities of the country.

3. AN, F15 3894, Société de charité maternelle, *Compte moral et financier,* 1871; Gille, *La Société de charité maternelle,* 109–111.

4. AN, F15 2564–65, 3561, 3806–3813, 3894 Société de charité maternelle à Paris, *Compte rendus,* 1810–1876; and Léonce de LaMothe, *Nouvelles études sur la législation charitable* (Paris, 1850), 70.

5. AN, F15 3799–3811, Société de charité maternelle de Paris, *Compte rendu* (Paris, 1866, 1876); Archives de la Ville de Paris et Département de la Seine (ADS) VD4/4994, Société de charité maternelle, *Compte rendu pour l'année* 1850; Gille, *La Société de charité maternelle.*

6. Gille, *La Société de charité maternelle,* 73; ADS, VD6/560 no. 3, Société de charité maternelle, *Compte rendu,* 1851, 3–4, 7.

7. Gille, *La Société de charité maternelle,* 71, 85, 100, 120, 130, 161, 164, 220, 274–276; Jacques Mornet, *La protection de la maternité en France (Etude d'hygiène sociale),* Thèse pour le doctorat en médecine, 1909, Faculté de médecine de Paris (Paris, 1909), 164; ADS, VD4/4994, Société de charité maternelle, *Compte rendu pour l'année* 1850; AN, F15 2565, 3799–3805, Société de charité maternelle, *Compte rendu,* 1876, 12–13.

8. ADS, VD4/4998. Mémoire du préfet de la Seine à la commission municipale sur la répartition entre divers établissements de bienfaisance du fonds de secours voté au budget de la ville de Paris pour 1854 (Paris, 1855); and ADS, VD4/4994, Rapport sur l'oeuvre des mères de famille dans le 12ème arrondissement, 1850.

9. Mornet, *La protection de la maternité,* 125.

10. Armand Husson, *Etude sur les hôpitaux* (Paris, 1862), 163; Paul Strauss, *Paris ignoré. 500 dessins inédits d'après nature* (Paris, 1892), 422. Archives de l'Assistance Publique (APP), l'Hôpital Port-Royal, Registres des entrées, 1860 to 1900.

11. In the first eight years of its existence, of the 7,339 women who arrived here, 80 percent had never been married. As in the other institutions, domestic servants constituted about half the women (57 percent) with day laborers comprising another 12 percent; 10 percent were seamstresses and 4 percent were laundresses. As many as 75 percent had been born in other departments. In the sample year of 1900 for which data on the 928 women admitted exist, 42 percent were between the ages of 21 and 25, with another 23 percent between 26 and 30. *La revue philanthropique* 8 (1900–1901):88–89; *La revue philanthropique* 11 (1902):504–505; Archives de la Préfecture de Police (APP), D/B 90; Mornet, *La protection de la maternité,* 141–142; Strauss, *Paris ignoré,* 423.

12. "Revue d'assistance," *La revue philanthropique* 27 (1910):73.

13. Victor Margueritte, "l'Aide Maternelle," *Journal* (16 December 1907), in Bibliothèque Marguerite Durand (BMD), DOS 362.

14. AAP, Fosseyeux 686, *L'Aide Maternelle,* préface.

15. Ibid.

16. Mornet, *La protection de la maternité,* 264.

17. In BMD, DOS 362 ASS, Cantines maternelles. *Les restaurants gratuits des mères nourrices. Recueil des documents relatifs à l'origine et à la propagation des établissements spécialement destinés à nourrir les mères qui allaitent leur enfant.* Publié par l'oeuvre Henry Coullet du "Lait Maternel" (Paris, 1912); Mlle Marguerite Jules Simon, *La vie de l'ouvrière* (Paris, 1911), 57–59.

18. Mornet, *La protection de la maternité,* 251.

19. Paul Strauss, "Variétés," *La revue philanthropique* 30 (1911–1912):202.

20. AAP, Fosseyeux 94, Procès verbaux 3ème arrondissement, Bureau de bienfaisance, séance 20 avril 1894; Mornet, *La protection de la maternité,* 122; Administration générale de l'Assistance publique à Paris, *Rapports des bureaux de bienfaisance des vingt arrondissements de Paris sur leur fonctionnement pendant l'année 1898* (Paris, 1900), 128–129, 184, 269–289. Sparse data indicate that the welfare bureau of the working-class nineteenth arrondissement provided aid ranging from Fr 10 to Fr 20 per month to 519 needy nursing mothers; the aid ceased by the thirteenth month after birth. Only forty women received the aid for a full year. The remainder received it for between two and four months. All the mothers were legally married. See also Ville de Paris, Bureau de bienfaisance du Vᵉ arrondissement, Antonin Papet, *Manuel de l'administrateur du bureau de bienfaisance, ses fonctions, ses devoirs* (Paris, 1902), 91–95; AAP, Fosseyeux 648, Procès verbaux des séances du bureau de bienfaisance, 3ème arrondissement, séance du 12 avril 1894; conseil général de la Seine, *Rapport* au nom de la 3ème Commission sur le service des Enfants assistés, présenté par Paul Strauss, 1894.

21. *Rapport des bureaux de bienfaisance des vingt arrondissements de Paris,* 65–66.

22. A. Boicervoise, *Rapport au conseil général des hospices de Paris sur le service des enfants trouvés du département de la Seine* (Paris, 1845), 64–66.

23. A. Valdruche, *Rapport au ministre de l'intérieur et au conseil général des hospices relatif aux enfants trouvés dans le département de la Seine, suivi de documents officiels* (Paris, 1838), 37–38. Valdruche discussed going with de Gérando and having these "paternal conversations."

24. Valdruche, *Rapport au conseil général*, 35–36.

25. Boicervoise, *Rapport au conseil général*, 66–67, 70–79; LaMothe, *Nouvelles études sur la législation charitable*, 110.

26. Valdruche, *Rapport au conseil général*, table 14; Statistique de la France, deuxième série, *Statistique de l'Assistance publique* XV (Strasbourg, 1861), xlix.; Administration générale de l'Assistance publique à Paris, *Dispositions relatives à l'admission des femmes enceintes dans les hôpitaux et la réception des enfants à l'Hospice des Enfants-trouvés et Orphelins du département de la Seine* (Paris, 1852), 12 (Document in Archives Nationales, C1039). Boicervoise, *Rapport au conseil général*, 65–68, tables no. 6 and 7.

27. Boicervoise, *Rapport au conseil général*. Computed from data presented in table 8; see also AAP, Fosseyeux 33. In 1838, for example, 1,272 women received relief before they left la Maternité; AAP, l'Hôpital Port-Royal, Registres des entrées; Fuchs, *Abandoned Children*, 82.

28. Jeanne Singer-Kerel, *Le coût de la vie à Paris de 1840 à 1954* (Paris: A. Colin, 1961) 299; Haussonville, *Salaires et misères de femmes*, 9; McBride, *The Domestic Revolution*, 61; Paul Leroy Beaulieu, *Le travail des femmes au XIXe siècle* (Paris, 1873), 73.

29. Valdruche, *Rapport au conseil général;* Boicervoise, *Rapport au conseil général*, appendix, no. 6 and no. 8.

30. Fuchs, "Legislation, Poverty, and Child Abandonment." This was determined by noting which mothers left la Maternité with the stated intention of abandoning their babies, then looking at the records of the Hospice des Enfants Assistés for evidence that the child had been abandoned within a year after birth.

31. Maxime DuCamp, *Paris: Ses organes, ses fonctions et sa vie dans la seconde moitié du XIXe siècle*, 6 vols. (Paris, 1869–1875), 4:124.

32. *Gazette hebdomadaire de médecine et de chirurgie*, 28 January 1870, Académie de Médecine. Addition à la séance du 28 December 1869. Discours de M. Chauffard, 53–57.

33. Procès verbaux, Commission des Enfants assistés, meetings of 22 April 1876, 4 May 1876, 6 October 1876, 9 December 1878, and 19 December 1879 in ADS, D1X4(12). AAP, Conseil général de la Seine, *Rapport* présenté par M. Clemenceau au nom de la 3ème Commission sur le service des Enfants assistés, séance du 24 November 1875, pp. 26–30. Hereafter cited as *Rapp. Cons. gén.* with the year and reporter.

34. Administration générale de l'Assistance publique à Paris, Service des Enfants assistés de la Seine, *Rapport* présenté par le directeur de l'administration générale de l'Assistance publique à M. le préfet de la Seine, 1888–1894. Hereafter cited as *Rapp. ann.* with the year. By 1876 the term enfants assistés in-

cluded all children aided through programs of assistance to their mothers. See also Rachel G. Fuchs, "Morality and Poverty: Public Welfare for Mothers in Paris, 1870–1900," *French History* 2 (September 1988):290–296.

35. *Rapp.* Cons. gén., Clemenceau, 1874, 12. He repeated this sentiment one year later: "Un secours de premier mois sera toujours insuffisant." *Rapp.* Cons. gén., Clemenceau, 1875, 32.

36. *Rapp. ann.* 1889, 41; 1892, 7; and 1895, 2–5. Greater detail on these programs can be found in Fuchs, "Morality and Poverty," table 1, 293.

37. Fuchs, "Morality and Poverty," 293; ADS, Service des Enfants assistés de la Seine, Rapports d'inspection, *Rapport de l'inspecteur principal à M. le sénateur, préfet de la Seine, 1876–1899.* Hereafter cited as *Rapport de l'inspecteur principal,* with the date.

38. *Rapp.* Cons. gén., 1894, 1896 (Strauss), and 1897 (Patenne); *Rapport de l'inspecteur principal* (Maichan), 1881.

39. Only by 1898 did the number of women receiving more than Fr 20 a month equal the number receiving less.

40. Fuchs, "Morality and Poverty," 295; *Rapport de l'inspecteur principal,* 1878–1898.

41. These percentages may be inflated, since some mothers (the figures do not indicate how many) were requesting aid for the same infant for a second time. All reports indicate, however, that almost all women seeking assistance were mothers of new infants.

42. Fuchs, "Morality and Poverty," 294.

43. AN, F15 3812–3813, Société des crèches, seventeenth annual public meeting, May 1869, *Rapport et compte rendu,* and Séance publique, 28 February 1875.

44. Ibid.

45. Speech of Marbeau before the séance publique, Société des crèches, 1875; *2ème congrès international des oeuvres et des institutions féminines,* vol. 2, 334; Dr. André-Théodore Brochard *L'ouvrière, mère de famille* (Lyon, 1874), 10.

46. Strauss, *Paris ignoré,* 230.

47. "La protection des nourrissons et la mortalité infantile," *La revue philanthropique* 28 (1910–1911):409; ADS, VD6/686; ADS, V bis 11 I5/3.

48. ADS, V bis 11 Q7, Register of admissions and attendance records of the Crèche Saint-Ambroise. See also ADS, V bis 11 I5/3 Procès verbaux, séances de la commission d'hygiène, 1851. These occupations are similar to those of mothers who put their baby in a different crèche, the Crèche Saint-Louis d'Antin from 1845 to 1851. See also Jean-Baptiste Durosselle, *Les débuts du catholicisme social en France, 1822–1870* (Paris: Presses Universitaires de France, 1951), 597.

49. Almost 90 percent of those babies who went to a wetnurse entered the crèche after ten months with a wetnurse. Over one-half of single mothers (53 percent) placed their babies in the crèche after the child was one year old; more married women waited that long (63 percent). ADS, V bis 11 I5 1, Register of doctors' inspections of crèche Saint-Ambroise 1847–1867 contains the descriptions of the babies' health that doctors noted as they made their daily rounds.

The usual problems were temporary outbreaks of diarrhea, eye disease, and sometimes bronchitis. Children who were sick were sent home, requiring a loss of time at work for the mothers.

50. Louis Henry Trigant de Beaumond, *Dépopulation de la France. De la conservation des enfants par les crèches* (Paris, 1883), 6, 10, 18, 39. See also Henri Napias, *De l'organisation des crèches* (Rouen, 1897), 28–33.

51. AN, F15 12529, Letter to ministre de l'instruction publique from mairie du Temple asking for support for a "spectacle" to raise funds for a crèche in his arrondissement, 1882.

52. Many of the Rothschilds also figured prominently on the list of benefactors as did the publisher Calmann-Lévy and the grand rabbi of France, Zadoc-Kahn.

53. AAP, Fosseyeux 686 *Une expérience sociale: La Pouponnière. Société maternelle parisienne;* AAP, Fosseyeux 686, Société maternelle parisienne, la Pouponnière, Exercice 1903; "Variétés, Assemblée générale de la société maternelle parisienne 'La Pouponnière.' Institut de Puériculture," *La revue philanthropique* 27 (1910):589.

54. Olga Veil-Picard, "La protection des nourrissons," *La revue philanthropique* 28 (1910–1911):413. Some mothers, especially the unwed, needed a, temporary place just for their babies in case of emergency. The Asile Léo-Delibes, founded in 1897, temporarily received infants from ages fifteen months to five years whom their parents could not keep at that moment because of temporary poverty, illness or imprisonment, or widowhood. Half of these children (56 percent) went back to their parents. "La vie de Paris à l'Exposition. Etablissements charitable et assistance par travail," *La revue philanthropique* 8 (1900–1901):89–90.

55. *Rapport général sur le fonctionnement des vingt bureaux de bienfaisance pendant l'année 1898*, 73–79; Strauss, *L'enfance malheureuse*, 227–232; Catherine Rollet-Echalier, *La politique à l'égard de la petite enfance sous la IIIᵉ République* (Paris: Presses Universitaires de France, 1990), 353–369.

56. Note by Pierre Budin in *La revue philanthropique* 1 (1897):35; Olga Veil-Picard "Causerie," séance du conseil d'administration de l'Oeuvre de l'allaitement maternel et des Refuges-Ouvroirs, du 5 décembre 1910, *La revue philanthropique* 28 (1910–1911):406–407.

57. E. Bonnaire, "La mutualité maternelle," *La revue philanthropique* 27 (1910):254–258; Mary Lynn [Stewart] McDougall, "Protecting Infants: The French Campaign for Maternity Leaves, 1890–1913," *French Historical Studies* 13 (Spring 1983):83; Jacques Mornet, *Les mutualités maternelles* (Paris: Bloud, 1911), 6–9.

58. Mornet, *Les mutualités maternelles,* 12, 16; [Stewart] McDougall, "Protecting Infants," 83; E. Bonnaire, "La mutualité maternelle," *La revue philanthropique* 27 (1910):267–269; M. Félix, "Mutualité maternelle de Paris," séance du mardi 19 juin 1900, *2ème Congrès international des oeuvres et des institutions féminines,* 2:16–22.

59. Mornet, *La protection de la maternité,* 151.

60. Mornet, *Les mutualités maternelles,* 16, 47, 53–55.

61. [Stewart] McDougall, "Protecting Infants," 83; Mornet, *Les mutualités maternelles,* 9–10.

62. The most easily accessible source for this law is Dalloz, *Jurisprudence générale. Recueil périodique et critique de jurisprudence, de législation, et de doctrine* (Paris: Au bureau de la jurisprudence générale, 1905), Lois, décrets et actes législatifs, IV, 16–26.

63. For a full discussion of the June 1913 law, see [Stewart] McDougall, "Protecting Infants," 79–105.

64. [Stewart] McDougall, "Protecting Infants," 103–104.

7. Mothers on Welfare

1. George D. Sussman, *Selling Mothers' Milk: The Wet-Nursing Business in France, 1715–1914* (Urbana: University of Illinois Press, 1982), 117–167, 169, and chaps. 5 and 7. The Nestlé company started selling infant formulas in 1897.

2. In the spring of 1901, 302 women from the department of the Nièvre alone were engaged in this service. Archives de la Ville de Paris et Département de la Seine (ADS), Dossiers Cour d'Assises, D2 U8 (21) Dossier 13 September 1873. For other examples, see (52) Dossier 6 September 1976; (62) Dossier 25 June 1877; (61) Dossier 23 June 1877; (135) Dossier 25 July 1882; (147) Dossier 8 June 1883; (208) Dossier 9 December 1886; (139) Dossier 9 November 1882. See also Ministère du commerce, de l'industrie, des postes et des télégraphes, *Résultats statistiques du recensement général de la population,* 4 vols. (Paris, 1906), 4:303–304. See also Sussman, *Selling Mothers' Milk,* 125 for what scant direct evidence exists for the mortality of the wetnurses' own babies. In one village, about 500 of the wetnurses' babies died "during the years 1858 to 1864."

3. Archives de l'Assistance Publique (AAP), l'Hôpital Port-Royal, Registres des correspondances, 29 March 1888. Throughout the century the percentage of women giving birth in la Maternité and sending their babies directly to a wetnurse was constant at 5.6 percent.

4. AAP, l'Hôpital Port-Royal, Registres des correspondances, 30 mars 1892. This was not the first time that the director of la Maternité made a special appeal to the director-general of l'Assistance publique for assistance to a mother of triplets. See AAP, l'Hôpital Port-Royal, Registres des correspondances, 22 December 1883.

5. ADS, VD6/1566, no. 5. Circular to the mayors of the arrondissements from the prefect of the Seine 28 December 1886. This declaration detailing the names, addresses, ages, and occupations of the parents as well as the birthdate and sex of the baby also included the name, address, and age of the wetnurse, as well as her wages and whether or not she breastfed or bottle-fed the infant. All wetnurses, and others, who received such a child had to make a similar declaration to the mayor of the commune in which they lived stipulating the child's arrival within three days of that arrival, any change of residence of the wetnurse, any return of the infant to the parent or other person, and the death of the infant

within twenty-four hours of that death. This information had to be forwarded to the mayor of the commune in which the declaration of sending to a wetnurse had been made. Some of these records, titled "Registres de placement des enfants en nourrice, en sevrage ou en garde," exist for the 1st arrondissement of Paris during the years 1878–1887 (V bis 1Q7 1 à 6); for the third arrondissement for the years 1879 to 1884, and 1894, with several registers missing (V bis 3Q7 1 à 6); and for the tenth arrondissement for the years 1879 and 1880 (V bis 10Q7 1). The tenth arrondissement's records are particularly sloppy. For the data analysis I drew a random sample of 566 entries.

6. Préfecture de la Seine, Service de la statistique municipale, *Annuaire statistique de la ville de Paris 1883, 1885, 1888* (Paris, 1885, 1887, 1890) 1883:216; 1885:192; 1888:200.

7. For one year in which data are available, 1888, the affluent eighth and sixteenth arrondissements sent the same small proportion of infants to a wetnurse as did the poorest thirteenth, nineteenth, and twentieth. *Annuaire statistique de la ville de Paris, 1888* (1890), 200.

8. For additional analysis see Sussman, *Selling Mothers' Milk,* 168–171. When the mothers declared that they were sending their baby to a wetnurse, they did not specify that they were living in a consensual union. The records either reveal the mother's and father's name and add that they were married, or the mother was named and the father not, with the notation that she was single. On rare occasions records provide both parents' names and specify that they were not married. In all cases in which the surnames of the parents were different and the addresses were the same but the records failed to reveal marital status, I assumed a consensual union. An estimated 20 percent were living in a consensual union.

9. On one-time aid to domestics see ADS, D1X4(13) Procès verbaux de la Commission des Enfants assistés, meeting of 6 April 1881.

10. Analysis of the 566 cases of women who made a declaration to their mayor that they sent their baby to a wetnurse, 1878–1894 (with some missing years). Whether a wetnurse breastfed or bottle-fed the infant was recorded. See also Sussman, *Selling Mothers' Milk,* 116–121, 138–139, 168–170, 181–182; Fuchs, *Abandoned Children,* 192–205.

11. Just Sicard de Plauzoles, *La maternité et la défense nationale contre la dépopulation* (Paris, 1909), 214.

12. AAP, l'Hôpital Port-Royal, Registres des correspondances, 17 octobre 1882.

13. ADS, VD6/1566, no. 5, letters to the mayors, 1870, 1887.

14. ADS, "Rapports d'inspection sur le service des Enfants assistés de Paris," MSS, M. Montravel, 1892 (hereafter cited as ADS, "Rapports d'inspection," MSS, author, and date). These are the manuscript reports made to the principal inspector from the field inspectors overseeing this aid program to prevent abandonment.

15. ADS, "Rapports d'inspection," MSS, Montravel, 1892.

16. AAP, Conseil général de la Seine, *Rapport* présenté par M. Patenne au nom de la 3ème Commission sur le service des Enfants assistés, (1897), 4; ADS

D1X4(12), Procès verbaux de la Commission des Enfants assistés, séance du 22 février 1877.

17. Administration générale de l'Assistance publique à Paris, Service des Enfants assistés de la Seine, *Rapport présenté par le directeur de l'Administration générale de l'Assistance publique à M. le préfet de la Seine,* 1888. Hereafter cited as *Rapp. ann.* with the year. Members of the Commission des Enfants assistés de l'Assistance publique complained that some employees lacked the qualities and sensitivity necessary for that job. They rarely offered assistance to prevent abandonment. ADS, D1X4(12), Procès verbaux de la Commission des Enfants assistés, séance du 22 February 1977.

18. ADS, Dossiers Cour d'Assises, D2 U8 (120) Dossier 27 September 1881, piece 68A, Interrogation of Pallet by Adolphe Guillot, the juge d'instruction on 26 July 1881; piece 55 A, letter to Dr. Brouardel from the director of l'Assistance publique, Michel Moring.

19. Bibliothèque Marguerite Durand (BMD) DOS 360 ASS, press clippings from *L'Aurore,* November 19, 1899, and *Le matin,* 27 January 1900.

20. Archives de la Préfecture de Police (APP), Dossier l'Assistance publique, B/A 1312, "L'assistance 'dite' publique."

21. Jeanne Leroy, "Lettre ouverte à M. Mesurer, directeur de l'Assistance publique de Paris," *La revue philanthropique* 11 (1902):641–648; G. Mesurer, "Réponse à la lettre de Mme Jeanne Leroy," *La revue philanthropique* 12 (1902–1903):32–34.

22. *Rapp. ann.,* 1888.

23. There always exists the possibility that Pallet was lying about going to l'Assistance publique, but her story is plausible in light of other information. Fuchs, "Morality and Poverty," 295, table 2.

24. ADS, D1X4(12) Procès verbaux de la Commission des Enfants assistés, meeting of 27 September 1877, 31 October 1877; 15 November 1877; ADS, "Rapports d'inspection," MSS, Dunas, 1889.

25. These reports provide valuable evidence of the way middle-class women and bureaucrats viewed the poverty and morality of unwed mothers. They also provide sufficient details of the women's lives to go beyond the perceptions of those in power and to understand something of the conditions of poverty and the functioning of the welfare system.

26. ADS, "Rapports d'inspection," MSS, Raoult, 1890, 1892; Lucas-Dupin, 1895.

27. ADS, "Rapports d'inspection", MSS, Bernard, 1890.

28. ADS, "Rapports d'inspection", MSS, Forgeot, 1890.

29. ADS, "Rapports d'inspection", MSS, Lucas-Dupin, 1891.

30. ADS, "Rapports d'inspection", MSS, Forgeot, 1890.

31. ADS, D1X4(18), Procès verbaux de la Commission des Enfants assistés, Conseil général de la Seine, séance 14 February 1906.

32. Each year different inspectors visited different arrondissements. No inspector was assigned any one area for more than two consecutive years.

33. ADS, "Rapports d'inspection," MSS, Brindejont, 1889.

34. ADS, "Rapports d'inspection," MSS, Montravel, 1890.

35. ADS, "Rapports d'inspection," MSS, Mulé, 1887, 1888, 1889.

36. ADS, "Rapports d'inspection," MSS, Raoult, 1890.

37. *Rapp. ann.* (1889), 29.

38. ADS, D1X4(21), Service des Enfants assistés de la Seine, Rapports d'inspection, *Rapport de l'inspecteur principal* à M. le sénateur, préfet de la Seine, 1876–1899. Hereafter cited as *Rapport de l'inspecteur principal,* with the date.

39. ADS, "Rapports d'inspection," MSS, Raoult, 1891.

40. ADS, *Rapport de l'inspecteur principal,* Maichan, 1881, 1888; ADS, "Rapports d'inspection," MSS, Raoult, 1890, 1891, 1895. Among the 25 percent of the mothers receiving all varieties of welfare who were married, 12 percent lived with their husbands, while 6 percent had been abandoned by their husbands, and 6 percent were widows with a legitimate infant. Only half of the married women who received welfare were living with their husbands, while one fourth of them had been abandoned by their husbands and one fourth were widows.

41. ADS, "Rapports d'inspection," MSS, Raoult, 1893, 1895; Lucas-Dupin, 1894. Sparse data, available from only two inspectors from the years 1893 to 1895, provide a glimpse into the status of women receiving aid. This is supplemented by a brief note for 1899 published in *La revue philanthropique.* H. Monier, "Les drames de la misère et la réforme des secours à domicile," *La revue philanthropique* 12 (1902):422n.

42. The work of Carol B. Stack on networks among the poor in a small midwestern American city during the 1970s is suggestive. See Carol B. Stack, *All Our Kin: Strategies for Survival in a Black Community* (New York: Harper & Row, 1974), 28.

43. ADS, "Rapports d'inspection," MSS, Brindejont, 1892 and Forgeot, 1892. There is scant evidence of a woman's street culture in nineteenth-century Paris, but sensitive analyses of the poor in nineteenth-century London and in a twentieth-century American city all describe women's domestic networks. See Stack, *All our Kin,* and Ellen Ross, "Survival Networks: Women's Neighbourhood Sharing in London Before W. W. I," *History Workshop* 15 (Spring 1983):5–19.

44. Conseil général de la Seine, *Rapport* au nom de la 3e Commission sur le service des Enfants assistés. Présenté par Paul Strauss, conseiller général (1895), 33.

45. *Rapp. ann.* (1888), 4–5; Fuchs, "Morality and Poverty," 305, table 4.

46. ADS, "Rapports d'inspection," MSS, Brindejont, 1892.

47. ADS, *Rapport de l'inspecteur principal* (1882), 10–11; ADS, "Rapports d'inspection," MSS, Raoult, 1890; Brindejont, 1892.

48. Inspector Raoult based his estimate on that of René Lafabrèque, who calculated that a payment of Fr 3.50 per day was essential for a single mother to maintain herself and her child. ADS, "Rapports d'inspection," MSS, Raoult, 1890; Brindejont, 1890, 1892.

49. ADS, "Rapports d'inspection," MSS, Mulé, 1885.

50. Ann-Louise Shapiro, *Housing the Poor of Paris, 1850–1902* (Madison: University of Wisconsin Press, 1985), 62–63, 76–78.

51. *Rapp. ann.* (1888), 4.

52. P. Leroy-Beaulieu, *Le travail des femmes au XIXe siècle* (Paris, 1873) 73; Haussonville, *Salaires et misères des femmes,* 86–103; Shapiro, *Housing the Poor of Paris,* 66–67.

53. ADS, *Rapport de l'inspecteur principal,* 1899.

54. Jill Harsin, *Policing Prostitution in Nineteenth-Century Paris* (Princeton, N.J.: Princeton University Press, 1985), 33, 244–5; Haussonville, *Salaires et misères des femmes,* 59–61; Commenge, *La prostitution clandestine à Paris,* 326–329, 337.

55. Pierre Guiral and Guy Thuillier, *La vie quotidienne des domestiques en France au XIXe siècle* (Paris: Hachette, 1978), 40–41.

56. ADS, "Rapports d'inspection," MSS, Montravel, 1890. Montravel mentions a family of several persons but does not even hint at who the others might be. Shapiro describes similar conditions of filth, smells, and lack of water. Shapiro, *Housing the Poor of Paris,* 72.

57. ADS, "Rapports d'inspection," MSS, Abbal, 1887; Capelet, 1890; Dunas, 1889; Forgeot, 1889, 1890; Lucas-Dupin, 1885, 1887, 1890, 1894; Mulé, 1889; Raoul, 1894; Raoult, 1889; Thirault, 1895; ADS D1X4(14), Procès verbaux de la Commission des Enfants assistés, 22 February 1888; Haussonville, *Misère et remèdes,* 33–35, 48–49.

58. ADS, "Rapports d'inspection," MSS, Lucas-Dupin, 1891, 1893, 1894. He estimated that 12 percent of the mothers lacked a crib or bedding for it and that those infants slept on the floor. See also ADS, "Rapports d'inspection," MSS, Dunas, 1889; Mulé, 1886, 1888 and Raoult 1893; ADS, D1X4(14), Procès verbaux de la Commission des Enfants assistés, 9 February 1887, 22 February 1888, and 25 October 1893.

59. ADS, "Rapports d'inspection," MSS, Lucas-Dupin, 1885, 1890; Dunas, 1889; Forgeot, 1892; Raoult, 1889; Capelet, 1890; Raoul, 1894. Doctor Marjolin, as head of the société protectrice de l'enfant, visited 600 *logements* and echoed the reports of l'Assistance publique's inspectors. He described revolting filth, windows broken and covered with paper, and garbage and debris all about. Quoted in Haussonville, *Misère et remèdes,* 70.

60. ADS, "Rapports d'inspection," MSS, Forgeot, 1891.

61. ADS, "Rapports d'inspection," MSS, Mulé, 1897; Lucas-Dupin, 1887; Roualt, 1897.

62. ADS, "Rapports d'inspection," MSS, Brindejont, 1893; Lucas-Dupin, 1891, 1893; Dunas, 1889; Raoult, 1890.

63. ADS, "Rapports d'inspection," MSS, Bernard, 1886; Mulé, 1886; Raoult, 1890, 1893, 1897; Lucas-Dupin, 1891; ADS, D1X4(14) Procès verbaux de la Commission des Enfants assistés, 25 October 1893.

64. Conseil général de la Seine, *Rapport* au nom de la 3e Commission sur le service des Enfants assistés. Présenté par Paul Strauss, conseiller général (1895), 33.

65. ADS, "Rapports d'inspection," MSS, Brindejont, 1890; Raoult, 1893; Lucas-Dupin, 1891; Mulé, 1889.

66. Fuchs, *Abandoned Children,* chap. 6.

67. ADS, "Rapports d'inspection," MSS, Bernard, 1893; Brindejont, 1895; Forgeot, 1891; Lucas-Dupin, 1890, 1893; Raoul, 1895.

68. In 1892, 15 percent of 238 unwed mothers under one inspector's jurisdiction lived with their families; in 1895, 23 percent of 219 did so. ADS, "Rapports d'inspection," MSS, Raoult, 1892, 1895; Brindejont, 1892.

69. Emile Zola, *Fécondité* (Paris, 1957). See *Fruitfulness,* trans. Ernest Vizetelly (New York: Doubleday, 1900), 380–383.

70. ADS, *Rapport de l'inspecteur principal* (1894), 21.

71. ADS, "Rapports d'inspection," MSS, Brindejont, 1893; Lucas-Dupin, 1893. See also *Rapp.* cons. gén., Patenne, (1898), 23. Quotation from Ross, "Survival Networks," 19.

72. Dr. A.-T. Brochard, *La vérité sur les enfants trouvés* (1876) 130; *Rapp.* cons. gén., Patenne, (1898), 23.

73. Paul Strauss, Commission de la dépopulation: Sous-commission de la mortalité, *Rapport général sur les causes de la mortalité* (Melun, 1911), 18–22.

74. AAP, Administration générale de l'Assistance publique à Paris, *Rapport à M. le préfet de la Seine sur la situation du service des Enfants assistés et provisions des dépenses pour 1885* (1885).

75. Information on the terminations of aid is derived from the numerous inspectors' reports and the préfecture de la Seine, *Annuaire statistique de la ville de Paris* (1897), 638.

76. ADS, "Rapports d'inspection," MSS, Brindejont, 1890, 1894; Forgeot, 1890.

77. ADS, D1X4(21), *Rapport de l'inspecteur principal à M. le préfet de la Seine* (1898), 25.

78. Other factors include accuracy of inspection reports and statistical errors. *Rapports d'inspection sur le service des Enfants assistés* présenté par l'inspecteur principal à M. le préfet de la Seine, 1879–1900. These data are corroborated by the data presented in Administration générale de l'Assistance publique à Paris, service des Enfants assistés de la Seine, *Rapport présenté par le directeur de l'Administration générale de l'Assistance publique à M. le préfet de la Seine,* 1877–1899. Twenty percent of the newborns (infants between one day and fifteen days at the time their mothers were aided) died. Of all infants whose mothers received monthly assistance, regardless of the age of the infant, 18 percent died. Conseil général de l'Assistance publique, fasc. 27. See also Fuchs, "Morality and Poverty," 309, table 5.

79. Strauss, Commission de la dépopulation: Sous-commission de la mortalité, *Rapport général sur les causes de la mortalité,* 18–22.

80. Paul Strauss, *L'enfance malheureuse* (Paris, 1896), 108–109.

81. For a detailed description of the data see Fuchs, "Morality and Poverty," 293, 295.

8.   *Birth Control and Abortion*

1. Archives de la Ville de Paris et Département de la Seine (ADS), Dossiers Cour d'Assises, D2 U8 (23) Dossier 10 December 1873. All information on

abortion, by necessity, reveals selection by the police and the doctors. Even women's testimonies, ostensibly in their own words, are actually filtered through others, such as court reporters. In every case, special attention was taken to discern outright lies or strategies that women employed in an attempt to secure an acquittal or conviction with extenuating circumstances. Furthermore, cases of infanticide and abortion brought before the courts by no means present a comprehensive picture of infanticide and abortion in Paris. Yet, given the absence of memoirs and autobiographies by single mothers, especially by those who committed crimes, court testimony is one of the few sources that can open even a small window on the lives of individual women. A careful reading of the interrogations, depositions, witness reports, character investigations, and letters that some of the women wrote to their parents or lovers should correct for possible distortions in the documents themselves. Surnames are fictitious.

2. ADS, Dossiers Cour D'Assises, D2 U8 (60) Dossier 10 April 1877. The heavy sentence for the midwife was probably because the police could associate her with many abortions, including several for married women, one resulting in death.

3. ADS, Dossiers Cour d'Assises, D2 U8 (219) Dossier 23 April 1887. She worked until 8 P.M. and the crèches remained open only until 7 P.M.; furthermore most still did not accept an out-of-wedlock child.

4. For selected works discussing contraception or the fertility decline, see John Knodel and Etienne van de Walle, "Lessons from the Past: Policy Implications of Historical Fertility Studies," *Population and Development Review* 5 (1979):227; Ansley J. Coale and Susan Cotts Watkins, eds., *The Decline of Fertility in Europe* (Princeton, N.J.: Princeton University Press, 1986); Norman E. Himes, *Medical History of Contraception* (New York: Schocken, 1970), 53–55; Angus McLaren, *Reproductive Rituals: The Perception of Fertility in England from the Sixteenth to the Nineteenth Century* (New York: Methuen, 1984); Angus McLaren, *Sexuality and Social Order: The Debate over the Fertility of Women and Workers in France, 1770–1920* (New York: Holmes and Meier, 1983); Linda Gordon, *Woman's Body, Woman's Right: A Social History of Birth Control in America* (New York: Penguin, 1977).

5. ADS, Dossiers Cour d'Assises, D2 U8 (39) Dossier 11 October 1875; (106) Dossier 9 October 1880. Fuye was sentenced to forced labor in perpetuity for rape, abortion, and corruption of a minor, but he served only nineteen years. His sentence was commuted in 1899 when he was sixty-five years old.

6. Angus McLaren, "Some Secular Attitudes toward Sexual Behavior in France: 1760–1860," *French Historical Studies* 8 (1974):605.

7. Francis Ronsin, *La grève des ventres: Progagande néo-Malthusienne et baisse de la natalité en France, 19e–20e siècles* (Paris: Aubier Montaigne, 1980), 123, 138.

8. See Angus McLaren, *Birth Control in Nineteenth-Century England* (New York: Holmes and Meier, 1978), 154.

9. See David Levine, *Family Formation in an Age of Nascent Capitalism* (New York: Academic Press, 1977).

10. Unlike in France, the birth rates of England and Germany had not yet begun to decline. At the end of the nineteenth century England's birth rate was

thirty per thousand and Germany's was thirty-six per thousand. The best discussion of Paul Robin and the issue of birth control can be found in McLaren *Sexuality and Social Order,* 2, 25–26, and chap. 6, and in Ronsin, *La grève des ventres,* 167–170. To try to garner some respectability, the League of Human Regeneration was quick to repudiate abortion. Members wanted to make clear that the league was to prevent pregnancies, not to terminate them. See Archives Nationales (AN), F7 13955.

11. Himes, *Medical History of Contraception,* 182.

12. McLaren, *Sexuality and Social Order,* 23.

13. McLaren, *Sexuality and Social Order,* 21; Etienne van de Walle, "Motivations and Technology in the Decline of French Fertility," in *Family and Sexuality in French History,* ed. Robert Wheaton and Tamara K. Hareven (Philadelphia: University of Pennsylvania Press, 1980), 135–178; Himes, *Medical History of Contraception,* 53–55, 191, 195, 226–230, 256–259.

14. The court cases of women tried for abortion between 1867 and 1892 reveal a higher percentage of married women than do the records of the public hospitals of Paris or the court cases of women tried for infanticide during the same years. Naturally, any figures based on criminal records are imprecise, and at best represent only those cases discovered and which had sufficient evidence to come to trial. On marital fertility control, see E. A. Wrigley, "Family Limitation in Pre-Industrial England," *Economic History Review* 19 (1966):82–109; James M. Donovan, "Abortion, the Law, and the Juries in France, 1825–1923," *Criminal Justice History* 9 (Fall 1988):171.

15. Ambroise Tardieu, *Etude médico-légale sur l'avortement suivie d'observations et de recherches pour servir à l'histoire médico-légale des grossesses fausses et simulées,* 4th ed. (Paris, 1881), 7–8. The first edition appeared in *Annales d'hygiène et de médecine légale,* 1855. Tardieu had been in forensic medicine (*médecine légale*) since 1844 and specialized in abortion and infanticide. Most references in this chapter are to the 1881 edition of this work. Two other editions, in 1863 and 1939, differ slightly from this middle edition and will be cited on points where they differ. Tardieu defines abortion as the "premature and violently provoked expulsion of the product of conception, independent of all circumstances of age, viability, or physical deformity."

16. E.-Adolphe Spiral, *Essai d'une étude sur l'avortement considéré au point de vue légal et spécialement de l'article 317 (1, 2, et 3) du code pénal relativement au concubinat suivi de l'examen de l'art. 340 du code civil* (Nancy, 1882), 6–9; Eugène Ferdut, *De l'avortement au point de vue médical, obstétrical, médico-légal, légal et théologique.* Thèse pour le doctorat en médecine (Paris, 1865), 97–98.

17. The law requiring the registration of all births and infant deaths within three days of birth was another means to exercise this control. Jeanne Gaillard, "Le médecin et l'avortement au XIXe siècle," *L'histoire* 16 (October 1979):35–37.

18. Angus McLaren, *Reproductive Rituals,* 115, 129.

19. Ferdut, *De l'avortement,* 102–106.

20. Roger-Henri Guerrand, "900,000 avortements en 1914?" *L'histoire* 16

(October 1979):38; Angus McLaren, "Abortion in France: Women and the Regulation of Family Size, 1800–1914," *French Historical Studies* 9 (Spring 1978):471–472; Tardieu, *Etude médico-légale sur l'avortement,* (1863), 93–96; (1881), 102–104; (1939), 102–105. The Academy appealed to the Pope to sanction their decision to allow therapeutic abortions; the Papacy took until 1895 to respond, and then said no.

21. Mme Giost, *Considérations sur l'avortement et l'infanticide dans leurs rapports avec la jurisprudence* (Paris, 1831), 22. Mme Giost was the directress of a maison d'accouchement. She wrote this short volume to magistrates, lawyers, and juries to enable them to acknowledge and judge spontaneous abortions and differentiate them from criminal abortions. She predated Ambroise Tardieu, the first and most famous medical-legal "expert" by twenty years. She differed significantly from Tardieu in her assertion that it was almost impossible to prove that an abortion had been criminally induced.

22. Paul Brouardel, *L'avortement* (Paris, 1901), 82, 117.

23. Stéphane Tarnier and Pierre Budin, *Traité de l'art des accouchements,* 3 vols. (Paris, 1888), 2:33–37, 363, 474–475; Dr. Antoine Corre, *Manuel d'accouchement et de pathologie puerpérale* (Paris, 1885), 320–321; Brouardel, *L'avortement,* 112–113.

24. Brouardel, *L'avortement,* 63–75, 109–111. Miscarriage during the second trimester is characteristic among women with syphilis.

25. Brouardel, *L'avortement,* 81–83; ADS, Dossiers Cour d'Assises, D2 U8 (139) Dossier 23 October 1882.

26. Brouardel, *L'avortement,* 84–85. The infant mortality figures were double that in the general population.

27. Tardieu, *Etude médico-légale sur l'avortement* (1863), 73–90; (1881), 82–100; (1939), 82–99. For specific hospital cases see Archives de l'Assistance Publique (AAP), L'Hôpital Port-Royal, Registres des correspondances, 24 June 1887. Letter to M. Lault, juge d'instruction; ADS, Dossiers Cour d'Assises, D2 U8 (221) Dossier 22 June 1887; (88) Dossier 22 August 1879.

28. Dr. Just Sicard de Plauzoles, *La maternité et la défense nationale contre la dépopulation* (Paris, 1909), 81–83. The data for my sample from la Maternité were identical. It is unlikely that more women resorted to abortion during these years, and more likely that they were willing to go to the now safer hospitals for problems.

29. Dr. Paul Bar, *La maternité de l'Hôpital St. Antoine. Description, organisation, fonctionnement du 18 mai 1897 à 1er janvier 1900* (Paris, 1900), 45–47; *La chronique médicale* (15 February 1909), 120, as quoted in McLaren, *Sexuality and Social Order,* 148.

30. McLaren, *Sexuality and Social Order,* 148.

31. Paul Delaunay, *La Maternité de Paris* (Paris: Jules Rousset, 1909), 136; Tardieu, *Etude médico-légale sur l'avortement* (1939), 127, 134.

32. Tardieu, *Etude médico-légale sur l'avortement,* (1881), 12–13. See also Spiral, *Essai d'une étude sur l'avortement,* 59; Dr. Ch. Floquet, *Avortement et dépopulation* (*Affaire Constance Thomas-Floury*), (Paris, 1892), 3; Brouardel, *L'avortement,* 44.

282 Notes to Pages 184–187

33. Tardieu, *Etude médico-légale sur l'avortement* (1881), 12–13; Brouardel, *L'avortement*, 44; B. R. Mitchell, *European Historical Statistics, 1750–1970* (New York: Columbia University Press, 1978), 4, 14.

34. Guerrand, "900,000 avortements en 1914?" 38, 45; McLaren, *Sexuality and Social Order*, 148. There were only 77,000 live births in 1904.

35. McLaren, *Sexuality and Social Order*, 148.

36. Paul Ponsolle, *La dépopulation. Introduction à l'étude sur la recherche de la paternité* (Paris, 1893), 16.

37. Marie Dh.'s lover did not want her to terminate the pregnancy because an abortion would have grave consequences for her health, but she had one anyway. Maria Da., who did not want a baby before marriage, had an abortion against her lover's wishes; and Eleanor S., a twenty-three-year-old domestic servant chose to have an abortion when she discovered her lover was married, even though he promised to support her. ADS, Dossiers Cour d'Assises, D2 U8 (218) Dossier Maria Da. 15 April 1887; (221) Dossier Marie Dh. 22 June 1887; (30) Dossier Eleanor S. 22 August 1874.

38. ADS, Dossiers Cour d'Assises, D2 U8 (35) Dossier 26 January 1875.

39. ADS, Dossiers Cour d'Assises, D2 U8 (48) Dossier 29 May 1876.

40. ADS, Dossiers Cour d'Assises, D2 U8 (122) Dossier 12 October 1881.

41. T. Galland, *De l'avortement au point de vue médico-légal* (Paris, 1878). The juge d'instruction and interrogators at the investigations for abortion often referred to the man who impregnated the woman as "the author of the pregnancy."

42. Eugène Ferdut, *De l'avortement au point de vue médical, obstétrical, médico-légal, légal et théologique*. Thèse pour le doctorat en médecine (Paris, 1865), 74–77; Tardieu, *Etude médico-légale sur l'avortement* (1881), 14, 17–18; Brouardel, *L'avortement*, 48, 116, 209. Tardieu places 44 percent during the middle trimester and Brouardel places 52 percent in this period.

43. For examples see ADS, Dossiers Cour d'Assises, D2 U8 (23) Dossier 10 December 1873; (35) Dossier 25 January 1875; (51) Dossier 19 August 1876; (122) Dossier 12 October 1881; (127) Dossier 14 February 1882.

44. Some of the more commonly used plants were savin, rue, yew, and rye ergot. Brouardel, *L'avortement*, 252–255; Tardieu, *Etude médico-légale sur l'avortement* (1939), 120; References to women making and drinking these concoctions abound in the court cases found in ADS, Dossiers Cour d'Assises, D2 U8, 1873–1889. For a detailed account of abortion methods see Edward L. Shorter, *A History of Women's Bodies* (New York: Basic Books, 1982), 177–223. Shorter provides great detail on the properties of the various herbs and drugs that women took to try to have an abortion. All of these drugs contained toxins which taken in sufficient quantities could produce contractions of the muscles of the intestines and uterus. Since the dosages are unknown, there is no way of ascertaining the effect they had.

45. Brouardel, *L'avortement*, 132; Tardieu, *Etude médico-légale sur l'avortement*, (1881) 31–32.

46. Tardieu, *Etude médico-légale sur l'avortement*, (1881), 50; Brouardel, *L'avortement*, 134.

47. Tardieu, *Etude médico-légale sur l'avortement*, (1881), 37; (1939), 116–117; Brouardel, *L'avortement*, 138.

48. McLaren, *Reproductive Rituals,* 104; Tardieu, *Etude médico-légale sur l'avortement,* (1881), 39–42; Brouardel, *L'avortement,* 142–150. Ergot is a mixture of alkaloids from rye fungus; some of the alkaloids cause uterine contractions. Its effectiveness in causing the onset of uterine contractions to provoke an abortion is more in doubt, especially in the first half of the pregnancy. It is only a secondary stimulant to uterine contractions, and in the doses taken by the women the results are not constant; much depended upon the freshness of the mold and the dosage used. It is still used by doctors today, in a form of ergometrine or ergotrate, to force uterine contractions to stop bleeding after a miscarriage.

49. Tardieu, *Etude médico-légale sur l'avortement,* (1881), 45–46.

50. Ferdut, *De l'avortement,* 63, 78–80. Tardieu, *Etude médico-légale sur l'avortement,* (1881), 26–27; Brouardel, *L'avortement,* 119–125. Despite the ineffectiveness of these measures, desperate women continued to try them, probably because a friend or neighbor knew of someone who tried one of these methods and aborted. The abortion may have been coincidental with the herbal concoction, but the word on the street was that there was a cause and effect.

51. Brouardel, *L'avortement,* 165–170.

52. For examples of advertisements for abortions see Jacques Bertillon, *La dépopulation de la France: Ses conséquences, ses causes, mesures à prendre pour la combattre* (Paris, 1911), 243–244; Madeleine Pelletier, *Le droit à l'avortement* (Paris, 1913), 8; McLaren, *Sexuality and Social Order,* 143.

53. Gordon, *Woman's Body, Woman's Right,* 70; Rosalind Pollack Petchesky, *Abortion and Woman's Choice: The State, Sexuality, and Reproductive Freedom* (Boston: Northeastern University Press, 1984), 33.

54. For examples see ADS, Dossiers Cour d'Assises, D2 U8, esp. (23) Dossier 29 December 1873; (48) Dossier 29 May 1876; and (51) Dossier 19 August 1876.

55. See the following court cases: ADS, Dossiers Cour d'Assises, D2 U8, (47) Dossier 10 May 1876; (51) Dossier 19 August 1876; (162) Dossier 24 May 1884.

56. ADS, Dossiers Cour D'Assises, D2 U8 (88) Dossier 22 August 1879. In some instances women made connections through others in the beds next to them in the hospitals. For example, Jeanne O. from the Morbihan had two "fausses couches" (miscarriages) noted on the registers of l'Hôpital Lariboisière. When in the hospital, she met another patient, B., whom she introduced to a midwife/abortionist in case the latter needed one. See ADS, Dossiers Cour d'Assises, D2 U8 (61) Dossier 12 June 1877.

57. Tardieu, *Etude médico-légale sur l'avortement,* (1881), 20.

58. "Mère Tiremonde" can be loosely translated as "Mother Pulling out All the World," or "Old Mother Pull out Everyone." Tardieu, *Etude médico-légale sur l'avortement,* (1881), 22.

59. Brouardel, *L'avortement,* 49; Tardieu, *Etude médico-légale sur l'avortement* (1939), 120.

60. Tardieu, *Etude médico-légale sur l'avortement* (1939), 122–123; Brouardel, *L'avortement,* 51; ADS, Dossiers Cour d'Assises, D2 U8 (24) Dossier 29 December 1873. The one midwife who allegedly charged Fr 500 performed services on a women who was married to a government official but was also the

mistress of a medium-level government employee who made her pregnant. The evidence in the court testimony is inconclusive about whether this Fr 500 was for an abortion or gynecology services.

61. ADS, Dossiers Cour d'Assises, D2 U8 (143) Dossier 24 February 1883.

62. Tardieu, *Etude médico-légale sur l'avortement,* (1881), 59. This procedure is borne out by the testimony, under interrogation, of many of the women accused of having had an abortion; see also Shorter, *A History of Women's Bodies,* 199–200.

63. Information on the midwives' abortion techniques in the above paragraphs comes from several sources: the women's and doctors' testimonies at the trials (see ADS, Dossiers Cour d'Assises—avortement); Tardieu, *Etude médico-légale sur l'avortement,* (1881), 52–56, 58, 60; (1939), 162–163; Brouardel, *L'avortement,* 152–165, 179, 181, 266, and 328–331 for a detailed description of intrauterine injection. Tardieu places the time of expulsion of the product of conception between five hours and eleven days after the provocation.

64. Corre, *Manuel d'accouchement,* 355, 362, 402–406; Tardieu, *Etude médico-légale sur l'avortement,* (1881), 58, 61; Brouardel, *L'avortement,* 174–196.

65. Tardieu, *Etude médico-légale sur l'avortement* (1863), 56; (1881), 62.

66. For an excellent discussion of the complex nature of these documents see Ruth Harris, "Melodrama, Hysteria, and Feminine Crimes of Passion in the Fin-de-Siècle," *History Workshop* 25 (Spring 1988):33. The court secretaries' reports are all available; they reveal that the interrogation of each woman followed similar lines with similar questions asked to try to establish what actually happened, motive, method, and the defendent's past moral conduct. These records of interrogations sometimes appear stylized or formulaic. Either they were not verbatim accounts, or the defendants and witnesses knew what was expected and had been coached to answer according to a formula. The accounts do record, however, when the defendant cried and when there was a conflict in the testimony. The Assize Courts consisted of three judges, the presiding judge, or president, and two assistant magistrates to assist the presiding judge in determining the penalty. For a detailed description of the criminal procedure *per se,* see James W. Garner, "Criminal Procedure in France," *Yale Law Journal* 25 (February 1916):255–284; Frederic R. Coudert, "French Criminal Procedure," *Yale Law Journal* 19 (March 1910):326–340.

67. Ferdut, *De l'avortement,* 90–92. The doctor's report in many of the court cases resulted from such "intensive questioning."

68. Brouardel, *L'avortement,* 45.

69. Brouardel, *L'avortement,* 58, 186–225; Tardieu, *Etude médico-légale sur l'avortement,* (1939), 6–10, 114.

70. Guerrand, "900,000 avortements en 1914?" 38; Garner, "Criminal Procedure in France," 278; Donovan, "Abortion, the Law, and the Juries in France," 163–164. Donovan's figures for acquittal are somewhat higher. He provides comparison figures: the acquittal rate for all felonies in France from 1825 to 1913 averaged 29 percent; the acquittal rate for abortion was thus twice as great as for all felonies.

71. Garner, "Criminal Procedure in France," 274, 279–280; Donovan, "Abortion, the Law, and the Juries," 164–165; Floquet, *Avortement et dépopulation*, 6.

72. The data are derived from Floquet, *Avortement et dépopulation*, 6–7, 11. Constance Thomas had worked as a domestic for a doctor, where she studied his books on female anatomy and childbirth and then became a practicing abortionist. At one time she plied her trade in the back of a wine seller's shop for a fee of Fr 10 to Fr 20, according to the ability of her client to pay. The case was far more complicated than this brief sketch indicates. For the best analysis of it see René Le Mée, "Une affaire de 'faiseuses d'anges' à la fin du XIXe siècle," *Communications: Dénatalité, l'antériorité française, 1800–1914*, no. 44 (Paris: Ecole des Hautes Etudes en Sciences Sociales, Seuil, 1986):137–174. For a sensationalist account of this abortionist see Maurice Talmeyr, *Sur le banc. Les avorteuses de Paris*, vol. 2, 2d ser. (Paris, 1890).

73. Floquet, *Avortement et dépopulation*, 11.

74. André-Théodore Brochard, *La vérité sur les enfants trouvés* (Paris, 1876), 98–99, as quoted by McLaren, *Sexuality and Social Order*, 139–140.

75. Maxime DuCamp, *Paris: Ses organes, ses fonctions et sa vie dans la seconde moitié du XIXe siècle*, 6 vols. (Paris, 1875), 4:123.

76. ADS, Dossiers Cour d'Assises, D2 U8 (51) Dossier 19 August 1876.

77. Dr. Antoine Corre, *La mère et l'enfant dans les races humaines* (Paris, 1882), 255; Sicard de Plauzoles, *La maternité*, 84–85.

78. See for example ADS, Dossiers Cour d'Assises, D2 U8 (60) Dossier 10 April 1877.

79. ADS, Dossiers Cour d'Assises, D2 U8 Dossier Marie Dh. (221) 22 June 1887; Dossier Englantine P. (47) 10 May 1876; Dossier Constance F. (219) 23 April 1887.

80. Paul Strauss, "Bulletin," *La revue philanthropique* 30 (1911–1912):239; Dr. Gustave Drouineau, *De l'assistance aux filles-mères et aux enfants abandonnés* (Paris, 1878), 18; "De l'avortement, mesures à prendre," *La revue philanthropique* 21 (1907–1908):145–156. The phrase "right-to-life" is a quotation from the times.

81. Drouineau, *De l'assistance aux filles-mères et aux enfants abandonnés*, 18; "Variétés," *La revue philanthropique* 30 (1911–1912):301–302.

82. Commission de la dépopulation: Sous-commission de la mortalité, *Rapport général sur les causes de la mortalité*, présenté par M. Paul Strauss (Melun, 1911), 1–30; see also Archives de la Préfecture de Police (AAP), D/B 614, avortement; "Variétés," *La revue philanthropique* 30 (1911–1912):302–303.

83. Dr. Gustave Drouineau, *De l'avortement. Mesures à prendre*, Rapport présenté au conseil d'administration de la ligue contre la mortalité infantile, 27 May 1907. Extr. du *La revue philanthropique*, 15 June 1907, (Paris, 1907):1, 6, 9; see also Commission de la dépopulation: Sous-commission de la mortalité, *Rapport général sur les causes de la mortalité*.

84. Spiral, *Essai d'une étude sur l'avortement*, 10–14, 19.

85. Ibid., 26–62; McLaren, *Sexuality and Social Order*, 149.

86. In France, as in England, the belief that unwed mothers would commit

suicide from an overwhelming sense of shame seems more in tune with bourgeois values of propriety than with the strategies of the poor for whom an out-of-wedlock child may not have been such an overwhelming stigma. Although there are some poignant pictures of a pregnant woman standing on the banks of the Seine, the suicide of a poor and pregnant woman does not regularly appear in the popular novels or in the tracts of social reformers. Louis Chevalier, in reviewing the literature on suicide, noted that only one-third of the suicides were committed by women. He asserts, without substantive evidence, that women commit suicide for the same reasons they commit infanticide. For a discussion of this theme in England, see Ann Rowell Higginbotham, "The Unmarried Mother and Her Child in Victorian London, 1834–1914," (Ph.D. diss., Indiana University, 1985), 207–210. See also Chevalier, *Laboring Classes and Dangerous Classes,* 285–286.

87. Pelletier, *Le droit à l'avortement,* 6–7, 13, 18.

88. Claire Galichon, *Amour et maternité* (Paris, 1907), 200–214.

89. As quoted by Sicard de Plauzoles, *La maternité,* 87.

90. Paul Strauss, "Bulletin," *La Revue philanthropique* 2 (1897–1898):798; *Conseil général de l'assistance publique,* fasc. 31 (1900), 114.

9. *Infanticide and Child Abandonment*

1. Archives de la Ville de Paris et Département de la Seine (ADS), Dossiers Cour d'Assises, D2 U8 (192) Dossier 17 November 1885; Archives de l'Assistance Publique (AAP), l'Hôptial Port-Royal, Registres des correspondances, L. 5, 3 August 1885, letter from director of la Maternité to the director of l'Assistance publique.

2. ADS, Dossiers Cour d'Assises, D2 U8 (48) Dossier 9 June 1876.

3. Peter C. Hoffer and N. E. H. Hull, *Murdering Mothers: Infanticide in England and New England 1558–1803* (New York: New York University Press, 1981); William L. Langer "Infanticide: A Historical Survey," *History of Childhood Quarterly* 1 (Winter 1974):353–365, and "Checks on Population Growth: 1750–1850," *Scientific American* 226 (February 1972):93–99; Maria W. Piers, *Infanticide Past and Present* (New York: W. W. Norton, 1978); R. C. Trexler, "Infanticide in Florence: New Sources and First Results," *History of Childhood Quarterly* 1 (1973):98–115; Sharon Begley, "Nature's Baby Killers," *Newsweek* (September 6, 1982):78–79; Mary Batten, "Slaughter of the Innocents: The Evolution of Infanticide," *Science Digest* (January 1983):38, 108; William A. Silverman, "Mismatched Attitudes about Neonatal Death," *The Hastings Center Report* (December 1981):12–15.

4. Philippe Ariès, *A Century of Childhood: A Social History of Family Life,* trans. Robert Baldick (New York: Vintage Books, 1962); Richard Lalou, "L'infanticide devant les tribunaux français (1825–1910)" *Communications: Dénatalité, l'antériorité française, 1800–1914,* no. 44 (Paris: Seuil, 1986), 175–200.

5. Farr, *The Wages of Sin,* chap. 4; Dominique Vallaud, "Le crime d'infanti-

cide et l'indulgence des cours d'assises en France au XIX siècle," *Social Science Information* 21, no. 3 (1982):476; Lalou, "L'infanticide devant les tribunaux français," 187.

6. Vallaud, "Le crime d'infanticide," 477.

7. ADS, Dossiers Cour d'Assises D2 U8 (83) Dossier 22 April 1879. In one particular way the nineteenth-century law and custom differed from that of the Old Regime. By the nineteenth-century Civil Code, in contrast with the terms of the Edict of 1556, it would do a pregnant woman no good to name the father. Forbidding the search for paternity completely undermined one of the central goals of the declarations of pregnancy—inculpating the father and making him share some responsibility.

8. Vallaud, "Le crime d'infanticide," 479; James W. Garner, "Criminal Procedure in France," *Yale Law Journal* 25 (February 1916):272, 279.

9. William Loubat, "Programme minimum de réformes pénales," *Revue politique et parlementaire,* 74 (March 1913):452.

10. See for example ADS, Dossiers Cour d'Assises, D2 U8 (4) Dossier 29 May 1869; (88) Dossier 4 August 1879.

11. Ambroise Tardieu, *Etude médico-légale sur l'infanticide* (Paris, 1868, 1880), (1880) 13–15.

12. AAP, l'Hôpital Port-Royal, L.2., Registres des correspondances, 28 February 1873.

13. See for example ADS, Dossiers Cour d'Assises, D2 U8 (17) Dossier 20 February 1873 and (53) Dossier 11 October 1876.

14. Victorine Mégin, a twenty-one-year-old unwed mother, had her baby at a welfare midwife's establishment, but just before her scheduled departure she notified the midwife that her infant did not appear to be alive. The midwife did not believe that the baby could have died from natural causes since it had been in good condition, and the mother had been preoccupied with ridding herself of the child by abandoning it. The midwife called the police and the infant's corpse went to the morgue for an autopsy. Mégin never went to trial. AAP, l'Hôpital Port-Royal, Registres des correspondances, L.5, 16 May 1892; for letters from the director of la Maternité to the police, and vice versa, see Registres des correspondances for 19 January 1873, 30 March 1883, 19 May 1883, 25 January 1885, 3 August 1885, 29 September 1885, and 4 February 1895.

15. Tardieu, *Etude médico-légale sur l'infanticide,* (1880), 3–5, 7–9; Lalou, "L'infanticide devant les tribunaux français," 180.

16. According to Paul Brouardel, from 1831 to 1880 there were 8,568 cases of infanticide brought before the courts of France. The number increased steadily from an average of 94 per year from 1831 to 1835 to an average of 214 per year from 1856 to 1860. It then declined to an average of 200 per year in the decade of the 1870s, and by 1892 only 163 women were brought to trial. By the eve of the First World War the numbers tried for infanticide had fallen to below 100 per year. Paul Brouardel, *L'infanticide* (Paris, 1897), 14; Emile Levasseur, *La population française,* 3 vols. (Paris, 1891), 1:313; Archives Nationales (AN), F7 12243 account from the Minister of Justice to the Minister of Interior, 30 October 1838. These data should be interpreted in terms of possible national trends. According

to Dr. Gustave Drouineau, for just the ten years from 1887 to 1896 there were an average of 447 cases of infanticide per year, almost double the number in the period from 1851 to 1865. It is likely that his figures were inflated by his advocacy for changes in the law to prevent infanticide and infant mortality in general. Dr. Gustave Drouineau, "L'assistance maternelle" (Rapport présenté à la ligue contre la mortalité infantile), *La revue philanthropique* 12 (1902):258. Historians Peter M. Smith and Frances Gouda carefully calculate that the infanticide rate in France from 1825 through 1913 more than doubled from .005 in 1825 to a peak of .010 to .012 in the years from 1850 through 1870. It then began its decline to less than .005 in 1900. Peter M. Smith, "Time as a Historical Construct," *Historical Methods* 17 (Fall 1984):188–189.

17. Tardieu, *Etude médico-légale sur l'infanticide* (1868), 11. Maxime Du-Camp's figures are greater than Tardieu's: the number of dead babies and fetuses fished from the Seine and brought to the Paris morgue increased from 78 in 1846 to 146 in 1866. In 1875 that number increased to 95 newborns and 70 fetuses. See Maxime DuCamp, *Paris: Ses organes, ses fonctions et sa vie dans la seconde moitié du XIXe siècle*, 6 vols. (Paris, 1869–1875), 1:339.

18. Conseil supérieur de l'Assistance publique, fasc. 91 and fasc. 31 (1900), 114. The number of extant court cases in the archival dossiers of the Cour d'Assises rarely exceeded ten per year. Numbers of infanticides, often widely discrepant, fail to reflect the true incidence of infanticide and only reveal the numbers of women either arrested or brought to trial. The proportion of those brought to trial out of those suspected and arrested was rarely more than one-third and sometimes not more than one-fourth. The data are important in that they provide a rough idea of the changing rate of reported incidence of infanticide and in that they were widely publicized at the time and used to support various arguments pertaining to women's morality, sexuality, crime, and public policy affecting the women and their babies.

19. Smith, "Time as a Historical Construct," 188–189; Lalou, "L'infanticide devant les tribunaux français," 192–193.

20. Edward L. Shorter, *The Making of the Modern Family* (New York: Basic Books, 1975), 168–195; Lalou, "L'infanticide devant les tribunaux français," 196.

21. Tardieu, *Etude médico-légale sur l'infanticide* (1868), 11; Smith, "Time as a Historical Construct," 188–189.

22. Vallaud, "Le crime d'infanticide," 480. Vallaud bases her data on Département de la Justice, *Compte général de l'administration de la justice criminelle, 1880* (Paris, 1882). Tardieu examined a shorter time period and demonstrated that of the 3,012 brought to trial in France from 1851 to 1865, 36 percent were acquitted. Tardieu, *Etude médico-légale sur l'infanticide* (1868), 8–9. It is difficult to obtain acquittal rates for cases of infanticide in Paris. The best figures are a 40–42 percent acquittal rate for cases of abortion and infanticide in all of France. In a similar time period, 30–40 percent of all other violent crimes were acquitted. See James M. Donovan, "Justice Unblind: The Jurors and the Criminal Cases in France, 1825–1914," *Journal of Social History* 15 (Fall 1981):93. Acquittal rates were also high in England, even when there seemed to have been evidence of the

woman's guilt. In England as well as France, women who killed their newborn infants met with sympathy. See Langer, "Checks on Population Growth," 96; and Higginbotham, "The Unmarried Mother and Her Child in Victorian London," 247–248.

23. Vallaud, "Le crime d'infanticide," 480. See also James M. Donovan, "Infanticide and the Juries in France, 1825–1913," *Journal of Family History* 16, no. 2 (1991):157–176.

24. Brouardel, *L'infanticide*, 77–78.

25. Brouardel, *L'infanticide*, 10–11.

26. Tardieu, *Etude médico-légale sur l'infanticide*, (1880), 19–20, 281–285, 333–345.

27. Tardieu, *Etude médico-légale sur l'infanticide* (1868), 99, 28–31; Brouardel, *L'infanticide*, 20–28. For his mention of much smaller infants being born at term and viable, see ADS, Dossiers Cour d'Assises, D2 U8 (146) Dossier 25 May 1883.

28. Brouardel, *L'infanticide*, 53–68; Tardieu, *Etude médico-légale sur l'infanticide*, 81.

29. Brouardel, *L'infanticide*, 82.

30. Tardieu, *Etude médico-légale sur l'infanticide* (1880), 122–124; for a statement that a woman fainted during the delivery and when she awakened found her infant suffocated between her legs, see ADS, Dossiers Cour d'Assises, D2 U8 (53) Dossier 11 October 1876.

31. Brouardel, *L'infanticide*, 45, 80–82, 329–330.

32. Tardieu, *Etude médico-légale sur l'infanticide* (1868), 99; Brouardel, *L'Infanticide*, 79–86.

33. Tardieu, *Etude médico-légale sur l'infanticide*, 152–155.

34. Brouardel, *L'infanticide*, 88; ADS, Dossiers Cour d'Assises, D2 U8 (48) Dossier 20 May 1876. In one case the woman testified that she pulled the baby by its neck to hasten the birth.

35. Examples of this excuse are numerous in the criminal investigations. For example see ADS, Dossiers Cour d'Assises, D2 U8 (114) Dossier 23 March 1881; (60) Dossier 25 April 1877.

36. Someone would have had to push the newborn down at the correct angles. In some instances, the body had been dismembered to more easily fit down the hole. Brouardel, *L'infanticide*, 92–101.

37. ADS, Dossiers Cour d'Assises, D2 U8 (135) Dossier 25 July 1882 and (247) Dossier 19 January 1889. Their cases rested on the concurrence of the doctor and the plumbers' reports that the hole and pipes were large enough for the infant. In neither case was Tardieu the doctor on the scene.

38. Tardieu, *Etude médico-légale sur l'infanticide* (1880), 159–160, 165, 172; Brouardel, *L'infanticide*, 102–103.

39. Tardieu, *Etude médico-légale sur l'infanticide* (1880), 133, 137–139, 142; Brouardel, *L'infanticide*, 53, 106–107, 111–113, 118–119. Brouardel, unlike Tardieu, admitted that occasionally a woman having unexpected labor pains could deliver as she was standing. The emerging infant could fall on the ground and fracture its head, and the cord would tear; but these events were

exceedingly rare, although at least one woman insisted this happened with her sixth child. ADS, Dossiers Cour d'Assises, D2 U8 (62) Dossier 25 June 1877. Even in a very rapid delivery, uterine contractions are not usually strong enough to push the infant toward the floor and tear the placenta. Furthermore, an infant never emerges all at once, and even if its head did hit the floor, the fall would not necessarily produce a fatal fracture. Only infrequently is the placenta expelled at the same time as the infant.

40. ADS, Dossiers Cour d'Assises, D2 U8 (21) Dossier 13 September 1873.

41. Tardieu, *Etude médico-légale sur l'infanticide* (1880), 99, 192–193; Brouardel, *L'infanticide,* 133, 328–335.

42. Tardieu, *Etude médico-légale sur l'infanticide,* (1880), 195–203.

43. Tardieu, *Etude médico-légale sur l'infanticide* (1880), 218–219, 229; Brouardel, *L'infanticide,* 147.

44. Almost every dossier from the Assize Courts mentions a woman's morality. See, e.g., ADS, Dossiers Cour d'Assises, D2 U8 (53) Dossier 11 October 1876, for "absolutely irreproachable conduct and services" and (62) Dossier 3 July 1877. For discussion of immorality see, e.g., (5) Dossier 8 June 1867; (61) Dossier 23 June 1877; (92) Dossier 6 January 1880.

45. See Robert Nye, *Crime, Madness, and Politics in Modern France: The Medical Concept of National Decline* (Princeton, N.J.: Princeton University Press, 1984).

46. For Ernestine Pallet see *Gazette des tribunaux* (28 September 1881), 1–2; ADS, Dossiers Cour d'Assises, D2 U8 (120) Dossier 27 September 1881; for other examples see (47) Dossier 11 May 1876; (71) Dossier 20 February 1878; (79) Dossier 9 November 1878; (120) Dossier 12 September 1881. See also Tardieu, *Etude médico-légale sur l'infanticide* (1880), 240–241.

47. Tardieu, *Etude médico-légale sur l'infanticide* (1880), 240–242. This is a very loose, often paraphrased, translation, but the intentions and words of the original have been maintained as much as feasible. See also pages 252, 338–340.

48. Brouardel, *L'infanticide,* 164–165. In one case of a woman tried for infanticide, her doctor from her hometown in Alsace vouched that since her birth "the accused had momentary madness." The woman was acquitted. Brouardel, the forensic doctor who served as the "expert" in this case, testified that there was absolutely nothing wrong with her mental health. See ADS, Dossiers Cour d'Assises, D2 U8 (148) Dossier 27 June 1882.

49. Vanessa R. Schwartz, "Dead Babies, Expert Doctors, and Crazy Women: Infanticide Trials in Nineteenth-Century France," seminar paper, 6 May 1988, Department of History, University of California, Berkeley, 22.

50. ADS, Dossiers Cour d'Assises, D2 U8 (48) Dossier 12 June 1876.

51. Tardieu, *Etude médico-légale sur l'infanticide* (1880), 230–233, quotation from 233; Brouardel, *L'infanticide,* 151–153.

52. ADS, Dossiers Cour d'Assises, D2 U8 (17) Dossier 20 February 1873; (58) Dossier 8 March 1877; (60) Dossier 25 April 1877; (62) Dossier 25 June 1877; (88) 4 August 1879; (135) Dossier 25 July 1882; (146) Dossier 25 May 1883; (153) Dossier 23 October 1883.

53. ADS, Dossiers Cour d'Assises, D2 U8 (17) Dossier 20 February 1873;

(21) Dossier 13 September 1873; (40) Dossier 25 October 1875; (60) Dossier 25 April 1877.

54. Doctors admitted that it was sometimes possible to deliver suddenly and to be unaware of labor pains, but at the moment of delivery the woman has to be aware that she is having a baby, unless, of course, she becomes unconscious. Tardieu, *Etude médico-légale sur l'infanticide* (1880), 235; Brouardel, *L'infanticide,* 154–155.

55. Tardieu, *Etude médico-légale sur l'infanticide* (1880), 239; for relevant court cases using this defense see ADS, Dossiers Cour d'Assises, D2 U8 (53) Dossier 11 October 1876 and (109) Dossier 7 January 1881.

56. Brouardel, *L'infanticide,* 13, 155–161, 327–335.

57. Brouardel, *L'infanticide,* 159.

58. Every court case included attestations of the suspect's morality and immorality. It would be impossible to cite them all. See note 46 above and ADS, Dossiers Cour d'Assises, D2 U8 (88) Dossier 4 August 1879. For conflicting morality reports on one suspect see (62) Dossier 3 July 1877; for one case of dubious morality see (139) Dossier 9 November 1882.

59. Camille Rabaud, *Le péril national ou la dépopulation croissante de la France* (Paris, 1891), 23.

60. Brouardel, *L'infanticide,* vii, 2–3; Tardieu, *Etude médico-légale sur l'infanticide,* 10.

61. Paul Ponsolle, *La dépopulation. Introduction à l'étude sur la recherche de la paternité* (Paris, 1893), 30. ADS, Dossiers Cour d'Assises, D2 U8 (48) Dossier 9 June 1876 for Anna B. See also (105) Dossier 5 October 1880 and (120) Dossier 12 September 1881, for examples of acquittals of women of good general morality abandoned by the father of their child after he had promised marriage, or who had been made pregnant by their employer. The jilted Anna Bordot was sentenced to six years of hard labor in part because Bordot emphatically denied her pregnancy, according to the testimony of her employer. Other suspects were never confronted with a denial of pregnancy because no one seems to have asked; some pled temporary insanity. Also, most acquittals of jilted women occurred after 1880 and rarely before—Bordot came to trial in 1876.

62. ADS, Dossiers Cour d'Assises, D2 U8 (120) Dossier 12 September 1881.

63. Brouardel, *L'infanticide,* 2–3; ADS, Dossiers Cour d'Assises, D2 U8 (128) Dossier 3 March 1882; (134) Dossier 6 June 1882, for dismemberment of the body into many pieces to better dispose of it, and (146) Dossier 24 May 1883, for conviction and violence to the infant. For a typical case of a woman who admitted premeditated infanticide, see ADS, Dossiers Cour d'Assises, D2 U8 (169) Dossier 22 September 1884.

64. In all of France, the infant's mother comprised 93 percent of those accused of this crime, and about three-fourths were single. During the first half of the century three-fourths were between the ages of twenty-one and thirty and illiterate. After 1876 those accused of infanticide were on the average younger (twice as many were teenagers as earlier in the century), and only half were illiterate. Almost three-fourths worked in agriculture or as domestic servants. Tardieu,

Etude médico-légale sur l'infanticide, 8–9; Brouardel, *L'infanticide,* 16–17; Vallaud, "Le crime d'infanticide," 496; Lalou, "L'infanticide devant les tribunaux français," 182–183. In England as well, 85 percent of the women tried for child murder were domestic servants. See Higginbotham, "The Unmarried Mother," 236.

65. ADS, Dossiers Cour d'Assises, D2 U8 (58) Dossier 8 March 1877.

66. ADS, Dossiers Cour d'Assises, D2 U8 (83) Dossier 22 April 1879. Others wanted to avoid la Maternité or were intimidated by the hospital's environment. See (58) Dossier 8 March 1877.

67. ADS, Dossiers Cour d'Assises, D2 U8 (146) Dossier 22 May 1883 and (148) Dossier 27 June 1882.

68. Vallaud, "Le crime d'infanticide," 485.

69. Piers, *Infanticide,* 39, 44.

70. ADS, Dossiers Cour d'Assises, D2 U8 (83) Dossier 24 March 1879; (276) Dossier 4 July 1891. Vallaud, "Le crime d'infanticide," 485; One twenty-two-year-old woman said that if her father knew she was pregnant it would kill him; see (58) Dossier 8 March 1877; see also (49) 20 June 1876; (48) 20 May 1876. Young Marie Melun from Brittany said that it was the "shame of admitting my fault that made me determine to have my infant perish." See also (90) Dossier 12 September 1879; (285) Dossier 14 October 1891.

71. ADS, Dossiers Cour d'Assises, D2 U8 (92) Dossier 6 January 1880. Marie Coudert, sad and sombre, came from a religious family in Brittany and wanted to hide her pregnancy out of shame. See (37) Dossier 13 April 1875.

72. ADS, Dossiers Cour d'Assises, D2 U8 (8) Dossier 13 June 1867. Widows, too, could shame their family if they had a child more than nine months after the death of their husbands. Magdelene Guyot, a thirty-six-year-old widow with two children, left her hometown in the Yonne when she was several months pregnant. See ADS, Dossiers Cour d'Assises, D2 U8 (32) Dossier 14 October 1874.

73. ADS, Dossiers Cour d'Assises, D2 U8 (8) Dossier 13 June 1867; (147) Dossier 8 June 1883 [Nauget]; (32) Dossier 14 October 1874.

74. Hoffer and Hull, *Murdering Mothers,* 147. ADS, Dossiers Cour d'Assises, D2 U8 (47) Dossier 11 May 1876.

75. ADS, Dossiers Cour d'Assises, D2 U8 (218) Dossier 19 April 1887; (37) Dossier 14 April 1875.

76. For just a few of many examples, see: ADS, Dossiers Cour d'Assises, D2 U8 (92) Dossier 6 January 1880; (109) Dossier 7 January 1881;

77. Joseph Marie De Gérando, *Le visiteur du pauvre* (Paris, 1820), 86–87. Efforts to prevent infanticide were not unique to France. In England, private charities founded maternity homes for the unwed and justified them as a means to decrease infanticide.

78. Adolphe Henri Gaillard (Abbé), *Recherches administratives, statistiques* (Paris, 1837), 342, 356, and *Examen du rapport de M. le Baron de Watteville sur les tours, les infanticides . . .* (Paris, 1856), 9–10; Brouardel, *L'infanticide,* 15; Rabaud, *Le péril national ou la dépopulation croissante de la France* (Paris, 1891), 39.

79. François Vidal, *De la répartition des richesses* (Paris, 1846), 285, quoted by

Angus McLaren, *Sexuality and Social Order: The Debate over the Fertility of Women and Workers in France, 1770–1920* (New York, 1983), 86 (emphasis in the original).

80. Tardieu, *Etude médico-légale sur l'infanticide* (1868), 6. In midcentury as well, reformers argued for keeping the *tours* and open abandonment. P. A. Dufau, *Essai sur la science de la misère sociale* (Paris, 1857), 211–217. Tardieu, *Etude médico-légale sur l'infanticide;* André-Théodore Brochard, *Des causes de la dépopulation en France et des moyens d'y remédier. Mémoire lu au congrès médical de Lyon, Septembre 1872* (Lyon, 1873), 20, and *La vérité sur les enfants trouvés* (Paris, 1876), 98–102; Dr. Gaston Variot, "Le secret de la Maternité et le rétablissement des tours," *Le Journal* (17 June 1913) clipping in Bibliothèque Marguerite Durand (BMD), 360 ASS PUB; Amédée Bondé, *Etude sur l'infanticide, l'exposition et la condition des enfants exposés en droit romain . . .* (Paris, 1883), 102–105. Tardieu called for statistical correlations between the incidence of infanticide and the existence of a *tour.* Such statistics would be welcome, but it is impossible to to obtain figures for incidence of infanticide. The best that can be done is to obtain incidence of arrests. The same desire to force women to keep their babies, or not to have them at all, motivated reformers both to curtail abandonments by closing the *tours* and also to intensify the efforts to arrest and prosecute people for infanticide.

81. Brochard, *Des causes de la dépopulation,* 20.

82. Paul Strauss, "Bulletin," *La revue philanthropique* 2 (1897–1898):798, and *Conseil général de l'Assistance publique,* fasc. 31 (1900), 114.

83. AAP, l'Hôpital Port-Royal, L.5, Registres des correspondances, 14 November 1883. Another time, a new mother planning on abandoning her baby was walking to the foundling home with a nurse's aid from la Maternité. They soon were accosted by a woman who said, "You are going to abandon your infant; give it to me. . . . I will raise it and give you a job" as a domestic. She offered the nurse's aid Fr 3 for her silence and complicity. They both refused. AAP, l'Hôpital Port-Royal, Registres des correspondances, 9 May 1889. In nineteenth-century England, as well, legal adoption was unavailable. Until the English Adoption Law of 1927, the "law made no provision for the surrender of parental rights to another individual as long as either parent was alive." Extralegal adoption probably also occurred there, as in France. See Higginbotham, "The Unmarried Mother," 163.

84. For a fuller discussion of abandoned children in diverse times and places see Fuchs, *Abandoned Children;* Claude Delasselle, "Abandoned Children in Eighteenth-Century Paris," in *Deviants and the Abandoned in French Society,* ed. Robert Forster and Orest Ranum (Baltimore: Johns Hopkins University Press, 1978); John Boswell, *The Kindness of Strangers: The Abandonment of Children in Western Europe from Late Antiquity to the Renaissance* (New York: Pantheon, 1988); David L. Ransel, *Mothers of Misery: Child Abandonment in Russia* (Princeton, N.J.: Princeton University Press, 1988); Volker Hunecke, *I trovatelli di Milano: Bambini esposti e famiglie espositrici dal XVII al XIX secolo,* trans. Benedetta Heinemann Campana (Bologna: Il Mulino, 1989); Joan Sherwood, *Poverty in Eighteenth-Century Spain: The Women and Children of the Inclusa* (Toronto: University of Toronto Press, 1988).

85. Valdruche, *Rapport au ministre de l'intérieur et au conseil général des hospices relatif aux enfants trouvés dans le département de la Seine, suivi de documents officiels* (Paris, 1838), tableau 11. The samples from AAP, l'Hôpital Port-Royal, Registres des entrées, 1830, 1837, 1838, generally concur with Valdruche's findings.

86. For further analysis of this regulation and these data see Fuchs, "Legislation, Poverty, and Child Abandonment in Nineteenth-Century Paris," 60–61, tables 1 and 2, and *Abandoned Children*, 77–87. The 10 percent of mothers who left la Maternité without their babies either sent their infant directly to a wetnurse, or else the baby had died.

87. Abandonment data for mothers who gave birth at la Maternité are available only up to 1869 and indicate that 38 percent of women who gave birth in la Maternité abandoned their infants that year, either directly from the hospital or several days after their discharge from la Maternité with their infants.

88. BMD, DOS 360 ASS, clipping from *Tribunal du Peuple*, 22 November 1899. Story is told by Michel Zevaco, in *Tribunal du Peuple*, with no mention of the child's return.

89. Statistics are marred because the category of "enfants assistés" included all abandoned infants as well as abused and neglected older children (the *moralement abandonnés*) who came under the protection of the state in increasing numbers.

90. Olwen Hufton, *The Poor of Eighteenth-Century France, 1750–1789* (Oxford: Clarendon Press, 1974), 318–351. Some married women who abandoned their babies may have been deserted by their husbands. The records are mute on this point. They were not, however, widows. For a detailed description of the statistics and the data bases, see Fuchs, "Legislation, Poverty, and Child Abandonment," 57–58, 64–65. By comparison, in Milan during the same time period and in Madrid in the previous century, a far higher percentage of abandoned children were legitimate off-spring of married women. In both of these cities, reclaiming an abandoned child was simple and commonplace, and a high proportion of legitimate children were reclaimed. The ease of reclamation perhaps made child abandonment a temporary solution to ease women out of a difficult time in the other cities, whereas in Paris it became a more permanent solution and therefore one chosen by only the most desperate—the single mother. In Russia, as many as one-third to one-half of the abandoning mothers were married, until the 1891 reforms excluded virtually all legitimate children from the foundling homes. Sherwood, *Poverty in Eighteenth-Century Spain;* Hunecke, *I trovatelli di Milano;* Ransel, *Mothers of Misery.*

91. For a discussion of the regression analysis employed to determine these results see Fuchs, "Legislation, Poverty, and Child Abandonment," 67–77, tables 4–8.

Conclusion

1. William Reddy, *The Rise of Market Culture: The Textile Trade and French Society, 1750–1900* (New York: Cambridge University Press, 1984), 165.

2. ADS, "Rapports d'inspection," MSS, Brindejont, 1893.

3. ADS, Dossiers Cour d'Assises, D2 U8 (166) Dossier 26 July 1884.

4. Higginbotham, "The Unmarried Mother and Her Child in Victorian London, 1834–1914," 37, 71, 149; and Ellen Ross, "Hungry Children: Housewives and London Charity, 1870–1918," in *The Uses of Charity: The Poor on Relief in the Nineteenth-Century Metropolis,* ed. Peter Mandler (Philadelphia: University of Pennsylvania Press, 1990).

5. Ransel, *Mothers of Misery,* 109; Seth Koven and Sonya Michel, "Womanly Duties: Maternalist Politics and the Origins of Welfare States in France, Germany, Great Britain, and the United States, 1880–1920," *American Historical Review* 95 (October 1990):1076–1108.

6. See Donzelot, *The Policing of Families.*

7. Paul Strauss, "Bulletin," *La Revue philanthropique* 9 (1901):654.

8. For a discussion of the issues surrounding childbirth in the twentieth century see Françoise Thébaud, *Quand nos grand-mères donnaient la vie: La maternité en France dans l'entre-deux-guerres* (Lyon: Presses Universitaires de Lyon, 1986).

9. François Ewald, *L'etat providence* (Paris: Bernard Grasset, 1986).

Archival Sources

Archives de l'Assistance Publique (AAP)

l'Hôpital Port-Royal, 1830–1900: Registres des correspondances, Registres des entrées, Registres des décès, Registres de sorties des femmes enceintes et en couches, Registres général de naissance des enfants, Registres de sorties des enfants, and Registres des femmes en couches envoyées chez les sage-femmes, 1869–1898.

Fosseyeux 33 Note sur le service de secours à domicile dans Paris, 1864.

Fosseyeux 94, 96, 228, 305, 648 Registres, Procès verbaux, Bureaux de bienfaisance du 3, 6, 10, 12 arrondissements.

Fosseyeux 101 Registres, Fondation Montyon.

Fosseyeux 151 Service d'Accouchement de l'Hôtel-Dieu.

Fosseyeux 577 Maternité Baudelocque, Répertoire de diagnostics, 1896–1897.

Fosseyeux 686 Brochures relatives à la mère.

Fosseyeux 690 Assistance en France: Assistance à la mère et à l'enfant.

Fosseyeux 707[2] Frigerio, "Rapport sur le service de santé de la Maison d'Accouchement [la Maternité]."

Fosseyeux 708[2] Recherches tendant à découvrir la cause de la maladie qui s'y produit sous le nom de fièvre puerpérale."

Fosseyeux 708[14] Société philanthropique de Paris, 708[19] Société charitable de Saint-Régis, 708[26] Bureaux de bienfaisance.

Archives Nationales (AN)

F7 12243 Infanticides 1838–1845.

F7 12379–12384 Sociétés de secours mutuels.

F15 1528, 1545, 1626–1632 Etablissements charitables, 1822–1835.

F15 2564–2566 Sociétés maternelles 1806–1820.

F15 3782–3798 Secours divers.

F15 3799–3813 Société de charité maternelle 1809–1876, Société des crèches 1853–1877.

F15 3865–3866 Etablissements de bienfaisance.

F15 3894 Société de charité maternelle. Comptabilité, 1862–1872.

F15 4257–4259 Aide à des oeuvres de bienfaisance, 1882–1913.
F17 12528–12537 Crèches, orphelinats.

Archives de la Préfecture de Police (APP)

D/B 90, proposals to amend the law of 1850 on the marriage of indigents, 1876, 1890; Circular from préfet de police to commissaire de police, 22 May 1847; Maison de refuge et de travail; Oeuvre de la maison de refuge de Bon Pasteur; Société philanthropique; Société St.-François-Regis; Société de patronage pour le renvoi dans leurs familles des jeunes filles sans place et des femmes délaissées.
D/B 614 Avortement.
B/A 1312 Dossier l'Assistance publique.

Archives de la Ville de Paris et Département de la Seine (ADS)

D1X1(9–11) Procès verbaux du Conseil de surveillance de l'Assistance publique, 1887–1917.
D1X4(1–4) Service des Enfants assistés de la Seine. Rapport du directeur de l'Assistance publique, 1874–1896.
D1X4(8) Rapports au Conseil général de la Seine sur le service des Enfants assistés, 1875–1892.
D1X4(12–18) Procès verbaux de la Commission des Enfants assistés, 1876–1906.
D1X4(21–25) Service des Enfants assistés de la Seine. Rapports d'inspection, 1875–1904.
D1X4(26–27) Rapports d'inspection sur le service des Enfants assistés de Paris, 1885–1895.
D2X4 Enfants assistés (cartons).
D1 U8 Arrêts de la Cour d'Assises, 1848–1914.
D2 U8 Dossiers Cour d'Assises, 1867–1891.
VD4/4989 La Société charitable de Saint-François-Régis de Paris.
VD4/4993 Société de patronage pour le renvoi dans leurs familles des jeunes filles sans place et des femmes délaissées.
VD4/4994 Société de charité maternelle, Compte rendu pour l'année 1850; Rapport sur l'Oeuvre des mères de famille dans le 12ème arrondissement, 1850.
VD4/4998 Mémoire du Préfet de la Seine à la Commission municipale sur la répartition entre divers établissements de bienfaisance du fonds de secours voté au budget de la ville de Paris pour 1854.
VD6/80 Procès verbaux de la Commission d'hygiène (crèches), 1852–60.
VD6/330–331, 337, 361 Commission d'hygiène et de salubrité, bureau de bienfaisance, 5ème arrondissement.
VD6/468–470 Mairie du 11 Arrondissement, Inspection médicale des crèches 1847–67; Procès verbaux de la Commission d'hygiène, 1853–1867; Rapports de

la Commission d'hygiène au préfet de Police portant notamment sur les crèches municipales, 1853–1869.

VD6/532–34 Mairie du 7 arrondissement, Certificat de vie et de moralité, 1827–1841.

VD6/560 Société de charité maternelle, 1851–1867.

VD6/561 Protection des enfants abandonnés, 1832–1854.

VD6/627 Inspection médicale des crèches, 1849–1851.

VD6/791(12) Assistance aux mères indigentes.

VD6/1230–35 Procès verbaux de la Commission d'hygiène, 1860–1893.

VD6/1388 Recensement des oeuvres de bienfaisance.

VD6/1398 Crèches municipales.

VD6/1463 Délivrance par le maire de certificats de vie, d'indigence et de moralité.

VD6/1503 Opposition aux mariages; Constatation des naissances à domicile 1860–69.

VD6/1566 Demandes de secours adressées au Maire, 1877–1888.

VD6/1689 Procès verbaux de la Commission d'hygiène, Crèches, 1852–1860.

VD6/1790 Réglementation des crèches, 1862.

VD6/1909 Oeuvre evangélique des mariages; Oeuvre des mariages des pauvres, Oeuvre de Notre-Dame de la persévérance, Oeuvre de St.-Antoine, Maisons de prévoyance pour les femmes sans place et les ouvrières sans travail.

V bis 11 Q7, Register of admissions and attendance records of the Crèche Saint Ambroise.

V bis 11 I5/1, Register of doctors' inspections of Crèche Saint-Ambroise, 1847–1867.

V bis 11 I5/3, Procès verbaux, séances de la Commission d'hygiène, 1851.

V bis 1Q7 1 à 6 Registres de placement des enfants en nourrice, en sevrage ou en garde, 1e arrondissement, 1878–1887.

V bis 3Q7 1 à 6 Registres de placement des enfants en nourrice, en sevrage ou en garde, 3e arrondissement, 1879 to 1884 and 1894.

V bis 10Q7 1 Registres de placement des enfants en nourrice, en sevrage ou en garde 10e arrondissement, 1879–1880.

Selected Bibliography

Accampo, Elinor. *Industrialization, Family Life, and Class Relations: Saint-Chamond, 1815–1914.* Berkeley: University of California Press, 1989.

Administration générale de l'Assistance publique à Paris. *Rapport général sur le fonctionnement des vingt bureaux de bienfaisance pendant l'année 1898.* Paris: Imprimerie Henon, 1899.

———. *Rapport sur le traitement des malades à domicile pendant les années 1890, 1891 et 1892 présenté au conseil de surveillance de l'Assistance publique par le directeur de cette administration.* Paris: Imprimerie de l'Administration de l'Assistance publique, 1894–1902.

———. *Statistique médicale des hôpitaux de Paris.* 4 vols. Paris: Paul Dupont, 1867.

———. *Dispositions relatives à l'admission des femmes enceintes dans les hôpitaux et la réception des enfants à l'Hospice des Enfants-trouvés et Orphelins du département de la Seine.* Paris: Paul Dupont, 1852.

———. Service des Enfants assistés de la Seine. *Rapport présenté par le directeur de l'Administration générale de l'Assistance publique à M. le préfet de la Seine.* Montevrain: Imprimerie de l'Ecole d'Alembert, 1877–1904.

Alter, George. *Family and the Female Life Course: The Women of Verviers, Belgium, 1849–1880.* Madison: University of Wisconsin Press, 1988.

Ancelet, Gabriel Paul. *Essai historique et critique sur la création et transformation des maternités à Paris.* Thèse pour le doctorat en médecine. Paris: G. Steinheil, 1896.

Ariès, Philippe. *A Century of Childhood: A Social History of Family Life.* Trans. Robert Baldick. New York: Vintage Books, 1962.

Ariès, Philippe and Georges Duby, eds. *A History of Private Lives: From the Fires of Revolution to the Great War,* vol. 4. Cambridge, Mass.: Harvard University Press, 1990.

Armengaud, André. *La population française au XIXe siècle.* Paris: Presses Universitaires de France, 1971.

Auclert, Hubertine. "Le féminisme, l'éxemption du bâtard." *Le radical,* 9 January 1899.

Balestre, A., and A. Giletta de Saint-Joseph. *Etude sur la mortalité de première enfance dans la population urbaine de la France.* Paris: Doin, 1901.

Bar, Paul. *La maternité de l'Hôpital St. Antoine. Description, organisation, fonctionnement du 18 mai 1897 à 1ᵉʳ janvier 1900.* Paris: Asselin et Houzeau, 1900.

Beaumond, Louis Henry Trigant de. *Dépopulation de la France. De la conservation des enfants par les crèches.* Paris: Huzard et Fils, 1883.

Becchia, Alain. "Les milieux parlementaires et la dépopulation de 1900 à 1914." *Communications: Dénatalité l'antériorité française, 1800–1914,* no. 44. Paris: Ecole des Hautes Etudes en Sciences Sociales, Seuil, 1986.

Berlanstein, Lenard R. *The Working People of Paris, 1871–1914.* Baltimore: Johns Hopkins University Press, 1984.

Bertillon, Jacques. *La dépopulation de la France: Ses conséquences, ses causes, mesures à prendre pour la combattre.* Paris: Félix Alcan, 1911.

Boicervoise, A. *Rapport au conseil général des hospices de Paris sur le service des enfants trouvés du département de la Seine.* Paris, 1845.

Bondé, Amédée. *Etude sur l'infanticide, l'exposition et la condition des enfants exposés en droit romain. De la condition civile des enfants abandonnés et des orphelins recueillis par la charité privée ou par la charité publique et du projet de loi sur la protection des enfants abandonnés, délaissés ou maltraités en droit français.* Paris: A. Derenne, 1883.

Boswell, John. *The Kindness of Strangers: The Abandonment of Children in Western Europe from Late Antiquity to the Renaissance.* New York: Pantheon, 1988.

Bourdon, Hippolyte. *Des maternités.* Paris: F. Malteste, 1870.

Bourdon, Mathilde Froment. *Antoinette Lemire, ou l'ouvrière de Paris.* Paris, Putois-Cretté, 1861.

———. *La charité en action.* Lille: L. Lefort, 1859.

———. *Charité, légendes.* 3rd ed. Paris: Ambroise Bray, 1864.

Bourgeois, Léon. *Solidarité.* Paris: A. Colin, 1896.

Brieux, Eugène. *Three Plays by Brieux.* Ed. and intro. George Bernard Shaw. Trans. Mrs. Bernard Shaw. New York and London: Brentano, 1911.

Brochard, A.-T. *Des causes de la dépopulation en France et des moyens d'y remédier. Mémoire lu au Congrès médical de Lyon.* Lyon: Librairie Médicale de J.-P. Mégret, 1873.

———. *Education du premier âge. Utilité des crèches et des sociétés de charité maternelles.* Saint-Etienne: Théolier Frères, 1876.

———. *L'ouvrière, mère de famille.* Lyon: Josserand, 1874.

———. *La vérité sur les enfants trouvés.* Paris: E. Plon, 1876.

Brouardel, Paul. *L'avortement.* Paris: J.-B. Baillière, 1901.

———. *L'infanticide.* Paris: J.-B. Baillière et Fils, 1897.

Buret, Eugène. *De la misère des classes laborieuses en Angleterre et en France. De la nature de la misère, de son existence, de ses effets, de ses causes, et de l'insuffisance des remèdes qu'on lui a opposés jusqu'ici; avec l'indication des moyens propres à en affranchir les sociétés.* 2 vols. Paris: Chez Paulen, 1840.

Burgière, André, and Tamara K. Hareven. *Family and Sexuality in French History.* Philadelphia: University of Pennsylvania Press, 1980.

Cère, Paul. *Les populations dangereuses et les misères sociales.* Paris: E. Dentu, 1872.

Chevalier, Louis. *La formation de la population parisienne au XIXe siècle.* Paris: Presses Universitaires de France, 1950.

Cheysson, Emile. *La question de la population en France et à l'étranger.* Paris: J.-B. Baillière et Fils, 1885.

Clark, Anna. *Women's Silence, Men's Violence: Sexual Assault in England, 1770–1845.* London: Pandora Press, 1987.

Clement, Ambroise. *Essai sur la science sociale: Economie politique, morale expérimentale, politique théorique.* 2 vols. Paris: Guillaumen et Cie, 1867.

Coale, Ansley J. and Susan Cotts Watkins, eds. *The Decline of Fertility in Europe.* Princeton, N.J.: Princeton University Press, 1986.

Coleman, William. *Death Is a Social Disease: Public Health and Political Economy in Early Industrial France.* Madison: University of Wisconsin Press, 1982.

Commenge, O. *La prostitution clandestine à Paris* (1894). Rev. ed. Paris: Schleicher Frères, 1904.

Commission de la dépopulation: Sous-commission de la mortalité. *Rapport général sur les causes de la mortalité.* Presenté par Paul Strauss. Melun: Imprimerie Administrative, 1911.

Commission extraparlementaire chargée d'étudier les questions relatives à la dépopulation en France et de rechercher les moyens d'y remédier (Instituée par décret du 5 novembre 1912), Sous-commission administrative et juridique, *Procès-verbaux des séances.* Paris: Imprimerie Nationale, 1913.

Congrès international des oeuvres et des institutions feminines, 1900. 4 vols. Paris: Charles Blot, 1902.

Corbin, Alain. *Les filles de noce: Misère sexuelle et prostitution aux XIXe et XXe siècles.* Paris: Aubier Montaigne, 1978.

Corre, Antoine. *Manuel d'accouchement et de pathologie puerpérale.* Paris: Octave Doin, 1885.

———. *La mère et l'enfant dans les races humaines.* Paris: Octave Doin, 1882.

Coudert, Frederic R. "French Criminal Procedure." *Yale Law Journal* 19 (March 1910).

Couturier, D. M. *Demain. La dépopulation de la France, craintes et espérances.* Paris: Maison de la Bonne Press, 1901.

Daubié, Julie-Victoire. *La femme pauvre au dix-neuvième siècle.* 2d ed. Paris: Ernest Thorin, 1870.

Dauphin, R. P. *Une plaie sociale, un remède.* Paris: Au Bureau de L'Oeuvre de St. Raphaël, 1900.

David, Edouard. *La fille Bazentin: Pièce sociale en quatre actes sur l'Assistance publique.* Amiens: Imprimerie du Progrès de la Somme, 1908.

Davin, Anna. "Imperialism and Motherhood." *History Workshop,* no. 5 (Spring 1978).

Delarue-Mardrus, Lucie. *Marie, fille-mère.* Paris: Bibliothèque Charpentier, 1908.

Delasselle, Claude. "Abandoned Children in Eighteenth-Century Paris." In *Deviants and the Abandoned in French Society,* Ed. Robert Forster and Orest Ranum. Baltimore: Johns Hopkins University Press, 1978.

Delaunay, Paul. *La Maternité de Paris.* Paris: Jules Rousset, 1909.

Desloges, Louis. *Des enfants trouvés, des femmes publiques et des moyens à employer pour en diminuer le nombre.* Paris: Chez Desloges, 1836.

Donovan, James M. "Abortion, the Law, and the Juries in France, 1825–1923." *Criminal Justice History* 9 (Fall 1988).
———. "Infanticide and the Juries in France, 1825–1913." *Journal of Family History* 16, no. 2 (1991).
———. "Justice Unblind: The Jurors and the Criminal Cases in France, 1825–1914." *Journal of Social History* 15 (Fall 1981).
Donzelot, Jacques. *The Policing of Families.* Trans. Robert Hurley. New York: Pantheon, 1979.
Dreyfus, Ferdinand. *L'assistance sous la Seconde République, 1848–1851.* Paris: Edouard Cornély et Cie, 1907.
Drouineau, Gustave. *De l'assistance aux filles-mères et aux enfants abandonnés.* Paris: G. Masson, 1878.
———. *De l'avortement. Mesures à prendre.* Rapport présenté au Conseil d'administration de la Ligue Contre la Mortalité Infantile, le 27 Mai 1907. Paris: Masson, 1907.
DuCamp, Maxime. *Paris bienfaisant.* Paris: Hachette, 1888.
———. *Paris: Ses organes, ses fonctions et sa vie dans la seconde moitié du XIXe siècle.* 6 vols. Paris: Hachette, 1869–1875.
Duchâtel, Charles-Marie Tanneguy. *De la charité dans ses rapports avec l'état moral et le bien-être des classes inférieures de la société.* Paris: Alexandre Mesnier, 1829.
Duesterberg, Thomas J. *Criminology and the Social Order in Nineteenth-Century France.* Ph.D. diss., Indiana University, 1979.
Dufau, P. A. *Essai sur la science de la misère sociale.* Paris: Vve. J. Renouard, 1857.
———. *Lettres à une dame sur la charité.* Paris: Guillaumin et Cie, 1847.
Dumont, Arsène. *Dépopulation et civilisation, étude démographique.* Paris: Lecrosnier et Babé, 1890.
Duroselle, Jean-Baptiste. *Les débuts du catholicisme social en France, 1822–1870.* Paris: Presses Universitaires de France, 1951.
Dutouquet, H. E. *Enfants trouvés. Création de la Société de Notre-Dame de Refuge et de ses asiles.* Paris: Guillaumin et Cie, 1858.

Echérac, A. de (G. Dargenty). *L'Assistance publique: Ce qu'elle fut; ce qu'elle est.* Paris: Steinheil, 1909.
Ellis, Jack D. *The Physician-legislators of France: Medicine and Politics in the Early Third Republic, 1870–1914.* Cambridge: Cambridge University Press, 1990.
Elwitt, Sanford. *The Third Republic Defended: Bourgeois Reform in France, 1880–1914.* Baton Rouge: Louisiana State University Press, 1986.
Esquiros, Alphonse. *Paris, ou les sciences, les institutions et les moeurs au XIXe siècle.* 2 vols. Paris: Raul Renouard, 1847.
Ewald, François. *L'etat providence.* Paris: Bernard Grasset, 1986.

Fairchilds, Cissie C. "Female Sexual Attitudes and the Rise of Illegitimacy: A Case Study." *Journal of Interdisciplinary History* 8 (Spring 1978).
———. *Poverty and Charity in Aix-en-Provence, 1540–1789.* Baltimore: Johns Hopkins University Press, 1976.

Farr, James R. *The Wages of Sin: Sexuality, Law and Religion in Burgundy during the Catholic Reformation (1550–1730).* New York: Oxford University Press, forthcoming.

Feillet, Paul. *De l'Assistance publique à Paris. Avec une préface par M. Paul Strauss.* Paris: Berger-Levrault, 1888.

Ferdut, Eugène. *De l'avortement au point de vue médical, obstétrical, médico-légal, légal et théoretique.* Thèse pour le doctorat en médecine. Paris: A. Parent, 1865.

Fleury, Pierre. *Des causes de la dépopulation française et de la nécessité de réorganiser les services d'assistance et d'hygiène.* Paris: Gueret, 1888.

Floquet, Charles. *Avortement et dépopulation (affaire Constance Thomas-Floury).* Paris: Policlinique de Paris, 1892.

Forrest, Alan. *The French Revolution and the Poor.* New York: St. Martin's Press, 1981.

Foucault, Michel. *Discipline and Punish: The Birth of the Prison.* Trans. Alan Sheridan. New York: Pantheon, 1977.

France, Bureau de la statistique générale. *Annuaire statistique de la France, 1835–1873.* 1st ser., 13 vols., 2d ser., 21 vols. Paris, Imprimerie Royale, Nationale, Impériale, and Strasbourg: Veuve Berger-Levrault, 1835–1873.

France, Bureau de la statistique générale. Statistique de la France. *Statistique annuelle.* Documents Rétrospectifs. 1871–1906. Paris: Imprimerie Municipale, 1872–1907.

France, Statistique de la France, Deuxième série. *Statistique de l'Assistance publique.* Strasbourg: Imprimerie Administration de Veuve Berger-Levrault, 1861.

France, Ministère du commerce, de l'industrie, des postes et des télégraphes. *Résultats statistiques du recensement général de la population,* vol. 4. 4 vols. Paris: Imprimerie Nationale, 1906.

Frégier, H. A. *Des classes dangereuses de la population dans les grandes villes, et des moyens de les rendre meilleures.* 2 vols. Paris: J.-B. Baillière, 1840.

Frey, Michel. "Du mariage et du concubinage dans les classes populaires à Paris (1846–1847)." *Annales: Economies, sociétés, civilisations* 33 (1978).

Fuchs, Rachel G. *Abandoned Children: Foundlings and Child Welfare in Nineteenth-Century France.* Albany: State University of New York Press, 1984.

———. "From the Private to the Public *Devoir:* Henri Monod and Public Assistance." *Proceedings of the Annual Meeting of the Western Society for French History* 17 (1990).

———. "Legislation, Poverty, and Child Abandonment in Nineteenth-Century Paris." *Journal of Interdisciplinary History* 18 (Summer 1987).

———. "Morality and Poverty: Public Welfare for Mothers in Paris, 1870–1900." *French History* 2 (September 1988).

Fuchs, Rachel G., and Paul E. Knepper. "Women in the Paris Maternity Hospital: Public Policy in the Nineteenth Century." *Social Science History* 13 (Summer 1989).

Fuchs, Rachel G., and Leslie Page Moch. "Pregnant, Single and Far from Home: Migrant Women in the Metropolis." *American Historical Review* 95 (1990).

Gaillard, Adolphe Henri. *Examen du rapport de M. le Baron de Watteville sur les tours, les infanticides, etc.* Paris: Parent Desbarres, 1856.

———. *Recherches administratives, statistiques et morales sur les enfants trouvés, les enfants naturels et les orphelins en France et dans plusieurs autres pays de l'Europe.* Paris: Th. Leclerc, 1837.

Gaillard, Jeanne. "Le médecin et l'avortement au XIXe siècle." *L'histoire* 16 (October 1979).

Galichon, Claire. *Amour et maternité.* Paris: Librairie Spirite et des Sciences Psychiques, 1907.

Galland, T. *De l'avortement au point de vue médico-légal.* Paris: Baillière, 1878.

Garner, James W. "Criminal Procedure in France." *Yale Law Journal* 25 (February 1916).

Gasparin, Comte Agénor-Etienne de. *La famille, ses devoirs, ses joies et ses douleurs.* 2 vols. Paris: Michel Lévy, 1865.

———. *Les réclamations des femmes.* Paris: Michel Lévy, 1872.

Gasparin, Comtesse A.-E. de. *Un livre pour les femmes mariées.* Paris: L.-R. Delay, 1845.

———. *Mariage au point de vue chrétien,* vol. 2. 3 vols. 2. Paris: L.-R. Delay, 1843.

———. *Il y a des pauvres à Paris . . . et ailleurs.* Paris: L.-R. Delay, 1846.

Gazette des tribunaux, 1872–1900.

Gérando, Joseph Marie de. *De la bienfaisance publique.* 4 vols. Paris: Jules Renouard, 1839.

———. *Le visiteur du pauvre.* Paris: Colas, 1820.

Gide, Charles. *La France sans enfants.* Commission d'Action Morale. Paris: Chez M. Léon Peyric, 1914.

Gille, F. *La Société de charité maternelle de Paris . . . Origine, fonctionnement et marché progressive de l'oeuvre de 1784 à 1885.* Paris: V. Goupy et Jourdan, 1887.

Gilligan, Carol. *In a Different Voice.* Cambridge, Mass.: Harvard University Press, 1982.

Gillis, John R. "Servants, Sexual Relations, and the Risks of Illegitimacy in London, 1801–1900." *Feminist Studies* 5 (1979).

Giost, Mme. *Considérations sur l'avortement et l'infanticide dans leurs rapports avec la jurisprudence.* Paris: Chez l'Auteur, 1831.

Goncourt, Edmond, and Jules Goncourt. *Germinie Lacerteux.* Paris: Société des Beaux Arts, 1910.

Gordon, Linda. *Woman's Body, Woman's Right: A Social History of Birth Control in America.* New York: Penguin, 1977.

Gossin, Eugène. *Vie de M. Jules Gossin, 1789–1855.* Paris: Librairie Religieuse H. Oudin, 1907.

Gossin, Jules. *Circulaire du président de cette société de charité à toutes les sociétés de Saint-Régis.* Société charitable de Saint-Régis de Paris. Paris: Vve Bouchard-Huzard, 1844.

———. *Manuel de la Société charitable de Saint-Régis de Paris.* Paris: Au Secrétariat de la Société de St.-Vincent-de-Paul, 1851.

————. *Note ayant pour objet d'obtenir une addition à l'article 9 du projet relatif au droit d'assistance.* Paris: Vve. Bouchard-Huzard, 1848.

————. *Recherches statistiques sur les 17,176 pauvres dont la Société charitable de St.-Régis, établie à Paris pour faciliter le mariage civil et religieux des indigents du département de la Seine, s'est occupée depuis le 1er mars 1826 jusqu'au 31 décembre 1841 inclusivement et résultats obtenus par la société sur les 8,588 couples inscrits entre ces deux époques.* Société charitable de Saint-Régis de Paris. Paris: Vve. Bouchard-Huzard, 1844.

Guerrand, Roger-Henri. "900,000 avortements en 1914?" *L'histoire* 16 (October 1979).

Guiral, Pierre, and Guy Thuillier. *La vie quotidienne des domestiques en France au XIXe siècle.* Paris: Hachette, 1978.

Gullickson, Gay L. *Spinners and Weavers of Auffay: Rural Industry and Sexual Division of Labor in a French Village, 1750–1850.* Cambridge: Cambridge University Press, 1986.

Harris, Ruth. "Melodrama, Hysteria, and Feminine Crimes of Passion in the Fin-de-Siècle." *History Workshop* 25 (Spring 1988).

Harsin, Jill. *Policing Prostitution in Nineteenth-Century Paris.* Princeton, N.J.: Princeton University Press, 1985.

Hatzfeld, Henri. *Du pauperisme à la sécurité sociale, 1850–1940.* Paris: Armand Colin, 1971.

Hause, Steven C. "Anti-Protestant Rhetoric in the Early Third Republic." *French Historical Studies* 16 (Spring 1989).

Haussonville, Comtesse d' (née Pauline d'Harcourt). *La charité à travers la vie.* Paris: Librairie Victor Lecoffre, 1912.

Haussonville, Othenin d'. *Assistance publique et bienfaisance privée.* Paris: Calmann Lévy, 1901.

————. *Misère et remèdes.* Paris: Calmann Lévy, 1892.

————. *Salaires et misères de femmes.* Paris: Calmann Lévy, 1900.

————. *Socialisme d'état et socialisme chrétien.* Extrait de la *Revue des Deux Mondes* 15 June 1890. Paris: Bureau de la Revue des Deux Mondes, 1890.

————. *Socialisme et charité.* Paris: Calmann Lévy, 1895.

————. *La vie et les salaires à Paris.* Paris: A. Quanton, 1883.

Hertz, Robert. *Socialisme et dépopulation.* In *Les Cahiers du Socialiste,* no. 10. Paris, 1901.

Higginbotham, Ann R. "The Unmarried Mother and Her Child in Victorian London (1834–1914)." Ph.D. diss., Indiana University, 1986.

Himes, Norman E. *Medical History of Contraception.* New York: Schocken, 1970.

Hoffer, Peter C., and N.E.H. Hull. *Murdering Mothers: Infanticide in England and New England 1558–1803.* New York: New York University Press, 1981.

Hufton, Olwen H. *The Poor of Eighteenth-Century France, 1750–1789.* Oxford: Clarendon Press, 1974.

Hugo, Victor. *Les Misérables.* Trans. Norman Denny. London: Penguin, 1976.

Hunecke, Volker. *I trovatelli di Milano: Bambini esposti e famiglie espositrici dal XVII al XIX secolo.* Trans. Benedetta Heinemann Campana. Bologna: Il Mulino, 1989.

Husson, Armand. *Etude sur les hôpitaux.* Paris: P. Dupont, 1862.

Imbert, Jean. *Hôpitaux en France.* Paris: Editions Privat, 1982.

Jacquemet, Gérard. *Belleville au XIXe siècle.* Paris: Ecole des Hautes Etudes en Sciences Sociales, 1984.

Jenson, Jane. "Paradigms and Political Discourse: Labour and Social Policy in the USA and France Before 1914." Harvard University, Center for European Studies (Working Paper Series). 1988.

Johnson, Christopher H. *Utopian Communism in France: Cabet and the Icarians, 1839–1851.* Ithaca, N.Y.: Cornell University Press, 1974.

Knibiehler, Yvonne, and Catherine Fouquet. *La femme et les médecins.* Paris: Hachette, 1983.

————. *Histoire des mères.* Paris: Editions Montalba, 1977.

Knodel, John, and Etienne van de Walle. "Lessons from the Past: Policy Implications of Historical Fertility Studies." *Population and Development Review* 5 (1979).

Laget, Mireille. *Naissances: L'accouchement avant l'âge de la clinique.* Paris: Editions du Seuil, 1982.

Lalou, Richard. "L'infanticide devant les tribunaux français (1825–1910)." *Communications: Dénatalité l'antériorité française, 1800–1914,* vol. 44. Paris: Ecole des Hautes Etudes en Sciences Sociales, Seuil, 1986.

Langer, William L. "Checks on Population Growth: 1750–1850." *Scientific American* 226 (February 1972).

————. "Infanticide: A Historical Survey." *History of Childhood Quarterly* 1 (Winter 1974).

Laslett, Peter, Karla Oosterveen, and Richard M. Smith, eds. *Bastardy and Its Comparative History.* Cambridge, Mass.: Harvard University Press, 1980.

Laurent, Emile. *L'Etat actuel de la question des enfants assistés.* Paris: Guillaumin, 1876.

LeFort, Léon. *Des maternités: Etude sur les maternités et les institutions charitables et d'accouchement à domicile dans les principaux états de l'Europe.* Paris: Victor Masson et Fils, 1866.

LaMothe, Léonce de. *Nouvelles études sur la législation charitable.* Paris: Guillaumin, 1850.

Léonard, Jacques. *La médecine entre les savoirs et les pouvoirs.* Paris: Aubier Montaigne, 1981.

————. *La vie quotidienne du médecin de province au XIXe siècle.* Paris: Hachette, 1977.

LePlay, Frédéric. *L'organisation de la famille selon le vrai modèle signalé par l'histoire de toutes les races et de tous les temps.* 3rd ed. Tours: A. Mame et Fils, 1884.

Leroy-Beaulieu, Paul. *Le travail des femmes au XIXe siècle.* Paris: Charpentier, 1873.

Levasseur, Emile. *La population française*. 3 vols. Paris: Arthur Rousseau, 1889–1892.

Lewis, Jane. *The Politics of Motherhood: Child and Maternal Welfare in England, 1900–1939*. London: Croom Helm, 1980.

Loubat, William. "Programme minimum de réformes pénales." *Revue politique et parlementaire* 74 (March 1913).

Lynch, Katherine A. *Family, Class, and Ideology in Early Industrial France: Social Policy and the Working-Class Family, 1825–1848*. Madison: University of Wisconsin Press, 1988.

McBride, Theresa. *The Domestic Revolution: The Modernization of Household Service in England and France, 1820–1920*. New York: Holmes and Meier, 1976.

———. "The Modernization of Women's Work." *Journal of Modern History* 49 (June 1977).

McDougall, Mary Lynn [Stewart]. "Protecting Infants: The French Campaign for Maternity Leaves, 1890–1913." *French Historical Studies* 13 (Spring 1983).

McLaren, Angus. "Abortion in France: Women and the Regulation of Family Size, 1800–1914." *French Historical Studies* 9 (Spring 1978).

———. *Birth Control in Nineteenth-Century England*. New York: Holmes and Meier, 1978.

———. *Reproductive Rituals: The Perception of Fertility in England from the Sixteenth Century to the Nineteenth Century*. New York: Methuen, 1984.

———. *Sexuality and Social Order: The Debate over the Fertility of Women and Workers in France, 1770–1920*. New York: Holmes and Meier, 1983.

———. "Some Secular Attitudes toward Sexual Behavior in France: 1760–1860." *French Historical Studies* 8 (1974).

Margerie, Eugène de. *La Société de Saint-Vincent-de-Paul*. 2 vols. Paris: Librairie Saint-Joseph, 1874.

Marthe. Paris: Editions du Seuil, 1982.

Marthe. A Woman and a Family: A Fin-de-Siècle Correspondence. Trans. Donald Frame. New York: Harcourt Brace Jovanovich, 1984.

Martin-Fugier, Anne. *La place des bonnes: La domesticité féminine en 1900*. Paris: Grasset, 1979.

Mée, René Le. "Une Affaire de 'faiseuses d'anges' à la fin du XIXe siècle." *Communications: Dénatalité l'antériorité française, 1800–1914*. Paris: Ecole des Hautes Etudes en Sciences Sociales, Seuil, 1986.

Michelet, Jules. *L'amour*. 3d ed. Paris: Hachette, 1859.

Monod, Henri. *L'Assistance publique en France en 1889 et en 1900*. Paris: Imprimerie Nationale, 1900.

———. *Ma mise à la retraite* (*Pour ma famille et quelques amis*). Paris: Société Générale d'Impression, Imprimerie Monod, Poirré et Jehlen, 1907.

Mornet, Jacques. *Les mutualités maternelles*. Paris: Bloud, 1911.

———. *La protection de la maternité en France* (*Etude d'hygiène sociale*). Thèse pour le doctorat en médecine, Faculté de Médecine de Paris. Paris: Marcel Rivière et Cie, 1909.

Moses, Claire Goldberg. *French Feminism in the Nineteenth Century*. Albany: State University of New York Press, 1984.

Nadaillac, Jean-François-Albert, de. *Le dépopulation de la France.* Extrait du *Correspondant.* Paris: DeSoye et Fils, 1891.

Napias, Henri. *De l'organisation des crèches.* Rouen: Imprimerie Gy, 1897.

Napias, Henri, and A.-J. Martin. *L'étude et les progrès de l'hygiène en France.* Paris: Masson, 1883.

Nourrisson, Paul. *La question des enfants martyrs et la protection des femmes à Londres.* Extract du *Correspondant.* Paris: De Soye et Fils, 1897.

Nye, Robert A. *Crime, Madness, and Politics in Modern France: The Medical Concept of National Decline.* Princeton, N.J.: Princeton University Press, 1985.

———. "Degeneration and the Medical Model of Cultural Crisis in the French *Belle Epoque.*" In *Political Symbolism in Modern Europe: Essays in Honor of George L. Mosse.* Ed. S. Drescher, D. Sabean, and A. Sharlin. New Brunswick, N.J.: Rutgers University Press, 1982.

Oeuvre des Mariages des Pauvres. *Rapports et compte rendu.* Paris: Au Secrétriat de la Société de Saint-Vincent-de-Paul, 1876.

L'Oeuvre libératrice, Société de réhabilitation. Paris: Siège Social, Avenue Malakoff, 1903.

Offen, Karen. "Defining Feminism: A Comparative Historical Approach." *Signs: Journal of Women in Culture and Society* 14, no. 1 (1988).

———. "Depopulation, Nationalism, and Feminism in Fin-de-Siècle France." *American Historical Review* 89 (June 1984).

Okin, Susan Moller. *Justice, Gender, and the Family.* New York: Basic Books, 1989.

Pateman, Carol. *The Sexual Contract.* Stanford, Calif.: Stanford University Press, 1988.

Pelletier, Madeleine. *Le droit à l'avortement.* Paris: Editions du Malthusien, 1913.

Perrot, Marguerite. *Le mode de vie des familles bourgeoises.* Paris: Presses de la Fondation Nationale des Sciences Politiques, 1982.

Petchesky, Rosalind Pollack. *Abortion and Woman's Choice: The State, Sexuality, and Reproductive Freedom.* Boston: Northeastern University Press, 1984.

Picon, Dr. *Aperçu sur les principales causes de la dépopulation et de l'affaiblissement progressif de la France.* Paris: Clément Larrieu, 1888.

Piers, Maria W. *Infanticide Past and Present.* New York: W. W. Norton, 1978.

Pinard, Adolphe. *Du fonctionnement de la maternité de Lariboisière et des résultats obtenus depuis 1882 jusqu'en 1889.* Paris: G. Steinheil, 1889.

Piot, Edme. *La dépopulation. Enquête personnelle sur la dépopulation en France.* Paris: Société Anonyme de Publications Périodiques, P. Mouillot, 1902.

Ponsolle, Paul. *Le dépopulation. Introduction à l'étude sur la recherche de la paternité.* Paris: L. Baillière et H. Messager, 1893.

Potash, Janet Ruth. "The Foundling Problem in France, 1800–1869: Child Abandonment in Lille and Lyon." Ph.D. diss., Yale University, 1979.

Préfecture de la Seine, Service de la statistique municipale. *Annuaire statistique de la ville de Paris.* Paris: Imprimerie Municipale, 1881–1885.

Rabaud, Camille. *Le péril national ou la dépopulation croissante de la France. Le péril, les causes, les moyens.* Paris: Fischbacher, 1891.

Rabinbach, Anson. "The European Science of Work: The Economy of the Body at the End of the Nineteenth Century." In *Work in France: Representations, Meaning, Organization, and Practice.* Ed. Steven Laurence Kaplan and Cynthia J. Koepp. Ithaca, N.Y.: Cornell University Press, 1986.

Ransel, David L. *Mothers of Misery: Child Abandonment in Russia.* Princeton, N.J.: Princeton University Press, 1988.

Reddy, William M. *The Rise of Market Culture: The Textile Trade and French Society, 1750–1900.* Cambridge: Cambridge University Press, 1984.

Remacle, B.-B. *Des hospices d'enfants trouvés en Europe, et principalement en France.* Paris: Treutel & Wertz, 1838.

La revue philanthropique (1897–1914). Paris.

Rigaudias-Weiss, Hilde. *Les enquêtes ouvrières en France entre 1830 et 1848.* Paris: F. Alcan and Presses Universitaires de France, 1936.

Rollet, Henri. *L'action sociale des catholiques en France (1871–1914)*, vol. 2. 2 vols. Paris and Bruges: Desclée de Brouwer, 1958.

Rollet-Echalier, Catherine. *La politique à l'égard de la petite enfance sous la IIIe République.* Paris: Presses Universitaires de France, 1990.

Ronsin, Francis. *La grève des ventres: Progagande néo-Malthusienne et baisse de la natalité en France 19e–20e siècles.* Paris: Aubier Montaigne, 1980.

Ross, Ellen. "Hungry Children: Housewives and London Charity, 1870–1918." In *The Uses of Charity: The Poor on Relief in the Nineteenth-century Metropolis.* Ed. Peter Mandler. Philadelphia: University of Pennsylvania Press, 1990.

———. "Survival Networks: Women's Neighbourhood Sharing in London before World War I." *History Workshop* 15 (Spring 1983).

Schwartz, Robert M. *Policing the Poor in Eighteenth-Century France.* Chapel Hill: University of North Carolina Press, 1988.

Scott, Joan Wallach. *Gender and the Politics of History.* New York: Columbia University Press, 1988.

Semichon, Ernest. *Histoire des enfants abandonnés depuis l'antiquité jusqu'à nos jours.* Paris: E. Plon, 1880.

Shapiro, Ann-Louise. *Housing the Poor of Paris, 1850–1902.* Madison: University of Wisconsin Press, 1985.

Sherwood, Joan. *Poverty in Eighteenth-Century Spain: The Women and Children of the Inclusa.* Toronto: University of Toronto Press, 1988.

Shorter, Edward L. *A History of Women's Bodies.* New York: Basic Books, 1982.

———. *The Making of the Modern Family.* New York: Basic Books, 1975.

Sicard de Plauzoles, Just. *La maternité et la défense nationale contre la dépopulation.* Paris: V. Giard & E. Brière, 1909.

Simon, Jules. *De l'initiative privée et de l'état, en matière de réformes sociales.* Conférence faite au Grand-Théatre de Bordeaux, le 7 Novembre 1891. Bordeaux: Gounouilhor, 1892.

———. *L'ouvrière.* 4th ed. Paris: Hachette, 1862.

Simon, Mlle. Marguerite Jules. *La vie de l'ouvrière.* Paris: Librairie Bloud, 1911.

Singer-Kerel, Jeanne. *Le coût de la vie à Paris de 1840 à 1954.* Paris: A. Colin, 1961.

Sismondi, Jean-C. L., Simonde de. *Nouveaux principes d'économie politique; ou, de la richesse dans ses rapports avec la population.* 2 vols. Paris: Delaunay, 1819.

Smith, Bonnie G. *Ladies of the Leisure Class: The Bourgeoises· of Northern France in the Nineteenth Century.* Princeton, N.J.: Princeton University Press, 1981.

Smith, Peter M. "Time as a Historical Construct." *Historical Methods* 17 (Fall 1984).

Société Philanthropique de Paris. *Rapports et comptes rendus, Annuaire de 1906–1907.* Paris: Bureau de la Société, 1906.

Spengler, Joseph. *France Faces Depopulation.* Durham, N.C.: Duke University Press, 1979.

Spiral, E.-Adolphe. *Essai d'une étude sur l'avortement considéré au point de vue légal et spécialement de l'article 317 (1, 2, et 3) du code pénal relativement au concubinat suivi de l'examen de l'art. 340 du code civil.* Nancy: G. Crépin-Leblond, 1882.

Stack, Carol B. *All Our Kin: Strategies for Survival in a Black Community.* New York: Harper & Row, 1974.

Stewart, Mary Lynn. *Women, Work, and the French State.* Montreal: McGill-Queens University Press, 1989.

Stone, Judith F. *The Search for Social Peace: Reform Legislation in France, 1890–1914.* Albany: State University of New York Press, 1985.

Strauss, Paul. *Assistance aux vieillards ou infirmes privés de ressources.* Paris: Cagniard, 1897.

———. *Assistance sociale: Pauvres et mendiants.* Paris: Félix Alcan, 1901.

———. *La croisade sanitaire.* Paris: E. Fasquelle et G. Charpentier, 1902.

———. *Dépopulation et puériculture.* Paris: E. Fasquelle et G. Charpentier, 1901.

———. *L'enfance malheureuse.* Paris: E. Fasquelle et G. Charpentier, 1896.

———. *Paris ignoré.* Paris: Librairies-imprimeries Réunies, 1892.

Sue, Eugène. *Martin, the Foundling: A Romance.* Dicks English Library, vol. VI. London, 1927.

———. *The Mysteries of Paris.* English translation. Translator not named. Philadelphia, Pa., 1912.

Sussman, George D. *Selling Mothers' Milk: The Wet–nursing Business in France.* Urbana: University of Illinois Press, 1982.

Talmeyr, Maurice. *Sur le banc. Les avorteuses de Paris,* vol. 2. Paris: Léon Genonceaux, 1890.

Tannenbaum, Edward R. "The Beginnings of Bleeding-Heart Liberalism: Eugène Sue's *Les Mystères de Paris.*" *Comparative Studies in Society and History* 23 (1981).

Tardieu, Ambroise. *Etude médico-légale sur l'infanticide.* Paris: J.-B. Baillière, 1880 (1868).

———. *Etude médico-légale sur l'avortement suivie d'observations et de recherches pour servir à l'histoire médico-légale des grossesses fausses et simulées.* Paris: J.-B. Baillière, 1863, 1881, 1939 (1855).

Tarnier, Stéphane. *De la fièvre puerpérale observée à l'hospice de la Maternité.* Paris: J.-B. Baillière et fils, 1858.

———. *Mémoire sur l'hygiène des hôpitaux de femmes en couches.* Paris: A. Parent, 1864.

Tarnier, Stéphane and Pierre Budin. *Traité de l'art des accouchements.* 3 vols. Paris: G. Steinheil, 1888.

Témoin, Sylvain. *La Maternité de Paris pendant l'année 1859.* Thèse pour le doctorat en médecine, 1859. Paris: A. Delahaye, 1860.

Terme, Jean-François, and J.-B. Monfalcon. *Histoire des enfants trouvés.* Nouvelle Édition. Paris: Paulin, 1840.

Thébaud, Françoise. *Donner la vie: Histoire de la maternité en France entre les deux guerres.* Paris: Université de Paris VII, 1982.

———. *Quand nos grand-mères donnaient la vie: La maternité en France dans l'entre-deux-guerres.* Lyon: Presses Universitaires de Lyon, 1986.

Tilly, Louise A., and Joan W. Scott. *Women, Work, and Family.* New York: Holt, Rinehart, and Winston, 1978.

Toubin-Malinas, Catherine. *Heurs et malheurs de la femme au XIXe siècle: "Fécondité" d'Emile Zola.* Paris: Méridiens Klincksieck, 1986.

Valdruche, A. *Rapport au conseil général des hospices sur le service des enfants trouvés dans le département de la Seine.* Paris: Mme Huzzard, 1838.

Vallaud, Dominique. "Le crime d'infanticide et l'indulgence des cours d'assises en France au XIX siècle." *Social Science Information* 21, no. 3 (1982).

van de Walle, Etienne. *The Female Population of France in the Nineteenth Century: A Reconstruction of 82 Départements.* Princeton, N.J.: Princeton University Press, 1974.

———. "Illegitimacy in France during the Nineteenth Century." In *Bastardy and Its Comparative History.* Ed. Peter Laslett, Karla Osterveen, and Richard M. Smith. Cambridge, Mass: Harvard University Press, 1980.

———. "Motivations and Technology in the Decline of French Fertility." In *Family and Sexuality in French History.* Ed. Robert Wheaton and Tamara K. Haraven. Philadelphia: University of Pennsylvania Press, 1980.

Vidal, François. *De la répartition des richesses.* Paris: Capelle, 1846.

Villeneuve-Bargemont, Alban de. *Economie politique chrètienne, ou recherches sur la nature et les causes du paupérisme en France et en Europe, et sur les moyens de le soulager et de le prévenir.* 3 vols. Paris: Paulin, 1834.

Villermé, Louis René. "De la distribution par mois des conceptions et des naissances de l'homme, considéré dans ses rapports avec les saisons, avec les climats, avec le retour périodique annuel des époques de travail et de repos, d'abondance et de rareté des vivres, et avec quelques institutions et coutumes sociales." *Annales d'hygiène publique et de médecine légale* 5 (1831).

———. *Tableau de l'état physique et moral des ouvriers employés dans les manufactures de coton, de laine et de soie.* 2 vols. Paris: Jules Renouard, 1840.

Watteville, Adolphe de. *Législation charitable.* Paris: Cotillon, 1863.

Weiss, John H. "Origins of the French Welfare State: Poor Relief in the Third Republic, 1871–1914." *French Historical Studies* 13 (Spring 1983).

Weston, Elizabeth A. "Prostitution in Paris in the Later Nineteenth Century: A Study of Political and Social Ideology." Ph.D. diss., State University of New York-Buffalo, 1979.

Zola, Emile. *Fécondité* (1899). Paris, 1957.

Index

abandonment. *See* child abandonment

Abbadie d'Arrast, Mme Andéria d', 91, 93

abortifacients. *See* abortion: methods of

abortion, 7, 8, 14, 57, 63, 66, 67, 69, 89, 93, 96, 97, 109, 148, 175, 177, 178, 206, 217, 219; acquittal, 176–177, 184, 194–195; as birth control, 180, 185–186; and child abandonment, 199; class and, 198–199; costs of, 189; criminal, 176–177, 180–181, 182, 183, 184–186; criminal proceedings, 175–177, 192–196; and depopulation, 177–178, 184–185, 195, 199; detection of, 192, 193–195; doctor-patient confidentiality, 183; doctors and, 180–183, 184, 187, 189, 193–195, 197; feminism and, 93, 198–199; juries and, 194–195; laws governing, 180, 196–199; legal reform, 196–199; married women and, 185–186, 196; and medical professionalization, 180–181; methods of, 175–177, 185–188, 189–192; midwives and, 13, 176–177, 184–186, 187, 188–191, 192, 193, 194–195, 197, 198; and morality, 177–178; numbers of, 183–185; public opinion, 195; reasons for, 175, 177, 195–196; spontaneous, 23, 24, 181–183, 186, 193; stage at, 186–187; therapeutic, 181

abortionists, 70, 188–191, 192; clients, 194–195; methods, 190–191. *See also* abortion; midwives

abstinence, 46, 52, 178. *See also* birth control; contraception

Academy of Lyon, 82

Academy of Medicine, 60, 62–63, 107, 181

Academy of Moral and Political Sciences, 39, 41–42, 50, 52

adoption, 220

Aide Maternelle, l', 131–132. *See also* Society of Maternal Aid

alcohol and alcoholism, 37, 39, 56, 57, 80, 103, 132, 160, 166; influence of, 11

Alsace, 27

Amour et maternité, 95

anticlericalism, 7, 59, 60, 72, 73, 84

Ariès, Philippe, 202

Asile George Sand, 110

Asile Maternel, 109–110, 133

Asile Michelet, 107–108, 133

Asile-Ouvroir de Gérando, 44, 129

Asile Pauline Roland, 110, 131, 133

Asile Sainte-Madeleine, 106

Asile Saint-Jacques, 108, 109

Asile Vesinet, 130–131

Asiles. *See* refuges for single mothers

Association of Mothers of Families, 129–130

Assommoir, L', 56

Auclert, Hubertine, 95, 98

Baudelocque. *See* Clinique Baudelocque

Bavaria, marriage laws, 46

Bécour, Julie, 84–85

Belleville, 11, 13, 32, 110

Béquet de Vienne, Marie, 88–90, 109, 158; and abortion, 198; and l'Aide Maternelle, 131–132; and Society for Maternal Breastfeeding, 133–134

Bertillon, Jacques, 62

birth certificates, 117, 156, 222, 225; midwives and, 117

birth control, 46, 52, 64, 97, 175, 180; abortion as, 180, 185–186; and depopulation, 177–178, 184–185, 195, 199; infanticide as, 201–202; methods of, 46, 52, 178, 180; and morality, 177–178; reasons for, 178–179. *See also* contraception